Also by n+1

P.S. 1 Symposium: A Practical Avant-Garde
What We Should Have Known: Two Discussions
What Was the Hipster? A Sociological Investigation
The Trouble Is the Banks: Letters to Wall Street
No Regrets: Three Discussions
MFA vs NYC: The Two Cultures of American Fiction

CITY BY CITY

CITY BY CITY

DISPATCHES FROM
THE AMERICAN METROPOLIS

EDITED BY

KEITH GESSEN AND **STEPHEN SQUIBB**

n+1/FARRAR, STRAUS AND GIROUX
NEW YORK

n+1/Farrar, Straus and Giroux
18 West 18th Street, New York 10011

Owing to limitations of space, all acknowledgments for permission to reprint
previously published material can be found on pages 481–483.

Library of Congress Cataloging-in-Publication Data
[Essays. Selections.]
City by city : dispatches from the American metropolis / edited by Keith
Gessen, Stephen Squibb. — 1st Edition.
    pages   cm
    Includes bibliographical references and index.
    ISBN 978-0-86547-831-2 (paperback)—ISBN 978-0-374-71340-9 (e-book)
    1. Cities and towns—United States—History.   I. Gessen, Keith, editor.
II. Squibb, Stephen, editor.

HT123 .C4976 2015
307.760973—dc23

2014041300

Designed by Jonathan D. Lippincott

www.fsgbooks.com
www.twitter.com/fsgbooks • www.facebook.com/fsgbooks

1   3   5   7   9   10   8   6   4   2

Furthermore:
a program of the J.M. Kaplan Fund

Published with the help of Furthermore:
a program of the J. M. Kaplan Fund

Contents

CANADA

MINNESOTA

WISCONSIN

MICHIGAN

MAINE

VERMONT

NEW HAMPSHIRE

Syracuse

NEW YORK

Boston

MASSACHUSETTS

Providence

RHODE ISLAND

CONNECTICUT

Milwaukee

Detroit

IOWA

Chicago

ILLINOIS

INDIANA

Cleveland

OHIO

PENNSYLVANIA

Reading

Brooklyn

NEW JERSEY

Philadelphia

Baltimore

DELAWARE

MARYLAND

Cincinnati

Washington, D.C.

WEST VIRGINIA

VIRGINIA

MISSOURI

KENTUCKY

Greensboro

TENNESSEE

NORTH CAROLINA

ARKANSAS

Arkansas River

Duluth

SOUTH CAROLINA

Atlanta

ALABAMA

GEORGIA

MISSISSIPPI

LOUISIANA

New Orleans

Palm Coast

Atlantic Ocean

FLORIDA

THE BAHAMAS

Gulf of Mexico

Lehigh Acres

Miami

0 Miles 500

0 Kilometers 500

CITY BY CITY

INTRODUCTION

KEITH GESSEN AND STEPHEN SQUIBB

When we began this project just after the start of the Great Recession, our working title was *City by City: The New American Poverty*. Struck by the intensity of the financial crisis, and inspired by Emily Witt's ingenious description of Miami's road to hell during the boom, we imagined a series of essays that illuminated the political and economic fallout of the financial collapse in cities across the country. In numerous books and articles, we had learned the view of the crisis from the office towers of Manhattan; we wanted a view that was a little more from below.

Many of the early essays, written in the immediate aftermath of the banking collapses, accomplished exactly this. They described the socialists of Milwaukee, the Walmart of banks in Seattle, and what it was like to work as a security guard in one of the last remaining denim plants in Greensboro, North Carolina.

Then, two years into the project, the cities themselves erupted. The various city-centric iterations of Occupy—Occupy Boston, Occupy Philadelphia, Occupy Oakland—seemed to both validate our idea and move beyond it. When Occupy was done, we felt that the project, and our curiosity about the cities of our country, could expand. We learned how different resources are managed in this country, from the Arkansas River to shale oil in North Dakota. We became interested in how gentrifying cities like Boise and Fresno are different from collapsing ones like Detroit and Cleveland. And how the process was taking place, or wasn't, in Atlanta; Reading, Pennsylvania; and New Orleans. Police violence anticipated in Cincinnati and Baltimore reappeared in Palm Coast, Florida, went missing in Boston right when we most expected it, and exploded again, dramatically, in an impoverished suburb of St. Louis called Ferguson.

Outside the project, we were encouraged by a huge increase in the amount of intense, intelligent reporting on American poverty, both in and out of the city, which freed our curiosity still further. Questions like "How do we reconstruct the urban economy?" and "How have the superhighway and the office impacted the city, really?" took place alongside ones like "What's it like to have Lil' Kim's brother as a landlord?" and "Where did Thomas Mann get his hair cut in Los Angeles?" Reality TV in Alaska. The invisible economies of San Diego. A mysterious disappearance in Duluth, Georgia. The intimate relationship between a mall and a lake in Syracuse. Mobsters in Providence, Germans in Los Angeles, marriages in Fresno, border crossings in El Paso, fires in Phoenix, running a brothel in our nation's capital, barely getting by in Kentucky, mapping the geography of Lehigh Acres, Florida, moving apartments in Hyde Park, growing up among the Dallas superrich, looking for health insurance in Florida, writing Las Vegas—what an incredible, confusing, prolific, and terrifying country we live in.

These essays were all written between 2008 and 2014, and they are all about the same thing—the way in which cities (and towns) have changed in the last five, ten, twenty years. Their methods of telling these stories are extraordinarily varied: Some of the essays are personal, others historical, others polemical. Several of the essays have clashing or contradictory attitudes toward the changes going on in the cities they describe. But overall this book is clearly the work of a generation of writers (and some of their forebears) for whom the city is, as it was not for their parents, a definite and final home, and who want to understand the forces that are shaping it.

Eduardo Galeano closes his epic three-volume history of the Americas by saying, "Forgive me if it came out too long. Writing it was a joy for my hand, and now I feel more than ever proud of having been born in America, in this shit, in this marvel, during the century of the wind." We don't know what the twenty-first century will be made of, but without minimizing the difference between his stories and the ones in this book—or the difference between writing and editing!—we know how he feels.

There are cities that did not make it and also broader themes that we missed, which we hope readers of the book will think about and adumbrate in future editions of *City by City*. In the meantime, we offer this collection to our contemporaries and to the future so they can know how it was here, between the day of the Lehman bankruptcy and the shooting of Michael Brown.

Brooklyn, New York, 2014

1

WELCOME TO SAN DIEGO

JORDAN KISNER

San Diego is famously mild, sunny, seasonless—and quietly extreme. A surf haven by reputation, it is also the largest and most important military outpost in the West, a leading national center of biotech research and development, and an exceptionally high-traffic site of smuggling contraband across the border, mainly weapons, human slaves, and stupendous amounts of meth. It is on the edge in the most basic geographic sense, all jammed up against the border and the ocean; the end of America or, depending on which way you're driving, the beginning. San Diego is *as far as you can go*. It's not just a military town; it's the *most* military. Its meth problem isn't just bad; it's the *worst*. The wealthy there aren't simply wealthy; they're Mitt Romney with his $12 million house expansion and his "car elevator." The wretched, farther south, are so unwanted and voiceless they functionally, civically, do not exist. The weather is perfect until the city burns.

You can see this, if you know what you're looking for, from the roads.

The most important roads in the county are its north–south arteries—the I-5 and the 805—and it's no accident that they extend between the county's two largest military bases: Pendleton in the north and Coronado down by the border. San Diego's self-styling as a "military town" began around the turn of the twentieth century, when politicians began vying for marine and naval contracts, hoping to use the money to expand the city. The existing army artillery base at Fort Rosecrans was joined quickly by the navy and the air force, and by World War II, San Diego was the country's biggest military town west of the Mississippi. The region swarmed with people and industry, and the city grew to accommodate them. Today, San Diego is still funded by the military and surrounded by the military: at its southernmost point lies Coronado Naval Base, the West Coast's primary center for warfare and Special Forces training. The naval base, which remains the largest single employer in the county, has fifty-seven thousand acres spread from Coronado Island back to the La Posta Mountain Warfare Training Facility fifty miles east into the desert. On the northern edge, forty minutes up the 5, there's Camp Pendleton, the largest West Coast expeditionary training facility for the Marine Corps. In between is Marine Corps Air Station Miramar, former home of Topgun. Many neighborhoods were once barracks. Fully a quarter of county residents work for the military and defense industries.

These last facts might be surprising to the average San Diego civilian. There are aircraft carriers in the bay and the occasional air show at Miramar, but otherwise the military's presence is inconspicuous. Most personnel live on or near the bases; you almost never see anyone walking around the suburbs in a uniform. Everyone knows there's a naval base on Coronado—it takes up more than half of the island—but you don't see it. Instead, you see the Victorian spires of Hotel Del, where Marilyn Monroe shot *Some Like It Hot*, and giant sand dunes and plazas made from terra-cotta tile. There are snipers being trained a mile or two away, but even if you drive to the base entrance, it doesn't look like much, and without clearance you can't drive any farther.

Total reliance on an industry that takes pains to remain out of sight can give a city a tensile sensitivity to what should be seen and unseen. North Torrey Pines Road is another hub of the San Diego economy but one that's deliberately visible, lined with the grand institutions and titans of local industry that the city is proud to exhibit. It begins at the UC San Diego campus in front of the La Jolla Playhouse, which sends a Tony winner from its gleaming, state-of-the-art theater complex to Broadway nearly every year. The La Jolla Playhouse's biggest patrons are its neighbors, the scientific research and biotechnology institutions that constitute the city's second most important industry and dominate the mesa that North Torrey Pines Road bisects. Many of them sit on land formerly owned by the city government, which donated large tracts to research institutions and defense contractors in the 1950s in another ploy to attract industry to the region. The grandest of them, only a few minutes from the La Jolla Playhouse, is the Salk Institute, the city's monument to the sciences, founded in 1960 as a collaborative environment for scientists to consider, rather loftily, the "wider implications of their discoveries for the future of humanity." Louis Kahn designed the complex, a dramatic modernist construction with a wide center pavilion and buildings set at rakish angles to maximize the cliff-top ocean view. It is so stunning that people come from all over the world to tour the grounds. Inside, Nobel laureates lead teams tasked with curing cancer, ending world hunger, and stopping global warming, and they're making progress.

Salk is the shining example: idealistic, innovative, rigorously productive, and—not for nothing—nice to look at. But there are also the labs at UCSD, where scientists are curing phantom-limb syndrome and mapping the way human memory functions, and the Scripps Research Institute next door, which is developing cures for deafness, obesity, Huntington's disease, and addiction—including a vaccine for heroin. Scattered between the biotech companies and the research institutions are the defense contractors: L-3, which does surveillance and recon for Homeland Security, and General Atomics, the region's largest and oldest defense contractor. General Atomics, which, like Salk, occupies land donated from the city, is responsible for everything from supplying nuclear research reactors to government agencies to developing the drones used by the military in Afghanistan. Right now it's also designing a series of theoretical nuclear reactors, as well as systems for hazardous material destruction, magnetic levitation systems, uranium processing, and "advanced laser technologies."

And it's attractive. The air smells of the eucalyptus trees that shade the sidewalks, which are clean, white, and trimmed with politely shaped hedges. The grass is very green, which means the grass is very expensive, maintained in defiance of the desert climate and water shortages. All the shiny buildings have cliff-top views of the ocean or of the thirty-six-hole golf course where pre-scandal Tiger Woods, looking handsome and correct in a bright red polo, won the U.S. Open in 2008 to the applause of day-drunk, suntanned men wearing Oakleys and carrying AmEx cards. Socialites swathed in Lululemon yoga pants, diamonds, and the same shade of blond flit in and out of the luxury resort spa at the Lodge at Torrey Pines. The most stunning views are privately owned, but the second best is publicly accessible from the dusty cliffs by the Gliderport, hidden on an unpaved road just behind the Salk Institute. Acres of undeveloped mesas and canyons roll back from the coast—dotted with multimillion-dollar homes—and there's so much ocean between the beach and the horizon that on a clear day Mexico emerges faintly in the distance. At the Gliderport, people strap themselves into paragliders and leap off the mesa into blue air, because the curvature of the coast is such that hanging above North Torrey Pines Road, you can see the whole county, from Pendleton straight to Coronado.

Some of that undeveloped land belongs to the Salk Institute, but most of it is the state reserve for which North Torrey Pines is named, dense with chaparral and pine trees and spiky plants that look like aliens made them. Just past the golf course, you can hike from the cliffs all the way down to the beach. There you will find old surfers and kid surfers and babies and runners and ladies in big hats and teenage couples and really every kind of person out for a walk on the beach. These beaches are not like the beaches of Cape Cod or Mykonos or Normandy. They are dramatic and wild looking and a little dangerous. The cliffs are sheer and unstable, hundreds of feet tall and given to crumbling and dropping lethal amounts of clod and rocks onto the sand below without warning. But it's hard to stay away from the cliffs; the beach narrows so precipitously in places that when the tide rises, the surf erases it entirely.

Once I was down on the beach in the haze. The sun became material, and there was so much of it: hundreds of feet of light swirling above the surf. The cliffs stretched higher. Everything grew huge. On the ground, the babies and the surfers, everyone, seemed wrapped in a heady gladness, reverent.

You can drive all this in five minutes, from the La Jolla Playhouse past Salk and the Gliderport and the Lodge and General Atomics through the reserve. There's a bend as the road dips down steeply toward the ocean, and the trees and sandy cliff faces lining the road fall away so that you're making a gentle left turn into panorama. This stretch of road is like a gift. No traffic, and the water glitters hard, and the car flies down the hill without any help from the gas pedal, and then you are blessed in a way only San Diego can bless you.

There's a phenomenon known to residents of San Diego, and Southern California generally, called the Santa Ana winds, which visit sporadically and reverse things. Normally, the wind blows through the county from west to east, carrying cool air from over the ocean out toward the desert, which accounts for both the breezy temperateness that draws tourists to its beaches and the way the mercury climbs by the mile the farther away from the shore you drive. But when the Santa Ana winds come, the whole thing turns around, blows east to west so the desert air sweeps back toward the coast, flooding the shoreline with air so dry and abrasive it feels as if it could light matches. You wake up in the morning, and the world feels thirsty and vaguely murderous. Your skin knows in a way your brain doesn't that something isn't right.

On these days, the weather report warns of brush fires, which overtake the county once every few years and incinerate houses and land and people until the wind changes again. In 2007, the fires flew from East County all the way to the coast. I was gone by then, but my parents still live near the beach, and over the course of two days the fire moved toward their house, uncontrolled, until it was less than half a mile away when the Santa Ana stopped, the wind reversed course, and everything blew back out to the desert. This is how Santa Ana comes and goes, like wrath.

The 805 crosses the 905 in Otay Mesa, a town featured prominently in the traffic reports because it's a major border checkpoint and there are always delays. Continue on the 805 for two miles past the 905, and you're at the end of California, Tijuana rising before you on a hill, the windows of its tightly packed box houses reflecting the vision of Otay Mesa back across the fence. When there's no traffic, the signs change quickly. IT IS ILLEGAL TO TAKE FIREARMS OR WEAPONS ACROSS THE BORDER, reads one. Another reminds drivers not to try to cross into Mexico with weed in the car.

The 905 runs parallel to the border, peeling like tape through land that was flat and arid to start but was bulldozed and stripped anyway, just in case. It's the east–west highways that move you from the tidy rows of palm trees and bright storefronts into a landscape that desaturates by the mile. Head east and everything gets browner and drier with every passing exit. Most of the east–west freeways are lined with tract home developments with inaccurate names like Sun Valley or strip malls full of Toys "R" Us stores and Paneras, but the 905 as it passes through Otay Mesa is all warehouses, scattered like overturned building blocks. Some are commercial— Performance Plastics, Martinez & Sons Produce—but most are unmarked storage or lie empty. SPACE AVAILABLE signs flap against corrugated metal or are driven on stakes into the dirt. There are no stores of any kind except for a few bodegas, a taco stand with a faded banner, and a gigantic Goodwill. To the right is the famous fence, miles of "climb-proof" chain link rising fifteen feet into the air and looped with barbed wire at the top just in case. Ahead—black hills.

The 905 is where San Diego's secret economies reside, only fifteen minutes from SeaWorld. The Sinaloa cartel took control of the smuggling corridor in 2006, and since then trafficking of both drugs and people has been on the rise. Over 70 percent of the methamphetamines trafficked into the United States pass through San Diego: between 2008 and 2013, three times more meth was seized at the Tijuana border than all other U.S.-Mexico border crossings combined. It comes in through cars, hidden in gas tanks or seat lining. There are also tunnels: in October 2013, Homeland Security found a smuggling tunnel more than six hundred yards long connecting a warehouse in Tijuana to one of the many unmarked warehouses in Otay Mesa. The tunnel was equipped with lighting, ventilation, and an electric rail system, and inside the authorities found 8.5 tons of marijuana and 327 pounds of cocaine. It was the eighth tunnel like this discovered since 2006. According to the special agent in charge of Homeland Security investigations in San Diego, Otay Mesa's claylike soil makes it "popular."

The weapons go in the other direction: the government did a study in 2012 which found that nearly three-quarters of the firearms recovered in Mexico over five years were traceable back to the United States. American gun suppliers make approximately $127 million a year on the guns smuggled across the border, and a lot of it comes through Otay Mesa. Then there are the people. Human trafficking is on the rise, and in 2012 the FBI declared San Diego a "high intensity child prostitution area." A few times a year the news reports surface: teenage sex slaves discovered, gang members arrested in "massive" trafficking conspiracies. The number of cases prosecuted tripled between 2009 and 2013. In October 2013, authorities found nineteen persons being smuggled through the Otay Mesa checkpoint inside air conditioners. It is also widely speculated that sexual assault of migrant women by Border Patrol is rampant, but those cases aren't prosecuted.

The word "pharmaceuticals" carries a different meaning in such a place, as does the word "innovation." The fact that both words are just as relevant in Otay Mesa as they are in Torrey Pines provides subtle justification for the dominance of the military and defense industries in the city, which are paid by government agencies in exchange for help regulating the border. But even their presence seems altered and cloaked this far east and south. You can drive within a quarter mile of the headquarters of San Diego Border Patrol and never know it is there. Blackwater is in Otay Mesa, the private military security company notorious for, among other things, illegal arms trading, killing sprees of unarmed civilians in the Iraq war, and creating a private special ops team of former CIA officers. But you'd never find it as such: its name has been changed twice— from Blackwater to Xe and then to Academi in 2011—and it doesn't advertise itself. The building, a giant cube with mirrored, opaque windows, lies several turns off the freeway among flattened fields, on the corner of Siempre Viva Road and a cul-de-sac to nowhere. It is, eerily, surrounded by roads to nowhere, neatly paved advances into the seven hundred yards of fields that lie between Siempre Viva and the border, tracing paths to corporate lots that were never developed. In the warehouse, Academi training sessions are in process, but outside it is silent. Like everywhere else in Otay Mesa, plenty is happening, but there's nothing to see. Scrubby trees poke up from the dirt in neat rows every thirty feet, shading empty sidewalks where no one walks.

The last time I was in San Diego, I drove to Otay Mesa and spent a morning cruising the dead ends. My brother, Griffin, rode with me and served as a kind of terse spirit guide, doling out dispassionate observations ("Well, the drag racers are using it," he said of Siempre Viva Road, noting the skid marks) and practical advice ("Get the fuck off your cell phone, you're going to get arrested"). When we agreed that we'd seen what there was to see ("Not very much"), we drove west on the 905, away from the mountains and back toward the 805 cross. A few minutes passed in silence, and then he spoke again: "Prisoners."

I jumped, scanning the cars in front of us. There it was: a white unmarked van that looked pretty much like any other white van except for a small floodlight attached to the back, angled to shine down on whoever might be stepping in or out. Through the tinted back windows, I could see that the inside of the van had been converted into a cage, like the ones used to transport animals back and forth from the pound, but the silhouettes inside were human profiles, sitting in two rows facing each other.

"ICE," Griff ventured. "Immigration. Some guys got picked up in the desert trying to cross the border." He was probably right. People come every day, alone and in groups. They scale the fence or attempt to walk across in the most remote, dangerous parts of the desert or just make a break for it and sprint up the freeway at the checkpoint, fleeing north and west. In November 2013, a crowd of a hundred stormed the border, hurling rocks and bottles at the agents.

At the border, the signage changes again when you head north on the 805. No more finger wagging about weapons or half-lit fluorescent advertisements for bail bonds. Instead, a warning to watch for something darting across the five-lane freeway. You see signs like these in other states, but the figures outlined in black are deer or moose or falling rocks. In this sign, it's a family—a mother, a father, and a little girl—running as if chased. The little girl has pigtails. Then, fifteen car lengths later, a larger and more colorful sign reads, in large, loopy letters, WELCOME TO CALIFORNIA.

2

LOS ANGELES PLAYS ITSELF

DAYNA TORTORICI

Traffic

In Los Angeles the freeways have definite articles, like rivers: the 10, the 110, the 101, the 405. The only one that doesn't is Pacific Coast Highway, or PCH, the segment of California State Route 1 that begins in Dana Point, just south of Laguna Beach, and winds up to the Oxnard Plain before turning due north to Mendocino, where an estimated two-thirds of the economy is based on the cultivation of marijuana. Approaching PCH from the 10 West, you must pass through McClure Tunnel in Santa Monica, a quick elbow that, despite frantic signage, cars fly through too fast. That tunnel spits you out onto PCH, and suddenly after so much concrete—the ocean. It's so bright you understand why even the least pretentious people here wear sunglasses. I've ridden this stretch of highway thousands of times since childhood, but it still feels like a small miracle every time, like the conversion of Paul.

After about a quarter mile, you hit traffic. If you're lucky, you stall somewhere with a nice view of the beach. If you're not, and it's June, you wait in a drab overcast, no view to speak of, and wait for the light at Sunset to change.

City boundaries are, to me, fuzzy. To know technically for sure, I have to look them up. From above, the mass of the city looks arbitrary, as if someone flung paint at a map and said, "That's L.A." A blob, with one skinny line dripping all the way to San Pedro. My sister lives in Westwood, with the UCLA professors and yoga teachers. Her boyfriend lives in the Valley, one of the nice parts. She refers to their relationship as long-distance. It takes her an hour to get to where he lives, so she stays for three days at a time, then comes home for one or two.

The most famous intersection in the city is a four-tiered overpass called "the stack," where the 110 meets the 101. There wasn't enough room to build a cloverleaf interchange, so the planners just piled the ramps on top of one another, like in the more boring, transitional parts of a roller coaster. Opened in 1953, it was the first such intersection in the world. If it wasn't the inspiration for the streetscape in *Blade Runner*, it could have been.

Traffic is a perennial struggle. In 1976, Caltrans, the state agency in charge of all transportation planning, introduced a program of "diamond lanes" to cut the number of cars on the Santa Monica Freeway by seventy-eight hundred, a model for high-occupancy vehicle (HOV) lanes that screwed up traffic forever. Joan Didion wrote about it in an essay called "Bureaucrats": they painted the lanes; the municipal engineer of L.A.'s surface streets was pressured to make traffic worse and force people *onto* the freeways, where they would be disciplined by traffic into carpooling. Accidents tripled; angry drivers scattered nails on the HOV lanes in protest. Diamond lanes were introduced to other major freeways anyway. In 2009, the city approved a $1.1 billion project to add, among other things, a ten-mile diamond lane on a stretch of the northbound 405 called the Sepulveda Pass Improvements Project. It's a kind of concession, half 1950s-era highway expansion and half 1970s-era environmental constriction: a new lane that only carpoolers can use. In 2011 and 2012, significant stretches of the freeway were shut down, and the radio DJs flipped out, saying it would be a CARMAGEDDON. They scared everyone off the road for two weeks. A record number of people took the Metro, though most stayed inside, as the *Los Angeles Times* had advised them to. As a result, traffic was lighter during the Carmageddon than usual. Air quality improved dramatically in minutes—83 percent better than usual, according to one study by UCLA environmental researchers.

"The air was amazingly clean that weekend," said a leading professor on the study. "Almost below what our instruments could detect."

In 2011, my friend Matt, a reporter for *The Huffington Post*, dug up a report from the Brookings Institution saying that Los Angeles gives people better access to public transit than any other city in the continental United States: 99.1 percent of no-car households have access. In the nation, only Honolulu is better. This seems unbelievable. Of course the commute, once accessed, is lousy: few people get to work in under ninety minutes. I recently watched the Blue Line, which runs from Long Beach toward downtown, pass through Watts; it was only three cars long. It looked kind of like the Franklin Avenue shuttle in Brooklyn, if the Franklin Avenue shuttle ran on the A line from Far Rockaway to Ozone Park and never touched a rich neighborhood.

Teenagers

To be in L.A. without a car is to be at the mercy of whoever will give you a ride. In this way, it both is and isn't a teenager's town.

Nobody knows where to go; it's not a city designed for accidental social discoveries. You think of a place, you look it up, you go; you look up the way back, you go home. I was always terrified to go too far. My little brother had his adolescence after Google Maps, so he went anywhere with a sense of ease and entitlement I found both repulsive and enviable. He could never get lost. I wasn't brave, but neither is he; I at least had to ask leering guys in academic Spanish how to get back to the 10. I asked my brother what he did with his freedom: Valley parties, he said.

All I ever did was drive the familiar loop of surface streets I knew, smoking cigarettes, blasting the heat with the windows down on winter nights. I drove from the Starbucks to the Coffee Bean where Perez Hilton wrote his celebrity gossip blog, to the other Starbucks and the other Coffee Bean where the girls in my class smoked Parliaments with homeless Vietnam vets as part of their Method acting research for the school play. We ate frozen yogurt for lunch and also for dinner and smoked and drove until we had to go home.

The other thing we did was drive up steep streets to look at the city from above. To the top of the Hollywood Hills, to the top of the Santa Monica Mountains, to Mulholland, to the Westridge fire road up the street from where Kobe Bryant's dad supposedly lived, in the house Kobe bought for him. There were rumors that the ceilings and appliances were built extra tall to accommodate him. From the fire road we could see the whole city, from the Pacific Ocean all the way past downtown, and on a clear day to San Bernardino and Catalina Island.

I mostly remember growing up as a series of establishment shots, like this one. There's not a lot of romance in ripping up Joshua trees and pumping water where it doesn't belong, but the result does look majestic at night, dense with lights as clear as the sky must have been before light pollution. This view is our compensation for smog, for never getting to see any real stars. (The star maps advertised on sandwich boards propped along Sunset Boulevard are not, as I thought as a kid, for astronomers.) Meanwhile, the smog, like the airborne toxic event in *White Noise*, creates vulgar, beautiful, sorbet sunsets.

It was reported that the city's most devastating wildfire, in 2007, was caused by a combination of drought, snapped power lines threaded through Malibu, a rogue pyromaniac, and a ten-year-old boy left alone with a box of matches. Before this was consensus, I was told that some teenagers hot-boxing a cave in Malibu left a joint burning: it caught a straw of dry brush and in days lit half the coast on fire.

Weed

The weed here is not for lightweights. I can't smoke it at all. The last time I tried, I drooled uncontrollably for several hours and couldn't stop touching my hair. Our brothers had cannabis club cards for "migraines," or our parents had them for cancer, which meant legal access to marijuana was easy.

Dispensary offerings have the stupidest names: Blue Dream, Berry White, Chocolope, Shark Shock, Sour Diesel Reserve, Super Lemon Haze, Green Crack, Cadillac Purple, OG Kush, Be Real, L.A. Confidential, Diablo OG, Girl Scout Cookies, Jedi, Skywalker, Yoda. On this dumb-named stuff you can get high just being in the room.

But you better have a club card. The L.A. County jail system is the largest in the world: eighty-eight municipalities, seventy-four law enforcement agencies, thirty-some criminal courthouses, and eight jail facilities. It houses an estimated twenty thousand people a year. Between 2004 and 2008, nearly 40 percent of arrests were for drug-related felonies or misdemeanors. Of those arrested for marijuana possession, only 23 percent were white, according to the FBI. But the FBI undermines its own data, lumping Latinos with whites where the LAPD doesn't. ("Latino" is an ethnic, as opposed to a racial, category, a distinction honored more in statistics than in everyday policing.) Although blacks make up a little less than 10 percent of L.A. County's population, they constitute 30 percent of marijuana arrests.

Speech

Actors and immigrants come here to have their speech scrubbed of regional inflection. Signs stapled to power-line poles say VOCAL COACH and SPEAK ENGLISH PERFECTLY and GET RID OF YOUR ACCENT and list a phone number. People like to say that everyone in Los Angeles is an arriviste or an immigrant, but that's no more true of L.A. than it is of any other big city. What is true is that the city does not aggressively remind you of its history.

I think vocal fry was invented here, that kind of sour, elongated, throaty way of talking that makes a long *a* sound slide into a long *i* sound, swaps "uh" for "ah," and nearly drops the long *e* altogether (as in "which wahy to the beach?" and "yer harcut looks rahlly good, whair'd you get et?"). Frank Zappa's 1982 song "Valley Girl" put L.A. speech on the map when his fourteen-year-old daughter, Moon, sang-spoke the lyrics "Like, oh my God, like, totally." This was notable. In L.A., people are supposed to sound like they're from nowhere, in order to sound like they're from anywhere: a central casting accent. The new vocal fry is like the Valley Girl sapped of enthusiasm: poolside, on Klonopin, constrained to the lowest register.

Los Angeles Plays Itself

The landscape has the ability to self-erase its particularities and become mutable. For decades, it has been forced to play other cities in movies.

In his incredible 2003 documentary *Los Angeles Plays Itself*, the filmmaker Thom Andersen chronicles every city Los Angeles has played in the history of American cinema. A video essay splicing together scenes from other films, famous and obscure, the movie draws out the city's architecture as a character. "Again and again it has played a city with no name," the voice-over says. Shots of nondescript nighttime scenes in front of hotels and movie-theater marquees loop again and again. "Its landmarks are obscure enough that they can play many roles."

In 1942, the Bradbury Building downtown played a Mandalay hotel in *China Girl*. In 1944, it played a London military hospital in *The White Cliffs of Dover*. It was the office of a New York publisher in *Wolf* in 1994. It played the future, most famously, in the climactic rooftop scene in *Blade Runner* in 1982. Frank Lloyd Wright's Mayan-revival Ennis House in Los Feliz, built in 1924, "transcends space and time." Andersen cites seven films in as many seconds: the Ennis House "could be fictionally located in Washington [*Timestalkers*, 1987], or Osaka [*Black Rain*, 1989]. It could play an ancient villa [*Howling II: Your Sister Is a Werewolf*, 1985], a nineteenth-century haunted house [*House on Haunted Hill*, 1958], a contemporary mansion [*The Terminal Man*, 1974], a twenty-first-century apartment building [*Blade Runner*, again], or a twenty-sixth-century science lab [*Timestalkers*, again], where Klaus Kinski invents time travel."

It's not that the buildings are indistinct. They look unlike anything else, which makes it even weirder that they're swapped in like it's no big deal; nobody would ever let the New York Public Library play a building in another city this way. What's made them interchangeable is the cultural dominance of Hollywood. Hollywood has denied Los Angeles the ability to be particular. We have monuments, but nobody knows what they are, except for the Hollywood sign. What says "Los Angeles" more than the Hollywood sign? Or rather: Does anything else say "Los Angeles" *but* the Hollywood sign? It's the only distinguishing symbol you'll see on souvenir key chains at LAX. You could get the one with palm trees, but then you may as well be in Florida or Hawaii.

Andersen observes that in movies villains often live in high-modernist International Style apartments, with living rooms enclosed in glass and cantilevered over a wide valley. The glass is an invitation for ejection: someone unfortunate will fly through it, grip the ledge of the building with a bloodied hand, and to the sound of screeching strings fall into the obscure mountain brush, never to be seen again, at least until the sequel.

Some of these houses for villains still stand. Richard Neutra's Lovell Health House in Los Feliz, made for a naturopath in the 1920s and reconceived as the home of a pimp in *L.A. Confidential*, is a favorite of architecture tourists. Many of the fakes, the prefab reproductions perched on the bluffs overlooking Pacific Coast Highway, detached and slid down the cliffs during the 1994 earthquake. Some have been rebuilt.

Herr Schmidt

Whenever anyone condemns the cultural vacuity of Los Angeles, defenders bring up the famous German émigrés who moved there during the war: Adorno, Horkheimer, Mann, Brecht, Neutra, Lang, Schoenberg. In *The Rest Is Noise*, the music critic Alex Ross describes a scene between Schoenberg and the wife of the novelist Lion Feuchtwanger at the Brentwood Country Mart, a grocery store with an outdoor fire pit where my parents used to take my sister and me to get fried chicken. Marta Feuchtwanger is handling some grapefruit when she sees the composer, wild-eyed, coming at her. "Lies, Frau Marta, lies!" he screams. "You have to know, *I never had syphilis!*" Since upgraded to an upscale shabby-chic boutique complex, where the General Store sells bubble mailers and Lacoste polo shirts, the Country Mart is now home to the Goop pop-up store, a physical-reality version of Gwyneth Paltrow's lifestyle website.

Bertolt Brecht, who was famously miserable here, wrote a poem about L.A. called "Contemplating Hell," after Shelley's "Hell is a city much like London." Hell, wrote Brecht, "must be even more like Los Angeles":

In Hell, too,
There are, I cannot doubt, these luxuriant gardens
With flowers as big as trees—which, to be sure, wilt
Without delay, if not watered at great expense.
And fruit markets with huge piles of fruit, which nonetheless
have neither scent nor taste. And endless trains of cars,
Lighter than their own shadows, faster than
Foolish thoughts, gleaming vehicles in which
Pinkish people, coming from nowhere, drive nowhere.
And houses built for the fortunate, which therefore stand
      empty
Even when inhabited.

The houses in Hell are not all ugly, either.
But the worry of being thrown onto the street
Consumes the residents of mansions no less than
Those who dwell in the slums.

He was wrong about the produce, but right about the houses.
There were other Germans. Three miles or so from Brecht's

house on Twenty-Sixth Street, tucked into the Santa Monica Mountains, stands Murphy Ranch, a fifty-five-acre compound built in 1933 by a small group of Nazi sympathizers. According to the sketchy historical record, they were also mystical cultists under the sway of a charismatic German, "Herr Schmidt," who claimed to have supernatural powers. The ranch was enormously extensive: there were plans for a mansion; a timed irrigation system for sustainable agriculture; a water tank and a power station. Hikers in Will Rogers State Historic Park still stumble upon the concrete infrastructure of their aborted fascist utopia. Now, though covered in graffiti, it's a nice place to walk your dog.

Fear

Thomas Mann used to love getting his hair cut in Westwood. "Gone to Westwood for a haircut," he'd write in his diaries.

I went to driving school in Westwood, but before I could drive, I had to beg my parents to take me there; they confused it for East Hollywood, Inglewood, or somewhere else. This was when in Mid-City and South Central L.A. there were three gang-related killings a day. The fact that they were nervous about Westwood, a UCLA candy land with two movie theaters and a California Pizza Kitchen, says something about how scared people were then or about how little people left their own neighborhoods in L.A.

In memoirs, in documentaries, in conversation, people often describe pivotal, fear-triggering events as having "changed Los Angeles overnight." After Sharon Tate was murdered by the Manson family, people in the city started to lock their doors at night. I was at a Christmas party when someone said to me that on the eve of the O. J. Simpson ruling everyone in Hollywood became a gun owner overnight. Nothing in Los Angeles happens overnight, but this is how people like to talk. Why, I don't know, but I think it has something to do with wanting the city to be either a dream or a nightmare, like in David Lynch's *Mulholland Drive*. Psychologically, there are two L.A.'s. One is where Naomi Watts gets to be the sunny aspiring actress Betty and have beautiful teeth and a gorgeous lesbian relationship with an amnesiac Laura Harring. The other is where Naomi Watts is Diane, with fucked-up teeth, an unrequited romantic obsession, and a bullet in her head. They're both the same movie, and none of it makes any sense. But it says something about how the city sees itself: things are one way, or suddenly another.

Self-Improvement

Growing up in L.A. taught me that beautiful people get away with practically anything: it is an aesthetocracy. To be beautiful is to transcend, to move through the world frictionlessly, as consistently pleasant as the weather: temperate, no clouds, photo ready. I no longer believe this is true. I don't live here anymore, but when I visit, I see many good-looking people getting in and out of cars in workout pants, going to and from spinning or the farmers' market, or driving to the outdoor staircases they will run up and down ten times before getting back in the car to drive home, where they will draw the blinds on the sun they moved here to see. I wonder if their lives feel easy or strained, if they're blissed out on endorphins and vegetable juice or if they hate themselves, only working this hard to remind themselves they have a body when the air offers no resistance. It is possible to become so healthy that you become sick. This way of life is kinder to the men than to the women, who are still promised more for physical perfection—a career, a love, a future. But the men do it too, pouring all of the energy and passion of a human life into their bodies, including the ones who have already won everything there was to win. It's a paradoxical lifestyle, self-improvement as an ethos. It demands one remain just shy of perfect, leaving some room to improve.

I once saw Paris Hilton walk, in person. I was at the Grammys.

She was late and walked around the front of the pit to her seat in the first row. Even when hardly more than a silhouette, she has an incredible walk. There's a real thrust to it; it was impossible to look away. I later learned from an MTV special that Paris wasn't always good at walking; to improve, she took lessons. Her how-to-walk-and-pose-in-photographs coach was interviewed for the special. A lot of three-quarter angling and triangle arm, that thing women are told makes their triceps look skinnier: one arm down, one hand on the hip, wrists turned in so the thumb digs unnaturally into the lower back.

I saw the special around the same time I was reading *The Magic Mountain* and had mono, and I read it as an L.A. parable: a perfectly healthy Hans Castorp plans a brief visit to his tubercular cousin in a sanatorium but stays for seven years, improving his own lungs, perhaps unnecessarily. "And life? Life itself? Was it perhaps only an infection, a sickening of matter?" Hans asks himself. Here, as in the Alps, self-betterment is a way of life. His permanent convalescence felt familiar.

Downtown

Slightly north of downtown, beside the L.A. River, sits Marsh Park. It is beautiful, but underneath the roped-off sections of grass are high levels of toxic chromium. My friend used to work for the Parks Department and told me she wanted to host an event there until she saw the reports about the soil. She says it's still bad: "Erin Brockovich bad."

Still, she says, the future is the river. Fifty-one miles long, the L.A. River is in most places just a concrete trough, fit for a car chase. If it were not fed with wastewater, it would be full only one or two months a year. But there is much talk of "greening" the river, replacing the concrete with a soft bottom, and developing the land that runs alongside it.

Downtown feels fake because it is; not many people go there.

Earlier improvement schemes have swept away affordable housing, and now all you see are mirror-paneled buildings that fling the wink of a merciless sun back into your eye. The people you do see downtown are taking a break from work at the Westin Bonaventure or one of the many $10-an-hour parking garages. Or they're visiting the library or homeless.

The week of Thanksgiving, I decided to drive through to see if it had changed. The five-block area east of Main that forms the heart of Skid Row was packed with people. Blue tarp tents rigged with plastic string, grocery carts, and crates lined the rows of low buildings on either side of the street, as if everybody were waiting for something. Between three thousand and six thousand people live here. Its sudden appearance, as I drove east through downtown, came as a shock. One block, deserted but clean downtown shopping streets, maybe a nice new bookstore. The next, hundreds and hundreds of people, families and junkies, crouched next to everything they own.

For years I heard about "sweeps" of Skid Row, periodic raids in which the police threw everyone's stuff indiscriminately into the garbage. In 2011, eight residents sued, and now there's a ban on the illegal seizure of homeless people's property that's left unattended on sidewalks. It makes sense: you can't take everything with you when you go to the bathroom or duck into a shelter for a shower. In 2012, the U.S. Ninth Circuit Court of Appeals upheld the ban under the protections of the Fourth and Fourteenth Amendments, against unreasonable search and seizure and the promise of due process. The difference on the street between before and after the ruling is huge, and illuminating. It's easier to ignore the existence of thousands of people when you're constantly erasing their traces, throwing away their belongings. Let them live there, and you really see them.

When I got home, I checked Google Maps to see what Skid Row looks like on Street View. I was stunned: block after block, nothing. Almost no people, and not a trace of debris—just pavement, drab buildings, a man with a blurred-out face frozen in the crosswalk, holding a bouquet of red roses to sell at the intersection for $5 each. I looked at the time stamp, which says the photographs were taken in May 2011—just before the ban. I wonder how long they'll keep it that way.

3

MODERN FRESNO

MICHAEL THOMSEN

Fresno was a mistake from the beginning.

I was five when we moved there. My dad and I drove from Texas in a rented Ryder truck; we finally pulled off the highway in a dingy business district north of the city's abandoned downtown. My mom had driven ahead of us, and we met her at a Motel 6 beneath sagging power lines and fast-food signs that had begun to crack in the harsh central California sun. My dad was starting a job teaching accounting at Fresno State, thinking a midsize farming city would be a good place to settle.

My parents were both born in Denmark. They'd grown up thirty miles apart but didn't meet until their mid-twenties, when they were both graduate students. They were brought up in the strict tradition of Seventh-Day Adventism, an Old Testament sect of Christianity that forbids alcohol, caffeine, jewelry, and pork and observes Sabbath from sundown Friday to sundown Saturday. When they discovered each other at a small religious college on Lake Michigan, they found ways to get together as often as possible.

My dad would pick my mom up when she finished a night shift at the school hospital, where she was studying to be a nurse. She'd stop by his bachelor apartment with fruits and baked goods on the weekend, and they'd go to the same church groups together, spending hours afterward debating the week's subject. They married a year after meeting and followed their hunger for novelty, moving from Michigan to Tanzania, then on to Italy, Germany, and—most novel of all—Texas, before deciding it was time to stop and raise my older brother and me. And so we drove to Fresno.

Fresno sits about two-thirds of the way down California's huge Central Valley, which runs almost the entire length of the state, bounded to the west by the coastal ranges and to the east by the Sierra Nevada. This is the most fertile farmland in the United States. The central and northern parts get plenty of rain, but the southern part, called the San Joaquin Valley, is dry and subject to droughts, though with a few nice months of green in fall and spring. It could not have looked very promising when Fresno first appeared as a small outpost along the San Joaquin River; the expansion of the California Pacific Railroad to Fresno in the 1870s helped, however. And soon enough it became clear that despite the difficulty of the land the connection to the farming infrastructure being set up to the north, including the railroad, made settling there worthwhile. Dutch and German farmers built irrigation ditches to make the land farmable. They were soon followed by immigrants from Mexico, Armenia, China, and Japan.

The first settlers decided to grow grapes to take advantage of the heat and the quick fruiting cycle. When the first crop of grapes proved too sour for wine, most farmers opted to make raisins: before long Fresno was the raisin capital of the world. It also established itself as the economic hub and northernmost outpost of the San Joaquin Valley, which in addition to raisins produced most of California's almonds, kiwis, cantaloupes, oranges, and figs. By the 1920s, the town had grown to forty-five thousand, and it became known as a "mini San Francisco" for its bustling streets, Victorian homes, and multicultural population. Another pattern also established itself: the area was close enough to Mexico, and close enough to the coast, that cheap migrant labor was always available. Farm owners cycled through laborers as quickly as they could. The bigger farms and processing mills offered single-room shacks to house their seasonal workers, some of which would later be converted into "Assembly Camps" to imprison Japanese-Americans during World War II.

In 1937, the federal government funded construction of Friant Dam, which blocked the upper San Joaquin River. The extra water turned the farming boom into an exponentially accelerating growth cycle. In 2009, agriculture revenue totaled $5.3 billion; Fresno County was one of the most productive areas of farmland in the world. That same year a report by the Federal Reserve used Fresno as a case study for American poverty, citing a Brookings presentation that found it had the most concentrated area of poverty in the country and the fourth-highest overall poverty rate.

After our stay at Motel 6, my parents moved us into an apartment complex in northwest Fresno called Cobblestone Village. In the 1980s, this was the scaffolded edge of the city, only half a mile from where the suburbs disintegrated at the sandy banks of the San Joaquin. The apartments were surrounded by acres of troweled lots. A wide pit had been dug in one with I beams and rebar sticking out of the dirt, the foundations of what would become a glassy real estate office.

My mom worked as a home hospice provider to cancer patients in the decrepit old neighborhoods left to rot around downtown. I sometimes went with her when my dad had to teach and none of the neighbors could look after me. Most of the houses had been built during the 1930s and 1940s. They sat on small squares of dead grass with no fences between them. The streets were always empty and dwindled into the dusty farmland abutting the southern end of the city.

Things smelled differently there. Rotting wood and years of piled junk crowded the light out of the windows. Inside each house lived a sad-eyed, slack-skinned person sitting in a wheelchair, plugged into a whirring ventilator. The small plastic tubes looked like bridles anchored against their noses. It was alarming to watch my mother speak kindly and confidentially to these collapsing bodies. The whooshing melodies of her Danish voice seemed strong enough to blow the walls over.

At home, her voice lost its volume, became a smaller part of the television racket, my brother's heartless teasing, and my dad's disruptive insertions of trivia from the news or whichever new book he'd come across in the academic lounge. My dad was tall and hunched; his head always seemed to be nodding upward with a grin, ready to announce some remarkable discovery. He had a bristly mustache and curly wild hair that grew around his ears to make up for his bald head. Otherwise he was like the male version of my mother, able to roll through any trough of gloom with optimism. They seemed like conjoined beings, the masculine and feminine variants of some eternal life, a Buddha with two faces and a billion arms.

When I finished second grade, they announced we were leaving the apartment to move into a house they had just built even farther north. The city was expanding, and we were trying to keep our dreams out of its reach.

On a map, Fresno is amorphous, a conical blob that looks like a piece of bubble gum squashed against a sidewalk. Downtown Fresno sits at the southwestern end of the blob, at the intersection between two freeways. California State Route 99 shoots diagonally northwest, marking the western edge of the city, while the 41—a smaller local freeway—goes straight north and connects with Yosemite sixty miles north. The two freeways form an inverted triangle with downtown sitting at the bottom tip.

The Tower District, a small bohemian neighborhood built up alongside Fresno City College and the eponymous Tower Theatre, is just north of downtown. The area thrived in the 1930s and 1940s with cafés, restaurants, and local nightlife; many of the buildings still stand, though businesses have struggled to keep the bohemian spirit alive as the city sprawls farther and farther away. Two miles farther north is the Old Fig Garden, an aging but opulent quarter of big lots and European-style country homes nestled into old fig orchards. Beyond Fig Garden is northwest Fresno, full of ranch homes and mini-mansions built in the 1970s and 1980s; this is where we moved when I was in second grade.

West Fresno is cut off from the rest of the city by the 99. It's a pockmarked encampment of fast-food restaurants and cheap trucker motels formed along the creaking, neon border of the highway. On the east end of the widening triangle of Fresno is Clovis, the white cowboy district. This is where the local chapter of the KKK used to be; as a child, I remember seeing flyers with strange symbols, which I learned in high school were taken from old KKK materials.

The push northward, away from the historical heart of the city, came with the jolt to the ag business following the Friant Dam project. Those who'd found their wealth in Fresno—mostly the white European settlers—began to build picturesque ranch homes in fig orchards a good distance from downtown. Stores soon followed. The downtown streets that had once been pedestrian-friendly, serviced by electric streetcars, turned into wide traffic gutters to accommodate the growing car culture. Aging industrial buildings and the decaying homes built by Fresno's early settlers were left to the migrant workers and the working-class merchants who sold them cheap imported goods.

The city saw what was happening to it and tried to make it stop. In 1958, the city council moved forward with a plan to fight against sprawl through its subsidiary the Redevelopment Agency of the City of Fresno. Victor Gruen, the Austrian architect and urban planner, was hired to draft a blueprint for Fresno that would once again make downtown its heart. Gruen's architectural firm was on the rise after its early successes designing America's first indoor malls in Detroit and Minneapolis. Gruen's proposal for a revitalized downtown was for another mall—but an outdoor one, made possible by Fresno's comparatively mild winters. The Fulton Mall project planned to convert Fulton Street—downtown's most congested commuter gutter—into a pedestrian shopping zone.

Gruen's plan called for new parking garages to be built nearby, a small secondary bus system for short-distance transport, and mixed-income apartment buildings along with a convention center, music hall, and hotels. Gruen hired the architect Garrett Eckbo to design the Fulton Mall itself; Eckbo filled the space with modernist fountains and statues that won Fresno national recognition. Its emphasis on modern design and public art was applauded. In 1968, a documentary about the Fulton Mall construction was shown at the White House to an audience that included Lady Bird Johnson; it was treated as a model for a wave of revitalization projects around the country.

It seemed almost perfect. And yet it didn't quite work. A few small shops and restaurants rented space, but with their customers moving farther and farther from the center, none of the big department stores that had left could be lured back downtown. Meanwhile, Fresno's new renown caused its own problems. In 1968, a Los Angeles–based developer called the MacDonald Group began appraising land for a private mall, a luxury facility called Fashion Fair, five miles north of downtown on the silken edge of the newest housing developments.

The company made a pitch to J. C. Penney, Gottschalks, and other department stores that still kept their flagship locations downtown while the neighborhood declined. The choice was a simple one: open exciting modern stores in the richest part of the city or wait things out where you are. The Fulton Mall was an important start, but many more steps were still necessary, including the funding and maintenance of new public transportation systems, the management and steady promotion of a new wave of apartment buildings, office space, parking lots, and a new freeway. It had taken six years to build the Fulton Mall itself; the planning of the subsequent infrastructure would take another decade or more.

With the federal money for the construction of the mall gone, the city council—a majority white and wealthy group—was left to manage the less glamorous parts of Gruen's plan. By contrast, the Macerich company offered thousands of new construction jobs and a new round of upper-income housing developments. So the council agreed to let the MacDonald Group break ground on Fashion Fair, making the Fulton Mall project a kind of hood ornament without a car to attach itself to.

The poor families still living downtown—largely black and Mexican—became increasingly isolated. They were joined by new immigrants in the 1970s, Hmong refugees who began settling in Fresno during the Vietnam War and the later rise of the Khmer Rouge in Cambodia.

For all these poor new residents, downtown provided cheap housing and access to manual labor in factories, truck depots, and the massive farming industry. The property values in downtown and the immediate vicinity continued to fall, school funding diminished on lower property taxes, and the bus lines that once adequately bound together the mini San Francisco became harder to navigate. A bus trip from downtown to north Fresno could take as long as two hours.

The contractors, carpenters, and masons who might have continued building up downtown were absorbed into the high-end projects around Fashion Fair. When it opened in 1970, the poverty rate in downtown and West Fresno had reached 43 percent.

Our new house was in Royal Coach, one of the most ostentatious developments in northwest Fresno. It was half a square mile of stucco mansions custom-built in a former fig orchard that had been rezoned for residential real estate. Our house was a two-story mansard with a circular driveway, three-car garage, pool, Jacuzzi, indoor atrium, and second-floor deck. It was so big there were rooms with no practical use beyond storing furniture. One of our neighbors was a man named John Bonadelle, one of the largest home developers in Fresno, pugnacious and ruthless; in the late 1990s, he'd be indicted for multiple counts of bribery, witness tampering, and money laundering. At the age of eighty, he eventually pleaded guilty to felony mail fraud as part of a corruption sting that saw twelve other developers and politicians convicted.

My mom was working three nursing jobs and had bought a used Jaguar to manage the tedious commutes between them all. She worked herself to exhaustion, but the cheap cost of wealthy living in Fresno was its own reward. Our house cost a quarter of what it would have cost in Los Angeles or San Francisco. And nobody could tell a used Jaguar from a new one on the highway. My mother soon developed a stubborn interest in beautiful and expensive things. She was hungry for them and discovered in the tiresome but feasible rhythms of working and commuting that the means to get these things were within her reach. This led not to satisfaction but to new levels of desire, with orbiting plates and vases and cars and Ellen Tracy jackets.

I wonder if this wasn't simply a survival instinct, the natural reaction of a lone woman in a house of selfish and emotionally distant men, each in his own way. My quiet and thoughtful brother had become a farting and burping jock with a propensity for womanizing and weekend parties. I had been an irrationally excitable boy, prone to wild swings of joy and unreachable fits of disappointment. Older, I kept the joyful outbursts more and more to myself and showed my mother only the sulking monosyllables of alienation. We all had our needs of one another, and those needs started to go unmet.

My dad had become a tenured professor of accounting. He'd also come up with a scheme to revolutionize the industry with a visual system for quantifying corporate profit, debt, and investment. His miniaturized graphs fit on baseball cards and could instantly show the proportion of a company's debt to revenue as black and white blobs. He performed minor miracles of craftsmanship around our house. One year he built his own two-story scaffolding and lined the entire ceiling of our massive family room with burnished wood panels that he designed and sawed himself.

These were distractions, complicated but logical problems that, once solved, left behind a satisfying object as evidence. And once their easy isolation was set aside for the day, my brother and I were easier company than my mother. We were a model audience, passively accepting his chatter about the day's projects and his newest discoveries pulled from *Scientific American* or *National Geographic* stories, offering only a head nod or "Cool" in acknowledgment while watching television or waiting for the phone to ring. My mother was not a passive audience. She asked questions back and wanted things that had nothing to do with quantum electrodynamics or anecdotes from Micronesia. She worked more and more.

As I started high school, my mom became convinced my dad had ruined her life. They'd married quickly and for superficial reasons. Two immigrants from the same country, raised in the manacles of an obscure religion, who both had a hunger to build a familial kingdom of their own. It could have been done with anyone. As my brother and I neared adulthood, the fervor of kingdom building had subsided, and so too the optimistic glow it had brought. My parents had their dream careers and their dream family and had just built their dream house. There was nothing more to want except each other. But they didn't like each other.

My mother seems to have figured this out first and began to scorn my father. A drawer left open in the kitchen was a subconsciously laid trap. The way he smacked his food at dinner was a sadistic screw boring into her psyche. She began reading books like *People of the Lie: The Hope for Healing Human Evil* and piecing together the ominous details of my father's upbringing. His severe parents had cared more about religion and appearance than they did about their own children. His business was a time suck that had only created tension with the accounting traditionalists in his department. His work around the house added to the uncontrolled mess that galled my mom. His slouch, eager curiosity, and willingness to go out of his way to help strangers were the dark shadows of his evil upbringing, about which he was perpetually in denial.

I had been in love with my mother as a child, but as I grew into a teen, I started to admire my dad's inexhaustible cheer and unconventional way of thinking. He never fought back when my mom would lose herself in anger. He would look at her momentarily and then look down. His eyes moved left and right, searching the floor as he listened to himself disassembled. I hated those moments and would regularly hurl myself in between my parents to beat back my mom's words. I'd launch my own rickety criticisms of her with no purpose other than to break back the expanding cloud of her rage.

Our fights grew more intense, inversely proportional to my dad's passivity. I hated our house. It was huge and incapable of muffling the sound of my parents' unhappiness. I could hear the faint stabs of anger coming from the garage, the kitchen, the bedroom. At night I would hear them through the walls, the cheerful Danish accent now spiteful and cutting. One night I heard my dad answer back. It was done, he told her. He wasn't going to be treated like trash anymore. A few minutes later, I heard the bedroom door open and close. My dad's footsteps went down the hall, descended the stairs, and stopped with the creak of his office door closing.

The end stage of both poverty and wealth is anarchic conflict. Short-term benefaction of the individual trumps social rule. Lacking bribe money and connections to contractors, a person will find other means to extract wealth from his surroundings. In the years after the Fulton Mall project was strangled by Fashion Fair, gangs began to proliferate in downtown Fresno. The most active of these were the Bulldogs (named for the Fresno State mascot), which had split off from the influential Mexican Nuestra Familia gang and its powerful drug distribution system and, left without a steady income, became a kind of anarchic, violent presence on the Fresno scene. In the first decade of the twenty-first century, police launched various initiatives to get them under control, with mixed success.

In 2009, a young Republican named Ashley Swearengin became mayor of Fresno (replacing the actor Alan Autry, who had served two terms) and brought with her another debate about how to revitalize downtown Fresno: Would the city declare the Fulton Mall a historic zone? The mall is currently at less than half capacity, and most of its tenants are Hispanic vendors who sell textiles and imports. Both Swearengin and a majority of the mall's vendors opposed the plan, as it would place new upkeep requirements on them. Meanwhile, the city council voted 4–2 to move forward with a 238-acre development of another mega shopping center built around a Target in the northwest corner of the city.

Another plan Swearengin pitched the council, with the backing of the Downtown Fresno Partnership, a nonprofit dedicated to revitalizing downtown, sought to reopen some of the mall to car traffic, citing the fact that more than 170 of the 200 pedestrian malls that had been built around the country in the 1960s and 1970s had closed. The dream of a bustling pedestrian downtown didn't seem to have worked out anywhere. Swearengin and the partnership filed a grant petition for their plan, worth $2.7 million, but a city council scoring committee rejected the proposal by a 6–5 vote, with several members objecting to the idea of spending more money downtown.

The council also spent more than $3 million investigating a proposal called the Southeast Growth Area plan, which would transform nine thousand acres of unoccupied farmland on the southern outskirts of the city into a planned community with parks, public spaces, water treatment facilities, and the potential to house 100,000 people. It would essentially be a separate city whose infrastructure and development costs would be paid for by a mix of bank loans, federal guarantees, and taxes collected from Fresno residents. Each successive generation builds its own version of the same basic escape plan, but it can only ever get as far as the city limits. Moving them farther and farther out has not changed the fact that they are still limits, encircling the inescapable.

I remember the last time I saw my parents kiss. I was twelve and caught them standing in the front entryway of our house one Sunday morning. I watched them through the loose foliage in the atrium. My mom wrapped her arms around my dad's neck and smiled her dimpled smile, entranced by his face. He was smiling too, in his overwhelmed and bashful way. They had been talking about taking a trip somewhere, and my mom, her heart still restless in its suburban stall, must have jumped. "Do you mean it?" she asked.

"Yeah, sure," he said, the idiom sounding like a pantomime with his Danish accent. "Why not?"

They lasted a long time together. They survived for twenty years, raised two sons, and built their own home in a place where a teacher and a nurse could afford a French country mansion. They sold the house after I left for college. But they stayed together, even though the only thing they had left in common was anger, sadness, and fear. They bought a new house, and then an empty lot, and then another house, as if they expected to find in them something other than themselves.

4

BANKRUPT IN SEATTLE

JENNY HENDRIX

In December 2008, a few days before Christmas, a rare snowstorm dropped a foot of heavy powder on downtown Seattle. The city does not as a rule deal well with snow: people panicked. Abandoned cars lined the freeway as drivers sought refuge elsewhere. Two charter buses carrying students home for Christmas break slid through the barrier of an overpass and teetered above Interstate 5. With transit at a halt and local roads unplowed, I, like most people, was unable to get to work, and my employer had no choice but to close. Garbage service stopped; on Capitol Hill, where I lived, a group of people went sledding on an old couch down Denny Way, the steep arterial connecting our neighborhood to downtown. Unable to shut down so close to Christmas, retail businesses counted on their employees to make it in somehow: Andrew, a housemate of mine, snowshoed half an hour each way to his job at the downtown Patagonia. Another housemate, Adam, a financial analyst, was able to stay home with a clear conscience: along with thirty-four hundred other Seattle-based employees of Washington Mutual, he had been laid off the month before. A number of former Starbucks employees were able to stay home as well: the coffee colossus was closing six hundred stores nationwide, including five in its hometown. Seattle was used to a little weather and the business cycle, but snow and subprime were something else. The city, like Starbucks, had overextended—and now, through these short, dark days and long, cold nights, it was hardly working at all.

Near the edge of the continent, where the United States crumbles into the Pacific and bleeds upward toward Canada, Seattle sits tucked into Puget Sound. The sound, a tatter-edged inlet, leaks down between the body of Washington State and the Olympic Peninsula: in late summer you can watch red hooknose salmon fight their way over the dam where the water enters the city via a system of locks to the north. From there, a channel empties into Lake Union, its houseboat-barnacled shores overlooked by a converted gas plant on a lumpish waterfront park. The city's easternmost border is formed by Lake Washington, the largest of its lakes: from the water you can watch cars stream across the floating bridge connecting Seattle to the largely suburban Eastside, where the towers of Bellevue rise below the snow-covered Cascades. Seattle is hilly: with the highest elevation located in and around the city center, it spills steeply down both sides of the ridge between lake and bay. The city grew by annexing surrounding small towns, neighborhoods that maintain their individual character—along with hyperlocal, somewhat separatist political bodies—and give the city a cozily suburban patchwork feel. Ten minutes from downtown, which is only about twelve blocks square, it's possible to find yourself on a street lined with verdant bungalows and Craftsman homes, patches of tomatoes and kale dotting the verge.

People have lived off this land for centuries. Even before the arrival of white settlers, the richness of the Northwest's natural environment supported one of the world's only settled hunter-gatherer communities. The Duwamish, Chinook, Suquamish, and Coast Salish tribes lived off salmon and shellfish and worked with cedar, developing highly sophisticated cultural and artistic civilizations. Settlers arrived via the Oregon Trail in 1851, gradually and sometimes violently annexing the land from the locals. An economy developed that was based on timber, which was shipped south to California; fish; and a seemingly indomitable optimism. When the

Northern Pacific Railway decided to locate its terminus in the tiny village of Tacoma rather than its larger neighbor to the north, Seattle's citizens began gamely laying track for their own railroad on the Duwamish River. Thanks to this independent railroad, a steam-powered sawmill, and the Territorial University (now the University of Washington), the town prospered, along with its sanguine pioneer spirit. After the Great Fire of 1889 destroyed Seattle's entire central business district, residents noted what a fine job it had done of ridding the city of rats. The Washington National Building Loan and Investment Association, later Washington Mutual, was founded to provide rebuilding loans—including the country's first amortized mortgages. The young city caught its first lucky break when in 1897, in the midst of a recession triggered by the panic of 1893, the steamship *Portland* docked in Seattle with a hold full of Yukon gold. As news of the gold strike spread, hundreds of thousands of unemployed men paid an average of $1,200 to go stake a claim in the goldfields up north. Capitalizing on this sudden flood of "sourdoughs," the *Seattle Post-Intelligencer*'s future editor Erastus Brainerd began to market Seattle as the "Gateway to Alaska." Over the next decade, the city tripled in size.

Seattle's next great boom followed World War II, when a struggling aviation company operating out of a barn by Lake Union began to exploit military technologies for commercial use. Boeing, founded by a Yale dropout who came west seeking a fortune in the timberlands, had paid for the construction of a wind tunnel at the University of Washington in 1917, allowing the university to offer classes in aeronautics and creating a reliable source of employees. As the war wound down, the Boeing engineer George Schairer was sent to Germany as part of Operation Paperclip, an OSS mission to recruit German scientists and keep their knowledge out of the hands of the USSR. In Braunschweig, Schairer discovered a mass of German research into "swept wings," a design in which an aircraft's wings were angled back to reduce drag and prevent the shock waves that came with high speeds. Schairer reported his discovery to his superiors at the OSS but also to Boeing, suggesting that the concept bore urgent study. Though the information was shared with other aviation companies in the United States, Boeing's wind tunnel enabled its engineers to get a head start on testing the swept-wing concept, leading to the development of the company's B-47 Stratojet. The plane never saw combat, but its design made the jet engine practical; Boeing's engineers soon adapted it into the "Dash 80" prototype passenger jet, which became the 707 in 1958. The jet age had arrived, and Seattle—now known as Jet City—came to rely almost entirely on its economic dividends. Boeing built the biggest building in the world for the production of its 747 in Everett, just north of Seattle, and by 1967 it was employing 100,800 people—known as Incredibles—throughout the region. When France's Concorde began to look like the future of aviation, Boeing won a contract to produce the United States' first supersonic planes. Seattle's ill-fated basketball team, the SuperSonics, was named in honor of the occasion. But in 1971, concerned about sonic booms and potential damage to the ozone layer, the U.S. government withdrew funding. A simultaneous recession in the airline industry meant no new orders for more than a year. Even as the 747 made its first commercial flights, Boeing fell on hard times, with employment dropping to 37,000. At the same time, the Northwest's traditional industries, like fishing and logging, had begun to suffer too, leaving the unemployed little to fall back on. For the first time, people began leaving Seattle. The population had dipped below half a million by the start of the next decade; it would take almost forty years for Seattle to recover.

But there was a silver lining to the Bust, economically speaking. In order to survive, Boeing began marketing the information technologies it had developed over the years, founding a computer-training center in Seattle. In 1979, a small software company called Microsoft relocated from Albuquerque to what was then the semi-rural city of Bellevue. Its founders, Bill Gates and Paul Allen, twenty-three and twenty-six at the time, had grown up in Seattle and attended the prestigious Lakeside School together. The Gateses had been in the city since 1880, their fortunes rising and falling with those of their home; the first Bill Gates used his delivery wagon to cart victims of the Great Fire to safety; when gold was discovered, the family tried their luck in Alaska. Yet it was Allen who pushed for the move. He argued that the Northwest guaranteed a more stable workforce than the already competitive Silicon Valley: the presence of the University of Washington meant a self-refreshing pool of computer scientists from which the company might draw. Nor was it insignificant, as the Gates biographers Stephen Manes and Paul Andrews write, that "the gray Seattle skies reinforced the Microsoft ethic of work till you drop."

Steely gray in winter, dim and dove-like in spring, and cloaked in fog in fall, Seattle is famous for its rain. The rain here is abstract, diffuse. More cotton ball than sheet, it is a woozy, three-dimensional rain that softens the city's hard corners. Calling up moss and mushroom and penetrating everywhere with a kind of psychic damp, the weather almost literally grows into you. For a few months in summer, when the rain dries out and the clouds clear up, the city is a different place altogether. Not for nothing did Perry Como sing "The bluest skies . . . are in Seattle."

For the most part, though, the weather offers a persistent gloom lending itself to introspection, bookishness, and a sort of unaffiliated mysticism, and for those who don't mind, it is quite cozy in its way. Seattle has been called the most literate city in the country—over half the adult population holds a bachelor's degree. More of us are atheists than anywhere else in the United States; many people meditate. Support for same-sex marriage, reproductive rights, and gun control is a given, and downtown's tree canopy is often a political issue. But beneath the tendency to quiet contemplation lies what Greil Marcus called "true grunge: not as some music-business catchphrase, but as dirt." Early in the city's history, workmen had used a chute, or skid road, to send freshly cut timber through what is now Pioneer Square to the sawmill below, and the drunks and derelicts who filled the area gave rise to the meaning of "skid row," which Kurt Cobain chose as an early name for his band. Grunge, that disaffected, famous-for-hating-fame ethos, captured something of the city's real romance with self-contempt, the sarcasm and despondency lurking beneath its cheerful facade. Augmented by the cloud cover, depression may send people to the bar or to the bridge, to the needle or off to California. For those who remain, there is a bitter pioneerish joy in living through the dark and the wet.

Grunge slouched out of Seattle to take the country's youth by storm in the early 1990s, and in doing so became exactly a "music-business catchphrase" deprived of the real dirt it wore at home. At the same time, a more insidious nationalization was creeping toward unsuspecting urban areas in the process of classing up. In 1971, two teachers and a writer had opened a storefront in Pike Place Market where they sold custom-roasted coffee beans. They named it Starbucks after the first mate on the *Pequod*—the one who didn't want to chase the whale. A decade after the store opened, the trio hired Howard Schultz, then running American operations for the Swedish plastics giant Hammarplast, as head of marketing and operations. Five years later, Schultz had bought the company from its original owners and started on a headlong drive to expand it all over the world. Starbucks opened stores in Chicago and Vancouver in 1987; the first New York store opened in 1994. That same year, a young hedge fund analyst named Jeff Bezos, noticing the astonishing growth in home Internet use, quit his job to move to Seattle and open a business, Amazon.com, out of his garage. In a month, he was selling to all fifty U.S. states and to forty-five countries around the world, and claimed to run "the World's Biggest Book Store."

Even the local bank got into the spirit of things: Washington Mutual took itself national, aiming to become, as its CEO said at the time, nothing less than "the Walmart of banking." WaMu launched an ad campaign, which debuted during the 2003 Oscars, featuring the rosy new slogan "The Power of Yes." "Yes" meant that

almost any loan, regardless of the income or situation of the borrower, would be speedily approved, and WaMu proceeded to ped-
dle its "flexible lending" with a sense of cheerful informality:
commercials ridiculed other lenders and their "rules." Even the
bank's casual new ATMs were on message, greeting customers with
a "Hi there! May I have your secret code?" Instead of "Yes" or "No,"
they offered "Sure" or "No thanks." It was as though someone had
boxed up a bit of Seattle nice: clubby, a little corny, resolutely laid-
back, and self-consciously inclusive to the point of noncommitment;
you needn't even bank with them to avoid a fee. "Whoo-Hoo!" their
other tagline went. It seemed as if WaMu wanted to be a friend to
its customers more than anything else: "If we've done our jobs," the
CEO, Kerry Killinger, said in 2003, "five years from now you're not
going to call us a bank." This turned out to be true, though not in
the way that Killinger probably meant.

Success was changing Seattle, burying its grittier place-bound
particulars under a smooth facade with broader appeal. A physical
transformation followed this change. In 2001, the city elected a
square-jawed, brush-cut Chicagoan named Greg Nickels to the
office of mayor. Widely seen as one of the most environmentally progressive politicians in the country—he urged cities to voluntarily
adopt the Kyoto Protocol after the Bush administration vetoed the
treaty—Nickels was able to forge (or perhaps force) an alliance between Seattle's developers and environmentalists. He advocated
transit-friendly, walkable urban villages as a way to save outlying
lands from development; in exchange, he was willing to sacrifice
some of downtown's trees. Through his efforts, the city council extended the downtown building-height cap from 240 to 400 feet,
allowing for the new crop of "tall and slender" residential high-rises.
In a skyline crisscrossed by the inverted orange L's of construction
cranes, these gleaming new towers began to rise like crisp stacks of
dollar bills.

Much of the construction was concentrated in South Lake Union,
the moribund area of warehouses and car dealerships between the

lake and downtown, where Bill Boeing had built his first seaplane in 1916. Its transformation was a priority for Mayor Nickels, who hoped to use it as a magnet for the biotech industry. The main development player in the neighborhood was and remains Vulcan Inc., a company owned by the Microsoft co-founder and now multibillionaire Paul Allen, which had quietly bought up a critical mass of properties there in the late 1990s and the first decade of the twenty-first century. In 2007, a Whole Foods supermarket arrived in the neighborhood, and a biodiesel station soon followed. Microsoft announced that it would move some of its employees from Redmond to a new Vulcan building nearby. After a special ruling by the city council to adjust some of its building codes, Amazon decided to relocate its headquarters from the looming, fortress-like Pacific Medical Center on top of Beacon Hill to a new 1.6-million-square-foot Vulcan development. Shortly thereafter, a new streetcar line opened, the neighborhood's first in over sixty-five years. The presence of this futuristic-looking orange and purple conveyance, which made no fewer than eleven stops in the half-developed area, looked to some like a symbol of the city's willingness to prostitute itself to private interests. In addition to Vulcan's contributions, the revamped South Lake Union had required $1 billion in public investment, including $45 million for the streetcar, $6 million for a new waterfront park that seemed to consist mainly of a footbridge, and $200 million for a new electrical substation. When bicyclists (of which the city, despite its hills, has many) began to complain about accidents caused by the tracks, a local cowboy singer wrote a song lampooning the "South Lake Union Trolley" as "a bump and grind machine"; a local coffee stand offered T-shirts reading "Ride the S.L.U.T.!"

Looking out the window at the construction cranes below, a new resident of one of the high-rises told *The Seattle Times* that she felt like a pioneer. But the neighborhood had never been empty. Its small residential area had once housed about nine hundred people, mostly artists and activists making below median wage. It included two hundred apartments for the homeless and mentally ill, co-op buildings, a soup kitchen, a women's shelter, and a treatment program for homeless men. After rolling out the multimillion-dollar streetcar, the city decided to cancel $600,000 in funding for the Cascade People's Center, a beloved volunteer-run community space that provided, among other things, free yoga classes, child care, and a community garden.

The April 2008 issue of *Forbes* included Seattle in its list of "recession-proof" cities, citing manufacturing growth, declining unemployment, and continued demand for local products like those of Starbucks, Costco, and WaMu. Amazon and Microsoft were still hiring. But that May something strange began to happen: with three new condo buildings in progress in South Lake Union, Vulcan rolled out an incentive program, offering to pay part of the closing cost for current renters who'd like to buy. Across the city, other developers followed suit, offering prospective buyers cars, vacations, and Vespa scooters in exchange for sales. The market for condos, it appeared, had stalled—the *Puget Sound Business Journal* reported that while the number of listings had risen by 43 percent over the previous year, sales had decreased by the same percentage. That summer my cousin moved into a building—the Aspira—that, like most of the other bright new residential towers, had converted from condos to rentals for lack of sales. After two years in the building, he estimated that it was still about half vacant. Even Microsoft decided against renting space in a second Vulcan building a few blocks away.

The situation quickly got worse. Developers could no longer receive financing without showing that their units could sell, and so while visitors marveled that the city still had cranes up in the midst of a recession, gaping holes at street level where towers should have been bore witness to the stillbirth of Seattle's new downtown. Developers also worried about WaMu, less as a source of financing than as a tenant: the bank leased about a million square feet of

office space downtown in addition to its own forty-two-story building. And by July 2008, WaMu's stock had dropped to $5 a share
from $45 a year earlier.

An acquisition spree in the early years of the twenty-first century,
and a decision to begin doing business outside Washington State,
had opened up the bank to the market for high-risk loans. By
2004, almost 60 percent of its loans were risky adjustable-rate mortgages, subprimes, and home equities. In keeping with Killinger's
plan for the bank to become the Walmart of home loans, under-
writers were told to make loans "work" regardless of a borrower's
ability to pay. As one appraiser who did business with WaMu later
told *The New York Times*, "It was the Wild West. If you were alive,
they would give you a loan. Actually, I think if you were dead, they
would still give you a loan." "The Power of Yes" fueled WaMu's
transformation from a frumpy Northwest thrift, which only made
loans to its customers, to a national powerhouse, which might have
made loans to the dead. *Forbes* dubbed it "the tallest midget in
the world." And, true to Seattle's spirit of cockeyed optimism,
WaMu kept most of these loans on its books—the feeling being
that the bank could get out of whatever trouble it was in. Yet by
mid-2008, a third of WaMu's loans in the ten cities hardest hit by
the mortgage crisis were in foreclosure, amounting to about $9.7
billion dollars in problems. The bank posted a $7.9 billion loss in
the first six months of 2008. My housemate Adam was a Financial
Analysis Analyst—that was his title—at the bank. His job involved
making models of the mortgage portfolio, and for months, he said,
each time he produced one showing that the bank was running out
of money, his superiors insisted it was wrong. Adam had signed a
nondisclosure agreement, which meant he could not share this
information with his co-workers, let alone with the news vans on
deathwatch outside the bank's downtown tower. He kept mum—in
fact, he estimates that only about half of the bank's corporate employees understood the severity of its financial position at the
time—but there was no disguising the beating WaMu was taking
on Wall Street. Beginning on September 15, 2008, in an old-

fashioned run on the bank, $16.7 billion was withdrawn by customers over the course of ten days—about 9 percent of WaMu's total deposits. The bank made round after round of layoffs. Even Kerry Killinger was fired, his portrait in the WaMu Center lobby replaced, according to an article in *The Stranger*, by a picture of an abacus. It was actually a relief, Adam told me, when, on the morning of September 25, he arrived at work to find fifty uniformed policemen waiting to escort the traders who worked on his floor out of the building. In the largest bank failure in American history, an illiquid Washington Mutual had been seized by the federal Office of Thrift Supervision and hastily sold to JPMorgan Chase. Its holding company filed for bankruptcy the next day.

Construction in Seattle, which had remained robust through November, dropped, as a local economic forecaster put it, "like a piece of concrete." Home prices fell 30 percent, and by the first quarter of 2010 the region had shed more than 130,000 jobs. I was working at Pacific Science Center (PSC), a nonprofit science education museum dependent on the largesse of corporations like WaMu, where one of our board members had been a senior vice president. With donations on the decline, foundations damaged by low interest rates, and an expensive exhibit that failed to draw, PSC instituted a mandatory five-day furlough and a wage and hiring freeze. When that was not enough, it laid off 8 percent of its staff. Around the corner, the Seattle Repertory Theater closed its production of *The Three Musketeers* a week early. Restaurants shuttered at such a clip that it was hard to keep track; a local news channel reported that north of the city, the Shell Creek Grill & Wine Bar had instituted a pay-what-you-like policy to get customers in the door. Reportedly, Seattleites only gave themselves a 25 percent discount, on average, but it wasn't enough to save Shell Creek. With WaMu, Seattle had lost a major civic sponsor too: the annual Winterfest parade, the Westlake Center Christmas Tree, and the Fourth of July fireworks on Lake Union had all been on the bank's dime. All over the city, WaMu branches had been draped in plastic banners that pictured a "Hello I'm" name tag reading "becoming Chase." They were meant to look friendly, I suppose, but as the city watched its basketball team—owned and then sold off by the Starbucks CEO, Howard Schultz—leave for Oklahoma, these were little grand openings that no one wanted to attend.

The other shoe was finally dropping for commercial real estate downtown. Chase's purchase deal with the FDIC allowed it to break WaMu's leases with impunity. When it did, vacancies doubled. The hardest hit by the loss was the Seattle Art Museum, from which WaMu had rented eight floors in a building adjacent to its tower. The rent the museum collected went to pay off bonds issued to finance an ambitious 2007 expansion. Chase gave the museum $10 million to lessen the blow, but WaMu's departure tore a $60 million hole in its budget. Across the street, at the Lusty Lady peep show—which, like downtown's sandwich shops and lunch counters, had depended on WaMu in an altogether different way—the dancers shimmied their last that summer. The Lady's beloved marquee, a reliable source of smartly topical smutty puns, bid the city farewell: "Thanks for the mammaries," it said.

The city felt small in the quiet after the blizzards of 2008. The warm conviviality of bars and coffee shops filled with fellow sufferers shaking snow from their clothes seemed suddenly too particular to be represented by the seventeen thousand identical Starbucks shops our home had inflicted on the globe. As we waited for snowplows to arrive from Oregon, Seattleites, at least for a minute, forgot about making it on a national scale and concentrated on getting things to work again here—if only a bus line or two.

Closed as part of the recession's cost-cutting, the Starbucks down the street from my house reopened under a different name the summer after the storm. Now called 15th Avenue Coffee and Tea, it was the first of three Seattle Starbucks franchises to abandon the national branding in favor of a more local, faux-independent feel. The siren logo was gone, as was the automatic espresso machine; the café served wine and microbrews and saved its grounds for neighborhood gardeners to use as compost. While Seattleites cheerfully protested the shop as "local-washing," it was hard not to admire the chutzpah of the thing. Yes, this franchise, disguised in salvaged wood, may well have been an admission of failure—of global ambition, of limitless growth—but it also suggested that a kind of lesson had been learned. Looking at the shop from the Starbucks across 15th Avenue, though, you might never have guessed what it was.

5

GOLD RUSH WHITTIER

ERIN SHEEHY

When I went to Alaska in December 2012, it wasn't the cold that surprised me but the light. The sun still rises in southern Alaska during winter, but it lies low in the sky, making long shadows, and the short days are bookended by stretches of cerulean twilight. It's a dream for filmmakers and photographers: the golden hour lasts most of the day.

I was in Alaska to visit Whittier, a small town on the western side of Prince William Sound, with my friend Reed, a photographer who shoots portrait series of communities all over the world. It was our third trip together. Earlier that year we'd photographed people in an El Paso neighborhood, and before that we traveled to a fishing town in Alabama that had been affected by the BP oil spill. It's not the type of work I usually do, but Reed needs someone to write profiles of his subjects, and I need an excuse to get out of New York. He also needs someone to hold the lights.

Reed is not a documentary photographer: his shots are posed, lit, edited. I think he makes his subjects look good—luminous, and a little bit proud. When people are on the fence about getting their picture taken, Reed shows them samples of his work, and they tend to agree to a portrait. Sometimes he tells people that they are "pieces of a puzzle"—a benign thing for a photographer to say, maybe, but I always cringe when he says it. We shoot and interview so many people during our two-week trips that it's hard for me to know how we'll possibly combine all those stories into a cohesive whole.

Whittier, however, seemed like it would be easy. We weren't headed to a sprawling city. The town was not racked with any controversy that we knew of. Reed had been in touch with the mayor, who said we'd be welcome there. We didn't even need to search too hard for an angle, because the town was a story unto itself: since 1960, almost everyone in Whittier has lived in the same building—a former army barracks called Begich Towers, built for military families during the cold war. We wanted to learn what life was like inside the building and to find out what sort of person would live there. We planned to photograph and interview at least fifteen residents in two weeks.

For Alaska, where many villages are only accessible by plane or boat, Whittier is relatively easy to get to. We drove some sixty miles down the Seward Highway from Anchorage, snaking along an inlet that during low tide looks like a pitted moonscape. The trees that lined the road were white with sparkling frost; fog hangs low there and freezes on their branches. The view is spectacular, but the highway is deadly. In most parts of Alaska, it's simply too cold to salt the roads: the salt refreezes and creates "chemical ice" that bonds even more tightly to the asphalt. Instead, they use sand and gravel for traction. In wintertime, the Seward Highway is often covered in black ice. Many people only brave it during daylight hours, but this can be logistically difficult when the sun rises at 10:00 and sets at 3:30.

The final stretch to Whittier is a two-and-a-half-mile, one-lane railroad tunnel that cuts through a mountain. Fifteen years ago, if you wanted to leave Whittier, you had to pay $75 to load your vehicle onto a train. In 2000, the tunnel was retrofitted to accommodate cars, so you can now pay $12 to drive slowly on top of the tracks. During winter months, auto traffic is allowed through twice an hour, at fifteen-minute intervals—one window for inbound traffic, another for outbound. But when the temperature drops below freezing, that window narrows to five minutes so that the internal temperature of the tunnel can be kept warm enough (opening the tunnel gates lets the cold air in). When we pulled up, we had just missed the window for Whittier-bound traffic, and our temperature gauge read minus thirteen. We waited at the staging area beneath a string of bleak, snow-covered stoplights, while a crew of burly ravens—the pigeons of Alaska—loitered nearby, puffing up their hackles. Fifty-five minutes passed, and finally we were let through.

Whittier is a product of World War II, when Alaska's proximity to the Pacific theater made it an object of interest to both the Americans and the Japanese. In June 1942, the Imperial Japanese Army launched two aircraft carrier attacks on Alaska's Dutch Harbor, a port town in the Aleutians—the string of islands that run southwest from the tip of Alaska. A few days later, Japanese forces invaded two of the westernmost Aleutian Islands, Attu and Kiska, occupying both until the summer of 1943. (Today, Kiska is one of the most intact World War II battlegrounds in the world, but so much unexploded ammunition is still buried there that visits are restricted.) Soon afterward, the U.S. Army completed a tunnel, a railroad terminus, and a port in present-day Whittier, using the area as its main supply link for the war effort in Alaska. The location was chosen not only for its access to Prince William Sound but also because the constant bad weather made it difficult for bombers to find.

In the summer, Whittier's population swells as thousands of pleasure boaters, fishermen, cannery workers, and tourists are drawn back to the harbor. Wildlife abounds: mountain goats graze on the green slopes across the water, black bears rifle through city Dumpsters, humpbacks and orcas breach along the shore. But in the wintertime, when the weather turns nasty, industry dies down. Whittier's harbor stays ice-free during winter, but sea air isn't much of a comfort when the wind blows hard enough to shatter windshields; if you're not careful, it will rip your car doors right off. Sustained winds of fifty or sixty miles per hour are so common here that they don't even merit weather warnings. (One night at the Anchor Inn—the only bar and restaurant in Whittier open year-round—a bartender nodded toward the snow whipping sideways past the window and said, "Down in the Lower 48, this would have a name.") Signs around town read, BE CAREFUL! ALWAYS WEAR YOUR ICE CLEATS! Come October, the "snowbirds"—people who head south for the winter—take flight, and the population dwindles to about two hundred people.

Even if there were demand for it, Whittier would have a hard time expanding, bounded as it is by water and mountains. The city mainly comprises low-lying industrial buildings, and from the harbor it slopes upward and inward toward Begich Towers, or BTI, the fourteen-story high-rise that sits atop a small hill. Following the war, the military decided to make Whittier a permanent base. In the 1950s, the army constructed what would become the largest and second-largest buildings in Alaska: the Buckner Building, a sprawling compound for enlisted men, and the Hodge Building, a high-rise for military families. The Buckner Building was promoted as the "City Under One Roof." It contained, among other things, a bowling alley, a movie theater, a shooting range, a barbershop, a darkroom, and a six-cell jail. Built in seven sections to prevent it from cracking apart in the event of an earthquake, its insides were labyrinthine. Though both residential buildings were occupied briefly, the Buckner Building was abandoned in 1960 when the army pulled out of Whittier because of a decline in military cargo. The remaining residents moved into the Hodge Building.

Throughout the 1960s, Whittier's population hovered between forty and seventy people. During the 1964 earthquake that destroyed Anchorage, thirteen of Whittier's residents were killed, swept out to sea by a forty-foot tsunami. The port, however, sustained less damage than the ports of other nearby cities, so for the next few years Whittier's port facility became the busiest in the state. Whittier incorporated in 1969, and in 1973 the remaining residents bought the city from the army. The following year they turned the Hodge Building into a condo association and renamed it Begich Towers Inc., after an Alaska congressman who'd died in a plane crash on the way from Anchorage to Juneau. Most people now refer to the towers as BTI. Behind BTI is Whittier Community School and, behind that, a mountain. The tower has been painted in a weakly cheerful combination of cream, peach, and blue, but when it was first completed in 1956, its concrete was left unadorned. Today, about 80 percent of Whittier's residents call it home.

Too full of asbestos and lead to demolish safely, the decaying Buckner Building still lies empty on the hillside, tucked into the trees like some sort of Soviet Overlook Hotel. The building has long been a teenage hangout; its interior walls are covered in graffiti, and hundreds of flattened beer cans are suspended in the thick layer of ice that coats its floors.

The first time we stepped inside BTI, we found a gray-haired man in slippers and pajamas scanning the bulletin boards that line the entrance. "You'll get a ticket if you park your car near the doorway like that," he snapped, then shuffled into an elevator. Most of Whittier's citizens are outgoing and friendly, but BTI has a few shut-ins, residents who never leave the building. They never need to: the first floor houses a post office, police station, grocery store, and Laundromat. (It used to house a combination video store/tanning salon, but then Netflix came along, and a resident moved the tanning bed into his apartment.) On the third floor, you'll find a health clinic, and in the basement there's a church.

As comfortable as it is, BTI can't shake its past as an army barracks. The hallways, with their fluorescent lighting and painted cinder-block walls, reminded me of an old public high school, and the condo we stayed in still had its military-issue metal cabinets, pale yellow 1950s electric stove, salmon-colored tile, and rattling wood-frame windows. Like the Buckner Building, BTI was built to be earthquake-resistant, made of three separate concrete sections connected by metal plates: if you run into the hall during a big tremor, you can see the sections swaying in opposite directions. It's also basically fireproof. On our second day in town, we were downstairs at the Kozy Korner grocery store when an alarm went off—an excruciating blare that wouldn't stop, like the horn that New York ambulance drivers lean on when people won't get out of their way. The man we'd been talking to put his fingers in his ears and screamed over the noise, "It's just the old military fire alarm system. Goes off around once a month. I'm sure the fire department is coming to turn it off." He tried to keep up a conversation, but Reed and I couldn't concentrate, so we escaped to the one set of functioning elevators. An older man wearing a track jacket got on with us. We explained that we were new to town and asked what he did during these alarms. He shrugged. "It's quietest inside the condos, so your best bet is to just go to your room and shut the door. It's a concrete building; nothing's going to burn down." When he got off the elevator, we noticed that the back of his jacket read, "Whittier Volunteer Fire Department."

Turnover can be high among newcomers here. Though there are plenty of summertime jobs, there is no year-round industry in Whittier besides the port, and the Alaska Railroad workers mostly commute in from Anchorage. When we visited, all but one of the police officers lived out of town, and even the mayor had moved to Anchorage. But people eke out a living somehow. The harbor and the tower and the city itself are in need of constant maintenance. Seasonal work is plentiful enough that residents work two jobs in the summertime to soften the lean months.

Most of the residents here are transplants from the Lower 48, though recent years have seen an influx of immigrants from American Samoa, the Philippines, and Guam. They come here the same way people come to Alaska in general: they hitch a ride on a whim, they come for seasonal work, they get word from a family member that money is good here, and they fly or drive up. Then they stay, perhaps because they are stuck, but usually because they fall in love with the landscape, the freedom, the ruggedness of Alaska living. Whittier is still an anomaly, though. Residents of BTI—and Whittier Manor, the only other residential building in Whittier—lack something that other Alaskans hold dear: privacy.

In some ways Whittier is a small town wearing big-city clothes. You'll find nosy neighbors in any small town, but in the high-rise you can hear your next-door neighbors' conversations through the walls, and most people have a view. All the residents on the harbor-facing side of BTI keep binoculars on their windowsills; when he first moved to Whittier, one man was warned to think twice before taking a piss outside. A lot of residents walk around BTI in their house slippers. We befriended a schoolteacher who told us that after she moved into BTI, it took her a long time before she felt comfortable going to a friend's apartment wearing pajamas or even holding a glass of wine. "I mean, I'm the teacher," she said. "But then I realized that the barriers were just going to be different here." When her students have problems with homework, they just knock on her apartment door.

After the alarm was finally shut off, we called up the mayor, who gave us a tour of the city in his truck. He drove us to the edge of town, where a new road was being built. A handful of Whittier's citizens and council members would like to see a resort area built farther out on the peninsula, hoping that it will bring in more tourist traffic. He then took us through the rail yards, back toward Whittier Community School—which is connected to BTI by an underground tunnel—and dropped us at our condo. "Well, I'm glad you guys arrived this week," he said, "because it's going to be crazy next week when those people from the Discovery Channel and the History Channel get here."

Sometime in the fall the mayor had told Reed that a couple of television production companies were interested in filming reality shows in Whittier. One company, Discovery Studios, had even started sending out contracts to "characters" that producers were interested in. Reed had planned to visit Whittier later, but when he learned that residents might be signing binding contracts, he changed his plans and moved up the visit. We thought we had beaten everyone else to the punch; we hadn't even thought of the possibility that the TV crews could show up while we were there. But the mayor had been fielding calls from everyone who was interested in documenting Whittier, and now it seemed that by trying to get there before the other New York media people did, we'd all accidentally scheduled our trips for the same time. It was just a minor annoyance for Reed and me, but the TV crews were being forced into a sort of showdown. The mayor told us that the city would be holding a special council meeting so that both production companies could pitch their show ideas to the people of Whittier. We were invited to come and watch. "A reality show could be good for bringing attention to our little town," he said, "but it does worry me, too. I don't want to be some Alaskan Honey Boo Boo."*

Over the past few years, the number of reality television series set in Alaska has skyrocketed. In 2014, more than a dozen aired on cable networks. Most of the programming is of the "man versus nature" variety: shows like *Deadliest Catch*, *Life Below Zero*, and even *Ice Road Truckers* tend to focus on the strange and dangerous professions of the Last Frontier. But forays into human drama have been made. The Oprah Winfrey Network ran a single season of *Married to the Army: Alaska*, about the "unique sisterhood" of military wives. TLC aired the short-lived *Big Hair Alaska*, a show about Wasilla's Beehive Beauty Shop, where Sarah Palin used to get her hair done. Alaskans have been both amused and frustrated by the explosion of media interest in their state. For a time the *Anchorage Daily News* even ran a blog called *Hollywood Alaska*, which reported on the latest industry news and routinely asked whether the state was getting enough return on this media gold rush.

*Alana "Honey Boo Boo" Thompson was the child star of *Here Comes Honey Boo Boo*, a reality show on TLC (formerly The Learning Channel) about a poor family living in the rural South. The series has been criticized as crude and exploitative, and the network was accused of ridiculing its own stars.

The Lower 48's obsession with the Last Frontier isn't the only cause of the boom. In 2008, the Alaska government began offering subsidies that allowed producers to recoup up to 44 percent of their spending in the state. The subsidy program—one of the most generous in the country—has been controversial. In previous years, shooting an entire feature film or TV series in Alaska tended to be prohibitively expensive. (*Northern Exposure*, the famous 1990s show about a Jewish doctor from New York who moves to a small town in Alaska, was shot entirely in Washington State.) More filming means more out-of-state film crews spending money on food and lodging, and could potentially be a boon for tourism, but the latest reports from the Alaska Film Office show that from 2011 to 2013, only around 15 percent of the total wages paid by these tax-subsidized productions have gone to Alaskans. On the seventh season of *Deadliest Catch*, Alaska workers earned less than $44,000, while out-of-state workers took home more than $1.3 million. And although an Alaska setting is central to the plotlines of most of the films and shows that are shot here, some production companies have come under fire for abusing the subsidy. *Baby Geniuses 3*, a movie about crime-fighting babies and toddlers, paid less than 6 percent of all wages to in-state employees, and its plot brought little attention to "Alaska issues."

Even when money or recognition does reach Alaskans, its effects are uncertain. Audiences typically tune in to Alaska-based reality TV for "real men in danger," not upwardly mobile characters. "Suddenly there's a lot of money floating around Tanana," a woman told us of the village where *Yukon Men* is filmed, "but no one can go out and buy a new Carhartt jacket, because on the show they're supposed to look like they're just barely hanging on." The Discovery Channel synopsis claims that Tanana is "part of an unknown America where men hunt and trap to survive, subsisting like modern day cavemen." One of the stars complained that after he brought home a deer he'd slaughtered, producers asked him to empty his fridge and freezer so that when he filled them with meat, it would look as if he'd had nothing to eat before.

At first I was surprised that people in Whittier were so nonchalant about being documented—media savvy, even. When we told one man with a Santa Claus beard that we'd like to take his portrait, he suggested he get a haircut first, but then his friend jumped in. "No, they want that swag. They want to see a guy who can hold a job with a beard like that. It's so Alaska." As long as the town of Whittier has existed, outsiders have been fascinated by the way its citizens live, but with the recent glut of reality television in the state it seemed that everyone we met knew someone who'd recently been on camera. The mayor had a friend on the taxidermy show *Mounted in Alaska*. A local had worked as a deckhand on a boat that was chartered for *Alaska: The Last Frontier*, and when she tuned in, excited to see her boat on TV, she was surprised to find that she herself was on the show. The day after the episode aired, someone belatedly called to ask for permission to use her likeness.

Our first week in town, we hurried to finish as many portraits as possible before the production companies showed up. We weren't exactly in competition with the TV crews, but we did worry that people would tire of interviews and cameras. "Are you the TV people?" they asked. So many residents were relieved when we said no that we began to introduce ourselves by saying, "Hi, we're from New York, and we're not with a reality show." Most of the town, it seemed, was murmuring about TV. Some feared they'd be made to look stupid. Others worried that on-screen drama would cause rifts in the community. Most thought the town was too boring for anyone to actually go through with a show. "People get scared about who will be picked to be on the show," said the city manager (who runs most of the day-to-day operations in Whittier), "because they all think their neighbors are idiots."

One morning we came downstairs to find casting call notices on the bulletin boards in BTI's lobby. "Today I saw a spiky-haired woman in a miniskirt," said the cashier at the Kozy Korner. "So I figured she must be from New York." We overheard the desk clerks at Whittier Community School double daring each other to go to the auditions that were being held that night. "Come on," said one, "I want that TV money!"

On the day of the council meeting, big lazy snowflakes fell on Whittier, blanketing the town. Reed and I walked down to the Public Works Building where council members and about thirty citizens had gathered. Cameras were rolling. A couple of men in skinny jeans and brand-new Sorel snow boots were fiddling with a DVD setup. Each production company would be given a chance to pitch its show: producers were to talk about the benefits of signing with their company and what would happen if the show got picked up by a network. People in town had been referring to the crews as simply "the Discovery Channel" and "the History Channel," but these labels were a bit misleading: one group was from Discovery Studios, the in-house production company for all Discovery-owned networks (including TLC, Animal Planet, and the Oprah Winfrey Network). The other group, though contracted by the History Channel, was from a small New York production company.

The representative from Discovery Studios gave her presentation first, leading off with a short reel of her company's reality shows. The video cut frantically between clips, from a hoarding show ("We have to clean this place up, starting now!") to a cop show ("The southern Texas border has become a war zone") to a diving show ("They want me to swim with sharks—what the hell was I thinking?"). The producer then explained that she had come to get a "sampling of flavors" in Whittier so she could make a "sizzle reel" to pitch to networks. She kept referring to the people in town as "characters."

The next representative called his Manhattan-based production company a "mom-and-pop shop" and explained that his show was trying to explore how real people lived in America. He argued that the History Channel was the right choice for Whittier because the network had an interest in "independent entrepreneurial-type people" and "unconventional lifestyles."

Both teams dispelled the rumors—widely circulating at the time—that if they requested it in their contracts, Whittier's "characters" could prescreen episodes to make sure anything they objected to wouldn't air. (This option, the producers explained, is typically only given to military and law enforcement agencies so that they can screen for classified information.) The floor was then opened up to questions from the audience.

The mayor said he was concerned that not enough went on in Whittier for a reality show to be sustained. "With *Gold Rush: Alaska*," said the mayor, "some of them tune in to see the characters, and some of them tune in to see if they strike gold. And the same thing with *Pawn Stars*. People tune in to see the pawn stars, and they also tune in to see what they're pawning and what they're selling. We don't have gold to find or Rolex watches that's being pawned to us. All we have is characters out here." Without an industry to follow, and with the main interest in Whittier being its unique housing situation, residents worried that producers would try to stir up interpersonal drama in BTI. People voiced their fears of being made to look stupid.

Not at all, said one producer. "You're Alaska," she stressed. "If anything, we'd be bragging about your extreme lifestyles." Someone asked if there was a difference between the concepts of the two teams' shows, and both said their theme would be "the story of a small town," an answer that did little to lessen residents' concerns about how they might be portrayed.

"Well, they're obviously going to show some of the bad side of Whittier," said a bottle-blond resident in a leopard-print coat. "That's what's going to make a show. But they're not going to make an intelligent person look stupid. And they're not going to make a negative, stupid person look good."

A woman in the back of the room spoke up. "This is the first time in a long time that our kids are getting confidence to go out on their own and to seek out new things to do, and I really don't want to see that damaged. Our EMS department is getting awards; a lot of people are getting awards. We've worked too hard for that to just go down the drain because somebody wants to be on TV." Schoolteachers expressed fears about how a reality show might affect their students. A relative newcomer to Whittier talked about how proud she was to call the town home and began to cry. I kept my eye on the cameras, wondering if the producers were telling the truth when they said that this footage was not for broadcast.

Though the meeting offered a forum for residents to raise questions and voice concerns, there was nothing, actually, to vote on. City councils can't determine whether or not a company should be allowed to film in their town. The Discovery producer explained that both companies could potentially go forward with their shows if they wanted to, though she suggested that the people of Whittier choose one company so the town would not be divided. Attendees suggested that everyone meet sometime at the Anchor Inn—not as a city council or a school board or a condo association, but as a community—so that if they went forward with a show, they went forward together.

The mayor, despite his reservations, was excited about the prospect of a reality show. "I just got back from the East Coast," he said. "One of my favorite things I did while I was in Boston was go to Cheers. I had my picture taken in Norm's seat at the bar, and I can see people wanting to come to Whittier and see where people sit at the bar or see where the city has their city council meetings. I could see some positive in this." The Discovery producer reminded everyone that having a whole TV crew in town, in need of room and board, would boost the wintertime economy. "If you have a favorite seat at the Anchor Inn," joked the History Channel producer, "you better write your name on it now."

"But they're going to become townspeople," protested the producer from Discovery. "They're going to become one of you. These are going to be your friends."

A production assistant was in her workout clothes, doing laps in the BTI hallway, when Reed and I were setting up one of our last shots of the trip. She had her headphones on, so we didn't bother to say hi. Soon afterward, the rest of her crew walked by and stopped to chat. "What are your names?" said the executive producer. "Maybe I've seen your work." It's always embarrassing the way media people talk to you when they hear that you are one of them. The local photographer wants you to look over his shoulder while he shows you his website and complains about his small-town neighbors. The film crew from New York invites you to the party they're having at a "rockin' space" in Bushwick. Their shoptalk has a competitive edge and shouldn't be mistaken for friendliness: "By the way, are there any cool people in town you think that we should talk to?" These interactions leave you with the same hollow sadness you feel inside an Apple store, but they also check the impulse to believe you're the tourist who's less touristy than other tourists.

A tide of out-of-towners has come and gone with every boom and bust in Alaska, from the Klondike gold rush to the World War II and cold war military growth that tripled the state's population. Most of the people we met in Alaska had arrived in the early 1980s, in the fat years after the completion of the Trans-Alaska Pipeline, which carries oil from Alaska's North Slope down to Valdez, just across the sound from Whittier. These were the people who came not for the oil but for the boom. They started restaurants and hotels and paint shops and craft shops; they stayed on and became Alaskans. But the people with their eyes on Alaska now are more voyeurs than adventurers. They are interested not in contributing stories of their own but rather in extracting and exporting the ones here already. The great part about TV is that you can watch all the excitement from the comfort of your own home.

On our last night in town, we went down to the Anchor Inn, but it was empty when we showed up, so we sat in the back with the bartender, watching the wind blow snow across the rail yard. "When I was younger," she said, "I was real thin, and that wind hit me so hard one time, I slid completely underneath my car." Customers started trickling in, but the place was quieter than usual; we had all become glued to the huge flat-screen TV, which was playing non-stop tragedy on the late-night news. A couple of guys from a TV crew came in with the bar's owner and sat down for drinks. A few of the regulars—Russ, Rusty, and Russ (one of the Russes is Rusty's son)—ambled in. Conversation picked up; the crowd started to buzz. But everything stopped when a woman at the bar whom Reed and I had been talking to all night got a call from a friend in BTI.

"Again?" she yelled. "Don't worry, I'm coming. Call Officer Dave." It was a domestic dispute in the tower. She said she'd be back as soon as she could.

"Okay," people called out to her. "It will be okay."

The producer from the TV crew was staring into his lap—texting rapidly beneath the bar.

"Are you trying to check out what's going on up there?" asked Reed.

"Yeah," said the producer, "I'm pretty sure we can get a ride-along."

"You know," Reed said to the producer. "I think TV people are real shitheads."

The producer was taken aback but didn't say much in response. We turned back to the flat-screen and ordered another drink. When we left, the crew was still there, sitting at the bar, taking up people's favorite seats, just as they'd joked they would. The next day, we left Whittier.

Throughout the second week of our trip, we kept seeing another man, all in black, walking through town with a tripod. We'd assumed he was with the television crews, but we only ever saw him alone. One night we went to the Anchor Inn, and he was sitting at the bar with a woman. We sat down next to them. It turned out that he was a photographer and she was a writer. We were all at the corner of the bar, each pair facing the other; it was like looking through some existential fun-house mirror. They told us they had met at Yaddo and were opaque about what they were doing in Whittier.

"I'm not exactly sure what I'm doing here," he said. "I'm mostly just taking pictures of piles of snow."

"I don't really leave the condo," she said. "I just stare out the window, write a little poetry."

After a while, we sussed out that they'd come to Whittier for a romantic getaway and a few weeks of artistic inspiration. It was such a departure from the mode we'd been in. We'd been surrounded by people looking for stories, and here they were, searching for something else, something they couldn't even name.

We explained to them that we had thought the photographer was with a reality show, but the couple had no idea what we were talking about. "I don't even say hi to anyone," the poet said. We told them about the crews in town and about reality TV's hunger for Alaska. They admitted that they could see the appeal, that they too were taken with the "realness" of Alaska living.

"We've been thinking about moving here," said the writer, "to one of the little empty cabins behind the Buckner Building."

Later I'd keep imagining them up there in the winter to come, freezing in one of those tiny cabins—previously abandoned because they were unlivably cold. Something about it seemed so silly, so arbitrary: if these two stayed in Whittier instead of going home to make their art about it, suddenly they'd have become insiders, or "characters" just like everybody else, and our lenses would have turned on them, too.

6

THE OFFICE AND THE CITY

NIKIL SAVAL

The wealth of capitalist societies, Marx wrote, presents itself as "an accumulation of commodities." One could just as easily say today that wealth appears as an accumulation of offices. If an emerging economy wishes to show off, it must immure itself in towers. In Chinese advertisements, lurid spaceship skyscrapers hover on the Pearl delta; in the United Arab Emirates, spindly, sinuous glass needles tower over the desert. The Indian state of Gujarat will soon finish a glassy showroom of office space in the wastes of its hinterland called Gujarat International Finance Tec-City, or—less cumbersomely, and more revealingly—GIFT. Not that the West is now free from the temptation of the office. Historically low-slung London has, in the last twenty or so years, succumbed—to towers that look like pickles and towers from which reflected sunlight melts cars below. The rosy granite hallucinations of postmodernism have come to a close, and a neo-modernism, exemplified by the dazzling glass skins of Sir Norman Foster, currently enjoys untrammeled triumph. Cities once again cloak their workers in curtain walls, striate them with mullions, cinch them shut in spandrels.

American cities, and the cities of the developed capitalist world more generally, are cities where white-collar workers are hegemonic, dominating the retail and service workers staffing the establishments where the white-collar workers shop for iPhone cases, eat Korean tacos, do hatha yoga, and drink coconut water. It was not always so. Cities used to be centered on manufacturing, and the change to other industries has been dramatic, nowhere more palpably than in New York. In the 1950s, New York had two workers in manufacturing for every worker in the finance, insurance, and real estate industries; by the early 1990s, the ratio had reversed. The shift made itself felt in the everyday street life of the city. On a sweltering summer day in 1998, construction workers picketed the Metropolitan Transportation Authority for using nonunion labor, shutting down Madison Avenue. Blue-collar strikes had by then become so uncommon that the *New York Post* ran a full-page article titled "Hunk Heaven," extolling the erotic fascination that the scene aroused.

New York has led the way in modeling how a city based on production can be transformed into one based on services and how a skyline of church spires and smokestacks can be elevated into a jagged, Tetris-like collection of tall glass boxes. At the same time, this process has been decidedly uneven. For every Chicago or San Francisco that survived the process of deindustrialization to maintain a salubrious connection to the global economy—evidenced by the continued resilience of their office skyscrapers—there are those like Detroit, whose central business districts are bywords for the windswept vacancy that has seized so many American downtowns. In some ways, the story of the office and the American city is here, in the development of the downtown central business district itself (for a time, a uniquely American phenomenon), its crisis in the postwar era, and its calculated resurgence in a few major cities and a handful of minor ones, with the rest of the cities expelled from a system that no longer needs them or their residents. Accompanying the resurgence of the city has been the gentrification of neglected areas, where white-collar workers from the glassy high-rise core "rediscovered" the pastoral pleasures (and low prices) of the brown-sandstone or brick row house in the low-rise periphery.

Central to this story is the question of class. The development of the original Gilded Age downtowns, as well as the refortified business districts of the American city, required planning, and planning very often meant encouraging the construction of office towers. To use the terminology of the political scientist James C. Scott: cities over time became "legible" to urban elites as essentially, perhaps even fundamentally, white-collar. The pollution, lower-classness, and urban unrest associated with manufacturing and other kinds of blue-collar employment were amenable neither to businesses, which professedly feared strikes and the contamination of their employees by unionization, nor to real estate developers, who saw higher returns on investment coming from office towers, nor city planners and politicians, who saw the tax base of white-collar professionals as preferable to that of laborers. This amalgam of interests and ideologies would help the American city become a white-collar phenomenon.

Office workers emerged as a distinct group in the mid-nineteenth century. In the 1850s, clerical workers were the fastest-growing segment of the largest American cities, Boston, New York, and Philadelphia. Until then, compared with the vast sweep of farms and the growing ranks of factory workers, white-collar labor was negligible in the eyes of commentators and went unnoticed by them. A new visibility, a sticking out, coincided with their burgeoning city presence, a fact as peculiar to themselves as to others. Clerks began to be . . . not conscious of themselves, exactly—that is, not in the Marxist sense of considering themselves antagonistic to other groupings and capable of action—but more vaguely aware of themselves as a distinct middle stratum, below the wielders of capital, whom they admired, but above those who worked with their hands, whom the office workers often seemed to despise. Clerks knew themselves to be part of a group, but it was a group marked by pervasive individualism, by a shared expectation that each individual would rise above his station by virtue of his own merit. This was class not as a restriction but as a viewpoint; the collective condition of clerks was just a temporary stopping place—a ladder rung that would soon be surmounted.

Office buildings took longer to emerge. For generations, the locations where clerks performed recognizable office work were known as "countinghouses," a term in use in mercantile England as well as in antebellum America. In their organizational form—a few partners employing a handful of clerks and bookkeepers—or their methods, such as double-entry bookkeeping, they weren't appreciably different from Italian banking offices several centuries older. Their imprint on cities was initially invisible by any exterior modeling; there were no office buildings to speak of. In antebellum New York, the countinghouses of merchants' clerks clustered around and below Canal Street, close to the busy docks, where the regular arrival of packet ships determined the broad outlines of the workday. Many mercantile concerns also operated dry-goods stores where they displayed their wares, such as textiles; the clerks divided their duties between manning the stores and keeping track of the stores' accounts.

The diaries of a merchants' clerk, Edward N. Tailer, give us some flavor of the geography of the white-collar workday, the sheer range of the city that it encompassed—achieving a level of mobility that even the more "nomadic" office workers today might envy. In one entry from 1848, Tailer records going to the Bank of Commerce on Nassau Street in the morning, going to two companies on Pearl Street to collect bills, making a deposit in the Merchants' Clerks bank on Beekman Street, meeting up with his friend on Broadway and Walker, and going to the gym in Greenwich Village by 9:00 p.m. Other days he stops at the Mercantile Library, an educational association specifically geared toward clerks seeking "self-improvement." Tailer's personal working and leisure geography overlaid that of the city's manual workers but was in various ways distinct from it. By demarcating institutions and spaces as specifically clerical, with accents, interests, and membership that distinguished one stratum of workers from the others, the office, and office workers, came palpably to structure the metropolis along the lines of class.

Eventually this took place in visible ways. Before long, the countinghouse began to separate itself from manual workplaces through distinctive architectural gestures. The specialization of labor within manufacturing enterprises prompted the need for more administration—for more clerks to keep track of bills and accounts and more bookkeepers to handle statements of profit and loss. Countinghouses and their stores participated in the Greek Revival movement of the period, framing their entrances with stiff lintels and fluted Ionic columns. City directories from the time began to note separate locations for company factories and company "offices"—the latter usually agglomerated in what also came to be called (around this time) downtown, though only in New York City was this business district actually located in the city's southern region.

The subtle demarcation of certain districts as white-collar, especially the downtown, lay the groundwork for the economic era to come. In the late nineteenth century, as a wave of mergers and forms of vertical integration swept through the American economy, cities began to swell with ever larger businesses, which began to devote more and more resources to specialized accounting and other forms of administrative bureaucracy—which in turn meant needing more office space. It does not necessarily follow that office buildings should therefore huddle together in a set of delimited square miles. But the swelling gigantism of the American economy led precisely here, and the reasons are complex. On the one hand, there were the simple communicational benefits of concentration. Specialization meant transactions that once took one meeting might now take several. It helped to have suppliers, customers, consultants, advertisers, and distributors all within walking distance or even under the same roof. W.L.B. Jenney, a Chicago architect who helped bring the steel-frame skyscraper into being, would note the benefits of Chicago's especially dense business district. "Business is so concentrated that strangers claim they can do more business in a given length of time here than in any other city," he wrote in the 1890s.

Ideology also justified the intense levels of concentration that American cities came to enjoy, or endure. Planning logic at the time operated according to a pseudo-anatomical ideology of what the urban historian Robert Fogelson has called "spatial harmony," according to which cities needed to have a strong central "heart" of workplaces and shops and restaurants and places of entertainment, connected to the periphery by various "arteries" of transportation: first streetcars and later subways and automobiles. For generations, and in European cities still through the nineteenth and early twentieth centuries, the separation of residence and business was not taken as a given. In the United States, however, downtown was for commerce; the periphery was for living. This was a formula that could encourage concentration in boom times, when the downtown looked good and people wanted to get to it, but could also encourage decentralization in bad times, when the outskirts and suburbs of a city looked better and people only came to the city to cruise in and out. (Over time, the ways into the city—first streetcars and elevated railways, followed by expressways—would become ways out of it, as masses of the residential population decamped to the newly accessible suburbs.)

The discourse of "spatial harmony" arose not coincidentally around the same time that the polarization between bourgeoisie and proletariat began to be remarked upon and lamented. Conflict within cities between capital and labor induced anxiety in city elites. One way to solve, or at least forestall, the conflict was to separate the administrative bureaucracy from the manual labor. The central business district in this sense became the image of a city that concentrated white-collar work and separated it from blue-collar work.

Chicago was an especially pure example of this enforced separation. In Chicago, the area that eventually became the Loop was originally a working-class district. Mahlon D. Ogden, a real estate developer, read this differently—an early example of the changing "legibility" of American cities. He saw it as "covered with countless old rookeries and miserable shanties, occupied, for the past twenty years, as dens of infamy and low gambling dives, the resort and rendezvous of thieves, burglars, robbers, and murderers of all grades and colors, to the exclusion of all decency, or business purposes." Mercifully for developers, the fire of 1871 tore through the area, leaving it pleasingly open for the planning imagination. Planners went to work, helping to move factories and warehouses out of the area, to the outskirts of the city, thereby allowing building owners to charge higher rents. The area became a singular white-collar concentrate, filled with towers whose beauty and innovative engineering feats belied their essentially speculative nature. It was here that the greatest skyscrapers of the Chicago school of architecture appeared, their entrances decorated in multiple kinds of variegated marble, their environs decked out in restaurants, libraries, and sitting rooms, all designed to point to the literally elevated nature of the work being done within. The city's factories, warehouses, and stockyards, stinking of smoke and cow dung, unions and anarchism, were moved far from the city center. They could be seen from the tops of the skyscrapers that occupied the areas where some of them once stood.

But why are the buildings so tall? The answer lies in the peculiar trajectory of American city development and above all in the misty realms of real estate finance. Like the central business district itself, the skyscraper was in its origins an American concept. It sprang up in cities that, unlike, say, Paris or Ghent, Rome or Warsaw, had only limited histories of development, and rarely along the lines of the tangled, insinuating medieval streets that characterized many European cities. These thickly populated, historic, communitarian cities would not permit the soaring individualism of a skyscraper breaking the low-slung skyline for decades to come. The rational planning of the American cityscape permitted greater freedom of upward movement. Following William Penn's plan for Philadelphia, American cities soon began to adopt grid-like forms for development; these allowed for the massive blocks that skyscrapers came to occupy—though the oddly shaped blocks of lower Manhattan also furnished opportunities for tall, albeit strangely shaped, buildings. It was comparatively easy, too, for developers to tear down existing buildings in order to build upward, because these—and the neighborhoods they were part of—were rarely old enough to justify any kind of preservation.

But the other, more consistently compelling reason is that tall buildings make money. For the office skyscraper is above all a speculative investment. "A machine that makes the land pay" is how Cass Gilbert, architect of the Woolworth Building, described the skyscraper. Speculation of course only means the forecast that rent income will equal or exceed the investment. But in commercial real estate, even more than housing, the delivery system encourages oversupply, because "demand" is only modestly related to the construction of office space. Offices don't necessarily come into being because people need them; after all, an office developer only has to lure tenants from another building. A city skyline is in some ways the reflection of a history of real estate cycles, and in boom times the skyline begins to burgeon and crane upward, seeking as much profit as the air, promise-crammed, will offer. Few of these buildings ever reflected the initiative or pride of the companies that owned them. The tendency to refer to the most spectacular instances by the names of corporations—Woolworth, Seagram, Lever (the soap manufacturer), Pan Am, Sears—obscures how often the buildings rented out space to other clients, as well as the horde of numberless knockoffs thrown up in haste to provide short-term leases for unknown future clients. In flush times, the number of these dreadful buildings begins to climb, as the value of the land becomes less grounded in predictable costs and more tied to the ballooning number of what someone will pay for it. Architects, developers, planners, and designers therefore collude in rushing to put out a building; it is in everyone's interest to throw caution to high-speed winds when the money is good. "Overbuilding of Offices Is Impossible," ran the chief headline of New York's *Real Estate Record* a brazen few months after the stock market crash of 1929.

And the form and height of the skyscraper in the early twentieth century depended to a great extent on the best way to make the land pay the investors and owners of a project. As the architectural historian Carol Willis pointed out in *Form Follows Finance*, the height of the building is achieved by compromising the engineering height—the structurally feasible number of stories that a building can go in the size of the location and geologic conditions of the plot offered to it—with the economic height, in Willis's words, "the number of stories that would produce the highest rate on the money invested." After a certain point, building higher begins to diminish returns, with extra stories failing to cover extra costs, chiefly because building higher required bigger elevator and service shafts, which in turn cut into the rentable area. One of the earliest examples of a speculative grand slam was the 1915 Equitable Building (now demolished). When completed, it was only the fifth-tallest building in New York, but thanks to its H shape it permitted four long lines of offices along the sides with shafts in the center and contained the world's largest concentration of office space in one building.

Buildings like the Equitable, with its monotonous, thick walls of limestone casting shade everywhere, prompted attempts to mitigate the scale of buildings. For a time, desperate height restrictions and frantic zoning laws provided the only municipal variation on what were largely similar-looking skyscraper shapes. In Chicago, an initial period of laissez-faire construction led to overbuilding and high vacancy rates following the panic of 1893. The city council moved to cap building heights at 130 feet, which over time gravitated toward 260 feet; during the same period, New York towers, unbounded by law, reached as high as 700 feet. Chicago investors, dissatisfied by the returns on their squat, fat buildings, sought money elsewhere, and they found it by constructing high-ceilinged,

ornate light courts on the ground floor, which they let out to retailers, who paid higher rents than office tenants. This eminently
commercial strategy had the added benefit of lending an air of aris-
tocratic comfort to "mental laborers" as they entered their lofty environs. New York, too, came to adopt restrictions, following a burst
of overbuilding in 1909 and a subsequent real estate recession in
1913. The zoning ordinance of 1916, rather than capping building
heights, forced builders to set back their buildings past a certain
height. In other words, a building within a certain plot of land could
rise, say, 150 feet from the corners of the plot before having to recede
into the plot 30 feet for the next 100 feet of space. Though building
heights didn't decrease (the Chrysler and Empire State Buildings
went up during this period), they acquired a ziggurat-like shape
that became characteristic of New York skyscrapers of the time.

Buildings get taller and more spectacular as booms come to a
close. Offices often survive the initial market crash, and periods of
recession are correspondingly marked by the absurdity of empty
office buildings going up based on previously spent cash. The Empire State Building in 1941, a decade after its opening, remained 75
percent empty. In New York City more generally, the vacancy rate
hovered around 30 percent well after the recovery began. The Depression had followed one of the wildest construction booms in the
history of the world; the vacancy rates that followed were, accord-
ingly, crushing. Skyscrapers began to be demolished to make way
for parking lots—"taxpayers," they were called, for their ability to
generate reliable and quick returns for developers.

Some of the poorest people live in conveniently located
slums on high-priced land. On patrician Fifth Avenue, Tif-
fany and Woolworth, cheek by jowl, offer jewels and jim-
cracks from substantially identical sites. Childs restaurants
thrive and multiply where Delmonico's withered and died.
A stone's throw from the stock exchange the air is filled with
the aroma of roasting coffee; a few hundred feet from Times

Square with the stench of slaughter houses. In the very heart
of this "commercial" city, on Manhattan Island south of
59th street, the inspectors in 1922 found nearly 420,000
workers employed in factories. Such a situation outrages
one's sense of order. Everything seems misplaced. One
yearns to rearrange things to put things where they belong.

—Robert Haig, chief economist, New York Regional
Plan Association (1929) (quoted in Robert Fitch,
The Assassination of New York)

By the 1940s, downtown was suffering. Vacancies still plagued
many downtowns well into the war-sponsored recovery. As a result,
laissez-faire development, which had produced all the empty buildings, came into serious disrepute, and it became an item of widely
held faith that the government—arm in arm with the power elites
of municipalities everywhere—would have to step in. The peculiarity of this, the third major phase of skyscraper construction (following the Gilded Age, and the 1920s, and preceding the surge of the
1980s), was its harmonization of two supposedly antagonistic forces:
architectural modernism and corporatist bureaucracy. A modernism that had begun as an avant-garde, and often explicitly socialist,
force, concerned with housing and shelter, found its greatest re-
alization and support in corporate America. In a way that few of
modernism's original proponents might have foreseen, some of
the classic works of international modernism would turn out to
be corporate office towers built for the purposes of speculative
accumulation.

Before the crash of 1929, a conception of the office as a solution
to the problems of the city had become internationally common-
place. Le Corbusier in his "Plan Voisin" (1925) had imagined an
ultrarational, orthogonal plan for the solution to Paris's housing
problem; he went out of his way to centralize business operations as
well, in evenly spaced, tall office towers. He rhapsodized the glory
of his business district in characteristically telegraphic sentences:
"From its offices come the commands that put the world in order.

In fact, the skyscrapers are the brain of the city, the brain of the whole country. They embody the work of elaboration and command on which all activities depend. Everything is concentrated there: the tools that conquer time and space—telephones, telegraphs, radios, the banks, trading houses, the organs of decision for the factories: finance, technology, commerce." In the American context, the Regional Plan Association of New York looked at the heavily blue-collar city of 1928 and produced a rezoned plan that would limit the amount of manufacturing and expel what remained to the city's edge. With the planning and creation of Rockefeller Center in the 1930s, the architect Raymond Hood brought the notion of a conglomerated, rational business-and-consumer center—against the individual skyscraper, which answered only to the irrational needs of speculation—to reality. In private, he imagined a total reorganization of New York along similar lines.

Though such enormous rational plans did not materialize, a concerted effort to reimagine the city as a pure, ordered, and—this part was usually unspoken—middle-class collection of office towers would broadly describe the postwar project known as urban renewal. Title I of the Housing Act, signed by President Truman in 1949, encouraged the demolition of "blighted" areas and the relocation of former "slum-dwelling" residents to public housing. Though it did not stipulate that federal authorities grant the newly vacated land to housing developers, that's what happened. Once the expulsion of hundreds of thousands of poor and working-class residents from the city center to housing projects on the periphery was complete, new office towers appeared on land granted to developers at below-market rates. The towers that sprang up in American cities during this era uniformly took on the cast of the International Style. Thanks to fluorescent lighting and air-conditioning, they had deep, wide, anonymous floor plates that could be partitioned according to the desire of tenants; their curtain walls were of pure, reflective glass, their crosshatched lines reflecting the gridded offices on the interior and the wider grids of the cities they towered over. Intended to be symbols of a progressive, technologically advanced civilization, in due course they came to look like icons of bureaucracy, indifferent to scale and human need.

Meanwhile, the cities they occupied were transforming at their base. Downtown business leaders and their allies in planning circles rarely countenanced any changes that would limit the scale of skyscrapers or the density of the business district. Rather quickly, business districts became unpleasant places to be and certainly joyless places to linger. Streets obscured by inescapable shadow and viscous with heat and sweat in the summer, crammed all the time with suits and construction, the rents climbing higher alongside the proliferating towers: it made sense that workers in these districts would come to seek homes, and other pleasures, outside the city. The highways that planners had constructed in order to encourage in-migration to the city began to facilitate the exodus.

Businesses, too, began to move out of downtowns, fleeing not only prices but restive unions, migrating African-Americans, and—a particular concern of the postwar era—the threat of nuclear war, which, business leaders assumed, would target centralized business districts. The 1950s and 1960s consequently witnessed a swelling trend toward the construction of suburban office parks. Not just a few of them emphasized the pastoral, contemplative pleasures of working in the "countryside." Some of them—such as Bell Labs—would enter the pantheon of American business. Most of them—thick, low-slung glass boxes encircled by fake moats that burgeon with reeds and stink of the ceaseless excrement of Canada geese—are among the most dreary and wasteful constructions known to man.

The subsequent flight of manufacturing from the urban core was not a placid, inevitable process, like water flowing inexorably downhill. In many cities, and in New York in particular, manufacturing was pushed out through a panoply of strategies—largely grouped under the rubric "urban renewal"—that left the city impoverished of blue-collar jobs but open to redevelopment for white-collar workers, or at least the office towers that were supposed to house them. From 1967 to 1973, sixty-eight million square feet of office space were constructed in New York—twice the amount of the boom of the 1920s. The lofts south of Houston Street, which housed the thousands of small-batch firms that were characteristic of New York manufacturing, were forced out through redevelopment. The landfill created by the monstrous World Trade Center and adjoining Battery Park City crushed the docks jutting out from West Street, helping to destroy the port of Manhattan and the jobs of the thirty thousand workers employed by the city's shipping industry.

Yet in the years that followed, New York and cities like it managed with relative success to reconstitute themselves entirely as powerhouses of media, banking, insurance, real estate, and, eventually, the proliferating, innovative instruments of high finance. These firms were networked with similar firms in similar cities (London, Tokyo, Frankfurt, and, more recently, Shanghai and Seoul) around the globe. Meanwhile, mid-level companies or smaller branches of what were increasingly multinational firms found homes (and generous tax credits) in the downtowns of cities like San Diego, Denver, Miami, and other cities of comparable size.

How could a city gut itself, as New York, Boston, and San Francisco did, and emerge to all appearances intact, not to say gleaming? In effect, deindustrialization encouraged the growth and concentration of white-collar work. Cities with diverse manufacturing bases, such as New York and Chicago, already had experience with concentrating various levels of white-collar management; this turned out to be one of the necessary foundations for what would be a new era of intense agglomeration. (In places like Detroit, where manufacturing was focused on a single commodity, the challenges of restructuring would prove insurmountable.) The push toward dispersing production across the globe that began to take place in the postwar era, accelerating in the 1980s, had the corollary effect of making it essential to centralize management services, for the ease and speed of communication.

Not only that: the increasingly complex network of factories that characterized manufacturing any commodity, as well as the intense competition engendered by firms having to fight for market share across the planet, augmented the tasks of management and the speed with which transactions needed to be conducted. Corporations required more lawyers, accountants, and advertisers. Universities not only provided future white-collar workers but also received grants from foundations and government bureaucracies to provide research that helped the growing network of firms. Finally, by the 1980s, the deregulation of the financial industry permitted the development of complex financial instruments, whose dubious value seemed to be based on the distance between the security (of, say, a collateralized debt obligation) and the underlying asset (the original housing mortgage). The multiple levels that lay between asset and security in turn inflated the numbers of white-collar workers, and especially rich ones, in American cities. In the classic analysis of the sociologist Saskia Sassen, these transformations in the nature of the economy ended up turning a few cities into the "command-and-control centers" of global capitalism. Many others, such as Detroit, St. Louis, and Cleveland, suffered from their reliance on nondiverse sources of manufacturing and went into unarrested declines. These developments were not necessarily predictable, and the reasons for the failure of some cities and the success of others are not always clear. Nonetheless, it seems likely that the cities that had an existing knowledge base (universities, hospitals, and associated research facilities), as well as major financial institutions, were best able to survive and prosper in the new era.

In this process, cynical New York again led the way, with cheery San Francisco not far behind, in encouraging the construction of office towers. Ed Koch in the former and Dianne Feinstein in the latter became infamous for luring developers and firms with luxurious offers of tax credits for new development, and for burdening their cities with some of the worst architectural excrescences in the history of the form. The 1980s skyscraper, with its nearly universal penchant for large quantities of granite massing on the exterior and high-ceilinged marble lobbies, became emblematic of the era's tasteless excesses. It had its roots in an intellectual movement, post-modernism, born out of an opposition to the inhumane, slick de rigueur gestures of modernism. In its corporate guise, whatever oppositional content postmodernism had enjoyed in the 1970s was buried under the mounds of cocaine and sushi and marble and granite. The signature architect of the era was Philip Johnson, the massing of whose AT&T Building was covered in acres-thick rose granite, its base circumambulated by a Renaissance-style loggia, and its very top capped by a silly Chippendale arch. Goofy, serenely nostalgic, and opulent all at once, the building and its descendants captured the Reagan era's schizophrenic desire to live in a glorious, fabricated past while ensuring the desecration of the past's actual remaining monuments.

But the increase in high-paying professional jobs and the relatively larger decline in decently paying blue-collar jobs would leave its mark on more than the city's skyline. As with the rise of clerical workers in the antebellum American city, the new middle classes (or "yuppies") of the post-manufacturing city transformed urban culture. Nowhere was this more a source of continual tension than with the rise of gentrification. The white-collar enchantment with places like SoHo and Park Slope in Brooklyn—more recent examples might be South of Market in San Francisco, Northern Liberties in Philadelphia, and sections of downtown Los Angeles—was in part a class-wide reaction to the stultifying nature of the central business district. Many workers in the suffocating, air-conditioned cubicle warrens of lower or midtown Manhattan had ceased to be content with the modern apartments that largely resembled the offices where they worked, let alone with the anodyne comforts of the suburbia where many of them had grown up. Seeking authenticity, the pleasures of village life, the ordinary pleasures of organic communities, they found solace in the air of craftsmanship that attended the modest ornamentation of sandstone row houses or the wooden beams and exposed pipes of formerly industrial lofts. These same workers opposed the lingering industries, helping to move factories and warehouses away from the neighborhoods they were rehabbing. The city that had supported industry was gone (and good riddance, the yuppies thought). But it still gave some pleasure to live where industry had lived, as in the lofts, or, in the brownstones, to relive the lives of the old Brooklyn bourgeoisie.

In his 1980 bestseller *The Third Wave*, the professional futurologist Alvin Toffler had imagined that the increase in telecommunication capacity would render office buildings obsolete. Human beings would no longer commute to work. Instead, they would work from home, in a decentralized network of glowing "electronic cottages." Downtowns in turn would depopulate, with office towers looming darkly over abandoned parking garages and streets bereft of any signs of life.

Toffler's forecast for what technology would do to city life has proven to be incontestably wrong. Cities wired beyond his imagination have repopulated; many downtowns have grown, and it has become common among people living in expensive, thoroughly gentrified cities like New York and San Francisco to speak longingly of other, cheaper places that are several stages behind in the process: "People tell me Columbus, Ohio, is really cool, that it's a great beer town" or "You can get a cheap place in Pittsburgh, and there are a lot of great bars in former steel factories," and so forth.

Why has the city center grown, when it no longer seems necessary? It is not only that a generation schooled on Jane Jacobs lite has come to prize the network of eyes and morning-to-evening ballet of street life. It is also that the city has become prized by workers as a supposed repository of knowledge and information, as a potential for random encounters and serendipity—not to mention as an inexhaustible source of baubles and entertainments for white-collar consumers. The faith of white-collar workers in the redemptive potential of the city has become absolute. In places like Las Vegas, venture capitalists and investors, led by messianic tech entrepreneurs, have seized derelict downtowns, in the hopes of turning them into conglomerations of cafés, bars, and other white-collar hangouts. Cities cater to white-collar workers by turning themselves into giant offices: every flat surface in any location with wireless access threatens to become an office, and service and retail establishments spring up with a kind of abandon to meet the demands of workers after or between their hours of work.

But one part of Toffler's prediction threatens to come true. In the wake of the crash of 2007–8, building office space in the old, enthusiastic way has become increasingly hard to justify. Space in cities is expensive, and office workers—who can work nearly anywhere—appear to need it less. According to a study by the design consulting group DEGW, employees are at their desks on average about 30 percent of the time, implying a tremendous amount of wasted space. What's more, firms employ fewer of these workers on a full-time basis; many more of them (around 20 to 25 percent, according to one estimate, and growing every day) work on a contract basis as "freelancers." These workers have no offices at all; they work at home or in cafés, or they pay for desks in increasingly popular "co-working" facilities. Office furniture manufacturers I have spoken to told me of a general crisis in their industry. Companies want less space to cram more workers into, as they directly employ fewer of them. The trend toward open-plan offices reflects this fundamental real estate concern, masked by depressingly ideological nonsense about "collaboration." The rise of metrics to record actual uses of space will likely put pressure on space to justify itself; it will undoubtedly mean that companies will use less of it.

The smart, or speculative, money has turned to condo development. Overall, though the United States has recovered the office worker jobs lost in the recession, the vacancy rate has increased. In cities like New York, the office-to-condo conversion rate increased dramatically in the 1990s and the first decade of the twenty-first century, thanks in part to incentives offered by the city to developers to convert commercial space. For the moment, the incentives are expiring, and the improbable growth of the tech industry in New York and elsewhere has increased the demand for space. But the bubble will burst, and the conversions will continue. In the cities of the West, the skylines are threatening to darken, and where people once worked, amid copy machines and phones, light gray partitions and withering plants, the rich will come to live.

7

THE MAKING OF LOCAL BOISE

RYANN LIEBENTHAL

The first thing I noticed was that somebody had finally managed to fill the hole. For more than ten years, an empty square pit split open the center of downtown Boise, Idaho, at Eighth and Main, just across from the indoor parking garage and the good sushi restaurant. One hundred forty-nine years earlier, the hole had been the Overland Hotel, a popular stop on the Oregon Trail, built the year after Fort Boise became a city. By 2001, when I graduated from Boise High School, the booms and busts of the 1990s had left us with just a mess of concrete and rebar and no structure to hold up. But now there was something going in. A bank or condominium or some other horrible thing, but at least it was something.

It was late March 2013, and I'd arrived from New York to spend four days at a new Boise music festival. I gazed out the plane window feeling, as I always do when returning to my hometown, as though I were preparing to watch a movie I've seen many times before. Getting closer, I could make out the LED glow of the suburbs, little thread-loop culs-de-sac, pools, tract houses. Out at the edges of sight are the foothills that bound the lights of the city, and beyond that is nothing. It always looks the same to me from up here, but I know there are these little changes, like 150,000 or so people who have moved into the area since I left for college twelve years ago.

•

Boise is in a valley north of the Snake River, stretching west from the foothills of the Rocky Mountains, which lumber up on the edges of the city, to the eastern border of Oregon. The basin in which the city sits is flat and low with long sight lines. In the early nineteenth century, French fur trappers are said to have descended from the surrounding desert and, spotting the verdant banks of a river, shouted with glee, "Les bois! Les bois!" (The woods! The woods!). A Fort Boise was erected, but it soon ran into what its drab historical placard calls "Indian trouble" and was closed in 1854. Eight years later, cast-iron pans plunged into the river's silty basin turned up little flecks of gold. To secure the ensuing flock of prospectors, the military revived the fort, placing it fifty miles downriver from its predecessor. By 1864, Boise was the capital of Abe Lincoln's new Idaho Territory. Any remaining natives were eventually removed to Fort Hall Indian Reservation, across the state, where their reservation now sits under skies thick with alfalfa and potato pollen, the horizon dotted with farmhouses of a single-level white-brick design I was taught as a girl to associate with Mormons.

As in many western towns, Boise's gold rush led to more traditional means of civilization, the Boise River remade into an irrigating and waste-management canal that foamed with the mingled effluvia of potato shavings, beet waste, grease, the rumina of slaughtered cows, and human excrement. In 1890, the year Idaho became a state, the population was four thousand; in 1891, a streetcar traveled from downtown to outlying neighborhoods; the railway came in 1925. Then sprouted industry: Boise Cascade lumber; Albertson's chain grocery stores; Ore-Ida frozen foods; and the potato-processing plant that paid for J. R. "Jack" Simplot's flag-marked mansion on the hill, the house the frozen French fry built. Boise was always clean-cut, conservative, conventional. "The 'beat generation,'" noted the local historian Carol Lynn MacGregor in 2003, "did not happen in Boise." The city is the only metropolis in Idaho, a state conceived of primarily as a growth medium for racist extremists; libertarian nutjobs; the nonironic-hat-wearing degenerates who drive pickups and semis across the flyover-imagined cartography of blue-state secessionists; and potatoes.

Henry Spalding, a Presbyterian missionary, introduced potatoes to Idaho in the 1830s via a Nez Perce tribe in the northern part of the state whom he was trying to civilize with agriculture, and in spite of the high cost of distribution across the undeveloped West, farming cooperatives run by Mormon colonists soon made the tubers a cash crop. A combination of high-desert climate, volcanic soil, and mountain snowpack—which can be harnessed in reservoirs for irrigating—makes Idaho an ideal potato clime, and revenue from potato farming in Idaho eventually grew to nearly $1 billion. In the early 1940s, the aforementioned J. R. Simplot, a prominent Idaho distributor who began his career as a farmer after dropping out of the eighth grade, patented the potato-freezing process that makes McDonald's French fries, which his company supplies, possible. Today Idaho is still the United States' largest producer of potatoes, at an annual output of about twelve billion pounds, which provides about one-third of the national supply.

But since the 1970s, Boise has quietly become a Silicon-offshoot tech hub. In 1973, Hewlett-Packard opened a plant in the city, then assigned to that site—which now employs nearly four thousand people—the development of its LaserJet printer, the company's most successful product. After that came Micron Technology, the country's largest manufacturer of computer memory chips, which was incorporated in 1978 in the basement of a Boise dentist's office. J. R. Simplot fronted the company $1 million and insisted that the board hold its weekly meetings over breakfast at Elmer's, a local diner. At the height of the memory-chip boom, in the early twenty-first century, Micron employed ten thousand people in Idaho, a state with a population of just over 1.5 million.

Meanwhile, by the late 1970s, Boise had grown from a hamlet

of thirty-five thousand (in 1960) to an almost city of seventy-five thousand existing increasingly in annexed suburbs. By then, developers, under the guise of the Boise Redevelopment Agency (BRA), had begun eagerly tearing down crumbly old downtown buildings, aiming for the kind of "revitalization" only sophisticated new commercial structures can provide. "If things go on as they are," wrote the Brooklyn-exiled Boisean L. J. Davis in *Harper's Magazine* in 1974, "Boise stands an excellent chance of becoming the first American city to have deliberately eradicated itself." That year the BRA, having already rid Boise of its Chinatown, was considering replacing the rest of downtown's charming historic core with eight blocks of an 800,000-square-foot self-contained "megastructure" at which 2,444 future Boise families could park their station wagons and shop until the end of time. For reasons that included the fierce resistance of preservationists, the megastructure project was never realized, and in the late 1980s residents instead got the million-square-foot Boise Towne Square mall nine miles away, to which was attached a six-lane freeway. The remnants of its downtown survived, but Boise, like many of its American counterparts, became a sprawl city.

When I was in high school, Boise had only one cool bar, the Neurolux. Built to Spill, Boise's only cool band, would sometimes play next door at the Record Exchange—Boise's only cool record store—for underage kids who couldn't get into the Neurolux. Down the street were the old headquarters of the only cool radio station, which called itself Pirate Radio and aired a lot of grungy alternative music from towns farther north and west. In 1998, the station, renamed the X, was sold to a national media conglomerate, and the original Pirate studio was taken over by a "gentlemen's club." This had happened before. In 1986, the president of Boise State University effectively sold the school's student-run radio station to the Corporation for Public Broadcasting, and by the early twenty-first century Boise's greater metro population, at about 450,000 and almost doubling every twenty years, had become the biggest in the country without a community radio station. To a certain set of young people, this absence communicated a larger message about culture and belonging: if we wanted anyone to hear what we were thinking, we'd have to go somewhere else.

In 2001, I left Boise to attend college at a liberal arts school four hundred miles west in much-cooler Portland, Oregon. After graduation, I moved briefly to France, then returned to Oregon to start my professional life in the low-wage retail industry that butters Portland's postcollegiate bread. Dismal job prospects aside, to be twenty-three in Portland, with its bookstores and coffee shops and thrift stores and beer theaters and naked bicycling and people-friendly city planning and cheap everything, meant believing the world was constructed just for you. There had been no making this mistake in Boise, where the hills are speckled with dot-com mansions and suburbs engulf each other in ever-widening circles. And yet, after a while in Portland, something about everything there had started to feel very predictable. So in the summer of 2008, I moved to New York, a city more or less indifferent to its residents, which I kind of liked.

There I spent three years acquiring a master's degree and touring the city's internship circuit. Meanwhile, I'd been hearing rumors about a Boise renaissance—new shops, clubs, arts projects. By July 2011, I hadn't yet found a paying gig, so I flew back to Boise on a lark for my ten-year high school reunion, expecting my geographic and academic superiority to buoy a sense of self-worth undone by student loan debt and self-inflicted unemployment. But many of the classmates I'd wanted to despise were, I found myself noting, "doing legitimately cool stuff now." They weren't earning a whole lot of money, but they had time and space to make music and art and hang out. An all-ages coffee-house venue had opened downtown, along with a nearby dive bar and several other new options beyond the few old standbys. And there was a real community radio station again, called Radio Boise, that played an exhilarating mix of music I'd never heard before. Blogs and online music magazines had started earnestly referring to Boise as "the next Portland."

The weather was beautiful—desert heat like an open-air oven. At night, talking to old friends against the burble of backyard irrigation canals, I heard myself utter the phrase "when I move back." I fell in love. I swam in the river. Two weeks later I was hired to work as a fact-checker at a women's fitness magazine in New York. I said yes immediately, but my first feeling was grief.

Back in New York, I listened nostalgically to Radio Boise through headphones from my office. The station's playlist has the feel of an astoundingly good public-access TV channel—indie rock shows followed by programs dedicated to Idaho real estate and interspersed with promos featuring Wayne Coyne (of the Flaming Lips) alliterating "Boise" with "Beyoncé." A Monday morning radio show, *Antler Crafts*, was hosted by Eric Gilbert, a charming young Boise guy who was the front man for Finn Riggins, a popular Boise band, and had begun devoting his life to the revitalization of Boise's music scene. Gilbert broadcast mostly indie rock and focused on bands that had been or were coming through town. That fall he also started talking about the Treefort Music Fest, which he was organizing. Gilbert was a good evangelist, and I was in a Boise reverie. One morning in early March, he hosted Josh Gross, a *Boise Weekly* writer, in the studio. "People talk about Treefort as this barometer of how the scene is growing," said Josh, who moved to Boise from Portland several years ago. "It's like getting called up to the majors." I decided to go.

How does a town, a fairly square town, producer of printers and potatoes, come to develop a "scene"? In Boise's case, there has been an interplay of a few factors. In 1998, the city hired a public arts manager and in 2001 passed an ordinance requiring new municipal developments to set aside up to 1.4 percent of their investments for public arts projects. Until then, downtown Boise had precisely five public works of art—one of which was a statue of an assassinated Idaho governor. Now there are nearly two hundred more, starting with the Basque Block, which turned a dilapidated historic cultural site into a pedestrian restaurant hub dotted with artistic representations of the Old Country (Boise is home to the largest concentration of Basques in America, descendants of a diaspora of sheepherders who settled here at the turn of the twentieth century). There are now also Idaho-historical works, abstract pieces, sound installations, a graffiti wall, and a whole proliferation of painted utility boxes.

Starting in 2005, Boise also saw the creation of the Linen District, a six-square-block downtown area that remade an old laundry into an arts gallery and events center and included a "trailer-park-cuisine" restaurant housed in an old tire shop (since shuttered), a visual arts collective (called the Visual Arts Collective—since relocated), and a retro-chic renovated Travelodge hotel called the Modern, which was reminiscent of Portland's Jupiter Hotel. In addition to successfully reviving an area of Boise I remember primarily for its parking lots, the Linen District provided a welcome counterweight to a burgeoning development down the street called BoDo (Boise Downtown) that evidently aimed to cash in on the city's momentum via a transparently cynical mix of hideous national retail chains and a multiplex cinema.

Finally, though I am somewhat loath to admit it, the Boise renaissance owes at least part of its instantiation to Richard Florida, theorist of the "creative class." In 2002, Jeff Abrams, a wildlife biologist for Idaho Fish and Game, listened to a radio interview with Florida while driving out on a fly-fishing trip to the Owyhee River. Before moving to Boise, Abrams had lived in Salt Lake City, where the local radio station KRCL was the only thing binding him and people like him to an alternative community. Hearing Florida encourage the local manufacture of a vibrant, creative environment and wondering what he should do with the rest of his life, Abrams had a thought: radio. Six years later, KRBX got its license, and in April 2011 Radio Boise went on the air. As his programming director, Abrams hired Wayne Birt, a former producer at KBSU who had quit on air when the administration co-opted the station and fired most of its student programmers in the 1980s.

In the fall of 2011, Lori Shandro, a local health-insurance agent, approached Eric Gilbert with an idea. For years Shandro and her husband had flown their private airplane to indie rock shows across the Northwest. He'd died in 2009 when his single-engine Cessna crashed into the Sawtooth Mountains. Shandro wanted to find a way to bring the music they'd enjoyed to Boise and suggested building a new local venue; Gilbert countered by proposing a whole festival.

And so it was that in March 2012, 140 bands from across the country filled out seven downtown venues and an outdoor main stage erected in a hotel overfill parking lot. Expectations were low. Others had tried similar things and nothing had caught, but Gilbert had been strategic. He'd chosen the week after SXSW to lure bands through Boise on their way from Austin to Portland or Seattle. The weather was unseasonably warm. I invited a friend over from Seattle and showed her around town on borrowed bicycles. It was absolutely delightful. Though the festival lost money, it drew about three thousand people a day, and Shandro wanted to try again. In 2013, Eric and company recruited 270 bands, filled eleven venues, and doubled sales; one thousand early-bird passes, released before the lineup was announced, sold out in seventeen minutes. At the last minute, after an upbeat invitation from the festival's press coordinator, I decided to go again.

This year I'm alone, and it's incredibly cold. On my first day, I'm shepherded about town by my mother; I sit in the sun-warm car watching people scurry about their business, and I drift into a sullen adolescent languor. "There's a feeling, from Ada to Irene," sings Doug Martsch (of Built to Spill) about the streets of Boise's North

End, a quiet downtown-adjacent neighborhood filled with old Victorian houses and European cars and giant trees lining wide empty boulevards. "There's something, there's nothing / You haven't seen." When I was in elementary school, my mother and I lived at the center of this stretch, in a low-income duplex on Fourteenth Street. The year I was born, my dad killed gophers and ran a postal route and made something like $5,000. My mom had grown up in L.A.; they'd met in Yellowstone, where he was working for the park, a couple summers before I was born, then divorced a few winters later. My mom worked full-time as a housekeeper until I was fifteen. Now my dad's a copywriter, and my mom, a social worker, finally has health insurance and a retirement account. But neither of them could likely afford to purchase a house in the neighborhood where I spent the first seventeen years of my life. Recently, my mom moved to the Bench, an up-and-coming neighborhood a couple miles west of downtown, and my dad resettled in Seattle. But I can still recall the name of every street between Ada and Irene, can see every picket fence and wraparound porch and gravelly alleyway, even feel the shade of the giant old hardwoods— except that actually it's been too long and now I can't.

I do a lot of aimless wandering. On the second morning, I duck into Big City Coffee, a café in the Linen District, to warm up. A guy slides in to the table next to mine and knocks off my shoe. His name is Steve. He heard about the festival on KEXP, the Seattle community radio station, and immediately decided to come. He's staying in the North End with this guy Matt he met via Couchsurfing.org. Originally from Alabama, Matt wound up in Boise at the end of a two-and-a-half-year journey the motivations for which I don't entirely understand but definitely involve use of the word "fate." Steve really likes Boise, too. Reminds him of Missoula. Or maybe Austin. Steve's tall, attractive, with short blond hair and a kind of amphetaminized energy. As he gets up, he grabs my foot again, letting his hand trail the length of my calf. I get hit on here. I'd forgotten that.

The next day my mom drives past the new downtown Whole Foods, which looks like every Whole Foods everywhere, and the site of the Trader Joe's that's going in next year. I'm reminded how dull this place can feel: pop-up low buildings all the same color, interiors lit by harsh fluorescents, the hills dead and brown, the people beautiful only by accident—ruddy, charming, the kind of beauty you make excuses for. I am entitled to this cruelty, I think, because I am one of them, no matter where I decide to live or for how long. In truth, I'm sad. The river romance I'd cultivated the summer before last year's festival had within months, via GChat, predictably faded. He has a girlfriend now, and because this town is so small, with that goes the majority of my Boise social circle. The moment I'd failed to seize in 2011, the one in which I got to escape New York and cheaply idle in a new young person's paradise where I fit in by default, has gone. And without friends, Boise is still—in spite of its supposed coolness—a relatively dreary place to be.

On the third night, I run into a high school friend playing pool by himself. I complain to him about New York, how I need to make more money, get out more, date. Three years ago, he moved back from Brooklyn—not just to save money and be closer to his family, but also to realize his dream of starting a hard-cider distillery. "Did I tell you I bought a house?" he asks. He just moved in with his girlfriend, who came here from Austin not long ago. "We should have you over for dinner."

In high school, I used to bike home past the hissing, clanking old Meadow Gold dairy plant at the edge of downtown, maneuvering around a collection of semis clumsily T-boning into the street. It's baffling to me that this thing is still in business. On Sunday morning, I pass the plant three or four times on breaks between back-to-back music panels across the street. Attendance is low, no more than a dozen or so at any time. During the first panel, "The Politics of Music," a gleamingly handsome local councilman named Ben

Quintana politely emits occasional platitudes about the city's investment in culture, by which he seems to mean business, which doesn't stop Brett Netson (frequent guitarist for Built to Spill and one-man Boise musical institution) from railing on corporations. "They should pay us just to exist. And in exchange, we display your logo one time and that's it."

The first Treefort festival had all local sponsors, but that year's festival didn't come close to breaking even, and this year it has taken a few thousand dollars from Whole Foods, a decision Eric Gilbert defends on the merits of the graciousness of the store's implantation in town. "I talked to a good friend who's a farmer in Boulder and has been very thankful for how Whole Foods works with her, in terms of buying local foods, and I know they've been reaching out to a lot of local folks in buying local produce," he says. "So it was like, okay, cool, we don't want it to be the Whole Foods–Treefort Music Fest, but if they want to partner with us in a smallish way, you know, I'm open to it."

That afternoon, I stop at the festival's main-stage-adjacent dining area, which is filled with carts offering local foods and craft beers—"the truck scene's really peaked," says a guy working an artisanal French-fry cart—and a clothing- and crafts-filled "Bricofort" run by a friend's sister, who moved back from Williamsburg several years ago and recently opened a modish downtown shop called Bricolage. As I continue to amble into the evening, I can hear the echoes of Youth Lagoon, the new up-and-coming Boise band, issuing from the main stage. Trevor Powers, a kid of twenty-three or twenty-four, is wearing a psychedelic muumuu-like caftan, his vocals so reverbed and woozy that I can't make out a single word. He became famous in 2011 after *Pitchfork* "discovered" a few songs he'd uploaded to Bandcamp. I run into my tenth-grade English teacher for the fourth time in four days. "My friend said this was like Beach House," she says. "And I love Beach House. But that builds to something. This just doesn't go anywhere." I shrug my shoulders. I've never really listened to this band, not even after I saw a giant promotional banner go up outside the record store near my office in New York. A few of my teacher's students are crowded around a fake, turret-like tree fort at the side of the stage. Styles have changed: a boy wearing a dangly feather earring stands next to his girlfriend, her face covered in a multicolored pattern of face-paint stripes. It vaguely hurts my feelings that all this exists and I didn't know about it.

Perhaps Boise is catching the tailwind of whatever pushed people into Portland a decade ago. Or Austin. Or Asheville. Or Seattle in the 1990s. Or some other town celebrated in a lifestyle magazine's top-ten list for its authentic "local culture." To counter the leveling influence of the Internet and the anonymizing vastness of the foretold megacity, maybe it just makes sense to stake out physical ground and build manageable little anthills of aesthetic and cultural kinship. In Boise, where the process has been especially painstaking, this still feels pure and exciting and enlivening—like watching your favorite band start to become famous—but I'm afraid of the gold rush, which might as well go by the name Whole Foods, or *Pitchfork*, or BoDo. And while I had no qualms about participating in Portland's metamorphosis ten years ago, here the prospect feels like a remapping of self. In New York, I hold a tiny claim to a seven-by-thirteen-foot bedroom and the view of the skyline I can access from my roof. But I still want to believe that in Boise everything belongs to me.

At midnight, I head to the Red Room, for TEENS, another band from Boise—by way of Philadelphia, Calgary, and Athens, Georgia. There are two lines out the door. A pudgy blond kid tells a stringy-haired guy to my left about his plans to move to either New York, Philadelphia, or Portland, Maine—"but I'm sure I'll have fun wherever I go." We wait for half an hour. I glance down the street, toward a defunct old punk house called the Sotano, which looks perfectly respectable now. My adolescent home, another block up, has new owners too; they've sodded over my mom's garden and staked decorative flags in the doorway. "You know, this place used to be called the Crazy Horse," says a middle-aged man to a tall, husky boy who looks too young to drink. "Oh. Cool," says the tall boy. "And in the '80s," the man continues, describing a place I'd been dragged to many times as a child but since forgotten, "this was Boise's only punk-band venue." "Yeah," the kid says, nodding vacantly. "I'm just here for the weekend."

8

MY LAS VEGAS

KATY LEDERER

Las Vegas has a story. Just like any other city. Most people know some part of it from watching documentaries or dark alluring dramas: Bugsy Siegel, played by Warren Beatty, bending down to grab a pile of sand; Nicolas Cage, drinking himself to death in the arms of his neurotic stripper paramour, Elisabeth Shue. In between the geologic shift from ocean bed to desert and the current economic slump, there was industriousness—the indigenous Indians charging traveling settlers exorbitantly for access to the local water supply—and glamour—crooning Blue Eyes and Dean Martin and the Marilyn Monroe of billowing white skirts and a seductively innocent innuendo. All the while, the city built and built, growing at a rate—more than 80 percent in the 1990s—that eventually made it the fastest-growing city in the country. An industry town based almost exclusively on gambling; who would think that such a city could exist? But then of course it could in the superficially Puritan, spiritually libertarian, and materially deeply frivolous United States. How we all love Las Vegas's story. It is our fulcrum. Rags to riches, sand to beaming lights so strong they can be seen from outer space. Please look at all these hurting hearts ablaze with the expensive immolation of their sadness and their need.

My family's humble story was far removed from Las Vegas's story until it wasn't back in 1987, when my brother came in fifth in the World Series of Poker, and we went. We had come from the cold—both literal and figurative—of New Hampshire, the small and frigid opposite of Vegas, where we lived on the large campus of a storied WASPy boarding school. Many years later I would write a full-length memoir about it, trying to make money so that I could be a writer, a poet (in the game of writing, poetry is always the short stack). But until then, it was neither here nor there, this story of a family living socially uncomfortably at a boarding school in the East. Some moderately interesting specifics: mother unusually intelligent and excellent at crosswords, artistically stifled, drawn to drink; father Jewish, teaching English to the WASPs, warm and garrulous, but emotionally out of touch; older siblings, good at games—sister jealously sadistic with the youngest, brother out of it on pot and so obsessed with the game of chess that he would, before graduating high school, reach the level of master. And of course there came with all of this the Brontëan frisson—upstairs, downstairs—of the story of the English teacher's family and the venerable, intimidating school, the chapel there a symbol of a civilized dominion, an imperialism of niceties and manners that we couldn't seem to live with.

I think we knew we'd have to leave. And in the end it was this leaving (to arrive in Las Vegas almost always means to have left some other place) that would make our story interesting to others. First my brother to New York, where he went to study chess, but, with a detour through homelessness and drugs, got deep into poker and sports betting; then my sister for college, but while there she would learn poker from my brother; and then, finally, my mother, who, with her new actor boyfriend, would work for my brother in his sports-betting operation. A story has a beginning, middle, and end. There was pain in the beginning. There was pain, too, at the end. The intersection of my family's boring story and Las Vegas's exciting and glamorous story was the middle. That was painful, too. The pain will make life interesting, dramatic, dark, and volatile, like gambling.

Life is what happens while you're making other plans. Life is what happens when the Department of Justice decides to bust your brother's sports-betting operation in New York, and he relocates to Las Vegas with your mother. Life is what happens when your sister decides to drop out of graduate school and move with her new husband and small children to Las Vegas to play poker. Life is what happens when your father—who, like you, is left, remaindered—remarries and moves with his new wife to San Diego. Now you have no home. You become truly an American—a settler, rootless, wandering, alone. The indigenous people will charge you an arm and a leg for a small sip of water. Life is that decadent part of the story, the part that is material and terribly expensive. I try to leave Las Vegas—I have tried to for most of my adult life—but I cannot seem to leave.

I went there after college, $1,000 in my pocket, and a vacant house to stay in that my brother's friend had lent me for the year. That Las Vegas was the first place that I moved to was unusual. Las Vegas is more usually the last place people live, the last resort. I told myself I was running toward my poetry—toward space and time to write—but really I was running toward my family, toward my mother. I was running fast, already lit. Nothing bad ever happens to a writer, as the cliché would have it. A kind of alchemy, the bad can be transformed into the good—into writing. The first night that I spent there, reading *The Theory of Poker* by David Sklansky, marking the book up like a student in a study hall, gazing out the window, thinking: now I am a writer and this story is material. I was playing against type: young, college-educated female *playing poker in Las Vegas*, melancholic poet *playing poker in Las Vegas*, in-pain and burning daughter *playing poker in Las Vegas*. Who was my audience? My mother?

My days then were luxurious. I would wake up in the morning, sip a coffee, and drive around in my brother's tricked-out Beemer, listening to the radio. I would drive the winding loop from his new house through Red Rock Canyon, past the gypsum plant and cactus store, and finally through the dully lit, exhausted, and hungover

Strip. I was waiting to clock in and play—I had decided to treat my voluntary apprenticeship as if I would be graded—usually at exactly 4:00 p.m. I would shower, dry my hair; I would prepare just like a schoolgirl who is packing a bagged lunch and sharpened pencil for the day. Sometimes, I would visit her—my mother—grab some lunch and chat. Or sit out on the shady porch behind her Tudor house and listen to the whirring of cicadas in the brutal heat.

And here, a run of stories, some are banal, some more interesting: me sitting at the $2–$4 table at the Mirage, playing "like a rock," as the expression goes, which means that I was playing "tight," playing conservatively. I was trying to learn poker in a systematic way—not in the typical way, in fits and starts, fueled by a burgeoning addiction or boredom or a childlike fascination with the mixture that is skill and luck and lying in the game. Or: me at the volcano at the front of the Mirage—the first time, the volcano spewing beautifully the fakest most natural fire in the world. "It costs them $40,000 a pop," my brother remarked. "Every couple of hours." The sums were disorienting, the scale of the place monumental, like Olympus or like hell. Delectable steak dinners, sometimes noodles, crab legs, fries galore; we would get a free voucher to eat at the buffet if we had been playing at our tables long enough, which is something I made sure to do. I would buttonhole my brother, make him sit with me and teach me what he could about the game. To him, I was beneath the level of a neophyte. I was a prudish little sister, there, in unrelenting pain, asking him to show me what amounted to some card tricks that made money.

At one of those dinners: the memory of my brother, sitting across a small table for two with a deck in his hands. "How many cards are in a deck?" he asked me. I didn't even know. "How many?" Pause. "There are fifty-two cards in a deck. Now, how many in each suit?" He was trying to get me to think quantitatively. This single interaction would change the way I thought about pretty much everything in my life and the world after that. "Thirteen," he said. He laid the cards out. Fifty-two cards in a deck, thirteen of each suit, each number and face card progressively trumping the lesser one that came before. It is a mathematical problem, but limited. Unlike the most high-profile mathematical problems of the day—statistical arbitrage, the national debt, or the chemical mechanics of global warming—this one had what you would call a limited downside. Poker, I saw then—intuitively, I did not yet have the vocabulary to describe it in this way—was a zero-sum game. You either have something—cards, a stack, a chance—or you don't.

And of course it was a metaphor for everything unfolding in my life. My family: five members, three of them had left, and two were shuffled back into the deck. Hand over. The old men trying to augment their retirement accounts who would sit at my table and play their stacks down; only a few winners, maybe 5 or 10 percent of those who played, and the house always taking it all in the end—incrementally, surreptitiously. *Don't mind me*, the dealer's hands would signal, raking $1 or $2 toward a slot in the felt, which is a metaphor for death. People both love and hate Las Vegas. While they love the spectacular immolations, the way they like fireworks on the Fourth of July, they despise the economics. At base, Las Vegas is an importer: food, love, money, dreams—all imported. And what it produces: stories, ashes. I had had enough of stories, so I left—at least I tried to leave—first for a master's in the writing of poetry and then for New York, where I would live among my type and barely make it.

In October 2001, after five years away, I would find myself vertiginously back where I started: in Las Vegas at the New York–New York Hotel and Casino. My sister-in-law had suggested we go. We were standing and watching "dueling pianos" from the back of a very large, very drunk crowd. That autumn: still warm, but I wore a thick sweater, and I pounded one screwdriver after another. My sister-in-law liked to drink. My sister-in-law liked to throw up her arms, close her eyes, and yell out to the dueling pianos. The Twin Towers had fallen. I had lost my apartment. I was broke, and my brother was taking me in. I remember looking up at the facade of the New York–New York. The skyline was cast in a series of colorful blocks—blue and green and salmon pink—but the towers were missing; they had always been missing. I would later find out that the designers of the building had decided the towers would throw off the proportions of the skyline if included. The designers had been prescient in that way; they had been practical. The frightened people of Las Vegas had laid flowers—heaps and heaps of them—and teddy bears and photographs of the missing and the dead, a kind of penance, at the gates of the New York–New York Hotel and Casino.

And so this is a penance, laid at the proverbial grave of my mother, who is literally ashes. A miniature urn of her sits on the mantel in my bedroom in Park Slope, New York, and I think of the times that I spent in Las Vegas, haunting her. And now she is haunting me. My mother in the yard, sitting—face wide open, like an owl's; we were discussing the poetry of Wallace Stevens. Whir and hum of AC, house lights shining on our faces as if the two of us were acting on a stage and nothing happening but talking. It is one of my favorite memories. Another: in the kitchen. She is sitting in her nightgown, running numbers for my brother. The savory smell of cooking food: lasagna, probably Lean Cuisine. My mother.

But I hardly saw her that long year I spent there after 9/11. Was I avoiding her? Or was it she who was avoiding me? I was working on the memoir that I hoped would get me out of debt—working, working every day, or at least very strenuously fretting. I try to craft a story, but in fact the recollections from that year bunch up into a ball I want to light on fire. I am always stuck in traffic, always going to the gym, where I would exercise until I couldn't think straight anymore. I am always on my way to the Bellagio casino, where the big games had been moved three years before, and very anxious. I didn't have money to play with anymore, but I was hungry, so I went there to beg for food and red wine from my brother. He would wave the waiter over as if swatting at a fly. Later, I would end up at my brother's house, passed out on the long couch, a kind of loneliness that maybe someone's mother could have cured, but not my mother, at least not that year.

She was mad at me. I had shown everyone my memoir: my brother, so he could verify the details of his New York years; my sister, who insisted that she hadn't in fact stolen from my mother's purse when we were small; and my father, who complained that I portrayed him as "a giant dork." Gripes, sure, but nothing particularly exposing or embarrassing. My mother, on the other hand, I did not show the memoir to. I was not ashamed of what I said and I had tried to be fair, but I had wanted her to read the final draft, the *perfect* draft, a kind of present. I guess she *was* my audience. I FedExed the clean manuscript to her the day before I finally took a plane back to New York—made my escape—and she had been sort of okay with it but not thrilled. "You made up a beautiful childhood for yourself," she said. "What happens in Vegas stays in Vegas," as the advertising slogan goes. The same is tacitly expected of a family or a childhood: what happens in a family should by all rights stay there—unarticulated, private.

I try to find the moment when my mother started dying. I see myself, a little girl, still sitting in the yard back east: toys, the square, dark, mossy bricks. I stared in through the sliding door. I stared in at my mother. The way the screen was black and light, its wires so tightly interlaced. Could I see her? She was crying on the green-and-blue-plaid couch. It was hard at that age to climb up without help, but I went to her. "What is wrong with you, Mommy?" I was up on her lap. I was stroking her hair and her face with my hands. "I'm so lonely," she'd said. She'd been drinking for years. She'd been smoking for years (for "pack-years," as the doctors would call them).

Or maybe it was later: she had moved with her new boyfriend to the Village in New York. They had met at the regional summer stock theater while my mother was still married to my father. (She would tell me much later that one of those summers I had talked to the boyfriend. How I'd said that they were using an "inordinate amount of paint" on the sets; how the phrasing from a little girl had charmed him.) She would always maintain she'd run away from my father, when really it seemed that she'd run from herself. Sad and privileged, bright and furious, she had wanted all her life to be an actress, but her mother had insisted that she study something practical like macroeconomics. After grad school, she had married, birthed three children, and—with an intransigent patience I have seen only in the very best gamblers and writers I've known— attempted a slow suicide.

When had she started? The day before her rehab when she drank herself near death on the brown love seat in the den? The day my father yelled, my sister left, the day the cat got hit by a car. The time I had gone to her apartment for the holiday; I had asked her out to dinner—just the two of us, no boyfriend, please. She balked and then began to cry. When we finally sat down at the table alone, the way that she casually averted her eyes. All the money she spent, decorating and redecorating, buying sweaters and jackets and black slimming jeans. To follow a dream you won't live is one way to not live, but to also not—technically—die.

I can see her, still sitting, her legs hanging down like a kid's from a bench. The emphysema had worked on her face and her hands, but she had tried to look her best for me. Dark mascara, two brief strokes of blush. My boyfriend and I—we would later marry in Las Vegas, but by then my mother would be dead—had brought Thai from downtown. We had eaten it, with gusto, from old plates we had found in the kitchen. We had talked about the family, its diaspora, life, love, and death. It was the last time I would see her sitting upright, sitting in a house. Her breathing was labored, but the two of us were able to pretend there was no rift, that nothing happened. Love. I can't describe it, but I know that I once felt it for my mother.

In the hospital later—it was maybe one month—someone had propped a black-and-white photograph of her as a child up against the far wall. In the photograph, which had once been in the living room of our old house and would later be hung in the nursery of my new one in Park Slope, she wears schoolgirl clothes, long brown braids, and a distant but contented expression. As I heard her breathing on the vent, I would stare at the picture and then back at her face. What would she have thought as a child of this death? Was this death the one she would have chosen for herself? What did I think? How was it my mother—a blue-blooded New England girl—could be dying like this in Las Vegas? One version might say that she left us and moved west because of feminist trends that had peaked in the early 1970s; another would say that she was simply a free spirit—the life of the party—and that the party was in Vegas; and yet another that my mother was depressive and emotionally unstable. My version: She was beautiful, confusing—charismatic. She lined all her words with a rumble that signaled an irresistible excitement. Around her: an abiding thrall. Within her, all the energy of someone who was sure she had been duped in her one life and wanted another. My mother might not have succeeded as an actress, but she succeeded as a character.

I go now to these literary parties in New York, where we shuffle around the bad wine and warm cheese and gossip about how someone horrible has won an important prize. Sometimes, during a lull in things or when a person has just come into the circle, it will be mentioned that I once lived in Vegas. People consider it a fun topic, a reliable conversation starter. They will say with a mischievously raised eyebrow that I play poker. I will say that I'm not very good, and the interlocutor will laugh, observing that this is exactly the sort of thing a hustler would say, and isn't that funny? Lately, we might talk about Tony Hsieh and his plan to transform the downtown into a new cultural and technological mecca. Previously, we would speak about white tigers or Celine Dion. A few years ago there was an article in *The New Yorker* about the new City Center's architecture. People would ask me about that for a while. I might tell a story about winning at craps or getting really drunk. Or I might try to talk about something more serious, like the immigrants who risked their lives by building Hoover Dam. But Las Vegas is the place my mother died.

9

PHOENIX RISING

EMILY GOGOLAK

I grew up in Phoenix in what they call a ranch-style house. The low, flat, very slightly sloped roof, the big lawn dotted with lazy eucalyptus and palm trees. But the name was misleading, because it was never a ranch. It was built on an old grove. The whole neighborhood used to be citrus.

My parents bought it when they moved to Phoenix from New York City in 1986: they didn't want to raise my sister in the city, Arizona is cheaper and more temperate, my mother refused suburban Connecticut, my dad refused anywhere my mother had family. They bought a house and gutted it and stuccoed it and painted the stucco very pale pink and roofed it with white tiles that are the same white tiles used to roof houses in Bermuda. They kept the palm trees and a few eucalyptuses, put in some olive trees and several big ficus. They planted what would be a giant grapefruit tree at the back of the lot. Ruby red, it blossomed in the wintertime, when its trunk was painted paper white for protection from the sun. Sunscreen for citrus trees—they were all painted white. This is only necessary until the canopy is thick enough to shade the trunk, but people keep painting trees anyway because they like the way it looks.

Just visible from the corner of our lot, over the hedge of oleanders, was Camelback Mountain, in the middle of Phoenix. Everything spreads out from there, into the low downtown and then, in all directions, to the suburbs. We lived near the center of the city, but the streets and lawns and buildings were as lazy and low and open as any suburb. If you climb to the top of Camelback, which is very steep, you see a lot of green from golf courses and lawns and some taller buildings to the west, but not a lot. On the other side of the mountain, the city stays small and stops when cotton and melon fields begin in chunks to the east. Then to the south the city starts up again, close to the ground. The sound of helicopters in my back-yard meant someone had climbed the mountain and gotten stuck.

One afternoon a few days before Halloween, I climbed into my tree house to practice batting my eyelashes. The air smelled as fall does in Phoenix, like grass wet from the sprinklers after a searing summer. When my eyes stopped fluttering, I saw two men and a woman talking in the empty lot behind us, too far to overhear. When the woman walked away, I noticed she had long red hair. Then one of the men started pacing, and the other hit him in the face, then the stomach, then the face again. The pacing man now lay motionless in dusty dirt, while the other walked across the lot to where the woman waited in a gray sedan. He got in and drove off. The fallen man started moving, slowly. I did nothing, then ran in-side, where I told no one and resumed batting my eyelashes.

Years later my parents said they wanted to "get out" before all of the other roofs grew higher and our house's value sank, before we were towered over. They sold for more than they'd hoped to people who seemed nice enough. They were extremely short.

Several years passed, and I went for a jog by the house. Its top and front were stripped. When I got home, I asked my dad what was going on. "They're making a fake second story," he said, but I didn't understand. He explained that the house was not constructed in a manner that could support a second story, structurally, so the new owners were adding a second story that made the house look taller. But it was just for the facade. It was a nonfunctional second story. You'd walk inside the front door and look up and see the same ceiling you saw before, but now it had the appearance of a place with two stories.

Our new house was two miles away, on a street called Casa Blanca. It didn't have palm trees or citrus groves, although we planted a hedge of ornamental oranges on the perimeter. They'd grow tall, but their fruit was bitter and inedible. We didn't know the neighbors really.

Then one night, three doors down, some construction caught fire, and there they were, the neighbors, out on the street. My dad and I speculated that it was one of the arsonists who did it, high on torching properties believed to be encroaching on precious desert land: one of our preservationist arsonists. But this made no sense because we were in the middle of the city, on land that hadn't been desert in decades.

In 2011 armed men broke into a house five minutes away and tied up the couple living there after making them empty their safe at gunpoint. Apparently, they were major art and jewelry collectors with a not insignificant security operation, and it was an inside job. Nobody got hurt.

A few months after that, an elderly couple came home from the opera and found an intruder in their home. They were tied up and shot in the head and were beyond recognition by the time the flames went out. The police believe one man acted alone and gave away stolen prescription drugs and jewelry to his friends. This second fire was too far for us to witness, but the first one was close; I remember the neighbors talking while the vacant house burned.

After that I drove to see our old house with its fake second floor. I wore sunglasses and tucked my hair under a sweat-stained baseball cap in order to look unrecognizable. My dog slobbered on the window. It felt like trespassing. I saw a very short woman walk out and go for the mail. Her hair was short and straight and tidy and blond. She looked at my car, and I drove until nothing was familiar, until I wasn't where I was from anymore. It felt good.

10

CROSSING EL PASO

DEBBIE NATHAN

The big desert city of El Paso, on the U.S. border with Mexico, for years felt like a lesson from the work of Giorgio Agamben. In his book *Homo Sacer: Sovereign Power and Bare Life*, Agamben analyzes a law from the Roman Empire specifying that if a man committed certain crimes, all of his citizenship rights would be revoked. This punishment, oddly enough, rendered the criminal a *homo sacer*, a sacred man, whom it was forbidden to ritually sacrifice to the gods. Yet in the everyday world the sacred man could be killed by anyone, with no penalty at all invoked on the killer. He inspired the highest veneration and the basest contempt. He constituted yet another category from Agamben's work: "bare life," or human existence stripped of its social nature and reduced to the purely biological. Bare life defines brutes. *Homo sacer*, brutes fetishized.

Fetish and brutish were everywhere when I lived in El Paso a generation ago. I'd moved there after wanting to for years, following a cross-country Greyhound bus trip my parents had let me take in the pre-civil-rights era, when I was a young teenager living in Houston. I'd seen a few Mexicans in my hometown, downcast speakers of broken English surrounded by a sea of whites who used casual epithets like "messkins" and "beaners." When the Greyhound stopped early in the morning in El Paso, not only did I see grand gray-silver mountains in the middle of town; I saw Mexicans, everywhere, and all I heard was Spanish, rolling, trilling, and glorious. After that I dreamed, literally, of El Paso.

When I moved there as a young adult, in the 1970s, I learned that the culture of my newly adopted city was defined by the fact that many of its people lacked immigration papers. "Wetbacks," the English-language morning newspaper called them. Articles about campaigns to apprehend them were headlined "Wetback Round-ups." At the U.S. Border Patrol Museum, a homemade place run by retired agents' wives, one exhibit featured a blown-up photograph of an officer yanking a frozen-faced, grade-school-age kid from under the hood of a car. "The Littlest Catch" was the smiling caption on the bottom of the photograph.

Meanwhile, local citizens—such as the author Raymond Carver, who wrote *What We Talk About When We Talk About Love* based on a year he spent living and teaching writing in El Paso— would gaily traverse the border to the sister Mexican city of Juárez, just across the Rio Grande. Carver enjoyed the dog races in Juárez, as well as the bullfights and bargain beefsteaks. Returning home on the high, arching international bridge, he could look down and see Mexican *homo sacers* crouched on the cement embankment of the river, nervously awaiting the Border Patrol's shift change so they could splash through the shallow water and disappear into the very first neighborhood in America, a hodgepodge of brick tenements laid out with tiny living rooms and bedrooms but not with bathrooms.

While the river crossers nursed their nerves, other *homo sacers* with little wagons and tinkling bells lurked beneath the bridge, hawking distractions to fellow wetbacks—peanuts, sodas, and Popsicles.

Most crossers made it over safely, but some didn't. Weekly, the El Paso papers ran boilerplate about nameless Mexicans who got caught in the river or its canals; their bodies sank in the current for days, then were spewed up as corpses ballooned with the animal gas of decomposition. Other *homo sacers* tried to hop Southern Pacific freights lumbering through downtown; they sprinted while the trains crawled, attempting to coordinate the two speeds and sometimes not succeeding. When the timing was wrong, the jumper was thrown under the train and had a foot crushed off, usually at the ankle. El Paso hospitals possessed medicine that could have saved the whole limb, but staff often juiced the patients on morphine and convinced them, while they were joyful and groggy, that they'd be happier back in Mexico with their families. After release papers were signed, the injured *homo sacers* were shipped to Juárez, where public hospitals were incapable of reattaching body parts and lacked antibiotics sufficient to stop infection below the knee. The south side of the border was populous with men amputated to the thigh. They leaned stolid on the international bridge on handmade crutches, shaking cups.

Back in El Paso, where thousands of legal people lived in comfort if not opulence, Mexicans who'd made it across knocked on doors. Residents answered and inspected little baskets. They contained one contraband cantaloupe sneaked in from Juárez, one lime, and one avocado—samples, and if the customer liked them, he or she placed an order. The Mexicans filled it by trotting back to their cars or trucks, stocking a bag, then returning to the door and politely waiting for a few nickels or dimes. In addition to its dazzling convenience, *homo sacer* produce was far cheaper than what was sold in El Paso's supermarkets.

The personalized home delivery of fruits was a border marvel, and so were other rituals, as when tired women knocked, not with fruit baskets, but begging for a little work—usually, cleaning windows by rubbing and rubbing and rubbing, not with pricey Windex, but with discarded newspaper pages, rendering the windows unbelievably sparkly, for a cost of fifty cents.

For the citizens, El Paso was clean and suburban and boring, while over in Juárez, things were grimy and noisy and wonderful. The streets teemed. There were Indians in rainbow skirts and Mennonite wives in bonnets speaking a curious German, selling homemade cheese produced on their nearby farms. Finches in wooden cages told your fortune for a peso. Native men beckoned in broken English to tourist men, something about women and shows and donkeys. Years before Starbucks was anywhere, you could get a cappuccino in downtown Juárez at a little café with a huge Italian machine, and you could sip it while reading the fat daily papers shipped up from Mexico City. The papers cost fifteen cents. The coffee, maybe a quarter.

These lovely rituals derived from two things. One: In Mexico, the economic gap between the poor and the rich was wider, deeper, and therefore uglier than in any other country in the world. Two: The political line separating America and Mexico, the border-patrolled border, with its armed agents and green vans and sensors, attracted an endless supply of people who crossed to America any-how, without anyone much caring, as long as they sold their fruits cheap and cleaned houses almost for free. Life under such circum-stances was fraught with risk, and when luck ran out, sometimes it was as though life had hardly transpired. A brief item in an El Paso newspaper from the period provided an example. It recalled a fourteen-year-old Mexican boy, presumably undocumented, who had hung around outside a barbecue stand on Doniphan Drive do-ing odd jobs for change until, one day, somebody noticed he was gone. Years later, a new owner demolished the barbecue stand to build another business. When the chimney came down, a dried and flattened thing dropped out. It was the boy. He'd been smoked, via recipes involving mesquite and spices and pecan wood, into jerky. No doubt this explained his disappearance, and upon publi-cation of the news article he was remembered for a day—as a prob-able illegal-alien delinquent who'd gotten stuck in the chimney while breaking in to rob the till.

And there was the poverty in Juárez. On the boulevards were ragamuffins and their scraggly parents, lunging to wipe your wind-shield. Or, more often, only to beg for your coins. Off the boule-vards, endless tar-paper shacks held endless, endless people. The Spanish-language papers covered the mayhem in these districts.

Toddlers fatally run over by cars and buses in areas unequipped with traffic lights or stop signs. Babies dead of dehydration in summer, caused by diarrhea caused by germs caused by no running water. Entire families suffocated on winter nights when their tinny heaters broke, releasing carbon monoxide.

Or maybe not whole families but only the little kids, and maybe not carbon monoxide but sudden flames, which took down everything and everyone before they burned themselves out. Fatal house fires in the slums could not be anything but common, when fathers and mothers left the tar-paper shacks with their children inside and locked the plank doors behind them by knotting a rope on a hook. They were employed during the day shift, the evening shift, the graveyard shift, and combinations thereof, in the maquiladoras—the hundreds of factories set up in Juárez to take this and that from the United States, assemble it into more complex thises-and-thats, then reimport them over the curving bridge, supplying necessary gizmos to the citizens of America, including but not limited to the wiring under your car dashboard, everything in your TV and your computer, certain tiny parts of your phone, your doctor's medical gloves. In Juárez, the parents who locked up their preschoolers earned about $10. Not per hour, but per day. It goes without saying they could not afford babysitters. This obvious fact inspired little practical concern among the citizens of El Paso.

They had their own problems, because El Paso itself was exceedingly indigent. In 1990, when the city was still considered a manufacturing hub for work clothes and refined metals, it was the third-poorest city in the United States, with over twice the percentage of people living in poverty as the national average. El Paso's poor were disproportionately Mexican-Americans. About a quarter of that group fell below the poverty line, whereas only a twelfth of whites did (the whites, as a matter of fact, were far better off in El Paso than whites in the state of Texas generally; they were also doing better than whites in the whole of America). Median family income in El Paso—again this applied disproportionately to

Mexican-Americans—was far less than the nationwide average. High school graduation rates were notoriously low.

These statistics were said to derive from a long-standing economic-development policy overseen by the local ruling elite. Its members were virtually all white men: bankers, lawyers, land developers, and manufacturers of commodities like sand, gravel, and work pants. Overseeing public education policy, these men ensured that Mexican-American and white children went to separate schools, schools in which the latter were tracked into academic courses while the former were taught car mechanics, air conditioner repair, and barbering. These men appointed others like them to the directorships of local law firms, banks, utility companies, and municipal boards, and they ran these institutions with the ease of powerful people who'd been on the border forever. Instead of dress shirts, many did business in the summer in guayaberas—traditional, short-sleeved Mexican garb for the well-attired man—and when one mayor saw neckties on men at city hall, he cut them off with scissors.

These men were barely interested in philanthropy, donating only piddling amounts during the Christmas season to safe, mainstream charities like Toys for Tots. I went to a benefit at one of these men's houses, in a beautiful neighborhood on a mountain in the middle of the city. This man's wife had hired a mariachi band for entertainment, and when she noticed one musician staring at the art on her walls and jotting in a notebook, she accused him of "casing" her collection in order to arrange a "heist." It turned out that when he wasn't playing mariachi violin and wearing silver-studded pants, the musician studied art at the local university. But he was a Mexican-American in El Paso, and the rich saw people like him as peons. The man who lived on the mountain had spent years trumpeting the city thusly during campaigns to lure out-of-town investment to the border.

In so many ways, El Paso did feel full of peons, both brown and white. Early in the afternoon, you could get The New York Times at a certain downtown newsstand, except for when you couldn't. The paper arrived via airplane, but occasionally it contained news—say, about *Roe v. Wade* surviving another legal onslaught—that offended the local distributor. When that happened, he refused to deliver the merchandise. Days would pass before you could get another *New York Times*.

Those *Times*-less days hardly bothered me. In a half hour, I could walk from my home to Juárez for the Mexican newspapers. I didn't go over the border directly. On the way, I always stopped at El Paso's *placita*, the town square and terminus for the city's bus system (SCAT, it was called: Sun City Area Transit. Derisively nick-named Shuttling Chicanos Around Town).

Because of its proximity to Juárez, thousands of Mexicans shopped near the *placita* every day, including Sunday. Little stores blanketed its periphery. They sold things moneyed people have no interest in: tube socks from China, bras from China, fake Nikes from who knows where, push-up-butt panties from China, and sec-ondhand clothing for fifty cents a pound (including, if you plowed deep through the piles, Diane von Furstenberg, Adrienne Vitta-dini, and other gently used designer items from the Goodwills of New York, making a final stop before continuing in bales to the Third World).

Sitting on a bench in the *placita*, I'd watch the housemaids and students greet one another and buy boiled, chili-sprinkled corn in Styrofoam cups as they waited for their buses. Hawk-eyed vendors with confidential voices hovered, offering untaxed cigarettes ($5 per carton for Marlboros, Salems, Kools), while clean-cut, well-fed guys wearing suspiciously crappy clothes, no doubt agents of the federal Bureau of Alcohol, Tobacco, Firearms, and Explosives, tried to purchase the product and bust the sellers. Hard-calved Border Patrol agents in spandex shorts parked their bicycles and wandered disconsolately on foot, attempting with spotty success to distinguish the legals from the illegals before stopping people and demanding their papers. The *placita* was home, too, to wizened guys in big Stetsons. To the homeless: schizophrenics, some of them handsome, gentle panhandlers; others handsome and overly aggressive; some ugly in all respects. To male-on-male hustlers, described so gorgeously in the opening pages of *City of Night*. (The author, John Rechy, grew up in El Paso and reportedly experienced his first gay trysts there.)

So many things seemed sacred. My daughter was entering adolescence. She was starting to cross the border with her friends, and not just to get drunk in the teen-friendly Jell-O-shot bars just over the bridge. On her own, she was visiting El Paso's *placita*, then continuing to Juárez's municipal market, speaking Spanish with the merchants, bargaining for clothes, exploring herbal folk medicine and folk-Catholic candles. I'd gone to the market, too, one time when I was pregnant. A fat old transvestite had wagged his tweezered brows and offered to read my palm—for free, he insisted, after I told him I didn't believe in that sort of thing and didn't want to pay. "It's a boy," he announced, peering at my hand. Then, "Tell me, why are you so cruel to your husband?" He smiled and walked away while I stood there, cut to the quick.

It *was* a boy.

When the boy got bigger, he played outside with the neighbor kids, with no adults in sight. In El Paso, children ganged up on their bikes and pedaled together for miles. Or they stayed near home and chased the ice cream truck, with no worrying about safety by their elders. A little boy on our block once streaked down the street on his skateboard, into the path of an oncoming car. My husband was the first adult on the scene: he did CPR, but it was too late. My kids were frightened the next day when they saw the daily paper with a front-page photograph of their father trying to breathe life into a dead child. The Mexican-American neighbor kids had it worse; for days, they saw the boy's ghost on the streets. They talked about it constantly, my kids listened raptly, and eventually the ghost was forgotten and the streets refilled with skateboards. The fruit vendors continued their treks, as did the window polishers, followed by the Border Patrol, who sometimes caught and beat their prey, sometimes locked them up for hours without water or a meal.

Some of us were disturbed by the brutality. We founded an advocacy group for undocumented immigrants. People would call our hotline with stories of mistreatment; we would make press releases and march downtown. The Border Patrol started building a big fence to block off Juárez from America. We waved angry signs and climbed a mountain. The city's coolest, most righteous people joined our group, or at least gave money. We gained members and got quoted in the national press. We starting holding annual fundraiser dinners, to which everyone came in dress clothes—even some local politicians, those not afraid to stand publicly for human rights.

In the early 1990s, dramatic, disturbing things began occurring on both sides of the border. One was that the North American Free Trade Agreement—NAFTA—created an explosion of big-box store openings in Juárez, and thousands of want ads appeared in the Spanish-language papers seeking more labor for the maquiladoras. These factories enjoy a special arrangement with U.S. Customs. When freshly assembled goods are sent north across the bridge, their owners pay import taxes, but not on the entire product, only on the quantum of value added by Mexican workers earning eight American dollars per day. Lured by the assembly bargain as it burgeoned after NAFTA, factories left El Paso and went south. By the turn of the twenty-first century, El Paso had evolved from a manufacturing town to a service economy in which unemployment went down—even as poverty went up.

Meanwhile, on the other side was murder. In 1993, the same year that NAFTA was passed, poor women in Juárez began to be brutally killed in unprecedented numbers, mostly by husbands and boyfriends gone berserk. Who knows why they started acting so violent? The maquiladoras preferred women workers, ostensibly because they were more docile than men and less apt to unionize. Some analysts noted that NAFTA was accelerating the movement of Mexican females from the home to factories and the streets, perhaps threatening traditional machismo and inciting rage in males.

Amid the domestic mayhem, scores of women were also offed by strangers in the most horrid, sadistic ways, involving rape both anal and vaginal, breasts cut off, the bodies buried in dumps. By the end of the decade, some four hundred women had been murdered, about a fourth of them victims of sadistic, ritualistic sex killings. When women's activists got interested in these murders, it became abundantly clear that the Juárez authorities could not or would not solve them. It was soon also obvious that men, too, were being slaughtered and that the homicide of both sexes was probably a by-product of narco-trafficking, which NAFTA had exacerbated by making it easier to ship both legal and illegal goods across the border.

By the turn of the twenty-first century in El Paso, people were getting so uneasy about Juárez that many stopped going.

In 2006, the newly elected president of Mexico declared a national war on drugs and sent troops to the areas considered most beleaguered by the cartels. Under fire, the various mafias jockeyed to redefine their turf. Spectacular internecine violence broke out in Juárez, and by 2010 more than three thousand residents a year were being slaughtered. The victims were men, women, children— people involved in the drug trade and many with no connection at all, innocent bystanders and those targeted by mistake. A quarter of a million people left Juárez—about a sixth of the population— abandoning thousands of homes and businesses. Large swaths of the city were painted with graffiti, torched, or left to the elements, crumbling to the ground. Areas of Juárez started to resemble the racial ghettos of the United States after the 1960s riots.

El Paso, too, was changing. The sacred rituals of bare life were starting to disappear, even as bare life became wider spread.

First to go were the vendors. They evaporated after 1993, when a new Border Patrol chief decided that rather than having personnel chase wetbacks through neighborhoods and the *placita*, it would be more efficient to line the Rio Grande with green-uniformed agents every few hundred feet and prevent people from crossing in the first place. Those still wanting to cross moved hundreds of miles west, into the broiling deserts of Arizona, where many over the next years would be broiled to death. Back in El Paso, door-to-door avocado peddling came to an end, along with the bare-bones income the saleswomen had carried from El Paso back to their families in Juárez. I visited my fruit vendor after the policy change, at her hut in a Juárez slum. The border blockade was only a few months old, but during that time she'd lost ten pounds, and her five daughters and one son also looked thinner. She asked about my kids and the other boys and girls in my neighborhood. But by then more children were staying inside.

On the adult-citizen front, a human-rights-oriented politician got hold of city government. He was Raymond Caballero, a Chicano lawyer who would never have assumed that a mariachi musician looking at art was thinking of pulling a heist. Caballero won a mayoral election and promptly started criticizing the corruption of the rich white business establishment—including one of its more powerful members, who'd recently been imprisoned on charges of bank fraud but received a presidential pardon from Bill Clinton when he was leaving office. The new mayor vowed to stop begging for investment crumbs from out-of-town, low-wage corporations and instead to encourage the development of local small business in El Paso. He also recruited young people—including Chicanos and the human rights activists—to join him in the practice of citizenship by running for city council and the county board of commissioners. The big-business men were miffed, and in 2003 they organized to successfully defeat Caballero when he ran for a second term.

But the young, self-styled progressives he'd recruited ran their own campaigns, and soon they were heading the local government. They were a new breed who had gone to great colleges and universities out of town. The sheepskins of El Paso's elite formerly came from the Texas College of Mines, Southern Methodist University, and Baylor. The upstarts sported diplomas from Princeton, NYU, Stanford, Emory, and Columbia. They'd absorbed the rhetoric of immigration and rights—as well as a painful understanding of how the Reagan era had withdrawn federal money from the cities of America, leaving them as desperate and pathetic as the women scrubbing windows with crumpled newspapers, the illegal lime sellers, the freight-train amputees on the international bridge.

Back in their new elected jobs on the border, these young people came to understand what almost every politician in the nation knew: that to get anything done, they would need to placate big business.

The big-business community in El Paso was developing its own new breed. Instead of stashing art collections in their houses, they were donating money to museums to purchase paintings for the public to enjoy. They were forming economic-development think tanks with which to approach the new politicians.

The new business elite was militantly Republican when it came to economics but pacifist in the nation's culture wars; abortion, birth control, and homosexuality didn't raise their hackles. And they were staunchly cosmopolitan when it came to transborder mixing with equals of their class. One transplanted El Pasoan, originally from Houston, had been married to a blond American and divorced. He remarried, to a blond daughter of the most affluent family in Juárez. This clan had roots in Spain and a history of higher education in Boston. Its matriarch was renowned for tireless charity on behalf of destitute Juárez women in need of doctors and contraception.

The family had amassed astounding wealth—wealth said to eclipse the fortunes of the richest of the rich in El Paso—by acquiring a virtual monopoly on the production and distribution of beer in Juárez. They also ran a chain of convenience stores there, stocked with their own private police, who were ordered, when confronted with beer-run kids and other would-be robbers, to shoot to kill, and often did just that. The patriarch of the family had funded the Juárez university and other good causes. The daughter had invested in a baseball team, and she was sponsoring the construction of a children's museum in Juárez that would dwarf anything north of Mexico City.

Her El Paso husband, an up-and-coming billionaire, had met her at a professional and social group for binational masters of the universe. After the wedding, he, too, became a superphilanthropist, giving El Paso $50 million for the border's first and only medical school. Wonderful, everyone said—everyone. A few old-school anticapitalists and die-hard Chicanos still mistrusted public-private partnerships. But who could argue with health?

Meanwhile, the young, progressive politicians were courted by yet another newcomer: the billionaire Bill Sanders, an inventor of the REIT—the real estate investment trust system of turning everything from skyscrapers to trailer parks into stock market shares. Sanders had spent his youth in El Paso, left to become a REIT master, then returned with dreams of "REITing" the entire U.S.-Mexico border on both sides. He planned to start this in El Paso by demolishing downtown and putting in upscale retail.

Sanders pitched his plan to the young, progressive politicians. They were studying the work of Richard Florida, inventor of the theory of the creative class. According to Florida, struggling American cities could redeem themselves economically by attracting young gays, bohemians, and Silicon Valley types who seek diversity, tolerance, nightlife, and fun on the streets. El Paso's young pols did not stop with Florida. They also looked at the New Urbanism, a challenge to Sunbelt-style sprawl. It emphasized city walkability, curbside intimacy, and, most of all, entertainment and shopping downtown. And so the progressives proposed a plan to renew the city, concentrating on its center.

Of course, there was already entertainment and shopping in downtown El Paso—the mom-and-pops with their steady customers, the embattled and often comical Border Patrol and ATF agents. But this was not what the pols had in mind. The businesspeople hired a focus group firm to go around asking people, if you could retool the city of El Paso into a person or persons, who would those people be? The answer, according to the firm's report: Matthew McConaughey and Penélope Cruz. And who, the focus group interviewers also asked, did the current, unrehabbed El Paso seem like? The report visually depicted the response as an anonymous Mexican geezer, a dead ringer for the elderly men in Stetsons over at the *placita*. The report labeled him "The Old Cowboy," describing him as "dirty," "lazy," "uneducated," and Spanish speaking.

The Old Cowboy could not have been more downscale and contemptible. The problem, however, was that he looked just like many El Pasoans' beloved *papás y abuelitos*. Indignant, many people began organizing against the downtown renewal plan. It eventually died, after courts outlawed use of eminent domain to tear down private buildings in the Old Cowboy's stomping ground.

By 2008, thousands of middle-class and rich people in Juárez, desperate to avoid shakedowns, murders, and kidnappings by cartel hit men, had begun packing up and fleeing to El Paso, where they bought houses and opened businesses. Their migration kept the northern side of the border economically afloat and turned Juárez into a pariah city—or worse, a ghost city that El Pasoans ceased thinking about.

Thanks to the well-heeled immigrants and their expatriate enterprises, gourmet restaurants flowered on the U.S. side of the border. El Paso's new medical school and other, related medical facilities bankrolled by the new elite created administrative jobs with salaries of $100,000 or more. Their wallets fat from the windfall, heretofore middle-class El Pasoans who'd spent years satisfied with the $7.99 Luby's cafeteria special now paid five times as much to dine on exotic cheeses, confits, and sauces, the names of which they'd never heard a decade earlier, much less known how to pronounce. People wanted booze with their fancy food: throughout the city, the number of business applications for alcohol licenses skyrocketed. Between meals, El Pasoans were now practicing yoga at new yoga studios. Women were having their legs waxed at new salons and patronizing new spas for new treatments: skin polishing, hot stone, mud.

The city was getting ready for Matthew McConaughey and Penélope Cruz.

But El Paso's poverty indicators continued to rise. By 2010, over a third of residents lived in areas of town classified by demographers as suffering from extreme destitution. In those slum areas—many of which lay right near downtown, near the offices of the rich businesspeople—public high schools were illegally kicking students out because they'd failed Texas's high-stakes No Child Left Behind exam. Children with limited English and poor, immigrant parents were labeled civic liabilities and expunged from civic institutions—further defined, that is, as bare life.

In Juárez, the adolescent cousins of the kicked-out El Paso students had no education at all. Public school in Mexico costs families money, and poor parents could not afford the price of uniforms, textbooks, lunches, and "tips" paid to teachers for teaching. *Ninis*, the poor teens of Juárez were called in Spanish, short for *ni estudian ni trabajan*—"neither studying nor working." Many did work, however, for the cartels. For a few bucks, on assignment with a handgun, *ninis* would murder disobedient drug dealers or ride the city bus downtown and extort $100 payments from store owners, keeping for themselves 10 percent. But then a rival organization would ambush and shoot the *ninis* with an AK-47. Or police would do the job. Cockroaches, the mayor of Juárez called the delinquent *ninis*.

El Paso was touted by the FBI as the safest large city in America, and while civic leaders celebrated this fact, no one understood why it was so. Some speculated that El Paso was a loving, caring place, and it takes a village to make a law abider. Some credited the city's huge immigrant population, praising them for being too busy working to cause trouble. Others wondered if the immigrants were simply too scared to do wrong, especially the undocumented ones, because even the lowliest crime could get a person without papers deported to Juárez.

Down by the river, drownings continued. Over the July 4 holiday in 2011, a Juárez man desperate for work tried to swim to El Paso while holding his five-year-old daughter, who was wearing a red-and-white dress. They went down together, and when they resurfaced days later, his body had so rotted that he couldn't be identified;

she was recognized because of the dress. Besides this father and daughter, two dozen other migrants died that year trying to cross to El Paso.

Meanwhile, the public and the private melded further. The gringo billionaire and his Mexican wife got interested in buying a sports team; so did yet another real estate investor, who was co-founder of the businesspeople's economic-development think tank. The two men and their families formed a partnership and asked the city to pay for an arena or a stadium to be located downtown, not far from several historic but decrepit buildings that the billionaire was lovingly rehabbing. The city joined the investors even as it was rerouting its buses away from the *placita*. With El Paso's Chicanos shuttled elsewhere around town, downtown had emptied out.

In El Paso in 2012, the rich people and the politicians presented voters with a "quality of life" bond-issue proposal. For nearly half a billion taxpayer dollars, El Pasoans were told, they could improve the city zoo, fix up the history museum, and add cool things to downtown, including a "multipurpose performing arts and education center," a.k.a. an "arena"—though the rich and the politicians avoided that term because they'd been advised by development experts that "arena" sounds controversial. It tends to remind voters of the many cities nationwide that have spent millions of tax dollars for sports facilities in the name of economic development, only to find later that no development has occurred. For the same reason, people also dislike "stadium," so in El Paso the prescribed term was "ballpark." A ballpark was needed now, for $50 million, to house the businesspeople's minor-league team.

Out in the neighborhods, many of El Paso's middle and working classes met this proposal with skepticism. At a meet up for constituents organized by a city council member who was planning to run for mayor, attendees stood and cursed taxpayer-funded stadiums for the rich and their private sports teams. "I used to feel the same as you," answered the council member. He'd changed his mind, he continued, because of the stunning generosity of the philanthropists, as well as—let's face it, he warned—the frightening possibility that they would relocate to Dallas or Phoenix if they didn't get their way.

The original bond proposal, drawn up by the city council in the spring, stipulated that voters would decide on the ballpark in the November general election. But suddenly, at a city council meeting in June, it was announced that the businesspeople had made an offer on a Triple-A team from Tucson and the deal could not go through unless the team's owners were *immediately* reassured that El Paso would build them a ballpark.

"Immediately?" everyone asked. "Immediately," the businesspeople insisted. And the ballpark simply could not be out on the highway; it *had* to be built downtown.

To make room, the city manager recommended dynamiting El Paso's ten-story, thirty-three-year-old city hall and moving its functions to various places around town—including the daily newspaper building, which was up for sale because, like the fourth estate everywhere, the *El Paso Times* wasn't doing so well. The move would work, the pols said, because the city no longer needed a unitary place for local government as much as it needed a brand-new, "quality-of-life" sports venue—a place even the people of Juárez would commute to, they insisted (though Juárez itself was almost finished building a big baseball stadium, but no El Paso pols knew this because none followed the Juárez media).

A vote was quickly taken. The instant it came out "yes," city council members responsible for the victory reached under their desks, whipped out baseball caps, and posed with wide grins for a photo op.

Civil war briefly erupted. Some people filed lawsuits to try to halt the demolition. Some organized an "Occupy" and spent a night in front of city hall. None of their efforts mattered. The courts ruled against them. The city manager called them "crazies."

A few weeks before the demolition, I took a walk to downtown El Paso. The streets in my neighborhood were as still as the surrounding desert: no fruit vendors, no ice cream trucks or little kids;

gentrification, with its cloistering of the young, was in full swing. Farther on I passed the *placita*, empty but for a man in a suit surveying the nearby old buildings that, because of the stadium and other impending downtown development, would soon appreciate in value.

Over at city hall, the parking lot was spray-painted with mystic arrows and numbers resembling those search-and-rescue hieroglyphs daubed onto dwellings in the drowned, post-Katrina neighborhoods of New Orleans. There the markings were inscribed to try to save homes and people. Here they augured an assault on civic life. Inarguably, city hall had always looked pretty awful—like a giant, glass toaster oven, roasting in the sun. It dated from the 1970s and was architecturally cheesy and funky. But in a sacred and moving way, funk in El Paso had once been a shared culture, embracing not just the person with immigration status and money but even, sometimes, the wetback *homo sacer*.

I walked on to the river, to a half-hidden break of wild bamboo, weeping willows, and discarded beer and soup cans. Deep in the brush were two plastic garbage bags jerry-rigged as tents, stocked with the minimal gear of bare people not at home; they must have been out on the streets, making a bare kind of living. I wasn't sure how they could do that anymore. Just after the stadium election, the city council had banned the homeless from soliciting in front of ATMs and restaurants, on the medians of wide streets, or on any commercial property whose owner disliked begging. (The language of the new law, the city council carefully noted, was devised so as not to violate anyone's rights under the First Amendment.)

It was also unlawful for garbage-bag dwellings to be pitched by the river, and their presence, just blocks from the upcoming stadium, could not be good for tourism. Some official would surely be along soon with a camera, pen, and clipboard, documenting the encampment for the commonweal, ensuring its eviction.

But what address would that official come from and return to, with one-stop government replaced by private stadium suites? *Sabe,* I thought—who knows? In the border's newly bare metroplex, it was hard anymore to see the civic, much less the sacred. What remained was corporate minor league. On the other hand, if we were lucky, the crazies would be able to afford tickets, at least on discount days. Old Cowboys all, they would replace their Stetsons with ball caps, sit in the nosebleed section, and like everyone else, even El Paso's billionaire, engage in the sacred ritual of gobbling concession popcorn. Which in Spanish is called *palomitas*, which also means "little doves."

11

UPSTREAM IN WILLISTON

NICKY TISO

Driving west toward the oil patch, across a prairie blinkered by wheat shocks and rusted machinery, dodging roadkill and semi-trucks, you learn that the untamed Great Plains of North Dakota alternate with bounded farmland. It felt American to stop for beef jerky at rest stops where the Cheyenne once hunted buffalo. I was on my way to Williston to see how the oil boom had changed a place I'd never been. It's not surprising that I'd never been there; North Dakota used to be the least visited state in the country. Then they figured out how to drill for oil two miles underground and horizontally. That changed things.

Williston is located in western North Dakota just below the Canadian border. The area used to be just another stagnating farming economy suffering population loss and brain drain. There are active Minuteman III missile silos in Stanley, North Dakota, just over an hour away. The Ronald Reagan Minuteman Missile State Historic Site is a five-hour drive east, in Cooperstown. The winters get very cold.

But the end of cheap, easy oil has led us to unconventional sources. The Bakken shale is a geologic petroleum formation located in a thin subterranean layer beneath the Dakotas, Montana, and into Canada. Lateral drilling technology combined with pressure injection (also known as fracking) opened this resource up to mining on a dramatically increased scale during the aughts. As of

2014, over ten thousand wells produced more than one million barrels a day and had nearly doubled North Dakota's GDP. North Dakota now accounts for 13 percent of all U.S. oil output. Williston is the administrative hub of the industry. The 2010 census population was 14,716. A North Dakota State University study estimates it grew to 17,792 in 2012; the figure jumps to over 30,000 if you include the tens of thousands of temporary workers living off the books in crew camps, tents, hotels, and RVs, making Williston one of the fastest-growing micropolitan areas in the nation (along with one of the most expensive).

The construction means you're getting close: a fourth lane is being added to Highway 85 and Highway 2, sprouting concrete overlays, turning lanes, bypasses, and shoulders. The town has a feeling of quaintness overlaid with unease. The downtown is a few blocks of boulevards lined with buckeye trees and flat brick storefronts, like a J. C. Penney from 1916, a pharmacy, a gift shop, mom-and-pop cafés, and a lone movie theater with vintage marquee. Most of the city is suburban: tracts of unassuming ranch-style homes and the occasional baseball field, driveways with old Ford trucks. The oversize developments of prefab housing encircle the old city in a cloud of dust. Drilling sites and finished well pads sprawl outward in gravel plots that stand out against the green prairie grass.

When I arrived, the Roosevelt Hotel was, fittingly, under renovation. Primer coated the walls. The wet polymer smell was oddly reassuring, like the whiffs of gasoline at the pumps one delighted in as a child. Oil-based paint is after all a petroleum distillate. The hotel was also totally booked. Not with tourists, but with roustabouts and roughnecks. As I walked to my room, I saw a piece of paper taped to a door that read in loud, angry Sharpie, "Do not disturb means do not fucking disturb!" I temporarily shelved my plan to knock on the doors and ask for interviews. Instead, I made some phone calls to the oil companies operating in the area. Nobody would talk to me. I kept getting circuitously transferred. I left Halliburton a voice message.

Eventually, I went for a drive. Derricks were everywhere: the tall steel scaffolding—erected to hoist pipes into place—was unmistakable. They were surrounded by shallow patches of water—prairie potholes—home to cattails, waterfowl, walleye. What had been a biodiverse sanctuary and a major hub for migratory birds was now punctured by boreholes and radioactive slurries.

I pulled off a gravel road to examine a finished well. Once the hydrofracking process is complete (it takes a few weeks), the borehole is capped with an artificial lift to pump the oil out—the "nodding donkeys" that dip up and down on a rotating piston. The oil and wastewater flows into separation and containment vats for transport. Around these, a spiraling white ladder leads me up to a catwalk with a view of the land hidden behind the folds of earth. I'm shocked to see the Missouri River, a blue crystalline ripple against white sandstone bluffs. Several hundred yards wide, winding from the Mississippi to the Rockies, the Missouri is the longest river in North America. I had no idea it was so close. Lewis and Clark had camped here more than two hundred years ago in search of a Pacific trade route, dressing skins and repairing canoes in a world of abundance we can only imagine.

Looking out over the shoreline, I thought of the Macondo well blowout, also known as Deepwater Horizon: the largest "accidental" marine oil spill in the history of the petroleum industry. It was caused by a flawed well plan that did not include enough cement between the 7-inch production casing and the 9⅞-inch protection casing, as well as a dead battery and mis-wired solenoid in the failsafe. The collusion of these factors was no anomaly; the question is one of overhead, not ethics. With fracking, the catastrophe moves inland. Train explosions, pipeline bursts, contaminated aquifers, flaming taps, seismic tremors. We've gone from the deep sea to the deep shale, looking for a clean vein.

At some distance, I saw a man standing by some excavating machines, which grew louder as I approached.

"What are you working on?" I asked.

"Do I look like I'm working?" he said.

"What?" The excavators were very loud.

"DO I LOOK LIKE I'M WORKING?"

"Oh, yes, very much so," I shouted. "Why, are you not?"

"Well, I'm just waiting on these scrapers to finish their job so I can keep irrigating."

"What's being built?"

"Something the town doesn't want us to build!" He laughed.

"What do you mean?"

"We're building housing lots for single-unit trailers, and they're afraid it's going to lower the property value of these half-million-dollar homes behind us."

I turned around and saw McMansions with granite facades in a newly paved cul-de-sac. Lawn ornaments peppered front yards.

"Who lives there?" I asked.

"Beats me, probably the professors." Williston State College was nearby. Deans, maybe, not professors, I thought, thinking of an adjunct's salary as I walked back toward the car. Then again, who knows? The inflation here is so extreme, because of the liquidity beneath our feet, that Walmart cashiers start at $17.10 an hour. The catch, as one employee candidly told me, is that "every day is Black Friday." In terms of the volume of shoppers, a regular day here is like the busiest day of the year everywhere else. Sure, there's town hall, but Walmart is the real civic heart of the city. Until a few years ago, you could camp in the parking lot, creating a quasi-permanent RV oasis for workers needing alternatives to the lack of housing, forcing Walmart to adopt a strict no-parking-lot-camping policy. It's still the one-stop supercenter for oil patch needs, from groceries to flame-retardant clothing. The ransacked aisles looked like the caricatured aftermath of a clearance sale. Clothes, bedding, canned goods—all sold out. There was plenty of memorabilia, though. Boom culture celebrates the Bakken as though it were a football team: bumper stickers, T-shirts, mugs, and the rest emblazoned with catchphrases like "Rockin' the Bakken!"

Like the ground stratified into columns and isolated for digging, the social and economic landscape of Williston is clearly layered.

You have your operators who contract service companies who subcontract a crew of workers to get the job done. These include truckers, surveyors, casers, drillers, finishers, mud loggers, and welders. In the end, it's hard to get a complete picture from anybody. Schedules are erratic and temporary, with workers cycling in waves every few weeks. When I asked one crew what they were working on, they mumbled about waiting for a callback from the supervisor in the morning to find out. But even the supervisors aren't omniscient; they implement plans developed by specialists headquartered in places like Houston, Alberta, Denver, Fargo, who analyze stratigraphic data and make the calls.

It is estimated that oil production in the Bakken shale will peak by 2016 and decline into 2040 with the number of wells in North Dakota alone totaling up to fifty thousand. There is an Achilles' heel to hydrofracking: every well's production declines by anywhere from 45 percent to 70 percent in the second year and upwards of 70 percent after five. New wells must continuously be drilled in order for production to grow, but we're already close to the peak, a dead end at odds with the investment brochures. The Bakken shale oil is considered "tight"; that is, it's a type of petroleum trapped in porous sedimentary rock with low permeability. Simply put, the rocks do not allow for an easy flow, which is why they must be blasted with millions of tons of water, chemicals, and proppants to wedge their cracks open and pressure the oil upward. The procedure is strangely energy intensive for such a short-lived phenomenon. Every well takes an average of one to five million gallons of to-be-contaminated freshwater delivered in over a thousand truck movements, most of it taken straight from the Missouri or its tributaries, with undetermined environmental impact.

At Wildcat Pizzeria, I met Dave, Stephanie, and Ron. Dave wore cowboy boots and blue dirtied jeans and a black T-shirt that read "I love to eat pussy" with a big graphic smiley face. Ron was heavyset with a beard and gleaming, childlike eyes, and Stephanie, thin, had her hair pinned up and a southern drawl to her voice. When I joined them, Dave and Steph were making out, and Ron was talking about the pros and cons of taking your wife to the strip club.

I asked if they work on the oil wells.

"Hell yeah, damn right," said Ron and Dave.

"What do you guys do?"

"I'm a driller, he's a foreman, and she's a whore, ha-ha!" Ron laughed.

"Oh, can it," Stephanie said. "I'm Dave's girlfriend. Moved here from Tennessee just a few weeks ago."

All three seemed perplexed by the lemon wedge in my Hefeweizen.

"Let me order you a real drink," Dave said.

After a few shots of whiskey and Red Bull, Ron got serious. He was from Texas and had come up here without his family so he could make some money. But there were problems at his work site. "It's my boss," he said. "He just gets high in his truck all day, and now he's saying he doesn't want to schedule work for tomorrow so his ass can sleep in. I need more money, but I don't—I don't want to rat him out; my daddy taught me not to step on anybody's toes."

"That's bullshit," Dave said. "You're not ratting on nobody, and everybody knows that. Tell me, what is he doing to you? What is he doing to you! Stepping on your toes, that's what! You have got to look out for yourself, brother. Shit, you've saved my ass before, and I'd see what I can do to get you put on our team." Ron listened. Stephanie leaned in: "The guy's a screwup, and everybody knows it. It's only a matter of time before he gets fired."

"Just tell him it's about money," Dave said finally, explaining how Ron could motivate his departure. "He can't argue with the fact that you got to make ends meet."

We had a few more drinks, then went back to the hotel (they were staying there too) and had some beers in my room. Then we went out. The last thing I remember was Dave taking a big gulp of beer and doing the shocker with his hand and fucking the air. "Rockin' the Bakken, baby!" he said.

"You're doing it wrong," Ron said softly, showing Dave which fingers go in the pussy, which in the ass.

Before leaving, I went back to the oil pump off the gravel road I'd come to know and listened to the thrust of pressurized gas releasing from the earthen pit, permanently aflame. Visible from space, these flares accompany every oil well and burn the natural gas trapped in the shale that we don't yet have the infrastructure or the inclination to capture, wasting it directly into the atmosphere. Meanwhile, the storms grow stronger as we take more and more carbon out of the ground and release it into the air. The controlled burn of methane hissed in my ear like a combustible seashell. I hopped back in my car, shifted into drive, and noticed the low-fuel light illuminating my dashboard.

12

LESSONS OF THE ARKANSAS

BEN MERRIMAN

The management of rivers in the American West has, at times, inspired great controversy. The Colorado, after lighting Las Vegas and watering Los Angeles, disappears into the middle of the desert; what reaches Mexico is so contaminated that it must go through a desalination plant before crossing the border. Salmon on Washington's dammed Snake River must return to their birthplaces with the help of special elevators. The bounty of California's Central Valley is fed by the pent-up water of four rivers. Throughout the West, some of the most famously beautiful landscapes of the nineteenth century have disappeared under impoundment lakes. And there is no relief in sight.

The Arkansas River forms in the Rockies near the old silver boomtown of Leadville, Colorado, then meanders east through Pueblo, Colorado; Dodge City, Kansas; and Wichita before turning southeast and moving at a stately pace through Tulsa, Oklahoma, and Little Rock, Arkansas, finally dumping into the Mississippi at Napoleon, Arkansas, a ghost town. At fourteen hundred miles, it is the sixth-longest river in America, behind the Missouri, Mississippi, Yukon, Rio Grande, and Colorado. It is the garden hose of the High Plains, sclerotic artery of midwestern commerce, and unamenable amenity in most of the towns and cities it passes through. Its history is, to a large extent, the history of all western rivers. It has been the subject of judicial whim, fractious legislative coalition, and blinkered administration, as well as, most recently, a major historical shift in attitudes about the environment.

Nineteenth-century colonization of the interior of the United States slowed significantly somewhere around the 96th meridian, which you can see on a modern map as the east–west border that runs between Minnesota and the Dakotas, Iowa and Nebraska, Missouri and Kansas, and Arkansas and Oklahoma (and Texas). Colonization slowed in part because the Plains Indian tribes fought unusually hard to keep their homelands; it also slowed because the plains were too dry for the agricultural practices carried by settlers from the eastern United States or Europe. The Dakotas, Nebraska, Kansas, and eastern Colorado are dry places, and for generations the colonizers had difficulty living in them. Before they arrived, professional soldiers and hired mercenaries killed and displaced the Plains Indian tribes. They also killed the American bison, of which there were as many as sixty million before the colonists arrived. Settlers claiming land under the Homestead Act, which gave ownership to those who could live on a parcel for several years, broke up the prairie sod and established farms with traditional crops. Certain crops, particularly drought-tolerant strains of wheat developed by Mennonites in Russia, enjoyed some success. The rest succeeded or failed depending on the unpredictable climate: natural cycles of drought and flood provoked economic cycles of boom and bust. Through it all, the settlers continued to impose old farming techniques on an unsuitable climate. They tore up the prairie grass that had sustained the bison and replaced it with uniform rows of corn and wheat. When the sky didn't provide enough water for these crops, they went looking for the water where they could.

In the late nineteenth century, settlers throughout the West began diverting rivers to the work of irrigating their arid land. This was a practice commonly called reclamation. Carrying water away from the riverbed for otherwise nonviable farms necessitated the development of a new form of water law. In the eastern United States, rivers were (and are) governed by riparian law, which holds that all people owning land along a river are entitled to use the water, provided that they do not unduly impair the use of the river by landowners downstream. The right to use water is tied to a claim to the adjoining land; if you sell the land, you can no longer use the water, but the person to whom you sold the land can. The eastern states inherited this form of law from the British common-law tradition, with which it shared the basic premise that people would use rivers for swimming, washing, boating, and shipping. Diversion of water for irrigation was never an important source of legal conflict: in England and the American Northeast, there was enough rainfall for the crops.

In the West, things were different. There was not enough rainfall, and so the use of the river could not simply be left to whoever happened to have settled on the riverbank. Nor was there enough river to share between all possible claimants. In this situation, riparian law did not provide a way of deciding whose demands for water should receive priority. Making use of a different line of law that tied property rights to productive use of resources, the courts in the 1870s developed a doctrine that came to be known as prior appropriation. Whoever was the first to develop a "beneficial" use of river water was allowed to keep using that amount of water henceforth, even if it meant that no one else got any. Beneficial use was construed broadly, with land reclamation—a human battle against climate—at its core.

By granting priority to historical levels of water use, prior appropriation also implicitly assumed that baselines of use and unpredictable features of the regional climate were, in fact, measurable. Answers to complicated questions about the amount of water appropriated, the proportion of the water that ran back to its source, and how much water existed in the first place were necessary for prior appropriation to be a workable system. Insofar as courts were able to determine historical baselines, the results were misleading: the settlement of the plains, and thus the establishment of baselines, coincided with uniquely wet conditions. Rights to water were thus set at levels that would be unsustainable in the drier years to come.

And so the lawsuits began. In 1902, after several dry years put a strain on both states' water resources, Kansas took Colorado to court. Colorado, Kansas wrote in its bill of complaint, had granted

> to divers persons, firms, and corporations the right and authority to divert the waters of the Arkansas River and its tributaries in Colorado from their natural channels, and to cause said waters to flow into and through canals and ditches constructed for the purpose, extending great distances away from the natural channels of said streams, and to store said waters and to empty the same upon high arid lands, not riparian to said streams, where large portions of such waters are lost from evaporation, and the remainder sinks into the earth, as a result of which all of said waters are forever lost to such streams, and are thus and thereby prevented from flowing into or through the State of Kansas.

Kansas was concerned that "it [was] the intention of the State of Colorado to divert absolutely all of the water that does, can, or might flow down the Arkansas River into the State of Kansas." Kansas asserted that riparian law, which would require that Colorado pass most of the water along, should take precedence over prior appropriation law, which Colorado claimed as an effective grant to keep the entire river for itself. The Supreme Court, the only court that could decide a dispute between states, refused to establish the priority of one set of laws over the other: doing so would deprive one state of the right to regulate its own affairs.

Setting aside these legal considerations left the Court with questions of scientific fact too complex to resolve with the available information, and so it gave Kansas what amounted to a massive homework assignment. "We think proof should be made," the Court ruled, as to whether Colorado is herself actually threatening to wholly exhaust the flow of the Arkansas River in Kansas; whether what is described in the bill as the "underflow" is a subterranean stream flowing in a known and defined channel, and not merely water percolating through the strata below; whether certain persons, firms, and corporations in Colorado must be made parties hereto; what lands in Kansas are actually situated on the banks of the river, and what, either in Colorado or Kansas, are absolutely dependent on water therefrom; the extent of the watershed or the drainage area of the Arkansas River; the possibilities of the maintenance of a sustained flow through the control of flood waters—in short, the circumstances a variation in which might induce the Court to either grant, modify, or deny the relief sought or any part thereof.

Furthermore, the Court appealed to a then-popular but entirely fanciful notion that irrigation and plowing actually *caused* rainfall. It therefore claimed that the more Colorado irrigated, the more rain would fall on Kansas. The Court was optimistic that things would work themselves out.

The farmers of Kansas knew otherwise, and five years later the state returned with what it believed was a stronger case, including many of the facts the Court had asked for. Colorado, for its part, countered with the dubious argument that the Arkansas River was actually two rivers, the Colorado Arkansas ("a perennial stream rising in the mountains of Colorado and flowing down to the plains") and the Kansas Arkansas (a stream from the south of Wichita to the mouth of the river), and that Colorado had only drawn from the former. The Court dismissed this claim out of hand but in the end sided with Colorado, for, whatever one might think about agriculture causing rainfall, irrigation *was* producing economic growth in Colorado. "The appropriation of the waters of the Arkansas by Colorado, for purposes of irrigation, has diminished the flow of water into the State of Kansas," the Court admitted. But, it went on, "the result of that appropriation has been the reclamation of large areas in Colorado, transforming thousands of acres into fertile fields, and rendering possible their occupation and cultivation when otherwise they would have continued barren and unoccupied."

Meanwhile, it was impossible to say how this use of the river might be harming Kansas, if at all. By the 1930s, monocultural row crops had replaced deep-rooted prairie grass. The huge swath of exposed soil turned to dust in a long drought and was taken up by winds and carried in huge masses throughout the country. The plains came to be known as the dust bowl.

The lack of water only spurred further litigation. In 1943, we see the states before the Supreme Court again, with Colorado asking the Court to force Kansans to stop suing. While the resulting decision ordered a particularly irritating group of Kansas farmers to stay out of court, the justices again avoided a resolution of the broader question of how the river ought to be shared.

In the 1950s, things became much worse when farmers in Colorado developed a new irrigation technology called the center pivot, which employed a wheeled irrigating arm rotating through a field centered on a well. One irrigation arm was able to water a 160-acre "quarter section" of land. It is these irrigation devices, still in use, that cause large parts of the Great Plains to look from the air like mosaics of green circles nested in brown squares. The center pivot effected a revolution in Great Plains agriculture and society. By drawing from deep deposits of subterranean water, center pivot irrigation made crops far more reliable than they had ever been before, tempering the boom-and-bust cycles of the plains economy.

However, center pivot irrigation does not buy prosperity; it borrows it. Extraction of subterranean water in Colorado meant even less of it flowed to Kansas, touching off two more generations of litigation. In 2001, Kansas finally won: the state was entitled to damages, because Colorado was using too much water. But the judgment was a Pyrrhic victory: Kansas would receive its reward only in money (not in water, as the state had hoped), and much of this money would go to pay enormous expert testimony fees not covered by the judgment. The dispute is in abeyance, though probably not for long.

Why do these people need so much water? The answer, in large part, is corn. In the nineteenth century, cattle raised on the plains were shipped off to Chicago for slaughter, but over time meatpacking moved progressively closer to the cow. The stockyards grew so huge that their size became inefficient. Improvements in the railroads and, later, the advent of the semitruck made it cheap to transport meat without a central site of production. Decentralization also enabled management to escape Chicago's strong labor movement. The industry is now dispersed across dozens of small plains cities: Dodge City and Garden City on the Arkansas in Kansas, and Liberal, which isn't far, as well as Greeley, Colorado, and Grand Island, Nebraska, along the Platte. Each city and its small hinterland is a vertically integrated unit for producing beef, and corn is the cheapest means to fatten cattle before they are sent to the slaughterhouse. Consequently, many plains farmers now grow corn instead of dryland crops like wheat. But corn is water hungry and must have twenty inches of rainfall a year to survive and at least forty to thrive. Only one of the corn-growing counties along the upper Arkansas receives twenty inches of rain a year, and some places are so dry that they are, both technically and in outward appearance, deserts. Although corn is manifestly unsuited to the climate, it is grown in enormous volumes, and irrigation is what allows this to continue.

Farmers have an added incentive to grow corn because the federal government underwrites it. Initially created to shield farmers from the instability of the open market and the rapacity of local grain elevator and railroad monopolies, government subsidies eventually became an ideological tool to protect the American farm as a real enterprise and national ideal. Since 1995, the irrigated counties of Kansas and Colorado have received $500 million in subsidies for growing corn. Stanton County, Kansas, which receives fewer than sixteen inches of rain annually, is showered by more than $2,000 per person in annual corn subsidies. Across the irrigated area, the government has spent another $225 million in disaster relief for catastrophic crop failure, mostly as the result of droughts that may well represent the long-term climatic norm in the region. Along the way, farmers have also drawn down the underlying aquifer, a subterranean reserve of water produced over millions of years and exhausted in a hundred. In many places the aquifer is already dry, and in most others it will be gone in the coming generation. Dryland irrigation leaves the river unsuitable for other use. It becomes salty and polluted, unfit to be drunk by humans or cattle, and at times fatal to aquatic life. That is, provided it flows at all. In the summer of 2013, the Arkansas was only inches deep at the Colorado-Kansas border, and the bed ran completely dry for a stretch of over a hundred miles. Irrigators, exercising their long-standing rights to the water, had used every drop. This is plainly an undesirable regulatory outcome: one arm of the federal government attempts to douse conflict over the water, while the other stokes it with piles of money.

The outcome is not simply bad for the local environment. Direct and indirect subsidies make American agricultural products such as finished beef extraordinarily competitive on the global market. This has harmed farmers in countries that abandoned subsidies and protections to join trade groups like the World Trade Organization. Competing with the United States can require rapid exhaustion of unprotected resources. Viewed in this way, the incineration of the Amazon basin was sparked in the American feedlot.

This is also not an outcome that could easily be changed if anybody wished to change it. As a constitutional principle, the federal government usually does not regulate land use. The individual states cannot easily stop ill-conceived farming practices, either. It is political suicide to injure farms, and though Colorado has made some limited attempts to rein in profligate use of water protected by prior appropriation, the main irrigators in Kansas, the Associated

Ditches, were granted irrevocable water rights in the 1940s and seem dead set on using them to the fullest each growing season.

Getting maximum agricultural use from the river has been one part of the effort to dominate the plains environment. Irrigation addresses the challenge of drought, but the Arkansas basin also suffers from floods that have, at times, been catastrophic. Before World War II, responsibility for flood control fell to states and localities, whose engineering resources were modest and protective works often inadequate. Furthermore, flood protection is zero-sum by nature: dikes and levees that protect one area raise the water downstream. This unsurprisingly led to another round of antagonism between the adjoining states along the Arkansas. Kansas felt that Colorado used flood-control works as a pretense to keep an unfair share of the river, while the Kansas congressional delegation sought to prevent the construction of dams whose purpose was to protect Oklahomans downstream. In 1927, floods overtook much of the middle of the country, including the Arkansas. Many towns mounted armed patrols atop their flood-control works; they had a well-founded fear that their neighbors would dynamite them.

After World War II, the Army Corps of Engineers intervened in flood protection on the Arkansas, building dozens of dams, dikes, and diversion channels, and, perhaps most important, elevating the issue above parochial interests. Of course, the Arkansas basin is still susceptible to severe floods. In 1998, my hometown in Kansas, on a tributary of the Arkansas, was flooded to the height of the billboards on Main Street.

Even as flood-control work progressed from the 1950s to the 1970s, a different attitude toward the environment was developing in parts of the American West. It came about from shifts in the larger culture, but also perhaps shifts in the nature of economic life. If the

"Old West" attitude treated the river as, simultaneously, an enemy and a source of profit, the "New West" treats it somewhat differently: The environment is something to be treasured, rather than something to be subdued and exhausted, though it is treasured as a sustainable source of wealth rather than as an intangible or innate good. As industries such as mining and farming became less profitable, in part because of their extraordinary efficiency, many communities sought to make use of environmental resources as attractive lures for those with excess money. The same technologies used for flood control, some thought, might also be used for development. Advocates revived an old ambition to use the Arkansas, as rivers are so often used, for navigation.

Conceiving of the Arkansas as a passable waterway required some imagination. In spite of its great length, there had never been any real demand for shipping. One early effort, in 1885, relied on the unpromising business model of carrying wheat upstream from Oklahoma to Kansas, making "coals to Newcastle" look like canny strategy by comparison. The business collapsed in 1886 after a bad storm. The hometown of the ship captain (and main investor) commemorated his effort by naming a street after him—always the first to flood in a heavy rain. Another venture, which shipped crude oil drilled on Indian reservations, folded within five years. Aside from flooding and the lack of a genuine economic need, all efforts faced the problem of seasonal low water. Even before irrigation began to affect the flow of the river, the Arkansas had trouble keeping its water level up.

All the same, after much lobbying and the passage of an act of Congress, the river was dredged, channeled, dammed, and locked. The project proceeded over two decades, continually funded through the efforts of powerful members of the Senate and against the better judgment and veto of President Eisenhower. The McClellan-Kerr Arkansas River Navigation System runs nearly five hundred miles from Napoleon to Tulsa. Tulsa's Port of Catoosa opened in 1971 at the final cost of $1.2 billion ($7 billion in today's money), greatly exceeding the price of more promising ventures such as the St. Lawrence Seaway or the Panama Canal. Activists immediately sought to extend navigation to Wichita. The Kansas congressional delegation had voiced support for the McClellan-Kerr boondoggle partly in hope of this eventual continuation. The lobbying lasted a decade before the idea of a Wichita port died. In addition to extraordinary engineering obstacles, lobbyists faced the mounting costs of the Vietnam War and the opposition of Oklahoma, which had no incentive to give the terminus away.

In any case, the treasure was fool's gold. Technological advances and deregulation in the railroad industry destroyed inland shipping almost immediately after the waterway opened. Today the Port of Catoosa is one of America's least used, ranking behind such shipping dynamos as Brunswick, Georgia, and Alpena, Michigan. In 2013, legislators from Arkansas and Oklahoma began to make rumblings about the need for new investment on the waterway. Many of the navigation locks had become structurally unsound, and the decision to build them, once made, cannot be unmade safely. Locks are pairs of gated dams that, when closed, create a pool of water that can be adjusted to raise or lower a ship. When they work, locks create smooth, level waterways in place of waterfalls, rapids, or shallows. If they fail, the result is what happens whenever a dam fails: a big flood.

Though the navigational possibilities of the Arkansas proved to be limited, the spirit of the New West continued to assert itself. Beginning around 2000, Wichita has sought to make the river into a tourist attraction. Imitating San Antonio, whose downtown is cut through by a shady path along the spring-fed San Antonio River, Wichita constructed the River Walk, intended to draw visitors to the city and anchor the attractions of downtown. This effort overlooks a central problem: after passing through hundreds of miles of irrigated farms, the Arkansas is all but used up and enters Wichita at a trickle, often no more than braids on a wide bed of mud and sand. When the river channel does promise to fill, part of the water is routed around the city in a flood-control device called, with lamentable accuracy, the Big Ditch. Oklahoma City, Wichita's more enterprising double, does not have a river and has turned this deficit into an advantage by building a much more compliant fake one.

The last time I visited the River Walk it was Christmas Day. My brother had just obtained his driver's license and drove me and my partner into Wichita. We parked behind Exploration Place, a science museum commanding the confluence of the Arkansas and the Little Arkansas. The Arkansas was, uniquely in my experience, more or less full of water, and the ground was uniquely covered in snow. I took a picture, my brother gallantly shielded me from snowballs thrown by my partner, then we left, having exhausted the pleasures the downtown could offer on what was, in fairness, a very quiet day. On the way out of town, we drove past what I consider a piece of the real Wichita, the Beechcraft plant, one of the several airplane manufacturers that dominate the commercial life of the city. (Though Kansas is poorly watered, it has plenty of empty sky.) At that moment, Textron, the parent company of Bell Helicopter and Cessna, was finalizing a deal to buy Beechcraft outright for $1.4 billion in cash. Massive layoffs were expected in the New Year.

The ecologist Garrett Hardin is well-known for describing the "tragedy of the commons." According to Hardin, certain kinds of resources, called common-pool resources, are particularly vulnerable to destruction. A common-pool resource is easily exploited by many people, but users may be overcrowded and the resource finite. The tragedy occurs through destructive self-interest; users, fearing the loss of access to the resource, draw upon it as much as they can, ultimately ruining it. This may explain how sensible people can fish a species to extinction, or cut down all the trees in a forest, or suck all the water out of a river.

This problem suggests two obvious solutions. One policy is complete privatization: a forest, for example, can be sold off into distinct parcels, each with an owner. The other is for government to take control of the resource and regulate who can use it. Both of these approaches can be undesirable. Privatization excludes people from accessing a valuable resource, and experience from many countries has shown that outright privatization of water can be extraordinarily destructive. Government regulation is liable to fail if the government doesn't understand the resource or can't provide credible enforcement.

The Arkansas River is a good example of the problems of government regulation. The government has not understood the environmental issues, so its restrictions don't restrict. The rules aren't coherently enforced, so people dispute them instead of heeding them. Kansas and Colorado have, in effect, spent a century arguing balls and strikes with an inconsistent umpire.

The political scientist Elinor Ostrom, who won a Nobel Prize in Economics for her work on common-pool resources, describes a major alternative approach. Against those who saw privatization or government regulation as the best way to protect common resources from destructive self-interest, she argued that the communities of people who make their living from such resources are best equipped to manage them responsibly. Though she examined many cases, some of her prime examples were irrigation systems, including one in Valencia, Spain, that has been sustainably self-regulated since the tenth century. Many of these systems, even the very old ones, function by the sale of transferable water rights. People with a claim to water they do not need can sell it to someone who does, preventing a scramble for the water and pricing the resource at its real, high cost. Prior appropriation law, for all its perversities, provides a possible framework for such a market: it offers well-defined rights holders fixed shares of water for specific purposes, and because the rights are not attached to landownership, they could conceivably circulate among bidders. Because the number of legal claims usually exceeds the available water, the cost of a right to water use would presumably vary depending upon the likelihood that one will be able to exercise this right.

In this view, the tangled regulatory apparatus produced by American federalism is central to the problems of the Arkansas River: the people making the decisions—courts and government agencies—are not the people most interested in the outcome, and the extreme administrative complexity assures that nobody is in a position to possess enough of the relevant information to act responsibly. On the other hand, these complex regulatory decisions have also produced a legal and material history that cannot simply be cast aside. Rights, once recognized, are not easily revoked. A physical legacy of older attitudes about the western environment exists in the form of dams, irrigation networks, navigation locks, and the like. Moreover, the residents of a watershed, who may be presumed to have a shared interest in its sustainable management, are divided by political boundaries and centuries of bad blood. The "watershed approach" to management, which views such preexisting political divisions as secondary and seeks a holistic approach to the governance of river systems, is particularly difficult to implement along lengthy rivers, especially ones with a fraught history and compromised ecological integrity. Toward the end of her career, Ostrom acknowledged all of these matters as major challenges to self-governance.

One of the reasons for Ostrom's influence is that her work is not prone to idle speculation: her argument is based on plenty of empirical evidence that communities can govern resources sustainably. However, the argument from actual communities disguises a cultural assumption: communities can only manage their resources sustainably if they are committed to their own long-term welfare. Yet the culture of the American West has rarely managed to produce such a commitment. When natural resources cannot be directly exploited, communities turn to boosterism, and when those ventures fail, people simply drift away. Part of the western sense of place is a sense that it is a big place, so big that opportunity—a new boom—can always be found somewhere else.

This culture becomes particularly pernicious in the American legal environment. Regulations and larger constitutional principles constrain local actors, often in ways that encourage destructive behavior, such as subsidizing the growth of climatically inappropriate crops while also guaranteeing access to artificially cheap water. Worse, the laws, and even the principles, keep changing, leaving people uncertain that what they have now can be relied upon in the future. This, in turn, reinforces the money-minded imperative that has always defined the culture of the American West: get yours or get out.

For many reasons, some of them non-environmental, "get out" has become the more common choice. The population of the plains is shrinking and aging, and nearly all of the plains, while remaining in extensive cultivation, has fallen well below the threshold of population density that once defined "frontier." These withering communities may feel little commitment to the region's future—*après nous, la sécheresse.* As Frank and Deborah Popper argued controversially in the 1980s, the collapse of irrigated society on the plains might not be a bad thing. The farming is economically marginal and ecologically ruinous, the system of property law ill-suited to the low density of resources, and the produce mostly destined for the feeding trough, not the table. Ruin could be a chance to start over.

But stopping the argument here misses a larger point. Major cities like Los Angeles and Las Vegas depend on western rivers for drinking water and electricity. Agricultural areas such as the Central Valley, which yield produce far more valuable and important than feed corn, make use of exhaustible irrigation waters. Though larger in scale, the basic problems are the same: complex, uneven regulations issuing from many different political authorities; strong water rights; and cultural indifference to long-term local sustainability. There is no easy solution. However, it is important to recognize that the problem is structural. Environmentally minded Americans often view ecological degradation as the result of conspiracy between political and economic elites, and there may be some truth in this. However, bad outcomes are much more likely to be the result of self-interest and regulatory accident than genuine bad faith. The American structure of government, which was designed to be inefficient, requires no special, malign effort to be dysfunctional. Yet dysfunction cannot go on forever. Though the exhaustion of the upper reaches of the Arkansas may not be of national or international importance, the drying up of the hydraulic civilization of the American West certainly is.

13

DALLAS AND THE PARK CITIES

ANNIE JULIA WYMAN

On the back of its state seal, Texas has six flags, one for each of the countries that have governed some or all of it at one point or another: Spain, Mexico, France, the Republic of Texas, the Confederate States of America, and the United States, also of America. All six—red, yellow, green, red, blue, white, with eagles and cacti and stars and bars—used to fly over every Six Flags theme park until the 1990s, when they were standardized into pastel putt-putt-style pennants presumably as the franchise expanded to places where the Confederacy has never been popular. I know all the flags in order and by sight because Texas requires that public school students dedicate the second and seventh grades to state and local history. From our state-issued textbooks, we learned our official heritage, flag after flag, and all the relevant victories and tragedies in between. Not many Americans know that General Antonio López de Santa Anna, the arch-villain who presided over the massacre of 189 Texas independence fighters at the Alamo, was given to wearing dresses in secret.

That wasn't the exact language our books used, but we took it in stride that any enemy of the Lone Star State must have been an involuted fairy. We made fun of him, all of us, growing up in what is called the Heart of Texas: the Park Cities, the small twin towns that form an "enclave" within Dallas proper. I came of age in the state's inner chamber of power, in its proud heart of hearts. In elementary school, we were given spiral-bound books containing the history of our two little towns and the larger city. These were especially good because they were our own property. We spent a great deal of time peacefully coloring them in with our map pencils: the hat on the cowboy was tan, with red trim; the Indians tan and sometimes red also; the Trinity River, which creeps along the southwest corner of Dallas, was brown, the color of dead grass and the saliva the football players spit in class, quietly, into enormous thirty-two-ounce plastic cups from the Dickey's Barbecue Pit on the other side of Central Expressway.

Dallas is flat, a car city, with forest to the east and prairie to the west, sliced through and through by superhighways whose cement walls are dotted with the state star. It is also a huge city, the ninth largest in the United States, and the D in DFW Metroplex, the largest landlocked metropolitan area in the country, with a population of 6.5 million and a GDP of $420 billion in 2012—this from oil, cattle, and related ranching, from an ever-increasing "technology sector" that includes Texas Instruments and, most recently, AT&T; before that it was cotton, alcohol, and railroads. The nearest body of water, White Rock Lake, is artificial; there is only one natural lake, Caddo, formed by an accidental logjam and named after the tribe who occupied north Texas before they were driven out.

Dallas's modern industries have erected a series of magnificent towers downtown, including a hideous rotating glass geodesic dome perched on 571-foot legs of poured concrete. Otherwise downtown isn't exactly inviting: in the 1960s, the city constructed the Dallas Pedestrian Network, a series of underground tunnels eventually stretching for thirty-six blocks and including a miserable simulacrum of a city beneath the city. If this wasn't the stupidest and most ill-conceived downtown revitalization project in the United States in those years, it was close. But so much in Dallas is ill-conceived, surreal, irrational, and even dangerous. A high school friend once showed me a state football championship ring with crud worked down into the settings of the diamonds and told me the crud was "black kid skin."

Dallas is the place where JFK was shot on a brilliant November afternoon half a century ago. I was driving through Dealey Plaza one evening, and my driver's ed teacher told me she was writing a novel wherein she traveled back in time to seduce Kennedy's grandfather and persuade him to warn his future grandson. "He has to call off the parade that will lead to his assassination!" she'd say in a breathy voice. She was bleached blond and middle-aged; there were always little scabs of mascara caught in her eyelashes. If I agreed to sit with her in the parking lot of McDonald's on Commerce and paid for our ice cream cones and helped her with her stories, she'd fill in more hours of driving than I'd actually completed. From what my public education had taught me, this seemed like a fair transaction. We'd learned the phrase "free enterprise system" in second or third grade. I assume the concept is included in the state elementary school curriculum precisely because all of Texas's major industries are monopolies and they wanted us to get a feel for that stuff early.

The more famous of the Park Cities is Highland Park (HP), which occupies only 2.2 square miles. George W. Bush goes to church in Highland Park when he isn't in Crawford. The second city is University Park (UP), 3.8 square miles; together these two bastions of whiteness in what is otherwise a multiracial city are known as the Bubble. Both places are fully Republican, though Highland Park is richer. Often people from UP, like me, say they grew up in HP. Maybe whoever you were talking to would assume you had more money than you did. And to say that you were from Highland Park was also the only way to feel as if you came from someplace—even if it was someplace famous for racism. In 2003, when I was a junior in high school, the *Park Cities People* ran a story about the first black family to move to Highland Park. The lede itself made national news: "Guess who's coming to dinner . . . and staying for a while?"

In 2005, the year after I graduated, *The Dallas Morning News* reported that Highland Park High School was 94 percent white. This was in the context of their coverage of Thug Day, an annual student-council-sponsored dress-up day the week before Halloween:

> Students at Highland Park High School dressed as gang members, rap stars, maids and yard workers this month during homecoming week—a tradition one Dallas civil-rights leader says is racially insensitive.
>
> On senior Thug Day, students wore Afro wigs, fake gold teeth and baggy jeans. On Fiesta Day, which was to honor Hispanic heritage, one student brought a leaf blower to school.

Every time we played "the black schools," Lincoln High or Lake Highlands, at football or even basketball, there would be rumors of fights, which led to SUVs full of players in grass-stained stretch pants being dispatched to Best Buy parking lots in rougher neighborhoods. I once covered an almost fight for the high school newspaper. I remember idling, smoking a cigarette out the window of my hand-me-down Ford Explorer, a car I drove to pieces, often while drunk. A dirty white Nissan lowrider—no one from my school would have been caught dead in it—circled the parking lot, and a kid got out, holding a tire iron. I watched as the other kids in their Chevy Tahoes stopped, too, and the cars themselves seemed to hold their breath in the humidity, waiting clownishly for the storm of violence and hatred to break and for blood to spill as it had been spilling forever in that city, at the edges of the enclave, on the flat gritty concrete acres of parking lots or the sticky asphalt of less-manicured, marginal streets. The moment passed, and the Tahoes drove away, the way predators will sometimes give up on something that stands up tall enough and looks them in the eyes—in the rare instance, for example, when they have mistaken a member of their own species for prey.

My parents—my mother a stay-at-homer with a JD, short, mixed race, uninterested in bouffant hair, and my father a neonatologist, white, eccentric, and enormously tall—moved us to the Park

Cities for the school district. This remains the dumbest decision of their lives. Perhaps there is something to be gained by firsthand knowledge of one of the earth's truly bad places—some wisdom in exposure to the dark heart of Republican power—but I don't know what it is. Dallas is something I am ashamed of and frightened to share. My family didn't go to church, and we had less money than almost everybody, far less than the Hunt family, owners of Hunt Oil ($4 billion in revenue in 2013)—Ray Hunt, later known for questionable dealings in Kurdistan and elsewhere, was on the board of Halliburton—or the Beecherls, of Texas Oil and Gas, or the Westcotts or the Wynnes, who were real estate magnates. At Highland Park High School, there was alcohol and there was football and every sport had a chaplain that led prayer beforehand, and anyone who didn't care about any of those three things—God, booze, touchdowns—was a leper. Weekly sports pep rallies were mandatory; once the high school celebrated academic achievers by standing us in the middle of the gym while the varsity cheerleaders ran circles around us, shaking their pom-poms to Outkast's "Hey Ya!"

It cost $400,000 every year to put the hundred-man varsity football team on the field; our stadium was the second in the country to have Astroturf, inside or outside the NFL. My friend Najib, the only Muslim I knew, used to faint during Ramadan, when he'd practice with the rest of the defensive line without food and water. The average high in Dallas in July is ninety-six degrees Fahrenheit, enough to kill a big kid who runs for two hours without a sip of Gatorade. Najib would practice anyway. The team wouldn't let him start varsity if he didn't drill during his fast. He stayed sharp, he said, by ducking his head into the team bucket of ammonia and water as often as possible.

It was near Christmas, when the snow wasn't falling—on those rare occasions, it was paltry and bitter, the consistency of frozen ash—that the piles of wealth towered highest. On lawns around Jerry Jones's house on Preston Road, trees were wrapped in hundreds of thousands of bulbs, while Escalade-size sleighs loaded with fake presents sported tags as big as street signs bearing the names of family members. There were gargantuan Nativity displays, where Baby Jesuses larger than spaniel dogs snuggled down in huge mangers. They knew, those Jesuses, that in Highland Park luxury goods and low property taxes were God's reward for acting right. No matter which church you attended—HPUMC, PCPC, PCBC, Methodist, Presbyterian, Baptist—wealth was simply His way of persuading other people to become Christians, too. It worked on my little brother, for a while; he had a student Bible in a zip-around cover. We must, said my mother, we must resist the urge to throw it away.

The word "Texas" comes from the Caddo word *tejas*, which means "friendship." When I was younger and wasn't friends with anybody, I'd pretend that I was one of the Caddo tribe, fishing alone in the creek in the park near my house. The fish were dirty, coated in brown mucus with worms on their scales and brown spines like razors that cut your palm while you wrenched the hook from their insides.

By the time high school started, I had secured two friends, Sarah and Kevin, drawn from the half a dozen of us who both ran cross-country and played in the marching band. We were a little flute trio and sent in recordings for interscholastic competitions; at meets we hung out together. It was nice to have a friend in Sarah especially, because there were about a hundred girls on the cross-country team, and most of them were religious, and all of them had better taste in charm bracelets and less body hair than I did. Sarah's father was the janitor at one of the middle schools, which was certainly one of the reasons no one else liked her. She had a slight lisp and couldn't dress to conceal her poverty and didn't go to church.

On Friday nights, after football games, we'd smoke pot and then worry, gigglingly, about getting up in time to catch the bus to that weekend's cross-country meet. Kevin was always with us. He liked video games and *Star Trek* and played the fife in Civil War reenactments, during which he was sometimes fake shot; he would have to lie still for hours, until a particular bugle blew and he could reconnoiter with the rest of the fake Confederates for IHOP waffles. Sarah and I often stayed at Kevin's house overnight, because his mother was a relatively absent divorcée. I still have one of his T-shirts, a soft orange thing from a private southern college he always let me wear as pj's. Eventually, after they left for state schools, Sarah and Kevin fell in love with each other, and we lost touch.

Sarah sent me a message on Facebook in 2011. She saw that I had gone to a good college and then a good grad school. She let me know that she'd always believed in me and that she'd found something I made her when she graduated, a photo collage including a picture from a cross-country meet: "i looked like i was going to barf after that race lol i don't know if anyone told you about Kevin. he died in december from a heroin overdose." At the end of the note was a passage from 1 Corinthians. He was at home with the Lord, Sarah wrote, "and we are always confident that while we are at home in the body we are absent from the Lord. For we walk by faith and not by sight." There was nothing in the note about Sarah's own addiction or how she had found God while serving three years in a state prison for heroin possession. She was wearing a prosthetic by then, having lost her left arm in a car accident in 2009. This was before Kevin died: she was speeding down the tollway, which Dallasites pride themselves on taking at about 120 miles an hour. Her arm was out the window holding a joint, and she swerved to avoid something. Her hand-me-down Explorer flipped, wrenching her arm off a little below the socket when it landed.

I often feel that if we had grown up somewhere else—somewhere money and religion and physical prowess as a football player or halftime dancer weren't the only paths to a safe place in the social order—then my friends might have survived. There were no openly gay students in Highland Park, though there were always a few kids who killed themselves or spiraled down into addiction about whom one never spoke. Whenever I think of Sarah and Kevin, I think of their unbelievable geekiness as teenagers, of all the things that marked them for exclusion and suffering. Kevin always wore a *Star Trek* costume for Halloween. He knew some Klingon and was unbearably dorky and sweet. I have a memory of Sarah and Kevin naked, kissing each other behind a pool table at his house, where we took Ecstasy to celebrate my sixteenth birthday. Seeing them, I felt immediately that something dangerous was happening. They would never leave, I thought, if they fell in love with each other as Dallas had made them, only half themselves, unhappy. That night I slept outside on the trampoline.

The next year I quit the band to be friends with the football boys in my Advanced Placement European history class. I didn't want to be different or weak or ugly. I taught myself to manicure my eyebrows and deal with the body hair. Also, my parents let us drink on our property, in the converted garage that used to be my older brother's room. I saw the opportunity to remove the given reasons for my sadness, and I took it. Like many female nerds in nerd-poor environments, I found that this attempted murder of my old self left me further from happiness than ever. At least a nerd knows why she's miserable.

I couldn't bring myself to go to school for most of my senior year. Some kids drank their way through the day—you could use a Dickey's cup, or you could inject vodka into an orange with a syringe—but I went only to work on the student newspaper or to paint on the little easel my English teacher let me set up in the back of his classroom. During my long truant days, I went to North-Park, the fanciest mall in Texas, home of the Neiman Marcus flagship, and to the Dallas Museum of Art (DMA), one or the other almost every day. At the mall, you could touch the expensive things that you couldn't afford, but otherwise the two spaces felt similar: with their white walls and glass panels and the gentle urging toward covetousness.

It was at the DMA that I met Jeremy. He was working the information desk under the manic glass epitome of nonspecific lobby art the world over, a Dale Chihuly anemone that looked like a fifteen-foot zit frozen in mid-burst. Jeremy'd lived in a car for a while, which impressed me then. We'd drive up to Denton, where the Polyphonic Spree played, and the Mountain Goats, and sometimes to little warehouse places in Plano. Plano is one of the meth capitals of America, where people set up their labs in empty Mc-Mansions and where there were strange explosions in the night. On a trip to Louisiana, Jeremy told me he'd used a student loan to pay for surgery for a dog with a terminal disease. That was why he'd been homeless. At the time, it seemed so softheaded and womanly that I couldn't look at him. When he told me the dog had belonged to someone else, I rolled over in my sleeping bag, and we didn't speak for thirty hours.

Unlike most even slightly arty people in Texas, Jeremy and I never went to Austin. Fuck Austin, I used to think. I still hate people who go to Austin and smoke a ton of weed and eat cardamom-flavored ice cream in the heat, who go to SXSW and come back to wherever and say, "Texas ain't so bad! Keep Austin weird!" These people are idiots, unaware that millions of Texas public school students are calmly coloring in the Indians with their red map pencils or that, not so far away in space or time, in the richest part of the most powerful state in the country, a student was arriving at my little brother's elementary school fair with a cake representing the Rio Grande, with Lego figures swimming across to "show the wetbacks," and that this had been his parents' idea.

After 9/11, when I was in ninth grade, the Texas legislature imposed a moment of forced prayer at all public schools, after we had said the Pledge of Allegiance and the Texas Pledge (the latter opens in an unnerving imperative—"Honor the Texas flag. I pledge allegiance to thee, Texas, one and indivisible"—and absents any mention of liberty and justice for all). I remember squirming and squirming. I knew enough about the Constitution to know that what was happening was wrong, but the Constitution was far away. For children who didn't believe in the Christian god, this was the daily minute of humiliation at the hands of our own, stubborn difference. (It was easier to externalize the youth group leaders loosed on us nonbelievers in the lunchroom on Wednesdays.) I never asked Najib what he did during the minute. But I had another friend, Alex, who was a Belarusian immigrant and who went to the University of Texas after we left high school for a triple degree. He used to stand up at his desk during the moment of reflection and just talk about whatever was on his mind because the moment of prayer was, according to him, total bullshit and against the separation of church and state and other things his family had moved to America to enjoy.

I asked Alex once if his parents couldn't have found a less terrible place to live, and he frowned at me and explained that as an infant he had spent several months in a Soviet quarantine center because he had been exposed to Chernobyl radiation while out for a push in his stroller. I took his point, even if my own exposure to the Fiesta de las Seis Banderas felt just as poisonous. The fiesta was the culminating pageant of debutante season, a charity bash tracing the history of the state with zero Hispanic people because anywhere from zero to three Hispanic people went to our school. A selection mechanism I never understood—a rich-mom cabal of some kind—picked out forty white high school women as debs. These were the duchesses, each named after a city in Europe that might or might not have ever been part of a duchy, past or present. The dresses were great billowy confections, tiers of lace and shawls and folding fans included; I read in the *Park Cities People* that the Duchess of the Confederacy got to wear the biggest dress, presumably because she was staring at the historical erasure of her nation by the Democrats and had to have a little more attitude than the other girls.

I never went to a debutante ball, was never invited, and I'm still mad about it. Mine was a local weirdo family, and I wasn't at ease with women generally. I certainly couldn't have hung with the blond girls long enough to provoke the necessary sympathy to be made sub-duchess of Chenille-sur-Chanel. But I know all about the dresses because beyond the pictures in the paper each duchess had a doll made in her likeness, complete with a dress cut from the same fabric as the original. These were prominently displayed in the windows of the nicer shopping villages. These dolls sometimes had human hair, cut from the real girls. As a test of my empathy, of the flexibility of my perspective, I sometimes try to imagine that I, too, am a woman who wants to be made into a doll. I could point to it and tell my granddaughters that once I was so beautiful that my people made of me this outrageous totem, a fetish of myself at peak value.

It's been almost ten years since I've seen any of those women, or Dallas itself. I went back to University Park once when I was in college, and then my parents moved to Northern California when my little brother graduated from high school, ending a decade of depression and status anxiety on the part of my mother. My father retired and began growing salad greens in old plastic buckets and let his teeth fall out because he, too, no longer felt he had to impress anybody. Most of my friends who left Dallas returned to spend money on bad art, guns, super PACs, loud silk tops, big jewelry, and plastic surgery. Theirs is a wickedness that knows not to stay too long from the nest. Texas power and money have concentrated themselves into a wise, far-reaching evil that knows it will be ignored—that is, left free to work, from Dallas to Iraq and back again—if its children stay in their prosperous enclave and talk like hayseeds and wear disarmingly dirty cowboy hats.

When I think of home, if home that was, I suppose I become as ruthless as the city raised me to be: I am most Texan when I talk about Texas. A few years ago, the fifty-five-foot-tall animatron that stands outside the fairgrounds in Arlington caught fire and made news all over my Facebook network. I watched several videos of the event: Big Tex's cowboy hat turned to ashes. His placid cheeks, his empty chest, his spindle legs, his big pale hand raised in friendship, were engulfed in orange and black and red. *Who knows*, I thought, *maybe there is a God.* All afternoon I kept my screen filled with images of the world's largest Texan as he crumpled into flame.

14

THE KINDNESS OF STRANGERS IN NEW ORLEANS

MOIRA DONEGAN

One of the things that happens when a corpse decomposes is that it fills up with gas and bloats. In New Orleans, I learned this when I asked about the cemeteries. The aboveground mausoleums there are made of carved marble and brick and look like teeny, tiny mansions. On the day that I was there, November 1, there were offerings lined up around them. I saw mostly candles and plastic rosaries but also pieces of chalk and toy cars, along with the flowers. I was in the cemetery with a friend who had grown up in New Orleans and wanted to show me All Saints' Day, a tradition where families bring gifts to the graves of their dead loved ones that in the United States now is widely observed in Louisiana and just about nowhere else. Aboveground cemeteries, it turned out, were a public health necessity. The southeast part of Louisiana isn't on the continental shelf; the land there is formed from a giant pile of silt, dumped by the Mississippi River and mounted up on the ocean floor. The land is literally made of the continent's trash: the dirt that falls into the river in Iowa or Tennessee and gets washed downstream ends up in Louisiana as a sediment deposit. Among other things, this means that the soil in and around New Orleans is thin and watery. If you bury a corpse there, when it bloats, it can eventually pop up again, like a beach ball pushed under the surface of a pool. The problem, he told me, is worst during floods.

I moved to New Orleans in the summer of 2012 because I didn't have much else to do. I had graduated from college in the spring and had been informed that there were no jobs—which was a relief, in a way, because it meant there was less pressure on me to find one. But I had spent a few college breaks on volunteer trips in New Orleans, and it seemed smart to move to a city that I knew I liked, where I already had friends, connections, and a favorite bar. I applied to a government AmeriCorps program that subsidized workers at nonprofits in Louisiana, and I was placed in a job screening phone calls in the volunteer services department of a food bank. The program would last for a year with an option to renew for a second. I figured that doing good was better than doing nothing and that by the time I finished, something else would have come along.

When I pulled off I-10 the day that I first arrived in town, a soldier in desert-colored fatigues stood beneath a blackened traffic light, directing cars with his stiff palms. On the road behind him, felled oak branches lay downturned on the asphalt like hands. I had to steer around them. This was August 30, 2012, and my timing could have been better. Hurricane Isaac had made landfall two days earlier, the first major storm to hit New Orleans since Katrina. Power was out in much of the city, and farther downriver, in swampy Plaquemines Parish, two bodies had been found floating facedown in a flooded kitchen. Isaac was the first real test of the new, $14 billion levee system that the government had built after 2005, and a lot of people had expected the levees to fail. Almost all of the friends I knew in New Orleans had evacuated to Austin, Memphis, or Baton Rouge; they sent me pictures of the traffic backed up on the outbound side of the highway. "I really don't know what's going to happen," one friend had told me a few days earlier over the phone. "But I don't want to be here when we find out." Before the storm reached land, the Army Corps of Engineers had been called in, to provide assistance and keep order. But the levees held, and while a lot of people lost power, the damage wasn't nearly as bad as what had been feared. By the time I reached town, there were soldiers standing in clusters at the major intersections along Claiborne Avenue, looking bored. The French Quarter even had its lights back on, and businesses were open in the tourist district. On Rampart Street as I made my way to my apartment, I saw an army Humvee stop to let a gaggle of drag queens cross the street. I watched them disappear into a bar.

Because of where New Orleans is, catastrophe is a promise. It is a cruel joke of nature that because of the way that land forms in a delta region, the levees that keep the city from flooding are actually also pushing it lower and lower, farther below sea level. Nearly everyone I met there agreed that eventually the city will flood again, worse than it did in 2005. In the meetings that were held in a church rectory every month for members of the AmeriCorps program, this came up a lot.

Like me, nearly everyone in the program was white, fresh out of college, and from out of town, and for the most part they were smart, ethically committed people who had taken the horribly paying AmeriCorps jobs in New Orleans because they wanted to do good. There was a time when such people were exactly what the city needed. In the months following Katrina, there was a lot of hard, unlovely, and sometimes weird work to be done. When houses lose power in a Louisiana summer, for instance, the food in their refrigerators rots quickly. After the storm, a city's worth of beer- and gumbo-filled fridges had to be duct taped shut, carted out to the curb, and thrown away without being opened. Houses flooded with a family's worth of books and clothes inside, and someone had to help throw out everything soggy and mildewed. Thousands of families and business owners had to file insurance and federal benefit claims, and somebody had to be there to help them with the paperwork.

But by the time I came to New Orleans, things were different. New Orleans was not what it had once been, but the heavy lifting of hurricane recovery was done, and a steady push of gentrification had changed much of the city. Now St. Claude Avenue has art galleries and a bike lane. There are bakeries that only make cupcakes. The Winn-Dixie on Tchoupitoulas started selling organic kale, which I bought and made salads with. Some of this, it turned out, was meant for the very people who had helped gut houses a few years before: of the thousands of volunteers who descended on New Orleans after the storm, a lot of them had fallen in love with the city and had chosen to move permanently to a place where they could enjoy mild winters and cheap rent. "We used to have a brain drain," one smiling city representative said. "Now we have a brain gain." After Katrina, New Orleans became a place where some people could live as yuppies. When the city was rebuilt, it was rebuilt largely in these people's image.

Of course, reminders of the storm were still all over. There were plenty of blighted houses, for instance; the few that hadn't been gutted since the storm had a smell strong enough that you could tell them from a block away. And many buildings still bore their X codes, the spray-painted symbols from different search-and-rescue teams that had inspected every building in the city after the storm. But with a few exceptions, most of the nonprofit work that my co-hort and I were assigned to had little to do with the flood. One girl was tasked entirely with helping the public defender's office process people who were arrested under a nasty state statute called the Crime Against Nature law. Another guy was working for a group that sent him door-to-door distributing those energy-efficient, corkscrew-shaped lightbulbs. The problems we were tasked with fixing had less to do with the fact that the city had catastrophically flooded than that it was in decline.

At the food bank, however, this wasn't the line we took. In the volunteer services department, it was my job to orient the church groups and sororities—many of them from out of town—who showed up to work in the warehouse. Before they started, we ushered them into an orientation room lined with photographs of smiling black children holding apples and bowls of soup. In this situation, it was useful to talk about the city's poverty—which was easy, because the poverty was real, trenchant, and bleak. "One in five children and one in three seniors in south Louisiana don't know where their next meal is coming from" was the statistic that rolled off my tongue with the neat rhythm of muscle memory. The volunteers would shake their heads slowly; motherish women in their forties would tut their tongues. Then I would take pictures of the volunteers in their lanyards and matching T-shirts and lead them into the warehouse to sort cans.

I wasn't technically a food bank employee but rather a "fellow." Every two weeks I got $415 from the government program and about $100 from the food bank itself. My rent was $450, and this wasn't enough. Somewhere along the line, one of my co-workers got me an extra job, working as a merch girl for a local record company that signed jazz acts. I went to the bar where the pianist or trumpet player was performing and sat in the back at a card table, selling CDs and T-shirts. Most of the bars I worked in were along Frenchmen Street, a brightly lit strip of music clubs that's within stumbling distance of the French Quarter and popular with tourists. Frenchmen Street got its name when five French rebels were shot on the levee during Spanish colonial rule, but this, it turned out, was not a good anecdote to charm tourists with at the bars. I wasn't very good at selling CDs and spent most of my time hanging out with Brandon, a fortyish black guy in thick glasses who kept his hair in tiny, perfect dreadlocks. Brandon was a drug dealer who hung around in jazz clubs selling small amounts of overpriced weed to out-of-towners in sweatshirts. He smiled too much and couldn't remember my name; Brandon always addressed me as "honey." But I liked him anyway, in part because I was lonely and in part because he could do magic tricks. "A magician is the most honest man in the world," he once told me in the back corner of the Blue Nile bar, "because he says he's going to trick you and then he does!" Then Brandon made the ace of clubs appear in an empty beer glass at the next table. Because we were both working, we were usually the only ones there who were sober.

Out-of-towners, I was learning, come to New Orleans either to perform charity or to party. The party industry is bigger. At the jazz shows, I saw a lot of people treating themselves to benders. There were groups of heavy-gutted men down for bachelor party weekends. There were girls in tiny sequined dresses, delightedly calling to each other, "It's so warm out!" It's legal to drink on the street in Louisiana, and in the tourist districts at night there is often a group of people clustered on the sidewalk, chanting, "Shot! Shot! Shot!" Bourbon Street smells like piss and disinfectant. It might sound far-fetched that I ran into volunteers from the food bank while I was there, but actually it happened a lot.

If you spend enough time around the tourists in New Orleans, you start to pick up on patterns. At the food bank and the bar alike, I was told that the city was "magical." People confessed to me that they were "under its spell." This attitude is partly a success of marketing: the city has undertaken a massive and ongoing campaign to make New Orleans a major center of domestic tourism, and it's working. But it's also partly a real phenomenon of the place. This kind of thing isn't easy to explain, but New Orleans is suffused with a seductive nostalgia that is surprisingly difficult to resist; it tricks you into participating in its own mythology in ways that you don't expect it to. Even now, whenever I go there, New Orleans seems to be trying to draw me into some kind of conspiracy of signification. When I lived there, my apartment was on Independence, a one-way street. Two blocks over was Desire, a one-way street going in the opposite direction. It was things like that.

Part of the reason why New Orleans plays so strongly on the imagination is that it looks just as it does in the movies. If you have never been there but have an image in your mind of a building with an iron lacework balcony and gas streetlamp outside, I can assure you that this building exists and that if you ever go there, you can track it down and take a picture of it. Most major avenues are lined with massive live oak trees, whose overhead branches are so broad and twisted that they always look as if they're moving. The mansions on St. Charles Avenue have big, toothy front columns, and in Mid-City the houses are low and painted the colors of makeup. I lived just a few blocks away from the Industrial Canal levee, a long, steep hill that's just wide enough at the top for people to jog or walk their dogs on. On my day off, I liked to climb to the top of it and take my shoes off on the grass. Like all the artificial levees in New Orleans, the Industrial Canal levee was built to keep the city from flooding, but from the top what was clear was how vulnerable the place was. On one side I looked down at the pitched roofs like lily pads below my feet, and on the other I would watch the tugboats on the canal push barges loaded with brightly painted Dumpsters.

In October, Hurricane Sandy started forming off the Atlantic coast. It became clear that the Northeast was in for something bad, and I started getting phone calls from friends in New York, who were worried about me because they had heard "hurricane" and thought that New Orleans might be in trouble. I explained to them that from where I was, Sandy was almost a thousand miles away. When the storm hit New York, in New Orleans it was a sunny day.

A few days later, the food bank had a volunteer group of teenagers scheduled. They were from a synagogue on Long Island, and we would be their first stop on a multisite volunteering tour of the city. In New Orleans, they were going to work in our warehouse, help canvass a neighborhood for a community organization, and raise a house for a Habitat for Humanity project, all before heading back to New York a week later. Before their bus pulled up, I was waiting for them in the lobby, talking to Miss Corinne, the ancient receptionist. "What are they coming down here for?" she asked. "They ought to be helping out back where they're from."

One of the most popular tourist activities in New Orleans is what is called a Katrina Tour. Coach buses pick tourists up from the downtown hotels and drive them into the Lower Ninth Ward to see overgrown lots and houses with weeds growing out of their roofs. A few years ago, Brad Pitt had a series of eco-friendly family homes built in the Ninth Ward, and now the buses drive past those, too. I lived near the canal that separates the Lower Ninth from the Bywater, and I used to see these buses driving over the bridge on my way to work at the food bank. Like everyone else in New Orleans, I was angered by the Katrina Tours, but increasingly the anger felt like something I didn't have much claim to. I had come to New Orleans first as a volunteer and then as a nonprofit worker and had only ever inhabited the city as someone who wanted to confront its pathologies. This was starting to feel like a kind of voluntary rubbernecking.

In the monthly meetings of my AmeriCorps group, there was a good deal of anxiety expressed about the politics of volunteerism. People were uneasy about being white social welfare workers in black communities. We held discussion groups with titles like "Privilege and Practice in Nonprofit Work," where we sat in folding chairs, nodding earnestly at one another; this felt helpful. But there were also people in the nonprofit world who were stridently defensive or condescendingly mollifying, the kinds of people who speak with the sinister optimism of ex-addicts. One of the problems with nonprofit work is that to think of yourself as doing good requires you to be certain of your convictions and your strategies. If you let it, this certainty can do violence to other kinds of understanding; it can transform your good intentions into obliviousness. Places and lives contain all sorts of self-defeating contradictions, and in New Orleans one of the most potent was that many of the people who had come to help the city were also hurting it.

In the cemetery on All Saints' Day, my native friend told me that I should take some of the gris-gris from the gravesides as a souvenir. "They're just going to come in and throw all this stuff away." He was right; as a party town, New Orleans has developed a sanitation system that is almost athletic in its efficiency. At the end of every Mardi Gras parade, you'll see twenty guys in jumpsuits hop off a street-sweeping truck and start picking up discarded beer cans and confetti with little brooms and pails. Soon they would come through the cemeteries and take all the offerings away, too. In the heat, a lot of it was already starting to look wilted: the teddy bear with the heart that said, "Grandma," the carnations wrapped in plastic. I looked at it all but couldn't decide what to steal.

15

M., NORTHERN KENTUCKY

GARY PERCESEPE

M. is a journalist in Kentucky who went through a nasty divorce a few years back. She was drinking white wine in those days and coping with an abusive ex-husband, but she pulled herself together, went through rehab, and raised two kids who adore her. The kids are out of the house now, and M. is six years sober. She lives alone in a small town along the I-75 corridor just south of Cincinnati.

During the recent recession, jobs went away for journalists in the rural part of northern Kentucky where she lives. M. found a job tutoring kids in English that paid $13 an hour, but a new Republican governor was elected and the program was cut. M. strung some freelance work together, found some other part-time work. But none of her three jobs come with benefits or health care. She has some help from her family, and her house is paid off. Of the ten million Americans classified as "the working poor," she is better off than most. Still, in 2009 she made $20,000. In 2010, she made $10,000, well below the poverty line.

I went to see M. just before Christmas. She'd just had some teeth pulled at the "free" clinic. Her mouth looked swollen and puffy. She'd been dreading the oral surgery for weeks, she told me on the phone. Every time she went to the "free" clinic, it cost $30 to be seen. Plus, getting there was a major pain in the ass. The clinic told her she wouldn't be able to drive after the surgery, so a friend drove her, a sixty-mile round-trip.

I was there to provide consolation, M. said when I walked through the door. In the Catholic sense, she added, presenting her tender mouth for a kiss. M. had a Catholic girlhood, eight years of private Catholic schools, and could quote Julian of Norwich from memory, but these days she refers to herself as a pagan and is more likely to invoke the Goddess. She is mad at Jesus, who spoke so glowingly of the poor. There is nothing fucking virtuous about poverty, she groused.

Leaving my house in Ohio to make the drive to see her, I had reached down and picked up from the floor the remains of a case of chicken noodle soup, as an afterthought. When I swung the soup onto her kitchen counter, I sheepishly counted six cans. Oh, she said. You brought soup!

I stayed with her two nights. It snowed both nights. The snow fell faintly through the air, and she took my arm as we walked to my car. The first night I took her to Olive Garden. Her little house is across the street from the railroad tracks, and as we backed out of her gravel driveway, we watched the headlamps play across the tracks. She ordered minestrone, and I was able to get her to eat some pasta. You always loved to feed me, she said. It was true.

The next morning two men showed up in a pickup. One of them was named Tommy. He was a family friend who'd been hitting on her for years, she explained later, though he was married to one of her best friends. With Tommy was a big guy with a long beard and a gray hoodie, who looked like he could have stood in on guitar with ZZ Top. Tommy and his friend hoisted a huge box of food onto M.'s counter, next to the remains of my case of soup.

The food was from the Good Guys Club, Tommy explained. Tommy had dark hair and a pencil mustache. He looked like Squiggy from *Laverne & Shirley*. There was a frozen turkey in the big box and a sack of potatoes. Bread, milk, eggs, peanut butter, cereal. It was a tall box, and it was full. M. squealed with delight. Don't thank us, Tommy said, thank the Good Guys Club.

I asked ZZ Top how long the Good Guys Club had been around. Oh, a long time, he said. He was new to it himself, but Tommy was a long time with the club. Tommy nodded his head. M. asked ZZ if he was still out of work. He said he was. Thirty years with the company and laid off before Christmas. But I expect to go back soon, he said. We all nodded and looked at our shoes.

M. asked me for a dollar. I couldn't imagine why she wanted a dollar at that particular moment, but I gave it to her. Here, she said, waving the dollar bill at Tommy, but Tommy wasn't taking any money. He looked at my BMW parked out front and said to M., If anyone wants to make a donation, they can just give it to the Good Guys Club.

M. used to write short stories. We had met at a writers' conference in Yellow Springs, Ohio. In those days, we were especially fond of Raymond Carver; now M. seemed to me more like a character from one of those stories. That was a dumb thing to think, but I thought it anyway. Seeing her again made me wonder, as I often do, about how we fall into narratives. Whether as readers and writers stories choose us, or we choose stories.

M. writes news articles for the small local paper. Her kids love to see her byline, and she is proud of her work. She feels like she is contributing to the community that she loves, that her work matters and helps people.

The next week I went back to see how she was doing. I saw her neighbor across the street eyeballing me as I got out of my car. Oh, M. says, yeah, him. Retired railroad guy. He's been after me for years to sleep with him. He's offered me $600 a month. He looks that way at all my boyfriends.

But I'm not your boyfriend, I said. She gave me the look, stuck out her tongue. Doesn't matter, M. said. To him you are.

The next morning she was up at first light and out the door, saying something about the magazine. I assumed she was out working on a feature story, but when she returned to the house four hours later, she told me she'd been stacking magazines at Kmart. She helps off-load the magazines from a truck. Then she loads the magazines into a shopping cart and wheels the cart onto the floor. She stacks and shelves the magazines, and she hates it. But what the fuck, I need the money, she said.

Stacking magazines paid $8 per hour. This was one of her three part-time jobs. M. told me she had a bead on a fourth. She was hoping that the local paper would be able to hire her full-time, but it didn't look good. She had interviewed for an editorial position in Cincinnati, editing a newsletter for a homeless coalition. She'd be terrific at it, and she is fully qualified for the work. I happened to know the executive director, so I called his cell phone and left a reference on voice mail, but she never heard anything back from him.

M. has an overactive-bladder condition. A simple procedure would fix it, but it would cost $200 up front, and there is the drive to consider, the sixty miles round-trip to the "free" clinic. This is the thing about rural poverty that I always forget (I am a city person). All the services are so far away. M. asked me if I had $200. I didn't. (I was going through a divorce myself, and money was tight.) She waved her hand and said, Oh, that's okay. Then I guess I won't get it. She didn't look disappointed. It was a long drive, the surgery would eat up a whole workday, and she'd been living with the bladder thing for years, she said. She'd get by.

M. wakes up thinking about being poor. She goes to sleep worrying about the bills. A robo-call from Kohl's department store comes every hour on the hour, wanting payment. I ask her how much she owes the department store. Five hundred, she says, matter-of-factly. She bought some Christmas presents, recently, for her kids. I wince when she says this, and she flashes on me and shakes her fine Irish head and says, Stop it. Don't fucking pity me. What, are you here to tell my story? Ha! Forget it. I'm one of the lucky ones, and we both fucking know it. Give it a rest.

But I can't. I think about the $200 that would fix her bladder. It angers me that I cannot fix things for her. I am not Mr. Fixit. Another one of Carver's characters.

A decade after the war in Afghanistan began, we were still spending $190 million on it every day. Who knows how much more in Iraq (the war no one would talk about any longer)? What could even a portion of that sum do if it were applied to the health concerns of people like M.? Or invested in job creation in northern Kentucky and Ohio?

I worked hard for Obama in 2008, as did many of my neighbors. In the precincts where we labored, day after day, door by door, and long into election night, we swamped McCain. We helped deliver Ohio, and the election. We were fighting for something.

But not this.

I used to work for a nonprofit organization whose mission was to reduce poverty in our community. We started a program called School of the Streets that mentored kids in the arts. Most of the kids wanted to sing or dance, but a few wrote poetry or painted. They would meet with their mentors once a week to work at their craft and to talk about what it took to be successful. The mentors were a talented group of musicians, teachers, ministers, social workers, and retired folks who enjoyed sharing their lives with kids. The program culminated each year in a talent showcase. Over a thousand people would show up for this event, and we often featured a "name" gospel group to headline the evening, which thrilled the kids and their parents. But we lost our funding during the recession when grant money dried up, along with everything else.

During the Clinton administration when welfare reform was instituted and the president was going around talking about all of the jobs that had been created under his administration, I heard a guy tell a joke. I liked the joke so much I started telling it myself when I was called on to speak about poverty at some civic function in our community.

The joke goes like this. The president (pick any president, any era) was speaking at a banquet in a ballroom of a famous hotel touting how many millions of jobs had been created under his watch. And everyone was applauding the president. Three million new jobs! And one old man who was working the event, busing tables, is heard to mutter, Yeah, and I got three of 'em.

Poverty takes many forms. Material poverty is not the only kind. There is spiritual poverty, civic poverty. I ask myself, what is the poverty in me?

I think of M. and her neighbor and the $200 she needs for her surgery and the way she works hard every day, and I think about her hands, which cradled my head last week as we talked long into the night about the way things were with us, once upon a time, when things seemed more hopeful, as if a future might open for us one day, and recall the way she rubs lotion into her feet each night, which are sore from standing on the days she stacks magazines early in the winter morning. I would like to find the guy who told that joke about the president's job creation and kick his ass.

I called M. today. She told me she was giving serious thought to letting the retired railroad neighbor across the street move in with her. She was obsessing about money, and the Kohl's calls kept coming. He'll want sex, M. said, and that's sort of repulsive, but he's not such a bad guy. He's been a good neighbor.

16

SIX HOUSES IN HYDE PARK

SAM BIEDERMAN

My family moved a lot when I was growing up. We didn't move around the world like a military family or around the country like a salesman's family. (I didn't even know what these two categories of family were, much less how we were or were not like them.) Instead, we hopped around a small rectangle of our small neighborhood, Hyde Park. The borders of our world were Fiftieth Street in the north and Fifty-Eighth Street to the south, Dorchester Avenue in the west, and, just five blocks away, the eastern limit of all of Chicago, Lake Shore Drive.

In 1983, the year I was born, we moved to 5000 East End, a Gothic high-rise along Lake Michigan. My sister, Lucy, was two. My father was a young real estate lawyer who practiced at a firm in the Loop fifteen minutes from Hyde Park on the northbound Metra Electric train. My mother had grown up in 5000 East End, and my grandparents still lived in the same ninth-floor apartment.

I loved the building basement's endless blue-gray hallways of narrow-doored storage closets. Its hypnotizing laundry room was home to vending machines with Coke so cold it didn't even taste sweet. But I barely remember our apartment; the clearer images in my hazy early memories tell me that I was far more fixated on our neighboring buildings.

Five Thousand East End was on the northern outskirts of Hyde

Park, in a four-block sub-neighborhood called Indian Village, after the tribal names of the skyscrapers in the area: the Chippewa, the Narragansett, the Algonquin, and my favorite, the Powhatan. Among my earliest recollections is my excitement at crossing two windswept blocks to the Powhatan, whose front door was gilt on glass and doorbells were inlaid with mother-of-pearl. The Powhatan had a doorman and an elevator man, and in the elevator there was a dignified little bench. And more than that—much more than that—the building had a pool.

A family in the Powhatan collected Joseph Cornell boxes, which my mother once took Lucy and me to see. Lining a dark dining room, the boxes held frightening arrangements of clock faces, newspaper cuttings, and birds, which I was afraid might start moving. Looking at the boxes was like listening to adults talk to each other, overhearing some words I couldn't understand but whose feeling I could begin to guess at.

Given how many times we moved, it's clear that I wasn't the only member of my family more interested in other people's houses than my own. Like the model Hyde Parkers they were, my parents read the weekly real estate listings printed on the back of the *Hyde Park Herald* like a gossip sheet. They were restless, but cautiously so. As often as we moved, we never risked a loss—which is, I suppose, the essence of upward mobility.

When I was in nursery school we moved to the Stein Building on Dorchester Avenue between Fifty-Eighth and Fifty-Ninth Streets, a safer, greener part of the neighborhood hugging the main campus of the University of Chicago. We spent only a year in this fifteen-story concrete tower set on a squat brick plinth. Our apartment overlooked the athletic field of the university's Laboratory Schools, where my sister and I (and decades earlier, my mother, my uncles, and my great-aunt) went to school.

From the third floor of the Stein Building, Lucy and I watched high schoolers playing soccer from the apartment's broad, west-facing windows. We watched with our housekeeper, Ruth, as our parents drove off to a private vacation. We watched my mother drive home from the hospital to tell us that our great-grandfather Sam had died.

Harold Washington, Chicago's first black mayor, also died while we lived in this apartment. That day, I came home from my half day at nursery school to find Ruth crying on the couch. Later, over a dessert of pound cake, I asked my mother why the mayor had died.

"He had a heart attack," she said.

How did people get heart attacks?

"He ate too much pound cake," she said. Understanding that it was somehow lethal, I didn't dare eat pound cake for years afterward, deep into the two-decade mayoral administration of Richard M. Daley, which ended in 2011.

Because Lucy was at school then for a full day, I got to spend a lot of time alone with my mother driving around the neighborhood, going to the grocery, the drive-through bank, the dry cleaner, and, for a treat, the Fifty-Third Street McDonald's, which was constantly getting held up. I don't recall ever being out of the house without my mother. Once I ventured into the hallway to look at the elevators.

"Psst," my mother said. "Where are you going?"

I had never heard the sound "psst" before, and I asked her what it meant. "It means come back to me," she said. I felt awful that she thought I was leaving, and I climbed into her lap.

From the start, we knew that the Stein apartment was only temporary. We were spending only a year there while we waited to close on our next place. The town house at 5522 South Harper Avenue sat a quarter mile northeast from the Stein Building in a row of identical town houses, on a block of the same.

Our new block and the four blocks surrounding it had landed in the late 1960s like Dorothy's house in Oz, flattening old tenements as part of what was then the nation's most ambitious urban renewal project. At the time, after weighing a move out of the city entirely, the University of Chicago decided to stay put instead in its crummy neighborhood and get rid of everything it didn't like. Chicago had no Jane Jacobs to stand in the institution's way, and so scores of town houses went up on Harper. Like its siblings, our house was three stories of khaki-colored brick, with a sunken first-floor lounge, two second-floor porches, one in front and one in back, and three businesslike, rectangular bedrooms upstairs. Each house had a little front yard and a bigger backyard and shared a common green on every other block. It was urban order by way of Levittown.

I can't say if this massive, top-down urban project destroyed any sense of community: I was still young enough that my world was confined mostly to the walls of our house. It was on Harper that when running circles around the living room, Lucy and I tipped over a bust of Abraham Lincoln, breaking off the nose. (The bust had been given to my rich great-grandpa Sam as a token of admiration from a business associate, who spontaneously reached into his file cabinet, pulled out the sculpture of history's greatest Illinoisan, and thrust it at my great-grandfather. "Here," he said. "I've got a ton of 'em.")

Still, Chicago was pushing itself into the corners of my vision. The house at 5522 South Harper was on the walking route of Throckmorton, who, without being too old-fashioned about it, was the local madman. He walked by our front door every morning around sunrise, carrying a freshly bloodied handkerchief and a closed umbrella, held upright. Hyde Park was full of homeless people, panhandlers, and familiar drug addicts who would scream at you as you walked past them on the street. (My father blamed their presence on the University of Chicago students, who tolerated and supported them with handouts.) But Throckmorton was distinct. Before he had lost his mind, he had been a scientist at the university. Before you saw him, you could hear him coming, singing his song: "Hey, loser, loser, loser, sexy, sexy, sexy, looo-serrrrr, looser!"

Driven by either principle or the fact that he just hadn't grown up in the neighborhood, my father did not take local eccentrics like Throckmorton in stride. He seemed opposed to the neighborhood's customary policy of salutary neglect. So Dad didn't laugh at Throckmorton, nor just quietly shake his head when his car window was smashed and his radio lifted, nor let teenagers' drunken Halloween antics go un-yelled at. He had grown up on the comfortable, suburban North Shore of Lake Michigan, and he had different expectations. I used to think that his submitting to live in Hyde Park was his labor of love for my mother.

Dad was also unhappy with the house on Harper in its own right. He simply didn't like the sparse modernism of the place. Starting when we lived in the I. M. Pei house, he would take me and Lucy driving through the South Side's un-renewed neighborhoods: we'd go west on Garfield Boulevard and north on Martin Luther King Jr. Drive between Hyde Park and the Loop. These broad streets were the scaffolding of Daniel Burnham's 1909 Plan of Chicago, and, but for the public park that ran along the lakefront, all that was left. The boulevards were blocks-wide, Champs-Élysées-style thoroughfares, with browning, trash-strewn lawns separating the north- and southbound lanes. Century-old mansions, either abandoned or carved up for apartments, lined the empty streets.

Dad loved the houses, and I think he loved the decay too. They were redbrick boats with slate turrets and Italianate flourishes in granite (also boarded-up doors and windows tagged with graffiti). They were the legacy of a city bursting with entrepreneurial genius and immigrant energy. Symbols of nineteenth-century Chicago, the center of the industrial world, they shamed the fumbling, postindustrial city Chicago had become. The 1960s, 1970s, and 1980s were rough on Chicago: civil unrest was followed by white flight, and the city rotted from inside out, hemorrhaging money, population, and influence.

My parents were very clear about why this had happened. First, when Mayor Daley's father, Richie senior, was mayor, he segregated the city by building expressways to separate poor neighborhoods from rich ones. He let places like King Drive go to pot. Second, Ronald Reagan was president, and he only cared about money. Finally, there weren't enough people like us, who were principled enough not to move to the suburbs even when things got rough.

The heavy hand of the University of Chicago had somewhat stayed this decay in Hyde Park, although we certainly had our share of crime and disorder. By the time Dad was taking us on drives through the wasted neighborhoods, the roaring 1990s were about to shake the whole city out of its mid-century torpor. We were looking to move for the last time.

In 1989, a realtor showed my parents a place that shared a backyard with Louis Farrakhan, then our neighborhood's most famous resident. My father couldn't resist looking over the high back fence. There, he told me and Lucy, he saw two lions resting in the garden. We bought the house around the corner.

Until we moved in, 5736 South Blackstone Avenue had for decades been occupied by a woman with the unforgettable name of Mrs. Raven I. McDavid. During Mrs. McDavid's tour of the house, Lucy and I fell down the curving basement steps, and upstairs we fell into hysterics over the wiggling of a spring doorstop, which we pretended was the flapping penis of a boy running to catch a school bus. The house had a back and front staircase, a laundry chute, odd dormers on the third floor, and a windy attic with nails sticking up from the floor. Lucy and I approved without reservation.

The house at 5736 Blackstone was in the quietest, safest part of the neighborhood, on a tree-shaded block of other town houses, only two blocks from our school. It wasn't on Throckmorton's route and was close enough to the University of Chicago campus to be patrolled by the university's private police. The place was big, big enough that when our brother, Felix, was born after we moved in, Lucy and I were able to avoid his crying by decamping from our bedrooms on the second floor to two vacant ones on the third.

Our new home was one of the last of its kind: an underpriced, decaying professor's house. Property prices had fallen along with the white population of the South Side in the 1960s. Low-paid university faculty who stayed in Hyde Park, out of convenience or a political belief in integration, snapped up mansions and town houses they could suddenly afford to buy, if not maintain. Now, thirty years later, it was time to start cashing in.

All of which is to say, the place needed work. In the first six years we lived there, my parents renovated the kitchen, the dining room, and then the living room; redid the second floor, which included removing a wall and installing rows of library shelves; redesigned the master bedroom; renovated all five bathrooms; made the prehistoric basement habitable; tore down and rebuilt the back porch; overhauled the back and front yards; and painted and wallpapered and tuck-pointed and did whatever else was needed. It seemed as if there were always someone redoing something in the house: Norman Letourneau, the painter, who smoked his cigar in the house; Ed Malm, the carpenter, who drove in from Indiana with his movie-star-handsome son John; Jack Spicer, the gardener, who seemed to have an instinctive understanding of what made Felix such an angry toddler.

And then, when the house burned, they did it all again, and all at once.

By the time we had our fire, we had lived at 5736 for nearly seven years, longer than we had lived anywhere else. I was twelve, Lucy fourteen, and Felix six. My father ran upstairs in the middle of the night to shake Lucy and me awake; my mother and brother were already on their way out of the house. I sat next to my brother and sister in the car and wailed as I watched flames curling out of my bedroom windows onto the roof.

The fire started in our neighbors' house as an accident of their own fevered renovation, but our house sustained just as much damage and had to be gutted and the inside rebuilt. This process took about six months, during which we rented an apartment in an old building by the lake called Jackson Towers that was—ridiculous, I think, is the right word for it.

We had a piss-elegant two-story unit with a spiral staircase up to the bedrooms, where, unlike in our thoughtfully decorated house on Blackstone, crummy rental furniture was thrown any old place.

The apartment had a plugged-up fireplace with fake logs illuminated by Sterno cans. And the building itself was in a no-man's-land, a part of the neighborhood you couldn't safely walk to at night.

But Jackson Towers did have one thing going for it: its views. From the living room, you could see the lakeshore stretching south to Indiana and, just below, the copper corkscrews topping the dome of the neoclassical Museum of Science and Industry, a well-kempt relic of the 1893 Columbian Exposition. From the west windows, you could see the whole South Side, broad and flat and infinite. Lucy, Felix, and I had spent so much of our lives in dark town houses that the brightness of the place seemed like a real liability. The apartment's owners had it on the market while we were living there, and Lucy used to walk around the apartment, squinting and saying, "This place gets so much natural light—how are they ever going to sell it?"

After six months, we got to go back home. It took six more months to finally complete all the renovations, but the house came out better than it was before the fire. No scars either, except for one: in late March, the melting ice on the roof stirs some old ghosts, and for a few days the closets on the third floor start to smell like smoke.

Around the time we moved back into 5736 Blackstone, the city had begun to do some of its own renovating. Through the 1990s, Mayor Daley blew up the failed public housing high-rises along Lake Shore Drive. He set up planters full of native prairie grasses in every neighborhood, including the poor ones. Having fallen in love with the semi-robotic street-cleaning machines he saw on a visit to Paris, he bought a fleet of them for Chicago. To capstone his career, the mayor built a giant park over the ancient train yards between the Loop and the lake (it came in $325 million over budget and four years late, making its already ridiculous name of Millennium Park additionally comical). By the end of the decade, Chicago's reputation for being beautiful started to rival its reputation for being corrupt, dirty, dangerous, and segregated. Rest assured, the city is beset by problems—endemic violence, crime, inequality, and the ever-present scourge of political corruption. But it's a safer place than it was when I was born.

We stopped moving, and I grew older in the same house; my parents still live at 5736 Blackstone. I got a driver's license and drove up and down Lake Shore Drive, up and down the Kennedy Expressway. But my mobility only showed how alien my city was, full of neighborhoods that kept their secrets. There was no room for me in Pilsen's Polish-Mexican mix. I never felt at ease among the cool art students in Ukrainian Village. The vast West Side was a hot-asphalt mystery to me. And even in my first, tentative explorations of Boystown, it seemed to me I had little in common with the guys leaning against the walls of the clubs. They were farm boys, thrilled to be in a lively, crowded place called Chicago.

Maybe it's just that old chestnut about Chicago's being a city of neighborhoods, maybe it's because my parents saw in Hyde Park a whole city's worth of opportunities, but I never felt more like a Chicagoan than I did like a Hyde Parker. Driving around the city was fine, but I liked coming back to Hyde Park. You knew you were back in the neighborhood officially when you drove over the satisfying bump on Forty-Seventh Street Bridge. My Chicago is as narrow and as deep as a well.

At my family's final home, the town house on Blackstone, my bedroom window had a view of the street, but you couldn't really see anything except the cars parked below. I preferred lying on my sister's bed after she left for college and looking out her window. Lucy's room was in the back of the house. Framed by the branches of the tall trees in the backyard, the steeples of churches and the tops of tall apartment buildings were visible. Below that were our neighbors' backyards. And sometimes the tenants in the building next door would start moving from room to room, as purposeful and mysterious as the birds in a Cornell box.

17

MILWAUKEE'S GILDED AGE
AND AFTERMATH

GREG AFINOGENOV

In February 2011, Governor Scott Walker of Wisconsin took a phone call from the blogger Ian Murphy, who claimed to be the far-right billionaire and Walker benefactor David Koch. Trying to play Walker for laughs, Murphy listened as Walker detailed his strategy for his infamous and successful assault on collective bargaining rights for all public-sector workers except police and firefighters. Murphy suggested planting provocateurs among the union ranks. Walker said they had considered it but dismissed it because the public was already turning against the unions anyway. As Murphy tried to wrap up the joke, Walker continued, comparing himself to Ronald Reagan at the fall of the Berlin Wall. When the transcript of the call went public and Walker survived a recall vote anyway, the governor claimed the call as the moment when he knew "God had a plan for me."

It is easy to see Walker's intransigence—and the popular groundswell that brought him to power—as part of a nationwide political conjuncture taking shape in the recession years: the rise of a new grassroots conservatism, an emerging popular hostility to neo-Keynesian economic policy, and widespread anger at politicians perceived to be part of a stagnant establishment. But despite the remarkable uniformity of the Tea Party's reactionary rhetoric, its politics remain local, and its antecedents go back much further than the 1980s. The comparison that was on everyone's mind was with the Gilded Age, when individual capitalists concentrated the reins of political and social power in their hands. In Wisconsin, the era arrived slightly late and was represented above all by one man: Mayor David S. Rose of Milwaukee, who came to power in 1898. Rose's corruption, lavish lifestyle, and kowtowing to municipal utility magnates were legendary; the most lasting legacy of his administration was a massive bribery scandal involving streetcar contracts. Walker, for his part, has become ensnared in controversy after hiring the son of a prominent construction lobbyist to head a state bureau responsible for environmental regulation. And his sniveling response to Murphy left little doubt about who calls the shots in his administration.

In Milwaukee, Rose's decade-long reign—punctuated by a two-year stint by Sherburn Becker, "Boy Mayor of Milwaukee," best known for his flashy cars and pink "Becker Hat"—came to an unanticipated end with an overwhelming Socialist victory in 1910. Milwaukee's Socialists, who were tied closely to the city's enormous population of German-speaking industrial workers, had gradually increased their share of the vote as the city industrialized and modernized in the 1890s and first decade of the twentieth century. Although they subscribed in principle to the goal of international social revolution, under the leadership of Victor Berger (who became the first Socialist congressman in 1911), they became firmly entrenched in electoral politics. In fact, they outdid their competitors: with an army of "bundle brigades" who distributed campaign literature and a network of well-organized locals and branches, they were a kind of forebear of the Obama presidential campaign. As Socialists, naturally, they stood for the rights of workers and the eight-hour day, but as it turned out, other aspects of their platform proved more decisive. In Milwaukee, a city riven by official corruption and dominated by leading industrialists, the Socialist Party above all stood for clean, honest, and efficient government.

In early-twentieth-century America—even before the Bolshevik

Revolution—no party calling itself Socialist could be allowed to escape the connotations unscathed. A 1910 Republican campaign ad declared that "Victor Berger promises, if his international party gains control, a bloody revolution. Victory for the Socialists means a conflict with the red flag of blood-lust, borne by such men as Berger . . . The time to kill the serpent of Socialism is now! Tomorrow may be too late!" Middle-class voters were unimpressed with the charge that the "many-headed reptile of Socialism" was more threatening than traditional politics and swept Mayor Emil Seidel, along with a broad slate of other Socialist candidates, into municipal office.

They were proved right. Once in power, the Socialists neither organized the working class for revolution nor threatened the Catholic Church (although Victor Berger made some loud anticlerical noises). It is true that the Milwaukee police, unlike that of almost any other municipality, was ordered to protect striking workers instead of shooting them. For the most part, however, the city's new masters showed that they deserved their derisive new nickname, "sewer Socialists": they cleaned up public utilities, established vocational schools, and expanded the park system. And they succeeded in cleaning up city government, too—so well, in fact, that they would have likely made further gains in the election of 1912 had the Democrats and the Republicans not realized the precariousness of their position and joined forces against them. The "Nonpartisan" reign proved equally short-lived. Four years later, the Socialist city attorney, Dan Hoan, became mayor, a position he was to occupy for the next twenty-four years.

The paradox of Hoan's mayoralty was his enormous popularity and influence in a city that had rapidly turned against the Socialists. As the United States entered World War I in 1917, support for the Socialist Party collapsed: not only were many of the Socialists proud Germans, but they supported a platform of pacifism and internationalism that was no longer acceptable in the jingoistic climate of the period. Victor Berger's *Milwaukee Leader* was one of the first publications to be targeted for suppression under the new

Espionage Act, and Berger ran his second campaign for Congress out of federal prison. He was popular enough among Milwaukee's voters that he was reelected, then reelected again after Congress refused to seat him in 1919. The Supreme Court eventually overturned the verdict against him, and he served in Congress from 1923 to 1929. Other Socialist politicians were less lucky, and Hoan never had the luxury of a city council majority to support his decisions; by the end of his last term, not a single Socialist remained.

As a result, Hoan and the rest of the Socialists focused again on what they did best: run a clean, efficient municipal government with a focus on public amenities and utilities. Everything Hoan did for the city, he saw in terms of helping the workers in whose name he governed. "Whether the worker be one who earns his livelihood by the sweat of his brow or a teacher in the public schools, or a small merchant or a member of the so-called white-collared class, he is very vitally and actively interested in clean government," he announced in a rather self-congratulatory book called *City Government*. "Workers are necessarily interested in ideal health conditions in the city. They cannot live in suburbs . . . All workers are interested in maintaining high standards in public school education . . . Workers are interested in parks and playgrounds, the health-building and character-building centers of the city." The Socialists' platform in 1932 was the same sort of mishmash of left-wing rhetoric and centrist practice, in which "the transition to a more humane system" entailed a tax credit for low-income homeowners.

Depressed Tea Party–era progressives tempted to find in Hoan a figure of nostalgia would be alarmed to learn that municipal debt was one of his principal targets. "A policy of extravagant borrowing," he insisted, "is the ruin of the entire municipal structure." He considered the "hard but sound road" by which the city "conserved and marshaled its finances" to finally free itself from debt in 1933 to be one of his greatest successes—a struggle he framed, in his characteristic rhetorical manner, as a battle against the bankers and the industrialists who were "not inclined to favor a pay-as-you-go policy." Hoan's attempt to run the city on a cash basis was not a historical accident or a vagary of the political context. The point of Socialist rule in Milwaukee, and the essence of its appeal, was that it could deliver better government and better services for less money. The consequence was a tightly wound and precisely balanced fiscal machine that performed well even as the city was devastated by Prohibition (which drove its famous breweries out of business) and the Great Depression.

Hoan's apparatus could deal with these crises, even when, as between 1940 and 1948, it was not run by a Socialist. Milwaukee had been an industrial metropolis since the last third of the nineteenth century; it was no stranger to busts and depressions. Industries had no choice but to rebuild, and when they rebuilt, they inevitably brought fresh waves of immigrants, jobs, and capital investment to the city. In short, for all Hoan's claims to the contrary, the large durable-goods manufacturers that employed the lion's share of Milwaukee workers were just as invested as he was in the city's success. Good government and ample city services kept the workforce growing and content, and the city's financial situation made it an excellent credit risk.

World War II promised a return to lasting prosperity for the first time since Prohibition. The enormous demand for machine tools and other durable goods produced by Milwaukee employers brought with it renewed employment needs and, with European immigration shrinking drastically, the need for a new population of workers to fill them. The ideal candidates turned out to be blacks, both independent migrants and recruits, brought to the city from the Deep South by industrial recruiting agents. Although Milwaukee had black citizens and black neighborhoods before this, they were not numerically significant until the 1940s. Even then, earlier clashes between unionized workers and black strikebreakers had shown how much industry could benefit from exploiting this population: deprived of access to unions, blacks would work for less money and in worse conditions than any of Milwaukee's existing social groups. It helped, too, that they could be more easily fired and replaced. In Milwaukee as in other large northern cities, it was this initial confrontation between, on the one side, the white working class and organized labor, which had fought so successfully for better working conditions, and, on the other, black migrants, who wanted the opportunities only industrial work could bring, that launched the still unresolved struggle for civil rights.

At the same time, there was little reason to doubt that as long as the alliance between industry, labor, and city government could be preserved, the pattern long established in Milwaukee and made efficient and streamlined by the Socialists could not fail completely. It would lead one wave of immigrants after another from menial unskilled labor to low-skill, well-remunerated union jobs and their children into colleges and white-collar careers. Fueled by industrial development, the rising tide really would lift all boats, and the city would remain a sterling exemplar of efficient and provident government. What Hoan and his successors could not have known was that the period of industrial recovery that accompanied World War II would be the city's last.

After the war, during the still relatively placid tenure of the Socialist Frank Zeidler (1948–60), it gradually became clear that the city was changing. Predictably enough (or so it seems in retrospect), the workers who were so necessary to industrial growth in wartime were easy to discard after the need for tanks and airplanes disappeared. The ranks of unemployed and underpaid black migrants began to establish themselves in what was now called the "inner core" of the city, north and west of the bend in the Milwaukee River. As black neighborhoods grew, they inherited increasingly dilapidated housing stock from departing whites. These were the skilled workers, craftsmen, and foremen who had formed the core of the Socialist voting bloc, the same people whom Hoan believed could not live in suburbs. Of course, when they got the chance, they showed with their feet that they could live in suburbs just fine. Independent of the city, with low taxes and ironclad closed housing codes, the wealthy ring of suburbs around Milwaukee expanded in both population and political power, and the people who filled them no longer had any interest in Milwaukee city government. Demographically, too, the white population of the city had less and less in common with the blacks who replaced them: the children of Socialist factory operatives were Republican and centrist Democrat white-collar workers and professionals.

Although these developments were only beginning in the mid-1950s, there was already a growing sense that blacks in the inner core were experiencing pressures rather unlike those felt by the Irish in the Bloody Third Ward in the late nineteenth century or the South Side Poles in the early twentieth. It took a series of increasingly violent and large-scale clashes between inner-core residents and police to bring this to the attention of city authorities, who up to that point had either promoted the traditional nostrum of "acculturating" black migrants or ignored the problem entirely. In 1959, Zeidler (who had been accused of being a "nigger-lover" during his mayoral campaign) offered a slightly more serious response; he organized several commissions to study "the problems of the inner core," which eventually resulted in a widely publicized report. The timing was convenient: by the time the report was completed, Zeidler was almost out of office, and his successor—the Democrat Henry Maier—was left to fix problems Zeidler had not even begun to address.

Despite his enormous popularity and staying power (he was to remain in office for twenty-eight years), Maier was far from the ideal candidate for the job of fixing the inner core. Whether or not he was a crypto-racist who deliberately held back the movement for civil rights in Milwaukee—or, indeed, whether or not his dilatory tactics were influenced by political calculations in a city where the segregationist presidential candidate George Wallace was to capture a third of the vote—it was clear that Maier did not see civil rights or engagement with the black community as major priorities. In 1962, for instance, he organized a social development commission aimed at addressing inner-core problems. One of its members, a sausage maker named Fred Lins, was soon quoted in the press as saying, "Negroes look so much alike that you can't identify the ones that commit the crime" and "An awful mess of them have an IQ of nothin'." Maier promptly circled the wagons; even in his 1993 autobiography, he was still making excuses for Lins, whom he painted as a victim of media scandalmongering.

Unable or unwilling to do much about civil rights, Maier fought desperately for the cause he actually believed in: mitigating the city's inability to fend for itself economically, as it did in the prewar era, at a time when both industries and middle-class white taxpayers were departing for the outlying suburbs. Maier used the opportunities provided by federal initiatives in the 1960s and 1970s to attract federal money to the city, especially in the form of urban renewal funds. He also began a desperate attempt to annex suburban land and force the suburbs to contribute to city coffers. His most prized effort was the creation of an industrial land bank from a large tract of annexed land in the northwest of Milwaukee County. Maier hoped that this would encourage industries to remain within Milwaukee city limits (and hence remain city taxpayers) even as they escaped the congested downtown. By redeveloping downtown areas and promoting festivals such as Summerfest, Maier intended to keep the city solvent and preserve at least some civic investment.

Meanwhile, in the 1960s, Milwaukee's nascent civil rights movement turned its focus to open housing, under the leadership of the white Catholic priest Father James Groppi. Both Milwaukee and its suburbs held to racially restrictive housing policies, making it almost impossible for blacks to live outside the increasingly blighted inner core. When Groppi and a contingent of civil rights activists marched across the Menominee River (from the inner core to the working-class South Side) in 1967, they were greeted by thousands of whites who shouted racist slogans and threw bricks at them. Similar incidents occurred throughout the city as pressure on the Common Council to pass an open housing ordinance grew. Activists accused Mayor Maier of avoiding responsibility for the legislation, and he in turn attempted to denounce them as irrational fanatics. For Maier, open housing became yet another battlefield in his endless struggle against the suburbs: if he refused to support a citywide open housing ordinance, it was because he was pressuring the suburbs to pass equivalent legislation. His motivations might or might not have been noble, but it is apparent that he wanted the suburbs to take some responsibility for what he clearly regarded as a toxic black underclass that was rapidly taking over much of Milwaukee proper. His attacks on the media's role in the conflict emphasized that a city-only provision was in the interests of insulated suburban editors, who could disparage the city's racist housing policies from the comfort of their own segregated communities. For his part, Groppi, although he supported a county-wide ordinance as well, stressed the necessity of immediate action: the needs of Milwaukee's black residents had to outweigh Maier's pet strategic priorities.

The open housing fight within Milwaukee was rendered moot by the Civil Rights Act of 1968, which included strong open housing provisions—and should therefore have been a major victory for both Maier and the activists who opposed him. In practical terms, however, the struggle ended in failure. According to a study by Richard Florida's Martin Prosperity Institute, Milwaukee is the country's most segregated large metropolitan area. With the exception of the northwestern territory Maier annexed to the city during his tenure, the demographic map of Milwaukee remains, as it was in the 1960s, a classic donut of wealthy, overwhelmingly white suburbs surrounding the economically depressed urban core. It is also clear that the late 1960s represented an important missed opportunity for cooperation between city government and activists. Maier was too blinkered to perceive the influence of structural discrimination and the racialized nature of the city's economic decline; Groppi's tactics eventually failed to effectively convert suburban complacency (the alternative to outright white supremacism) into positive change. Their common failure has shaped the outline of contemporary Milwaukee.

The economic changes of the late twentieth and early twenty-first centuries provided the other component of this outline. As an industrial metropolis, Milwaukee was already declining in the 1970s, helped along by the recessionary climate. It was only in the 1980s, however, that deindustrialization began in earnest across the Rust Belt. Nearly all of the manufacturing companies and breweries that had anchored the city's economy went bankrupt, moved their operations elsewhere, or introduced large-scale automation to save on labor costs. Even if the new black working class had been in a position to take advantage of them, the well-paying but low-skill jobs that had sustained previous working-class generations were simply no longer available. Poverty, unemployment, and crime grew rapidly, and, even worse for Maier's vision of the city, the Reagan administration drastically reduced federal subsidies to urban areas. (In Maier's memoir, the city-oriented Nixon is a hero, while Reagan is essentially a criminal.) Beyond the mayor's personal preoccupations, the loss of federal funding had significant long-term effects: working-class white neighborhoods had benefited much more from federal funding than the black inner core, and now the opportunity to right the balance had vanished.

John Norquist, the Democrat who succeeded Maier in 1988, anticipated the third-way appeasement tactics of the Clinton era. He denounced Maier's practice of rooting out and exploiting any available source of federal funding as "tin-cup federalism." Instead, he relished the title of "fiscally conservative socialist" and offered the city a new age in which progressive policies were married to free-market solutions. The most immediately visible feature of his policies, however, was an embrace of the New Urbanism, an architectural and urban-design philosophy that emphasized mixed-use, low-rise pedestrian zones and traditionalist aesthetics. Norquist was opposed to freeways and helped demolish an unfinished freeway spur that had served as a lasting reminder of the failures of postwar urban planning. While his preferred solution—light-rail—was never brought to fruition, he did oversee the creation of notable new architectural developments, such as the Santiago Calatrava–designed wing of the Milwaukee Art Museum that opened in 2001.

Norquist's New Urbanist style, which primarily targeted the downtown and wealthy East Side areas, went hand in hand with an increased emphasis (which continued under Norquist's successor Tom Barrett) on making the city attractive to young professionals and the creative class. Milwaukee was now presented as a city that had successfully negotiated the transition from an industrial to a postindustrial economy. To replace the continually declining manufacturing sector, the city attempted to attract service, technology, and knowledge-based industries, particularly health and financial services. To a certain extent, this succeeded, because companies like Aurora Health Care are now among the city's largest employers. What it resoundingly failed to achieve was the citywide diffusion of walkable New Urbanist affluence: the creative class was increasingly concentrated in a handful of white-dominated enclaves surrounded by urban decay. The Norquist era was not good news for the city's poor, especially urban blacks. Those who were employed were overrepresented in what low-wage manufacturing jobs remained, and the catastrophic situation in the Milwaukee Public Schools system left few graduates in a position to take advantage of the growth in professional jobs. As it was elsewhere in the country, for many black men incarceration turned out to be the only alternative to unemployment.

The Clinton era brought Milwaukee two high-profile attempts to address the problem: school vouchers and the Wisconsin Works (W-2) welfare-reform program. Both were conceived in the context of conservative political dominance and a renewed emphasis on the power of free markets. The object in both cases was to improve outcomes for target populations and reduce government spending on social programs, though not necessarily bureaucracy, because the monitoring these programs require often implies an equally cumbersome support apparatus.

The Milwaukee Parental Choice Program, supported enthusiastically by Mayor Norquist, was intended to allow some parents to pull their children out of public schools and use government-issued vouchers to fund private school educations, including religious and charter schools as well as former public schools reopened as charters. Although studies suggest that the program has been fiscally beneficial for the city government, none of the measures of academic achievement appear to have improved in any noticeable way among the students who participate in the program. The charter schools that the program supports, meanwhile, are plagued with constant scandals revolving around mismanagement and misappropriation of funds. The public schools are doing no better: although vouchers were supposed to encourage public-private competition, reform efforts have repeatedly failed to deliver meaningful results.

The situation with the W-2 program is little different. At the time of its introduction, it was hailed as a revolutionary statewide attempt to replace welfare with temporary aid intended to encourage participants to return to work ("workfare"), and it served as the blueprint for the federal welfare-reform legislation passed under Clinton in 1996. Initially, it proved successful at reducing the welfare rolls—an outcome cited to the exclusion of any other indicators—but subsequent progress has stalled, and participants have generally shifted to other forms of aid (such as food stamps). In the meantime, the program's term of eligibility has expanded from twenty-four to sixty months, a tacit recognition of failure. Not unexpectedly, the outcomes in Milwaukee, where 80 percent of the recipients are concentrated, are worse than in other parts of the state. In a Clintonesque attempt to encourage public-private competition, the government agencies that were charged with distributing aid in Milwaukee were themselves deemed failing and replaced with a combination of six different for- and nonprofit companies. No fewer than three of these have been found mismanaging or illegally misappropriating their funds. (The for-profit corporation Maximus Inc., for instance, was forced to pay the city of Milwaukee a total of $1 million as compensation for large-scale billing violations.) Meanwhile, the computerized participant-tracking system that was supposed to ensure that all enrollees were actually working or participating in other assigned activities is widely ignored, leading to a general inability to track aid recipients.

W-2 and school vouchers have been more successful at cutting spending (and funneling it to private contractors) than improving outcomes, which suggests the nagging thought that the real purpose all along was to quietly divest from a city given up for lost. In 1990, the black Milwaukee alderman Michael McGee threatened to organize a violent black militia—"I'm talking actual fighting, bloodshed and urban guerilla warfare," he was quoted as saying—if progress toward racial parity was not made within five years. Yet little has changed since then. The numbers from the latest American Community Survey estimates paint no clear picture, but they do suggest one thing: the new, post-housing-bubble poverty in Milwaukee is not all that different from the old poverty, at least if you happen to be black. The inner core derived little benefit from the bubble and suffered little fallout from its burst. Its desperation is decades old, backed up by the stubborn facts of economic history. As white Milwaukee lived through its crisis—first abnormally high unemployment, now a partial and perhaps abortive recovery—black Milwaukee simply experienced more of the same. If a full recovery does come, it won't be black Milwaukee that benefits from it: years of decline and Walker-era austerity have left the city's residents less able than ever to take advantage of jobs requiring advanced degrees, even as those jobs themselves become more precarious.

I spent most of my teenage years in Wauwatosa, one of Milwaukee's oldest suburbs. In the 1960s, at the height of the city's civil rights struggle, it was one of the hotbeds of racist resistance: when Father

Groppi led a protest march into the town, he was met by Klansmen and other onlookers who waved signs reading KEEP TOSA WHITE. By the early twenty-first century, such explicit racism was rarely seen, and most young people were in the dark about the role their grandparents' generation had played in those events. We knew the facts in the abstract, of course, and those who were particularly engaged with politics could even get direct experience with "the issues" by volunteering in Milwaukee itself. But that, of course, was "over there." We went to the good public schools and joked about the bad ones; we had white neighbors and were uncurious about the real meaning of the epithet "ghetto."

When I was sixteen, I began taking long nighttime walks. They served at first as an outlet for angst, but soon they all started to follow a similar trajectory. I would go as far east as I could in one night, and this always meant crossing the invisible line of privilege that walled Milwaukee off from its central city. I was, of course, slumming, daring myself to face the ghetto, and one night a black passerby stopped me in the street and told me, in no uncertain terms, that I did not belong. I did not cross the line in my walks ever again.

The next year, I started taking classes at the University of Wisconsin–Milwaukee, which meant a daily bus trip east along North Avenue. It turned out that seeing the same burned-out blocks and faded hair salon displays from a car and from a bus offered two very different experiences; for one thing, overhearing conversations about crack addiction and casual murder tends to change one's relationship to urban space. But it would be a stretch to say I was enlightened. The bus simply took me from one bubble, the suburban idyll of Wauwatosa, to another—the old-timey movie theaters and alternative coffee shops of the East Side. Like the other young whites on the bus, I wore headphones as often as I could. I did not nod or smile, and I was left alone in return. To ask me to be concerned about the city was one thing; to ask me to live in it was another.

In 2011 I went back home and repeated the trip, in an attempt to determine what, if anything, had changed in the recession years. The only change that I could find was a raft of BRONZEVILLE REDEVELOPMENT INITIATIVE signs in the windows of empty buildings. This, apparently, is the only visible trace of an attempt to bring back the tiny black downtown district of prewar Milwaukee. It is too early to tell if the project will change much, but its website is a worrying sign. "The primary African-American economic and social hub of its time," it cheerily announces, "Bronzeville brought all ethnicities together to celebrate African-American culture." There's no mention of the exclusion of blacks from labor unions, of black strikebreakers used to ratchet up racial antagonisms, of neighborhood self-segregation adopted as a survival strategy by the city's embattled black community. It's all Satchmo and black-and-tan clubs.

This whitewashed leftist pseudo-history is mirrored today on the right: in his inauguration speech, Scott Walker—who began his political career in Wauwatosa—appealed to Wisconsin history to call for "frugality and moderation in government." He could not, of course, acknowledge the socialist Hoan as a predecessor. His goal, though perhaps more radical and invidious than that of the Bronzeville project, is fundamentally similar: it is to enroll history in a project of legitimation, to portray a Wisconsin without unions as a return to the historical mean.

Walker is right, in a sense. With government ranged against labor, austerity budgeting chopping off public services, and official venality a basic assumption of political life, 1900 does not seem so far away anymore. What is becoming increasingly clear, however, is that it is one thing to turn back the clock and quite another to make it stop there. The crowds that surged into the state capitol in 2011, in what now looks to have been a futile gesture of protest, are not just the soggy remnants of the Obama coalition. They are also the heirs of the Socialist bundle brigades that eventually drove Milwaukee's bought-and-paid-for politicians out of office. If they failed in their attempt to recall Walker in 2012, so did their Socialist antecedents. They and their children proved, if nothing else, that the call for "frugality and moderation in government" is a much more ambiguous—and potent—demand than Walker would have us believe.

18

SAVING DETROIT

SIMONE LANDON

Dale Brown started what would become the Threat Management Center in the early 1990s, not long after moving to Detroit. He was living in an apartment building on the east side of the city, which saw about as much crime as any other: annually, Detroit averaged five violent crimes per thousand residents back then. One day, a fight broke out in the street. A crowd of people had surrounded a young woman, beating and kicking her. Brown came outside and tried to clear some of the people away. Eventually, the police came. They told Brown he should mind his own business.

He had always respected men and women in uniform; his mother was a rifle team commander in the U.S. National Guard. But this encounter with the Detroit police—Brown subsequently failed to get them to look into the woman's beating even a little bit—caused him to consider other policing options. If the city couldn't do it, perhaps Brown, who had attended paratrooper school and then trained to be a private investigator, could.

He began developing a system he called the Eclectikan—an intense regimen that combines mixed martial arts with knife, baton, and firearms training and tactical psychology—and recruiting trainees he called VIPERS, the Violence Intervention Protective Emergency Response System. He and his recruits began patrolling the streets around Brown's apartment building. In their flak vests and camouflage fatigues, they were both more menacing and, importantly, more present than the Detroit police. Crime decreased noticeably. Brown started getting calls for private security jobs, including from trucking companies that feared hijackers. At the same time, he and his team began training women and children in self-defense and what Brown likes to call "urban survival tactics."

In 2000, just as Detroit's population dipped below one million for the first time since 1920, Brown opened the Threat Management Center down by the river just east of downtown. The police force was embarking on a decade-long hemorrhaging of personnel, and Brown started getting more jobs doing security for local businesses, covering big events, and providing bodyguard services to celebrities like Bill Cosby and Sylvester Stallone when they passed through town. He was able to invest in his new training facility and administrative headquarters, a Quonset hut that sat between some abandoned lots and old warehouses still years away from being transformed into apartment lofts. He bought body armor and communications systems and guns and cars and dogs. He was building a paramilitary organization that would be superior to local law enforcement, though he was careful to work with the police when possible.

Fifteen years after its opening, the Threat Management Center is still very much in business. In addition to their traditional camouflage fatigues and flak vests, contemporary VIPERS are kitted out with earpieces and smart phones. They are not armed when on community patrol, though they are when doing private security work, but Brown owns many, many guns and displays them prominently at his center. While the organization is equal opportunity, the VIPERS program seems to attract, on average, bodybuilders who enjoy playing laser tag. Demographically, their ranks come close to the Detroit Police Department, one of the more diverse major city squads in the country: about two-thirds black and a quarter women. (Brown is black.) Like him, they devote their lives to the center, sometimes putting in eighty to ninety hours a week. They call him Commander Brown. Everyone gets a code name.

Brown doesn't like it when Threat Management is referred to as a private security company, and while his team is often hired to patrol wealthier areas of Detroit, he resents the term "private police force." To him, the Threat Management Center is an educational institution and a community service organization. He uses the money earned from protecting his corporate clients to subsidize his work with victims of domestic abuse, effectively redistributing public safety. To "pay" for their training in the Eclectikan, VIPERS must volunteer hours to Threat Management's community defense forces. Some of this volunteer work, not unlike police work, can seem a little comic; in a city that still sees fifty-nine carjackings a month, uniformed VIPERS sometimes bring extra gas to stalled-out motorboaters on the Detroit River. But most of the time, they offer the invaluable service of protection for local women. These clients, mostly poor and mostly black, are under threat from their male partners or ex-partners, often the fathers of their children. Threat Management walks them through the paperwork needed to file police reports and enforces personal protection orders when the cops can't or won't. In certain cases where child custody is in dispute, the VIPERS will intervene to return babies to their mothers. They stand guard at these women's houses, escort them around town, and find safer places for them to live. Most important, they remain on call should anything bad happen—something no one can any longer expect of the Detroit police.

To a lot of people, Dale Brown is a hero, even a superhero. Some of that is physical: he's as thick with muscle as the Hulk and embraces technology rivaling that of Detroit's other vigilante, RoboCop. Some of it is earned from his work with women who are in danger. And at least some of it is fantasy, a belief that the presence of one good man, or even a collection of them, can save a city long since abandoned to lawlessness.

I first heard about Brown from my friend Jacob Hurwitz-Goodman, who followed the VIPERS around for two years to film a documentary. Jacob grew up in one of the tonier Detroit neighborhoods that now pays Brown's company for security services, but he discovered the organization when he moved into one of those now-renovated lofts kitty-corner from the Threat Management Center. We were both back in Detroit after attending college in other cities, trying to make sense of our hometown as adults. It was the middle of the recession, and Detroit had gotten a lot worse for most residents: foreclosure after foreclosure surrounded my parents' house in Mexicantown (which is what Detroit's predominantly Latino neighborhood really is called). But for young white kids like us, it was getting better. We could ride our bikes without worrying about traffic and buy cheap beer at the liquor stores that still sat on every corner, the only businesses aside from the gas stations to weather the crisis, just as they'd weathered every crisis to hit the city since the 1967 riots. Detroit was starting to attract civic do-gooders, investors, and turnaround specialists whose zeal and confidence outstripped the city's desperation. Some of these people would say Detroit was a blank slate, just an empty canvas they could write their lives onto. Some of them would get mugged at gunpoint.

Jacob's parents were civil rights lawyers who were always suing the Detroit police for force and abuse, and we'd attended the same private Quaker elementary school in a middle-class neighborhood of town houses between Lafayette Park and downtown. He was interested in Threat Management, and Brown's self-described mission of nonviolence, as one alternative to what was clearly a broken civic infrastructure. I had a hard time getting past the commando uniforms. But Jacob was also interested in the appeal of the superhero, the desire to save someone or something, even a whole neighborhood, an entire city.

The Detroit we knew growing up in the 1990s was poor and underpopulated, but Detroit was once a wealthy city. In the first two-thirds of the American century, driven by demand for its signature product, the automobile, and the solid wages won by the autoworkers' unions, it boomed. Detroit first appeared on the list of top-ten most populous American cities in 1910, doubled its population between 1910 and 1920 as Henry Ford perfected the Model T, and remained fourth (behind New York, Chicago, and Philadelphia) or fifth (after the rise of Los Angeles) until 1970.

These good years let Detroit build many beautiful buildings—the Art Deco Penobscot Building, the neo-Renaissance David Whitney skyscraper, and the Beaux Arts public art museum, with its Diego Rivera murals—and expand its grid to 139 square miles, a scale fit for the cars its factories produced. The city filled up with immigrants from Poland and Greece and white migrants from Appalachia and black migrants from the Deep South. This latter group found the middle-class life promised by a union job at the auto plants harder to purchase. Even as their share of the population of the city, and of the auto industry workforce, grew, blacks couldn't cross the red lines encircling the neighborhoods of neat brick bungalows.

The red lines shifted after the war with the construction of new suburbs centered on new car factories and open only to white residents. Eventually, 8 Mile Road, the city's northern limit, became the official and metaphorical divide between mostly black Detroit and its mostly white suburbs. The city lost a third of its residents between 1950 and 1980 and has lost another third since then. The people who left took tax dollars and other resources with them.

Rust is the metaphor most often used to describe Detroit's extinct industry, and the rust really does tinge even the muntins of the windows of the shuttered parts factories, their panes long since smashed. But on the blocks and blocks of once-residential city streets, the deterioration is due less to rust than to char: dozens of blighted, burned-out houses lost to neglect or arson, the rest on the brink of catching fire. In many ways, Detroit has become a city of negative spaces: one-third of the land is vacant; more than half the population is long since gone.

All this empty space is hard to control. The grass grows tall in city-owned lots while thieves strip the copper from streetlights, leaving block after block in the dark, the better for more thieves to break into cars and homes. Detroit routinely records thousands of burglaries and stolen cars, and hundreds of homicides, each year. Late-night drivers are advised to skip red lights to avoid carjackers; if there aren't enough cops around to protect them, there aren't any to write traffic tickets.

The police department refuses to say how many officers it employs. The best guess is somewhere between two and three thousand, though the more important, or at least more often cited, figure is how much the force has declined in the last ten years: by 40 percent, through layoffs and attrition. Detroit residents know the police dispatchers only respond to violent crimes, and even then it takes the police an hour to show up. For a while, the precincts closed their doors from four in the afternoon until eight in the morning, ostensibly the hours when more police were needed out on the beat, but also shuttering stations during the period when members of the public were more likely to report crimes. They were directed to call a hotline instead.

At least fifty women were killed in Detroit in 2013. One was shot by a group of men who entered her home by pretending to be cops. Another who was raped and beaten was killed outside her home days before she was set to testify against her attacker, who had been released from police custody on a tether. In 2009, a special forces cop shot a sleeping seven-year-old girl in the neck—on camera—and a jury couldn't agree whether he was guilty of involuntary manslaughter. The city left more than ten thousand rape kits untested and sitting on a shelf in an evidence warehouse for years. In 2003, the Justice Department found Detroit's police guilty of beating up too many people and launched an oversight program, which lasted a decade. (The city was happy to see this oversight end in 2014, because it was paying the monitor a salary of nearly $1 million a year.)

You can begin to see why someone would think self-styled commandos patrolling the abandoned streets in black Hummers was a good idea. And you can begin to understand why even the city government would prefer a vigilante superhero to its own law enforcement. There's a feeling that ordinary civic approaches no longer apply, and organizations like Threat Management provide necessary backfill for the void of once public services. The city, long since exhausted and incapable, is put in the position of endorsing these efforts because they let it off the hook. When the city accepted an $8 million gift from eight private companies and foundations to buy new ambulances and police cars, the weary mayor said, "Anything helps."

In 1805, the entire city of Detroit burned to the ground. The complete leveling allowed for a new city plan, designed by Augustus Woodward and modeled after Pierre Charles L'Enfant's design for Washington, D.C. With a bit of accidental prescience, Woodward laid the city streets on a spoke system, with major thoroughfares radiating out from a downtown hub. Detroit also took its motto from this great fire: "Speramus meliora; resurget cineribus" (We hope for better things; it shall rise from the ashes).

In July 2013, Detroit filed for municipal bankruptcy, the largest American city ever to do so. Bankruptcy was supposed to be a new kind of leveling, a fire sale that would provide for a fresh start. The man in charge of seeing the city through this process bore the title emergency manager, a position created by Michigan's governor and state legislature to gut financially distressed towns and school districts in the name of solvency. Detroit was the sixth and the largest of the cities to fall under this augmented state receivership. Legally, the manager had unilateral control over the city's finances and government; he could fire the city council and rewrite contracts with service providers and the public-sector unions. This immense power was supposed to forestall bankruptcy, but the governor gave the job to a Washington bankruptcy expert who'd helped Chrysler through its restructuring just a handful of years before. The emergency manager called Detroit "the Olympics of restructuring," but there wasn't much left for him to cut. The city had already turned the schools into charters, paid contractors to take over the bus system and the lighting department, and secured corporate sponsorship for the rec centers. The water department quietly went up for sale, and Christie's came to appraise the museum's art collection. Four months after the emergency manager arrived, he was in court filing the city's bankruptcy papers.

The emergency manager was really an undertaker. His task was to help the city into its coffin, to bury the old Detroit and begin again. In a narrow, accountant's view, once the balance sheet returned to zero, the city would be good as new. But the city still needs someone to cut the grass, teach the kids, police the streets. Under such circumstances, each new volunteer or entrepreneur offering a private solution to a public problem is treated as a savior. There are plenty of examples more and less innocuous than Dale Brown's VIPERS. A group of groundskeepers that gets together to mow the grass at parks the city closed because it couldn't maintain them. A company that billed itself as a reimagined bus system that would run between Detroit's richer enclaves for $5 a ride. (Eventually, the money was supposed to trickle down and let the company serve the poorer neighborhoods, but it turned out that shuttling yuppie bar hoppers wasn't enough of a business model, and the company closed.) A luxury watchmaker that installed four $12,000 clocks as somewhat anachronistic public landmarks. A plan from local tycoons for a 3.1-mile-long light-rail line running down a single street.

This last one counts among its investors Dan Gilbert, the billionaire owner of both the Cleveland Cavaliers and a company called Quicken Loans, the country's largest online home mortgage originator. The light-rail would connect Downtown, where he recently re-headquartered Quicken Loans, and Midtown, where he offers rent-voucher incentives for his employees to live. Gilbert has been buying up property since the market hit its nadir and now owns fifty buildings downtown, many of them the skyscrapers of

Detroit's prime, ready for rehab. He plans to turn them into start-up incubators (he already has the M@dison building, formerly the Madison building, where the walls carry inspirational quotations written in Comic Sans) and housing and retail for the urban new-comer millennials who will work there. (Owning so much comes with the benefit of getting to be choosy about the tenants.) All this property needs protection, and Gilbert has installed his own secu-rity infrastructure, including private patrols and three hundred sur-veillance cameras. He's often called a superhero for his revitalization endeavors, though left unsaid is how much they're clearly designed to bring an enormous return on his investment.

This handover of power to the few who can afford it—and the near elimination of the public sector in favor of the private—has been under way for a long time; the bankruptcy has only acceler-ated it. The previous mayor, a former steel executive, produced a plan for a shrunken Detroit; any residents who lived outside his new borders would have to move or wait until the cutoff of water and lighting drove them out. The new mayor, a former hospital executive (and the city's first white mayor in forty years), has a simi-lar vision, though he'll need the bankruptcy judge's permission to implement it. Detroit is looking forward to a system of patronage and paternalism, depending on the kindness of strangers, men from out of town who have the means and the power to do just what they like.

Superhero movies usually end with the protagonists safe but the landscape in ashes. My friend Jacob's movie about Threat Management ends a little differently. Commander Brown has fallen in love with another VIPER, a Bosnian immigrant and sin-gle mother named Mirela Mesinovic who works as the organiza-tion's office manager (even superheroes need bureaucrats). Her French-manicured hand rests on his black glove as Brown explains how they got together after he had an elective surgery related to weight lifting, when she acted as his nurse. Brown admits that he took the step of asking for her help, then realized that her caretaking was the stuff of a real relationship. It's a neat reversal of the superhero fantasy. Detroit doesn't get to ask for help very often, deemed as it is so far beyond redemption. Even less often does anyone ask Detroiters if they want help or what that help might entail. Superheroes want to know what it feels like to save someone, but a better question is this: What should it feel like to be saved?

19

THE CLEVELAND MODEL

INTERVIEW WITH GAR ALPEROVITZ

Gar Alperovitz is a historian, political economist, activist, and writer. He has written many books, including The Decision to Use the Atomic Bomb, *and, more recently,* What Then Must We Do? Straight Talk About the Next American Revolution. *He grew up in Racine, Wisconsin, and has contributed to numerous efforts at economic reconstruction, including in Youngstown and Cleveland, Ohio. All of which he discussed with n+1 in between panels at the annual conference of the New Economy Coalition at Northeastern University in the summer of 2014.*

n+1: You were born in Racine?

GA: I was.

n+1: When?

GA: Nineteen thirty-six. I'm older than I look.

n+1: How long did you live there?

GA: Until I went to college, University of Wisconsin, so until eighteen or nineteen.

n+1: What kind of town was Racine?

GA: Racine was, in those days, an industrial town. It was said to have more small-manufacturing businesses per capita than any other city in the United States. I don't know if that's true, but probably approximately it was a kind of truth.

n+1: What do you mean by small manufacturing?

GA: My father was a small manufacturer. Ten employees or less. Usually specialty work. My father was an engineer. He and two other guys ran this little company.

n+1: What kind of engineer?

GA: He was a civil engineer, but he actually practiced mechanical engineering. His company made specialty parts for small tractors and mowers. On the other hand, there were also very large manufacturers in Racine at that time, mostly oriented to manufacturing for agricultural use. Case was the big tractor company, and Massey-Harris was a big agricultural company. Case still has a plant in Racine, but Massey Ferguson, as it's now called, moved to Duluth.

n+1: Does Racine have any sort of indigenous political tradition?

GA: It was a labor town; it had strong labor unions. But the actual First District of Wisconsin, which is the congressional district in which it lives, has gone back and forth between right and left over the years. Les Aspin was a liberal congressman and later became the secretary of defense, and the current one, Paul Ryan, is very conservative. There was a strong Danish population, a German population, there was an Armenian population. And at the time I was in high school, Racine did not have a large black population. And slowly, because of World War II, blacks became drawn in to work in the defense plants. To give you a sense of the kind of town it was: my high school had three black students who came up, and of course we elected one president. That was the kind of liberal midwestern flavor of the town. It's changed radically since then. I go back occasionally. Different town now.

It was a wonderful place to grow up. My experience of it was wonderful. It was a small high school. I was involved in the activities. I played football.

n+1: What position?

GA: I played left guard. And I was 167 pounds and a pulling guard. I was successful; I was a very good guard because I had a 300-pound tackle next to me.

n+1: Have you been back recently?

GA: I was back last year. I was at a conference at Wingspread, which is a big conference center outside of Racine. I keep in touch with one of my high school buddies, who is interesting—extremely conservative. But also very smart, and a really good guy to talk politics with.

n+1: Do you have a sense of where that conservatism comes from?

GA: His family was Catholic-Italian. He's very religious. But he was always one of the smartest kids in the class. Very nice; very principled; very conservative. But here's Wisconsin for you—he always calls me on my birthday—this last time I said, "Well, you must have had some difficulty with Senator Russ Feingold. You know, very liberal." "Well," he said, "no. I voted for Russ. He's a good man. He's a man of principle." Very conservative, but that moral aspect registered with my friend.

n+1: Our essay on Milwaukee discusses that city's strong socialist tradition. Is that something you saw in Racine, or is that a purely Milwaukee thing?

GA: Well, Milwaukee socialists were still called socialists in the mid-1950s and '60s, and you could still use that term, but it was a liberal Democratic community, nothing more than that. Growing up, I never heard the word "socialism" in Racine. Labor unions, however, were active. My parents were Eisenhower Democrats— moderates—and they had some thoughts about the left-wing lawyer whose daughter I dated.

n+1: How are American cities, north or south, different from European ones?

GA: I think the really big difference between European and American city politics is that here, if you're corporate, you can pull the rug out from under the cities all across the continent. In the global market you can move around, and in the American market you can move around.

But it's different in Europe. I once was at a Brookings Institution seminar. And some guy from Germany was saying, "America, it's wonderful. You can just get up and move, and the workers will take it. In Germany, we can't do that; there's no place really to go. In America, they play the different regions off against each other. You just move the game."

The term I use now is "throwaway cities"—Cleveland, Detroit, of course. I mean it's brutal, because it's not only corporate policy. The U.S. has such an unconsolidated social democratic system: liberalism is so weak that corporations encounter very little constraint. Also, transportation policy is pitifully weak as it relates to city policy. A few weeks ago, I had to go to Cleveland for a meeting from Washington, D.C. The airfare was $850. You can't do business very well if transportation costs that much.

n+1: Huge transaction—

GA: Yes. Amazing. And the same thing in Cincinnati. There's no attempt to coordinate the development of transportation policy and city policy. And furthermore there's nobody with power in the city who gives a damn. By pulling transportation out of the city as has happened with some airlines in Cincinnati—or making it costly as in both Cleveland and Cincinnati—they're making it so expensive that you can't run a large business in the city. It isn't quite so bad in European countries, where there is an attempt to stabilize with regional policy, as they call it, and to coordinate it with transportation policy.

n+1: So what you're describing then is that, for lack of a better term, the mode of distribution in Europe is smaller—

GA: Scale matters. This is historian William Appleman Williams's influence, because he made me think about it in a way I hadn't before. The founding fathers—especially Madison—understood that if you spread people you can divide them, you can conquer them. That's straight Madison. Federalist No. 10 also says explicitly that power is based on who owns the wealth. And the problem from Madison's point of view is to spread out those people who want to take the wealth. So we spread them out around the continent. And expand. We divide and conquer.

In the United States, you can drop Germany into Montana. People don't realize the scale that we live in; the same thing that goes on in the global empire is being done in the continent. They just keep sprinkling jobs and moving them around. So it's a very difficult system—very different. There's no other place quite like this in the advanced world.

n+1: What can cities do?

GA: Some cities still have a political structure that can tax, and allocations can be used for interesting purposes. More important, many of the larger cities established universities and health systems during the era of industrial development. And these institutions are anchored—they don't get up and move—and are actually channels for a lot of public money.

They also have populations that are under intense pressure, so there's the possibility of different politics, and you can begin to generate models that are essentially quasi-socialist models. Not around state ownership, but around more complex communities/worker structures. In Cleveland, for instance, an integrated group of large-scale worker cooperatives and other firms are in part supported by the purchasing power of hospitals and universities that, in turn, have a good deal of public funding.

It's also a model that in many cases is workable, politically, but one that also introduces entirely different principles. I'm as interested in what principles such models teach as in the terms of the models themselves. This is a country with little socialist tradition in the modern era. So it doesn't know that changing the ownership of capital is important. It matters who owns capital, and this idea is not widely understood. It's not an idea in the times, and it's not even an idea in the culture. How do you introduce the notion that common ownership and democratic ownership is an important principle in the political economy in such a culture?

In cities it can be done. Cities can do that. In real-life terms. Not bullshit terms. Not ideology.

n+1: How do you understand this term "ideology"?

GA: The term that's most interesting would be the German term *Weltanschauung*, the encompassing understanding, which is part ideas, part values, part theory. That which tells us where it is we stand and how we are proceeding in the world. Ideology is the ground on which people come to that question.

And in terms of future American politics, unless we begin to build that in a way that coheres with a concrete political strategy and a concrete institutional strategy, we lose.

n+1: What is the Cleveland Model?

GA: The idea is to set up an institution, not a corporation, but something else, within a geographic community. And then on that structure you build worker-owned and multi-stakeholder firms that cannot be sold off, which is critical. This means that any growth that happens is distributed more equally because everybody collectively and individually owns a piece of the asset whose value is appreciating, whose revenue is growing.

Then you've got these anchor institutions I was talking about earlier: hospitals and universities—Case Western, Cleveland Clinic, University Hospitals. Medicare, Medicaid, education efforts—lots of public money in the area: Those three Cleveland institutions alone purchase $3 billion in goods and services a year. That's leaving aside salaries and construction—just what they buy. And, until now, none of it from that area. So the model directs some of that purchasing power to the multi-stakeholder firms and co-ops.

Now, these are not your traditional small-scale co-ops. The model draws heavily on the experience of the Mondragon Cooperative Corporation in the Basque Country of Spain, the world's most successful large-scale cooperative effort, which now employs around eighty thousand workers in more than 250 high-tech, industrial, service, construction, financial, and other largely cooperatively owned businesses.

In Cleveland now, there are three such firms. The Evergreen Cooperative Laundry [ECL] is the flagship, and it capitalizes on the expanding demand for laundry services from the health-care sector, which is huge, something like 18 percent of the national GDP and growing. After a six-month initial "probationary" period, employees begin to buy into the co-op through payroll deductions of fifty cents an hour over three years (for a total of $3,000). Employee-owners build an equity stake in the business over time—a potentially substantial amount of money in a tough neighborhood. Also, it's totally green, with the smallest carbon footprint of any industrial-scale laundry in northeast Ohio. Most industrial-scale laundries use four to five gallons of water per pound of laundry; ECL uses eight-tenths of a gallon to do the same job.

The second employee-owned enterprise is Evergreen Energy Solutions, which does large-scale solar panel installations on the roofs of the city's largest nonprofit health, education, and municipal buildings—again, those anchor institutions I was talking about.

The third enterprise is Green City Growers, which operates a year-round hydroponic food production greenhouse in the midst of the Glendale neighborhood in east Cleveland. The 230,000-square-foot greenhouse—larger than the average Walmart superstore—will be producing more than three million heads of fresh lettuce and nearly half a million pounds of (highly profitable) basil and other herbs a year.

There is also significant support from local foundations, banks, and the municipal government. The Evergreen Cooperative Development Fund, initially capitalized by $5 million in grants, expects to raise another $10–$12 million—which in turn will leverage up to an additional $40 million in investment funds. So, for example, the fund invested $1.3 million in the Evergreen Cooperative Laundry, which was then used to access an additional $4.2 million in financing, a ratio of over three to one.

An important aspect of the strategy is that each of the Evergreen cooperatives is obligated to pay 10 percent of its pretax profits back into the fund to help seed the development of new jobs through additional co-ops. Thus, each business has a commitment to its workers (through living-wage jobs, affordable health benefits, and asset accumulation) and to the general community (by creating businesses that can provide stability to neighborhoods). It is community reconstructive, sustainable, and democratic. So that's what's going on. And it's very difficult to do. As of my last reading, all three are in the black or in line to be in the black shortly.

This experiment was totally top-down. However, it's a demonstration that the model works, and it gives people something that's practical. Small-business men see it as positive. Why? Because it helps the local market, people are working hard, they're getting a piece of the action, it's not welfare, it's constructive, it's practical. No rhetoric. And it gives the mayor another option when corporations come around asking for something. Most important, it introduces the democratization of wealth, and it introduces a planning model. That is, a quasi-planning model in that the market is stabilized by quasi-public—hospital and university—procurement. And that's very interesting, because you could do essentially the same thing at scale with, say, national mass-transit production when the next General Motors goes down.

n+1: Parts of it sound like the theory of competitive advantage: this city has these anchor institutions, and these other cities have these other anchor institutions. So what about those cities without anchor institutions?

GA: Any large system has a lot more of these than you think. Hospitals are significant, they're a very large part of the economy, the health-care systems, the university systems, they're always around. If you also throw in utilities, which also can't move, museums and city government, those are also anchor institutions, you'd be surprised. And you have a multiplier—one dollar spent leads to another dollar spent and so forth—and if you can expand the multiplier, you'd be surprised by how much stability you could build in to most cities.

n+1: What is it that allowed this to happen in Cleveland? Is this possible in cities undergoing rapid gentrification?

GA: In highly gentrified cities this is not going to happen. There the question is whether or not gentrification will continue. There's some fragmentary new data that's suggesting that it's slowing down—if not reversing—but in cities where the gentry is moving in, young people, people without families, you just don't have the political economic preconditions to attempt something like this. Nor is it is going to solve the problem of affordable housing in gentrifying areas.

Though the economics of the model make sense anywhere, the politics are, at this stage, only possible in places like Cleveland. The question is whether or not politics can build these new ideas into larger systems down the road. At this stage, we're introducing elements, not solutions. And in many cities you can begin to see a whole set of ideas shift. It's been extraordinary. Two or three years ago, the word "worker-owned co-op" was regarded as ridiculous.

n+1: It's heartening.

GA: It's heartening, but there are no other options left. We must democratize. The pain will just continue. Period. It just gets worse, and worse, and worse and worse. And if democratization of wealth is a possibility, it's going to start small. So that's how you get your co-ops.

That's a premise I've been working with for many years. It's interesting to see it pop, and I think it's over-popped, because now people think worker ownership in a worker-owned co-op is the answer. It's not an answer. It's an element of an answer. Worker-guild socialism develops competitive worker-owned companies in a culture of competition, not a culture of cooperation or socialism. And it is appropriate in some cases. But that's not what the Cleveland Model's about—certainly not at this stage.

n+1: Is there a role for traditional political or labor conflict at this stage?

GA: You know, that model—labor against corporations to get unions—is a dead-end model now. Liberal strategy has always largely depended for serious policy change on the political strength of organized labor, and labor unions have dwindled from 35.4 percent of the labor force organized to 11.3 percent now, with only 6.7 percent in the private sector. I think we need to try to hold the line as best we can. I'm not against labor unions in that respect; indeed, I am a strong supporter. But their power is decaying right before your eyes. If the name of the game is systemic change, then the introduction of a different thematic and different structural principles is critical at this stage.

The horror story in the back of my mind is always Russia in the late nineteenth century. The Narodniks were looking at a vaguely similar problem when the Russian peasants exploded. Enormous conflict. But they didn't know where they were going in any serious and widely understood programmatic sense. And then they got killed. We may see explosions and not know what to do. There's already a lot of conflict, but it has no other goal other than "Stop the pain" or "Give us a break." It doesn't have a direction. So how do we generate that direction both in ideology and also in learning enough on the ground so we actually know something? So we ultimately can propose and demand something real!

n+1: What happened in Youngstown?

GA: Youngstown was fortuitous. It was the first major plant closing in modern American history. Or at least the first one that got major publicity. Five thousand people lost their jobs. It was national news. September 1977. Big news, national. Now it happens all the time; it's not news.

The steelworkers, a couple of them—there was the Sadlowski movement, which was an activist steel movement in Gary, Indiana, and there were some activists in Youngstown too—and they were saying, "Let's take over this mill," and "Why can't we run it?" And a deeply concerned ecumenical coalition got together and also said, "What are we going to do?" This was a really big crisis in the community.

At the time, I had been doing a lot of Left-liberal economics. I was a public figure. On *Meet the Press* and in *The New York Times*, et cetera, I was everybody's Left-liberal-Left economist, supported by labor, environmental groups, consumers, black organizations, et cetera. I was doing something with the press all the time. The point is people in Youngstown knew of me, and so they called me: "Would you come and try to help?" And I said, "Yes, of course." And I helped them shape the idea that they could go forward with a worker-community ownership model. Just buy the plant and run it as a community. And second, I urged that if we dramatized it nationally—politically dramatized it, get the national religious coalitions and so forth behind it—it could be a big enough story that they might very well pull it off. And even if·you didn't pull it off—this is what I liked about them—you would at least spread the idea. Which they did. So they asked me to do it, and I was able to help them get a significant grant from an assistant secretary of HUD who was willing to take a risk and financed a very, very, very professional top-of-the-line study on how to do it. So they had it nailed. And then it was a matter of politics.

So the community mobilized, there was revenue, people set up "Save Our Valley" accounts, they mobilized the national religious community, they mobilized the press, it was a big story in the press, very exciting. And much more important than all of that, the Mahoning Valley, in which Youngstown is situated, had given Carter the state of Ohio. So they had muscle, too. And the Carter administration pledged $100 or $200 million in loan guarantees to do it. And we had the study by the top guy in the steel industry, so it was a viable study. Then the election of 1978 occurred, and after the congressional election, the Carter administration disappeared. So the money disappeared—not really a surprise.

What was really interesting about Youngstown was that they understood that that might happen. And they saw their mission—partly the religious guys—as spreading the word, which was important for other futures. Somebody in Ohio—a wonderful professor named John Logue—set up a little Kent State University institute, and you now find a lot of worker-owned companies that came out of that. And you find a lot of activists still inspired. Barack Obama was hired in Chicago for the first time by such people. Somebody's doing a biography of Obama who told me that.

What you notice, if you think about this as a political economist, is that steelworkers are now the strongest proponents of worker-owned companies.

n+1: So where is Youngstown today? It's shrinking—

GA: Definitely!

n+1: Radically.

GA: It's a Detroit.

n+1: It's happening in Detroit too.

GA: If you accept the larger argument that stagnation, rather than collapse, rather than boom, is the economic context we're living in, you have to ask why. Why stagnation, in this context, rather than collapse?

Political organizing in a context of stagnation is very different from the political organizing predicting collapse. The question to ask about any of these shrinking towns is, where did the people go? Nobody asks. They had to go somewhere.

n+1: And where is Racine today?

GA: Racine is about the same size as it was: eighty thousand. What has largely happened in Racine is that it's got a beautiful waterfront on Lake Michigan. So it's become a waterfront town. If you go there, you'll see the small yachts of people from Chicago and Milwaukee and a beautiful harbor. So it's got that going for it.

n+1: You mentioned the waterfront. What do you think of Richard Florida?

GA: Not much. [Laughs.]

n+1: I mean, what function does he serve?

GA: Well, you live in Cambridge. You see a lot of smart people, and they invent companies, and they spin off ideas. And it's true that there's a creative, inventive class that does do those things. So it's like bird feeders for Florida. If you put out bird feeders, then the birds will happen here; if you put them there, the birds will happen there. So let's create nice cafés and art galleries and the like and attract some creative birds. And there is some element of truth in that, no doubt.

But there are only so many places that you can put the birds when there's no larger market developing. And what usually happens is you're moving the checkers around the checkerboard. A couple years ago, I was out in some little town in Pennsylvania at a conference. And every town is trying to set up interesting coffee shops and art galleries, and maybe the birds will come. And they're getting the local chambers of commerce around that idea. Now, any new business helps the chamber, but as a community policy and as an industrial policy it was absurd.

n+1: So it's bird feeders as economic strategy.

GA: And only so many birds. It doesn't tell you anything about the capacity of the political economy. So that is one of the reform models liberals now work with. On the other hand, Marxists have traditionally worked with a collapse model. We could talk a long time about why stagnation and political stalemate is the likeliest of the options. It's a very different political landscape than the reform context or the radical revolution context. You know, in the radical revolution context, collapse would probably go to the Right, not the Left. I spend a lot of time thinking about the emerging context. The emerging stagnating context of "neither collapse nor reform" allows for time to learn something new. You wouldn't know how to run the system today if you were to take it over. We may actually be able to learn things like the Cleveland Model and hopefully well beyond, and then develop a politics with it.

Put another way: it's potentially the most interesting time in American history because we've run out of options. The imperial option's dead, the reform option's dead, the collapse option's dead. So the reconstructive option may be the only one left. Another overly simplified way of saying it: They ran a system by taking a continent in the nineteenth century. Then they ran out of land. Then they ran a system using war in the twentieth century—not by decision, I don't think it was intentional, but war was a fundamental economic stabilizer in the first, second, and third quarters of the twentieth century. Then they ran out of war. And we're now into a whole different context. It's not without possibilities. A lot of Marxists don't know the difference between a tendency and a trend. And that's really critical if the context is shifting.

You know, I love the conversation we're having, but I'm not sure we have yet figured out how to have a deep conversation on these issues beyond academics and activists. It is really important that the conversation be put in terms that ordinary Americans understand.

We've got a great deal of work to do, in part to break out of our own political-intellectual ghettos. These issues are where I live. This is important stuff. To get out of the radical bullshit and ideological stuff and career making; it's time to get serious about what makes sense and how to talk about it.

20

NEIGHBORHOODS OF CINCINNATI

JAMES POGUE

Cincinnati isn't a place prone to the usual cataclysms. We had a big flood in 1937 and a locally memorable one sixty years later, but today we're cut off from the river by levees and highways, and for most of us all that Ohio can threaten is annoyance, not damage. We had a little earthquake a few years ago, so weak that it barely registered on my Facebook news feed, and our tornadoes are usually about as fierce. The Depression was mild here because it led to a resurgence of river traffic. We had no real housing bubble. We were never burned by the British or Sherman or terrorists.

It's a quiet town of about 330,000 people bedded down into the hills of southwestern Ohio, which is a confusing area to be from. East Coasters usually call us midwestern, which is just wrong, topographically speaking, because midwestern cities are flat, and Cincinnati is almost all hills. Truly midwestern cities remember that they were on the frontier not so long ago. They're grafted onto the landscape, not a part of it. When Norman Mailer wrote about seeing Chicago as a "city on the plains," he meant that on some nights even the burliest midwestern city looks alone and defenseless on the prairie, as if a tornado or a tribe of Indians could sweep it away. Indianapolis feels that way to me, and so does Omaha. But safe in the Ohio River valley, Cincinnati feels as smugly permanent as Boston.

Because we're just barely north of the Mason-Dixon Line,

Cincinnati is often included on lists of northern industrial cities, but that's not really right either. A few weeks before writing this I was in Nashville, a city I love, and a friend from Canton, in Ohio's flat midwestern north, told me, "It figures you'd like it here. You guys are already southerners." We did develop a manufacturing economy, and Cincinnati is still known as "Porkopolis" for all the pigs that used to be processed here. But even that name is misleading. As much as anything we were, like Atlanta and Knoxville, a transit center on the way north for all those stuffs that did so much damage to the southern soil: cotton, tobacco, coal. In the 1880s, at the height of the pig years, we earned two and a half times as much distilling bourbon as we did producing pork.

Even the truly southern Cincinnatians get confused sometimes. Riding back on the Greyhound from Nashville, I sat next to an electrician on his way home from Dallas to Covington, Kentucky, right across the river from downtown. When I asked him how he liked Texas, he said, "Man, fuck those guys. They hated me because I'm a Yankee."

Things change so slowly that lovers of the city have developed a whole disorganized campaign to convince people that things really do happen here. Every Cincinnatian my age can probably remember a social studies teacher or parent, flush with civic pride, saying, "You know, the Russians pointed a missile at us too." Walking down Spring Grove Avenue near JD's Honky Tonk and Emporium a while ago, I passed a big brass sign marking where, in 1932, some long-gone company produced the world's first glass-door oven. Growing up here felt like living outside of history.

So our cataclysms have always been riots, because you riot when you think that nothing will change otherwise or when you're very, very bored. Researching this piece, I went to the big library downtown and asked the local history librarian for a general-interest history of the city. She thought for a minute and said, "Honey, I don't think anyone has ever written one of those," but she was game to look. In the end, we found a book in German from 1896.

I flipped to the table of contents, and almost every single entry that wasn't a sketch of an eminent German dealt with some kind of social uprising. In 1789, "die erste Volksversammlung" appointed William McMillan, a Virginian, like most of our early settlers, to be magistrate of the new city, and soon afterward he led an attack on a military garrison he thought too rowdy. In the 1830s, a free black community established itself here, leading to the "Abolitionisten Aufruhr," and by the 1840s Cincinnati was a Dubai-style boomtown, a swaggering, tough, proto-industrial city of the future. This was when we began getting the only serious influx of immigrants in our history. There were some Jews and more Irish but mostly Bavarian Catholics. They established themselves in Over-the-Rhine and the West End, the two neighborhoods surrounding downtown, and opened beer halls and parish churches, which, in the name of temperance, native Cincinnatians occasionally tried to burn down. This led to both "der erste Kampf gegen die nativistischen Loafer" and "der Kampf mit den Know-Nothings."

Once the Germans settled in, they even joined some of the later riots, which were all directed at the state: "Der Sturm auf die Jail," "Das Niederbrennen des Courthauses," and "Der grosse Courthaus-Riot."

One such riot, in 1884, was among the bloodiest in American history, and it's classic Cincinnati: forty thousand brewers and clerks rose up demanding cleaner government and ended up behind barricades shooting at the Ohio National Guard. Fifty-three people were killed, and two weeks later the city held an election in which it returned the same political machine it had risen up against.

The Germans came to Cincinnati thinking it would grow into an industrial giant, and you can still sense in them an unfulfilled ambition. Procter & Gamble and Kroger groceries were founded here, and in the late nineteenth century we became a world capital of machine tool milling. But our fundamental bet was on the river, and we realized far too late that Chicago would eclipse us by becoming a rail hub. There never was another boom time, and the Slavic and southern European migrants who came to the United States in the early twentieth century mostly avoided Cincinnati and went to Cleveland and Pittsburgh. Instead, we had people better suited to the local spirit—blacks leaving the Deep South and Appalachians, who began fleeing the coalfields in the 1940s.

Now the Germans mostly live on the bluffs and in the suburbs of the West Side, and the German men especially are easy to spot at a baseball game, loud and red-nosed from years of drinking and lawn mowing. The Appalachians took the Germans' place in Over-the-Rhine and the West End, before they too left and moved out along the river and up into the little choke valley that separates the eastern and western hills.

Slum clearance began in Cincinnati in the early 1960s.

In 1962, the city replaced the narrow and hilly old Mill Creek Expressway with a new section of Interstate 75, running it through the heart of the West End, one of the city's densest neighborhoods. "They got the word and they had so many days to get the hell out," a city councilman later said. At least fifteen thousand people, mostly poor blacks and Appalachians, were forced out of their homes.

Fifteen thousand people would have been about 4 percent of the city's population at the time. Displaced black families moved into neighborhoods like Avondale, where my moneyed grandfather was living, Walnut Hills, and Mount Auburn, all on the central East Side slopes up the hill from the West End and Over-the-Rhine. These areas were early suburbs for the carriage-owning set of Cincinnatians looking to get away from the factories and the Germans in the basin, and many of their old mansions were subdivided and rented. Whites began trickling out of what were briefly some of the only integrated neighborhoods in the city, and middle-class blacks struggled to accommodate the refugees. Then we had a serial killer.

No one knows if the Cincinnati Strangler was just one person, and the suspect police eventually settled on was only convicted of one murder. But someone, or some combination of people, began raping and garroting middle-aged and downright elderly white women in the same central East Side neighborhoods that were just beginning to decline.

The most common story was that a black man, sometimes short, sometimes tall, sometimes mustachioed, sometimes clean shaven, would show up at the door of an apartment house, ask a woman if he could speak with the caretaker, and subdue her when her back was turned.

Seven women were murdered between 1965 and 1966, and several more were attacked. I asked my mom about the time, and she said, "It was like everyone was on house arrest. My friend and I snuck out one day to walk to the Frisch's Mainliner," which is a diner in one of the whitest, safest suburbs in America. "The Mariemont police picked us up, because we were white girls walking, and lectured us all the way home," back within the city limits. Hardware stores and locksmiths ran out of dead bolts. Finally, in December 1966, police arrested a former cabdriver named Posteal Laskey for the killing of a woman four months earlier. That night, with Laskey in custody, a seventy-nine-year-old white woman was attacked in her apartment by a black man who came asking for the caretaker.

Laskey was convicted anyway, without physical evidence, by an all-white jury. The attacks did stop, but Black Power groups began putting up posters in Avondale calling him a martyr. In May 1967, he was sentenced to death. On June 10, Martin Luther King came to Avondale and gave a sermon on nonviolence. The next day a cousin of Laskey's was arrested for blocking an Avondale sidewalk. Riots broke out, and eventually spread across the central East Side and down into the West End and Over-the-Rhine.

We had more riots after MLK was assassinated, but neighborhood ties are very strong, and we didn't have a great white exodus the way many cities did after the riots of 1967 and 1968. Instead, we developed a simple, quiet system of segregation. Hyde Park and Mount Lookout were white; Walnut Hills, Over-the-Rhine, and the West End were black. But it was complicated. White people were able to eat in a white-owned diner grandfathered into a newly black neighborhood and could continue to live in some of the more extravagant Walnut Hills mansions, but black people did not cross from Walnut Hills to all-white Hyde Park unless it was to wash dishes. White people could go to Over-the-Rhine, because it had Music Hall and some historic restaurants, but they would never go into the West End. It wasn't, demographically speaking, more or less of a ghetto—just somewhere we didn't mix.

I'm living in Little Rock, Arkansas, now, where one of my regular bartenders told me that he roots for the Cincinnati Reds because there aren't any black guys on the team. (This is actually untrue; there are two African-American Reds, and one of them, Brandon Phillips, is an All-Star.) Still, I'm always shocked when I drink with him, because black men—guys in white T-shirts who say, "You know what I mean, mane?" trap-music style, every third sentence—can come in and drink, in pairs, without his caring or seeming to notice. You get the sense in Little Rock that there are white-on-black brawls every so often, and someone will occasionally call someone a nigger, but the social order seems totally safe.

This is the exact opposite of Cincinnati. An Over-the-Rhine bar owner once explained the success of his place to a local journalist by saying that he "wouldn't let the locals come in and panhandle the customers, use the bathroom, and steal the toilet paper." On Main Street, I've seen black men come into a bar and watched the bartender pick up the phone to dial the local precinct before they even sat down. "You're disturbing people" is what they usually say—and, in a sense, that's true.

•

I was born in 1986 in a big house in Mount Auburn, an old annexed suburb just up the hill from Over-the-Rhine, and for the eleven years I lived there, I was the only white kid on the street. It was the kind of street white Cincinnatians patronizingly call "black middle class"—as though if you're black in Cincinnati, and you live in a neighborhood where only 25 percent of the population lives below the poverty line, and there are only dope boys at one end of every block, you're doing pretty well.

I had a great time, playing baseball down the block at the dead end and eating pork chops at the neighbors' after school. I played outside every night until dark, and no one messed with me unless they weren't from the neighborhood, in which case they were usually just shocked into saying something mean. One of my strongest childhood memories is of riding my bike past a girl standing at the corner of Earnshaw and Burnet and hearing her involuntarily blurt out, "Ew! A little white boy!" As soon as she said it, she covered her mouth and walked away.

Anywhere else we would have been gentrifiers. My dad had raised my sisters from his previous marriage poor in Over-the-Rhine, but my mom came from a diminished East Side fortune, and they settled somewhere in the middle. But in Cincinnati in those days, serious gentrification just wasn't something that seemed as if it could ever happen. The city was too divided. We had the second-highest income inequality rate in the nation, the sixth-highest level of segregation, the third-highest poverty rate.

The actual city of Cincinnati is about 55 percent white and 43 percent black, but there are only a couple central neighborhoods that are even close to integrated, and surrounding Hamilton County is chalk white and conservative. Whites dominate the city power structure almost completely. City government has remained largely an exercise in carrying out the will of certain families, like the Lindners of Chiquita and the Peppers of Procter & Gamble, associated with our big corporations. In 1948, corporate money pushed through a referendum ending proportional representation on the city council, and for much of the 1950s, a local historian told me, "city policy was decided over lunch with Neil McElroy," then president of P&G. They would eat, and McElroy "would point his finger at the business leaders and tell them how much they had to pay for each policy initiative."

Cincinnati's leaders avoided full-scale white flight by giving middle-class whites everything they wanted, subsidizing downtown department stores and building freeways and stadiums, and paying for it all through sales, not property, taxes. And the police department remained a province of ambitious German and Irish boys from the West Side. In 2011, after years of federal consent decree, nearly 20 percent of the police force still came from just two predominantly white West Side high schools.

Between 1995 and 2001, this police department shot and killed fifteen black males under the age of forty. The last shooting, of an unarmed nineteen-year-old named Timothy Thomas, set off the latest riots, but things were so bad that I think they would have happened anyway.

The 2001 riots in Cincinnati were the biggest American riots since Rodney King, and they unfolded slowly, without the sudden flash of violence that would have suggested a response to a single injustice.

Thomas was killed at 2:13 on the morning of Saturday, April 7, five months after another unarmed black man, Roger Owensby Jr., was killed by police who sat on his chest until he suffocated. The weekend passed peacefully. A local group called the Black United Front organized a community cleanup of the vacant lot where Thomas was shot.

On Monday, April 9, the city council's Law and Public Safety Committee held a meeting at 3:00 p.m. at city hall. The entire council came, as did Mayor Charlie Luken and Chief Thomas Streicher. About 150 protesters came, led by the Black United Front.

The meeting started, if not calmly, then not unlike many city council meetings, where black militants occasionally show up to yell "nigger" at council members and screaming matches are just a fact of city business. But Streicher refused to give an account of the shooting, arguing that he'd be commenting on an open criminal investigation, and after years of protecting police officers, he finally tipped over the bucket. The protesters became so angry that he was given a three-officer "human shield" detail, as the *Enquirer* described it. Fed up, Mayor Luken left the room, and a teenage protester took over the mayor's chair. Trying to prevent what was occurring "was like trying to push water back up a hill," Streicher said later.

Around six, the crowd debouched from city hall and moved four blocks north, to District 1 Police Headquarters, where it swelled to about a thousand people. At this point, some in the crowd, like Obalaye Macharia—a poet I know as the guy who sometimes does Wednesday night readings at the public library—clearly wanted to start a riot, and people began throwing bottles at the police officers blocking the entrance to the station. "I left to round up the members of the artistic activist group I belong to. I ran from City Hall all the way to the West End. It was like—it's on," Macharia later told *Cincinnati Magazine*.

But all of the larger local black organizations tried to calm things down, to the point that the local Fruit of Islam spent several hours guarding District 1 from black protesters. "We're here protecting the community. We're here to keep order in the community," one of them told the *Enquirer*. Eventually, the Nation of Islam left but the crowd stayed, and around midnight police officers began firing beanbag ammunition and tear gas into the crowd, which dispersed into Over-the-Rhine and the West End.

Things had stayed mostly peaceful for three days, longer than the entire life cycle of most riots. By comparison, the Rodney King verdicts came down at 3:00 p.m., and looting had begun by early evening. In Cincinnati, there were reports of white and black strangers hugging and crying at the site of Thomas's killing.

But on Tuesday, a youth protest began at an Over-the-Rhine corner just north of the downtown business district. It moved south, and people began attacking hot dog vendors and smashing windows. Then suddenly the whole downtown area ringed by Over-the-Rhine and the West End was completely lawless. Police held the line at Central Parkway, the border between Over-the-Rhine and the downtown business district, and the looting and burning spread up to Avondale and Walnut Hills, where the last riots occurred. Dozens of whites were attacked by black rioters in a city where black-on-white crime is very rare. The attacks became the story of the riots for many white Cincinnatians, and a decade later, if you Googled "Cincinnati Riots," the second hit was a video put up by a white supremacist titled "2001 Cincinnati Race Riots—over 100 Whites Assaulted." I was in eighth grade, and I remember realizing how serious things were while waiting at a friend's house to meet a group of German exchange students coming to tour our school. The bus driver who brought them from the airport hadn't been listening to the radio and drove straight through Over-the-Rhine. He got them caught in a rain of thrown objects, and the bus showed up windowless, the German teenagers cowering on the floor. The unrest went on for four days, and the city was shut down under curfew for two more.

The period immediately after the riot was a chaos of ideas. Liberals started putting cheery bumper stickers on their cars that read, "Work for Peace and Racial Harmony in Cincinnati." Jim Tarbell, a bar owner and city council member, convinced much of our artsy population (there are no hipsters here, just "artsy people") that the destruction that occurred during the riots had created one last best chance to save Over-the-Rhine by gentrifying it. Carl Lindner—then chairman of Chiquita and by far Cincinnati's most important political figure—seemed to think a new baseball stadium would bring us all together. The United Nations sent a team to ask our police to be nicer to black people.

The only thing everyone agreed on was that we could never, ever have another riot. We're a dowdy city, as *Life* once put it, and it wasn't fun getting calls from acquaintances who saw the riots on CNN.

Two concrete things happened. First, the Cincinnati Police Department entered into a collaborative agreement with the Black United Front, among other groups, and agreed to set up the Citizen Complaint Authority and restrict its use of force. This appeased no one, and national black groups launched a boycott of the city. Bill Cosby wouldn't even come here.

Then, sensing that race relations weren't improving, our local patricians decided to make them a nonissue. In 2003, P&G, Kroger, Chiquita, and others came together to form the Cincinnati Center City Development Corporation (3CDC), with the explicit mission of "revitalizing" the basin neighborhoods. 3CDC is an almost entirely corporate project, with a mandate to build condos (you used to be able to buy one direct from its website) and attract "diverse businesses" to areas of Over-the-Rhine that used to be almost completely black. Since 2004, it has spent $206 million to buy up historic buildings and convert them to market-rate apartments, in a neighborhood where the median household income was, at the beginning of the campaign, $8,600.

This campaign is by far the biggest change the city has seen in my lifetime. Over-the-Rhine is on the National Register of Historic Places, which means it's essentially illegal to tear a building down. 3CDC, a corporate creation, is the first serious group to come in with the money to do renovation up to both the National Register's standards and the city buildings code. So it has been able to write the future.

It's very hard to say how many people have been displaced by the renovations, partly because a lot of Over-the-Rhine buildings were already vacant and partly because 3CDC usually refuses to buy and upgrade inhabited buildings. Which means that the hard work of emptying rent-controlled buildings goes to landlords before they sell, and every month or so you hear stories like the one about 1316 Race Street, where thirty-three residents were offered $75 each to leave within two weeks so that the building would be empty at the time of sale.

A little before the riots, my mom inherited some money, and we moved to a house way out east, near the city limits. The East Side is the kind of place where people remember where you went to school, who your parents dated before they married, and where your grandparents liked to sit at Music Hall. In the 1880s, the Culbertson family used to have a mansion next to the Pogues' up on Grandin Road, and they still come over to visit us on Christmas Eve. I know a great number of families who have fallen from wealth, but almost none who have risen to it.

I commuted every day to a high school in Over-the-Rhine, where 3CDC was just beginning its campaign. We weren't rich, even by Cincinnati standards, but life on the East Side hills, where almost every neighborhood is clearly black or white, poor or well-off, let me think that at least the white middle class was holding steady.

It was, on the East Side. But on the West it was crumbling, in part because the riots gave us an excuse to ignore the poor white neighborhoods that line the valleys along the Ohio and the Mill Creek. Next to the gelled class structure of the East, the West Side and its suburbs always seemed different. It was rougher—I've been beaten up twice on the West Side, never on the East—but freer. Over there the culture was one that made it seem possible to start a plumbing business or a car dealership and get Cincinnati rich, like Marge Schott, the openly racist, dog-loving, bibulous former owner of the Cincinnati Reds. East Siders would cringe at the sight of you, as they did at the very thought of Marge, but then East Siders never seem to rise out of the city as she did. All of Cincinnati's national luminaries—Schott, Pete Rose, John Boehner, Charles Manson—are from the West Side.

Through my dad's work and because I had a girlfriend over there, I got to know some of the Appalachian areas of the West Side well. They are very poor and deeply strange but also magically close and caring, little urban settings for a Synge play. There were always stories like that of my dad's friend Walt, an ex-con who helped me rebuild our roof in the summer of 2010 and froze to death sleeping on a porch the next winter, but also clean and sober local characters with names like Hubcab Bill and Snake-Man Scott, whom you could visit if you wanted to buy things like hubcaps or snakes. There were a lot of kids born with fetal-alcohol syndrome, but there were also many of those scolding, white-haired women who sit on porches and keep the whole block in line. I remember one charity Thanksgiving dinner where Roscoe Morgan, a local bluegrass musician, played the Woody Guthrie song "Hobo's Lullaby." There was a fat, genial German cop in the audience, and when Roscoe sang the line about how "there'll be no policemen" in heaven, he stopped and smiled and said, "Except for this one here, that is." All the women in the audience cooed, "Yeah, except for this one." It was that kind of neighborhood.

These quarters always seemed like separate domains, literally looked down on by their neighbors up the hill and removed by class, family ties, and dialect from the rest of white Cincinnati. But of course they aren't really, which makes it all the more disturbing that they're falling apart. Stable poor neighborhoods don't spread their problems around. Collapsing ones do. Black Cincinnati already learned this lesson.

This is the problem: Cincinnati is trying to become a pleasant, livable, twenty-first-century city without solving its twentieth-century problems. When I was a kid, our model seemed to be Memphis—a diffuse suburban metropolis powered by company headquarters and with a downtown kept alive by a destination entertainment district. The city even hired the developer behind Memphis's Beale Street to come and help turn Main Street into the same sort of party strip. Now, predictably late, the model has shifted to something closer to Portland. What has stayed constant is an understanding that Over-the-Rhine is the city's key neighborhood and a blindness to the problems in the rest of the region. The city has put its full force into remaking the area, with plans for a streetcar running through it and 3CDC advertising page after page of condo developments on its website, not quite grasping the extent to which "condo" has become a dirty word to the creative-class types it's trying to attract. But these efforts have been shockingly successful. In 2011, *The New York Times* did a "Surfacing" piece on Over-the-Rhine, which included the words "rockumentary," "mixologist," and "textured-cotton sundresses" in fewer than five hundred words of text. All of the stores and restaurants the article mentioned had opened just the year prior. The city is still losing population—according to the 2010 census, it had shrunk to fewer than 300,000 residents from a high of 500,000 in the 1950s—and the hope is that Over-the-Rhine, the largest intact nineteenth-century neighborhood in the country, larger and frankly prettier than Greenwich Village or the French Quarter, will become cool and that its transformation will bring the city back from the brink.

Nothing unexpected so far. Every midsize city in the country is trying something similar. And Over-the-Rhine is just one neighborhood. But no other city has our recent history, and we've seen these conditions before. When huge sections of the West End were razed to make a path for I-75, sending poor blacks to East Side neighborhoods that couldn't absorb them, the displacement precipitated three riots and the decline of entire sections of the city.

Though Cincinnati has not collapsed, like some cities in the industrial North, it is worse off now than it was then. It has lost jobs, though not catastrophically. Cincinnati was always a headquarters town first, industrial center second. Kroger, Chiquita, Macy's, Great American Insurance, and Procter & Gamble are all still based downtown, though the city has had to give many of them tributary payment in the form of tax breaks and subsidized parking garages. P&G continues to make soap in the original Ivorydale plant.

But what that has meant is that the better-off East Side neighborhoods have been able to ignore our deindustrialization, while the Appalachian neighborhoods and blue-collar West Side have suffered it quietly. And of course our black neighborhoods, like black neighborhoods across the country, have gotten much poorer.

East Price Hill, which is overwhelmingly white, saw its poverty rate triple in the 1980s. By 2000, even Westwood, which used to be a fortress of the Bavarian bourgeoisie, had whole census tracts where the median household income was only about $16,000. Mike Maloney, a demographer who moved here from eastern Kentucky, told me that "the basins and valleys on both the Ohio and Kentucky sides of the river form one contiguous poor area fifteen miles long" and that now on the West Side there isn't one solidly middle-class area left between the far reaches of Westwood and the Mill Creek. Add to this the East Side, still starkly segregated between the poor black areas that developed in the late 1960s and the rich white neighborhoods, and there's nowhere stable for people priced out of Over-the-Rhine to go.

Now that formerly middle-class West Siders "are losing Victorians and moving to trailer parks in the suburbs," and the plan in Over-the-Rhine is explicitly to drive criminals, drug addicts, prostitutes, and implicitly a large portion of the area's poor black residents into the hills, it's hard to drive around without feeling as if the whole project were falling apart. Cities are compacts: middle-class West Siders, our property tax base, used to agree to help inhabit Cincinnati because it was cheap, the schools were serviceable, and everyone from the local parish lived around the corner. But we have nowhere to absorb refugees from Over-the-Rhine, and it makes sense that many of them will move to the partially integrated neighborhoods that suffered most during the recession. "White people still live in North Avondale because they can—barely—still find schools where their kids won't get beat up," Maloney told me, reflecting a basic fear here. Now two very twenty-first-century processes—city-sponsored gentrification and the decline of the white lower-middle class—threaten to force on us two very twentieth-century urban processes: ghettoization and white flight. "We're not yet at the tipping point of becoming a poor black city with just a few white enclaves," he told me. "But we're close."

•

I left Cincinnati, but I come back often, and when I visit Over-the-Rhine, I'm always surprised to see how cruel a little city can be. This rapid change doesn't suit us. In 2010, the School for Creative and Performing Arts (SCPA), the jewel of the Cincinnati public schools, moved to a shiny new building on Washington Park, around the corner from Music Hall and from the Drop Inn Center, our local homeless shelter. The city and 3CDC are building an arts quarter around the square.

A decade after the riots, the homeless people in Washington Park are literally so thick on the ground that in July 2010 a police officer who used to joke with me outside school accidentally ran over a sleeping woman in his patrol car, killing her. Just a few weeks later, my mom, who is on the Drop Inn Center board, got a call from the mayor, under pressure from 3CDC. You have to move this place, he said, somewhere farther from all the beautiful new stuff. "Don't you care about the city?"

In 2009, Esme Kenney, a white eighth grader at SCPA and a friend of the family, was murdered by a black man who walked away from an Over-the-Rhine halfway house. The killing, like the Cincinnati Strangler trial, became one of those low moments of urban life, when unspoken mistrust and tension find an outlet in a news story. SCPA is central to the plan to remake Over-the-Rhine, and politicians and radio hosts quickly tried to turn Esme into a symbol of why the area needs to be remade right now. Roxanne Qualls, the vice-mayor, gave an interview after the killer was sentenced to death, suggesting that the Drop Inn Center would be guilty if it stayed in the arts quarter and a homeless person attacked a student. She didn't mention that the killer had left Over-the-Rhine, and that Esme was actually attacked near her house, on the West Side.

I came to town in October 2010 for the dedication of a memorial to Esme, at SCPA. It was a cold, rainy day, and after I left, I ended up wandering around Over-the-Rhine, trying to buy a bottle of water. I found myself in one of the remaining no-go areas, a maze of old row houses a few blocks away from the streets targeted for redevelopment. I was looking for a corner store that must have closed years ago and stopped a woman to ask where it was. She shook her head and said, "Come in the house, we have water." I went up into a classic old Over-the-Rhine apartment: grates, not just bars, at the windows, linoleum floors half a bubble off level. I gave her daughter a dollar for the water and mentioned how much things had changed since the riots. "Not really," she said. "They talk about they're going to sell this building. It's still Cincinnati, wherever we go."

21

FIVE JOBS IN READING

CHRIS REITZ

The game of Monopoly has four railroads: B&O, Short Line, Reading, and Pennsylvania. As a child I assumed that Monopoly took place in my hometown of Reading, Pennsylvania. It doesn't; it takes place in Atlantic City, even though the B&O didn't send trains to Atlantic City and the Short Line isn't real.

But the Reading Railroad was. In addition to the rails that moved the coal, the Philadelphia & Reading Railroad owned the mines that held it and the ports that shipped it—it was one of the largest corporations in the world. The Reading also had a modest passenger line; you could at one time ride the rails between Harrisburg, Shamokin, Jersey City, Philadelphia, and of course the city of Reading. A wealthy iron and garment manufacturing town in the nineteenth century, Reading continued growing into the 1930s, before beginning a long process of decay as the railroad vanished with the coal industry. Highways were built, American car culture exploded, and in 1976 the Reading ceased to exist. CONRAIL now runs much of what remains, although there are no passenger trains and less coal to move. The tracks persist, however, crisscrossing the city as they make their way along the coast.

Although Reading's decline was similar to that of many other industrial towns on the East Coast, the path it took was not uniform. It has had many "rebirths," promises of renewed glory ending in the recalcitrance of poverty and crime. Reading was once "famous for its outlet shopping," a phrase I heard frequently from moms in other towns. And Reading had in fact built a fairly large industry around closeout, mis-sized, as-is "designer brand" apparel and home goods. Buses would bring in shoppers from all over the East as restaurants, hair and nail salons, and çoffee shops sprouted to feed and pamper them. But now there are outlet malls all over the country. Designer brands have even created outlet labels so that retail customers can shop without fear of accidentally purchasing the same shirt as some deal-hunting cheapskate. The outlets are still in Reading, but they don't host the same crowded, frantic weekend shopping orgies I remember. Why travel to one of the most dangerous cities in America when discount jeans are as common as stucco in strip malls in New Jersey? Without such an attraction there was little to draw out-of-towners into the city limits. The West Shore Bypass, which opened in 1965 but remained an ongoing project until 1998, allowed traffic to avoid downtown entirely, starving small businesses. The 2010 census declared Reading the poorest city in America.

Even when I was in elementary school, Reading was something driven over on the way to a mall or a restaurant. Any trip downtown involved a bridge. I remember annual visits to a vacuum cleaner repair shop and a ceiling fan store and the bureaucratic issues that could only be resolved in the city courthouse, a building so big and old and beautifully out of place. Then, from ages fourteen to twenty-one, I spent summers and weekends collecting jobs in Reading.

I began at a Subway on the very edge of downtown. A sandwich artist, I rotated the syrup on the soda fountain and illegally operated the industrial slicer. I made sandwiches for two months before the store was robbed by masked men with shotguns two hours after my shift ended and my parents made me quit.

I took a job pumping gas and working the register at an auto shop nearby. I wanted to learn to repair cars. The mechanics and shop regulars wanted to teach me other things. They told stories about wild nights of hooker sex and boner pills, often while staring at women through a pair of binoculars kept at the shop's window. They explained that a woman working as a stripper wears a certain kind of shoes, or carries a certain kind of bag, or pays with lots of singles. When a shop regular had to go downtown for a blood transfusion, he speculated about how to avoid getting a black guy's blood. The owner told him to settle down. "Blood is red, not black. You'll take whatever blood they give you and be grateful." Later he confided that he too would prefer to avoid black blood, but because you can't prevent these things, why let the poor guy worry about it?

I left that job after some teenagers stole a bunch of car keys hanging on the peg board in the office while their friend distracted me by asking for help with his bike chain. That night they drove off with three cars, including a Corvette. "Damn Mexicans," the owner said when I told him.

"What makes you think they were Mexicans?" I demanded.

"Well, they weren't white kids, were they?" he said with a laugh. I wanted to tell him in my indignant sixteen-year-old voice that it was impossible to know exactly what country they or their parents or grandparents had come from and that they spoke American English just as I did and that I assumed they were American because they live in America. But I was already in trouble, and his point had nothing to do with where they were from. Everybody was from Reading now anyway, and that was the problem. Everyone but me, that is. These stories are what a suburban kid remembers from negotiating urban conflict on the weekends. They're not mine to write, or rather, they're only mine. But they are stories about Reading, and there aren't many of those around.

With each new job I moved deeper downtown. When I was sixteen and driving I took a school-year internship at the local office of the federal congressman. I wanted to know about national politics. I learned instead that constituents treat representatives as a kind of concierge. And that representatives use interns to oblige them. I was honestly impressed by the diversity of problems we sought to resolve and deeply frustrated by how little I cared. Lots of people complained about their neighbors. One needed clarification about venomous reptile laws and help finding a mediator for a dispute with a local herpetology enthusiast. Many thought nearby roads were too noisy. A few complained about the lack of trains downtown.

At the end of the school year and wanting money, I got a job as a busboy at a dining club on the edge of the city. I was quickly promoted to server. As anyone who has worked in a restaurant can tell you, service jobs are often divided along racial lines, and mine was no exception. The kids with Spanish accents bused tables, black people cleaned dishes and stocked the kitchen, white people with neck tattoos cooked, and white people without neck tattoos waited tables and tended bar. The job afforded me no other insight into Reading. However, my commute through downtown took me past a bustling tattoo shop. At the time, I was nearing the peak of my punk rock phase, and so I returned to work there as a body piercer after my first year of college.

Mostly the shop did tattoos. Body piercing was a recent addition, treated with skepticism by the veterans. The artists were bikers and so were the clients. Many were former addicts. One of the steps in hard-drug recovery is apparently addiction substitution. Tattoos and body piercings, which offer a quick burst of adrenaline followed by weeks of involved aftercare, can fill the niche perfectly. Heroin users, in particular, seemed to gain something from the association with needles and pain.

Although the shop refused to do gang tats, various members would come to us for unaffiliated, decorative ink. I learned that Reading's gangs are primarily Mexican and Dominican and that they have managed to successfully do what countless rehabilitation projects haven't: turn Reading into a thriving commercial hub. By setting up elaborate cocaine and heroin distribution networks between New York, small Pennsylvania cities, and drug import locations like Florida and the Mexican border, the gangs have turned Reading into one of the largest drug hubs on the East Coast.

But despite such connectivity, the rise of crime within the city limits has only increased the city's isolation, leading residents to add baroque ideologies to their guns and gods. The shop also refused to do swastika tattoos, white power symbols, or anything hate related. But that didn't stop people who already had such identifiers from coming in for other things: angry white men upset about the wave of Puerto Rican residents on the run from Giuliani's New York. White was still the largest demographic in Reading, but many were otherwise convinced and wore their paranoia, very literally, on their sleeves. Unlike the suburban, gas-station racism espoused by the lower-middle-class men who drove the bypass, city racism was active. It attended meetings at Reading's KKK-operated church and had a public-access show that aired every Tuesday at 3:00 a.m. I stayed up one night to watch two men in full Klan regalia review *The Bell Curve* and admonish "Uncle Adolf" for book burning, despite his other redeeming qualities.

Body piercers maintain a fairly fixed apprentice system. New piercers spend a week or two watching the master at work. After this they assist for a while before moving on to ears and then, slowly, to more challenging holes. Eyebrows bleed a lot; cartilage can too if you don't check for veins with a flashlight first. Belly buttons are tricky and don't heal well. Tongues are easy if the person doesn't move. Learning to pierce genitals takes longer. This is because genital piercings are less common, which means less practice. It can take years before someone has done enough supervised genital piercings to do one solo. And as my teacher was quick to remind me, "You can really fuck someone up down there." There's no sense rushing it.

I had no intention of rushing it, or of ever learning that side of the business. This wasn't my career; it was self-exploration. By August I had pierced exactly one nipple when Marco walked in for the first time that month. We had seen him weekly since the beginning of the summer, when he began heroin recovery, often for multiple piercings. When he stopped showing up, I just assumed he had fallen off the wagon.

"I joined the army," Marco said. "Had to get out of Reading."

"Congratulations," I said. "Are you getting pierced to celebrate?"

"Actually no. No piercings in the army. That's why I'm here. I need you to take out my dick ring."

I couldn't take out his dick ring. The boss was off for the day and I was expressly forbidden to work on genitals. And besides, I really, really didn't want to. Marco had what is called a Prince Albert, where the ring penetrates the underside of the head of the penis and exits through the urethra. In Marco's case, a stout 8 gauge—3.25 millimeters or roughly the size of a quarter-inch audio jack—making the removal more challenging. As I began to explain my inability to remove the ring, a uniformed army officer entered the shop and listened until I was finished.

"Son, your friend here enlisted two weeks ago. We informed him that he was required to remove all piercings. We discovered yesterday at inspection that he had failed to remove a ring from his penis. Basic begins next week, and if you do not remove the ring today, in my presence, Marco will be dishonorably discharged for not complying." I escorted Marco to the piercing chair and got my tools ready.

"Do I take my pants off or just pull it out through my fly?" he asked. I had no idea.

"Whatever you're comfortable with." He decided to go through the fly.

First I spread the ring and removed the captive bead. I had hoped to open the ring wide enough to just slip it off, but it didn't work. The amount of penis captive was larger than could comfortably fit through the hole in the ring. Unlike normal earrings, body piercing rings have no moving parts. If the hole is too small the only way to remove the ring is to physically bend it so that it can corkscrew out of the skin. Marco's ring was thick, and my hands were shaking.

Using two pliers I clamped down on the wire ring and pushed in opposite directions. Just as the jewelry started to bend, one of the clamps slipped off with a loud metallic snap. Everyone jumped.

"What the fuck is wrong with you people," whispered the commander.

No one was injured. I apologized to Marco and told him to sit still. I continued to bend the ring, this time without incident. Once bent, the ring easily slid out of Marco's urethra. I put it down on the table and took a few deep breaths.

"Do you want me to do your nipples next?" I asked the officer. "I'm much better at those."

On the way out I asked Marco what motivated him to join the army. He said it was because he needed to feel he was part of something. Drugs had stopped working for him, Narcotics Anonymous hadn't been enough lately, and he was running out of things to pierce.

"Any idea where you'll be stationed?" I asked.

"Basic training is down south. Then there's a reserve base here in Reading where I'll probably be stationed for a while. Hopefully they get me the fuck out of here soon, though."

I didn't think to charge Marco for the extraction, and he didn't think to pay. He left the shop without a single metal ring in his body, a stupendous transformation considering the number of holes we'd put in him that summer. I like to think of him as a specialist who returned home with an in-demand skill who now makes tons of money consulting, again covered in piercings. But that doesn't sound like Reading. Instead, his military career was likely short-lived. Because of drugs or insubordination or some medical condition he didn't know about, Marco was probably discharged and rejoined the 40 percent of Reading's population living below the poverty line. Do not pass "Go"; do not collect $200. And if that's the case, then perhaps Marco has resumed his search for exits and connections. Maybe through a biker club this time, maybe tattoos; more false starts drafted in needlepoint on flesh, crisscrossing his body like the train tracks to nowhere embedded in the streets downtown.

22

LATE SHOW PHILADELPHIA, 1999

CHANELLE BENZ

The summer of masturbators, I wore long socks. This was a preventive measure for a former soccer player who was nectar to mosquitoes at night. It was 1999, and I was living in Philadelphia.

On a walk home like any other, I passed Dirty Franks, a perennial dive at the corner of Thirteenth and Pine, where a friend worked as a bartender. She had a voice like Tallulah Bankhead playing the Black Widow in old episodes of *Batman* and had played my mother in a Vietnam War drama staged in the basement studio of 1619 Walnut Street, where *The Mike Douglas Show* had been filmed and the NBC peacock was still etched on the floor. A realistic actor, she cooked us breakfast onstage every night. The sizzle of eggs in a pan meant I was a couple of minutes away from being slapped by my soldier stepbrother.

That night, I took Pine Street toward Broad, the flag-lined central artery leading to the bronze statue of William Penn standing atop city hall, his ruffles and broad Quaker hat incongruous with the neon-yellow clock under his buckled shoes. Lit by the clock face, the city seemed at its most abstract and sinister; a Gotham with no Batman perched above monitoring my progress.

Philadelphia could change moods in a single block then; you could pass from landscaped front gardens and brick buildings with star-shaped washers that kept them from collapse to an abandoned house, windowless and boarded up. I'd heard that they were crack houses and sometimes people found bodies. But I'd walked through Center City about a thousand times and didn't worry about how quiet Sixteenth Street had gotten along its flat-faced brick houses. It was late. A few cars on the road, passing me every other minute, and so I imagined I was safe.

Near Rittenhouse Square, I crossed over to Spruce, a couple blocks from my house. But before I could cross Nineteenth, a car braked red at the corner, and something nagged at me. Where it had stopped, so close to the corner, was not a parking spot. Then, a mistake: I looked as I passed. The driver, a pasty dark-haired man with a grim smile of effort, was pumping his equally pasty schlong for all it was worth. I ran.

After I called the cops, a rookie showed up to take me to the police station. He drove so fast that I kept sliding around in the back on the plastic orange seat. Despite our speed, the drive took long enough that I started to worry about where he was taking me. Finally, in what seemed the middle of nowhere, he turned in to a complex surrounded by a stone wall with barbed wire on top. This was the Special Victims Unit at Frankford Arsenal, an old military ammunition plant where moths flocked thick in the cobwebbed warehouses full of old evidence no one would throw away. He pulled up at a brick building with globed streetlamps, reminding me of nineteenth-century London, something out of Sherlock Holmes. I was brought to a middle-aged detective in a cluttered, poorly lit room. This would be my first visit.

A few days later, as I was walking home from the subway, a man not unlike the masturbator was sitting in a car outside my front door. When he saw me, he tried to smile but seemed nervous. Because it was daylight, I whipped out a sheet of notebook paper, marched to the front of his car, and took down his license plate number. What was the problem? he wanted to know. I ignored him until I was on my front step. He was frightened and drove off. I went inside, shaking as badly as he was, and called the cops again. They told me that they would pay him a visit.

Back then, I could divide public life into two categories: being invisible and being harassed. As a teenager, I was shy and didn't belong to any cliques. I'd never had a boyfriend and didn't go to prom. My first date ended in tears, and my second stood me up. Everything changed when I straightened my hair. Men in the street began testifying loudly to the existence of my physical self: yelling out windows, honking their horns, following me. Smile and you might escape. Reject them and you might get spit on. Though I had suitors as well, gentlemen callers who had grown up in the Philadelphia suburbs at addresses like 123 Pennsylvania Avenue. They couldn't believe I was a virgin and found out the hard way that I didn't even know how to kiss. Those were the rare moments when I wanted to be seen by those who wanted to see me; intimacy is reciprocal. Being masturbated at is like being a captive audience for a rabid soliloquy, except there is nothing separating you from the performance.

The second masturbator was less committed but more creative. And to add to his victory, I'll never rid myself of the image of his brown cock.

Same summer. A swamp-thick midnight. No socks. I was with a roommate walking around the marble fountain in Rittenhouse Square, which, while not packed, was not deserted. But as we passed a man reading a magenta romance novel upside down, again I looked. Squatting on a bench in silk red basketball shorts, holding the weathered pages of a virgin-giving-up-her-tender-bud-to-his-hard-brutal-passion with one hand, he rubbed one out with the other. This time, he ran. In my outrage, I actually chased him for a second and he stopped. There was a fleeting, uneasy standoff as I froze, gripping the Mace I'd bought for just such an occasion. But I couldn't decide if I should spray it, couldn't get my thumb to flip the cap. All I could do was offer up variations on "fuck." He pondered this with large eyes, then was gone.

My roommate and I ran over to the other side of the park where a police car was parked and told the officers what had happened.

They asked for a description and took off. Soon after, they came back, they'd found a guy in red shorts, but it wasn't him. We got in the car. At a traffic light, a beat-up brown car full of big, rough dudes pulled up for a chat. It took me a minute to understand that these men were undercover cops. I wondered why they would blow their cover. But as I listened to their casual banter, I realized how little they thought it mattered.

On my second trip to the Special Victims Unit, there were three strippers ahead of me, scratched and bloody from a fight, or from being attacked. I studied the mug shots in the dim light while I waited, looking for people I might recognize. Indecent exposure. Rape. Last seen: a gentlemen's club on Delaware Avenue. I had been told to audition at a place called Delilah's by a young chef on a smoke break when I worked in the men's department in the basement of Strawbridge's. He knew someone who worked there and told me that she had no tits and was a coke addict and still made good money. I was broke and disenchanted with helping old men pick out khakis. The dancing I pictured was around a pole, not on a lap. I pictured a spangled emergence from offstage; I did not picture the patrons or imagine them touching me. I liked to think I was hard and being a stripper wouldn't hurt me. But I ended up lying, saying that I couldn't dance, when the truth was that I was afraid.

One thing you learn in acting school is that we spend most of our lives on the edge of our flight instinct: bugged-out eyes, tipped-up chin, shortening the back of the neck. We don't breathe fully. We don't take up space. The longer we live like this, the more we acclimate to the feeling of panic that accompanies our perpetually startled posture, the physicality of the hunted.

The detective remembered my name, chuckling to see me back. A female detective told me I should have just made fun of the guy. You have to humiliate them, she said. Say, is that all you got? Tell him how small it is. Anyway, it's a humid night, she said, laughing. The Mace would have blown back on you. But it wasn't small, and I felt as if she were telling me I shouldn't have used the Mace. I was told to look through mug shots on an old computer, but we all knew I'd never find him among the smear of faces. I was being humored like a child reporting a lost parakeet.

The year before, a Wharton grad student named Shannon Schieber was found naked and strangled. Her neighbors had called the cops when they heard her screaming, but when the police came, they knocked on the door and left because she didn't answer. Her apartment was three blocks away from where I lived. The police eventually matched the semen found on her bed to the semen of five other rapes, two of which had been downgraded to 2701, a code that technically means "investigation of person" but in practice not even that. Sketches of the "Center City rapist" appeared all over the city, warning us of a man who could slip through the bars on the windows. Alone in my apartment late at night, I wouldn't sleep until someone came home. *The Philadelphia Inquirer* wrote a series of articles detailing how the police department was misclassifying rape cases as lesser crimes to keep the numbers down; Special Victims was nicknamed "The Lying Bitches Unit."

The next summer, the first of the new century, I moved to the center of Center City at Thirteenth and Walnut up on the eighth floor in an apartment building across from a gay bar, Woody's. Down the alley was a lesbian bar, Sisters, and on the other corner was Signatures, a gentlemen's club. At the corner opposite was a mix of low-ranking drug dealers and transgender prostitutes. Guessing which direction people were headed was a favorite pastime. I didn't stick out, and I felt safe, for the Fruit Loop never slept.

One afternoon, as we watched strippers going to work, a friend from across the hall asked me to go for Indian. The proprietor had a glass eye, a beautiful wife, and a gut-busting buffet. But as we walked out onto the sizzle of Thirteenth, we saw that a crowd had gathered to watch a fight. I'm not sure if I actually saw the guy getting hit in the head with a brick, but I saw the blood. It was redder than I thought it should be. Next to the brick, a young face topped with short dreadlocks lay in the street, toes pointing up like in a cartoon. People who had seen him get hit waited for someone else who had seen to get help. It was forever before an ambulance came. We hung about in a loose circle of inaction, an invisible audience. That was the summer I decided to leave.

23

THE HIGHWAY AND THE CITY

DAN ALBERT

The interstate highways, everyone agrees, killed the city. It started in 1939 with six simple lines on a map, lines that would later become I-5, I-55, and I-95 going north to south and I-94, I-80, and I-40 going east to west. In the next two decades, these highways destroyed everything in their path and changed the way everyone lived. With their limited-access, grade-separated interchanges, they allowed people to travel in comfort and safety at great speeds. Wealthy whites used these highways to move at great speeds out of the city, taking their property taxes with them, returning only once in a while to go to work in office towers with underground parking. And if it wasn't enough for the highways to work through simple subtraction, they also worked through outright destruction. Highway men plowed interstates through the poorest and politically weakest parts of cities so as to remove "blight." They also consciously used the highways to segregate rich from poor and black from white. In the thirty years after World War II, suburbanization and "slum removal" delivered a one-two punch to American cities from which they are only just now, and only in some places, recovering.

The familiar story has much truth to it. But there was also a time when, far from hoping that the highway would kill the city, urban planners and architectural visionaries believed that only the highway could save the city from the suburbanization and traffic congestion that were thought to be destroying it. To understand the history of the postwar interstates, we need to go a little further back.

Before the cement highways killed the city, natural highways, the winds and currents that circulated the people and goods of the Atlantic world, gave birth to them. New Orleans, sitting as it does at the mouth of the continent's natural highway network, the Mississippi River system, was once second only to New York as an entrepôt. Boston and San Francisco are so alike because of their shared history. Though landfill now obscures this, the narrow Boston Neck was once the only connection between the urban island and the mainland. So too was San Francisco merely a toehold for ships until technology and competition drew the main port south to Los Angeles. Likewise, Boston's trade moved southwest to New York, where the first important artificial highway, the Erie Canal, provided a better link to the burgeoning hinterland.

In the middle of the nineteenth century, the iron road quickly supplanted the canals and dirt and gravel turnpikes. Cities that had been sited by the hand of God began to compete with cities arranged by the hands of men. Chicago displaced St. Louis not by virtue of its lakeside location but because the railroads came. Atlanta, Georgia, far away from river, ocean, or mountain pass, is where it is because the builders of the Western & Atlantic Railroad chose the spot for its easternmost terminus. It takes imagination now to realize how difficult overland travel was before the railroad. It moved at walking speed. (The famed Pony Express carried mail for a year and a half before the telegraph killed it.) The railroads changed that forever.

Strangely enough, the railroad had limited impact on the city form. Between cities, the rail lines followed the easy route through the mountains that nature had already found when it made rivers, and once the rails reached a city, no one objected to their staying on the riverside. In our era of high-priced waterfront real estate and city parks, it may be strange to think of the riverbank or shoreline as the best place for a sooty, coal-fired railroad. But at the time, the waterfront, with its ships, warehouses, odoriferous cargoes, and perhaps equally odoriferous and transient seamen, became home to saloons, brothels, and other undesirable forms of commerce. Sewers, such as there were, also ran untreated through storm drains into the water. To separate the city from that mess seemed to many a blessing.

Across the tracks from the riverfront, the American city remained the merchant's walking city with land at the top of the hill most valuable, as long as it was close to the action. A wealthy shipowner could stroll from his mansion atop the hill the short distance down to the New Bedford docks to check on his cargo of whale oil. The working and middle classes lived "above the store" or otherwise close to their places of employment; the word "commuting" only took on its journey-to-work meaning near the dawn of the twentieth century. Poor and rich lived side by side, though in different conditions. City streets became increasingly congested as the city grew, congested not only with traffic but with commerce (pushcarts) and leisure (a good game of stickball). Density choked out light and air. In Chicago, the slaughterhouses blackened the sky and turned the water into industrial waste. Cleveland's Cuyahoga River is best known for catching fire in 1969, but its industrial waste had caught fire thirteen times before, including in 1868, 1883, 1887, 1912, 1922, 1930, and 1952. The ever-increasing number of horses in the city fouled the streets, though their waste made a thriving business, as did their carcasses.

As if these forms of pollution were not abhorrent enough to the upper-class, native-born white Protestant population, the cities were becoming "polluted" as well with new migrants. Irish and Roman Catholics, Jews, and other un-American types were settling in. The WASPs wanted to get out of town. Horsecars (horse-drawn trolleys on iron rails) and then electrified trolleys allowed them to do this. Electrified trolleys especially, with their standard nickel fares, brought the dream of an English country home down the economic ladder.

Two things are worth noting at this point. First, just as the inter-states eventually created and reinforced geographic segregation by race and class, so too did the streetcars. As the urban historian Sam Bass Warner has shown with regards to Boston, the "streetcar sub-urbs" created concentric circles around the central city. The layout of the lines ensured that the wealthiest would be able to live far-thest from the city; they had stable jobs and could locate their homes along the longest lines. For those one step down, employment was less stable, so they often needed the flexibility of crosstown lines. And the lower class was still stuck in the city.

In other cities, segregation was more explicit, as developers cre-ated "whites only" communities at the ends of streetcar lines. The legacy of these racist policies endures. For example, Chevy Chase, on the border with Washington, D.C., began as an exclusive com-munity. Today African-Americans make up about 1 percent of its population, while in the surrounding areas blacks make up 18 to 25 percent of the population.

The second thing to note is that the same forces of land specu-lation that built the streetcar suburbs would also build the postwar automobile suburbs. The United States developed rich in land and relatively poor in population compared with its European fore-bears. It lacks the tradition of regional, centralized planning found in Europe and elsewhere, so developers have fairly free rein to lo-cate their subdivisions. Absent any transportation or land-use plan-ning, housing developments pop up as randomly as mushrooms, driven ever outward by subdivision economics.

Given that there is more continuity than change between the forces that shaped the pre-automobile city and the automobile city, one might conclude that the automobile just brought more of the same. And it did. More segregation by race and class, more spread-ing of the city. There are, however, important differences.

The automobile as a vehicle of individualized mass transporta-tion was new in its profound incompatibility with urban density.

Cars simply need far more real estate than mass transit, whether they are moving or parked. The space problem also reflects the new ownership pattern. All previous forms of mass transportation were sold as a service—buy a ticket, get a ride. With cars, individuals buy the vehicle itself. Individual ownership means cars are parked much of the time, taking up space in the middle of the city for hours and days at a time. Their right to use the streets for moving and storage was challenged in the early years but upheld by the courts. In 1925, the nation's leading municipal traffic engineer, Miller McClintock, complained that the public at large, rather than the motorist, bore the cost of parking in the city. "After all," said McClintock, "the ability of a transportation vehicle to bear the terminal charges at both ends of the run is not a very severe test of its utility." The car would have failed that test, but it was never administered.

Resident car owners wanted free parking on the streets, and so did downtown business owners, who feared a loss of the high-value "carriage trade." City leaders wanted to ensure that there was enough space for street parking lest businesses move out of the central business district to cheaper land where they could offer free parking. In the face of all this, off-street garages that might have kept the cars out of the way rarely made sense, competing as they were against free alternatives. Surface lots meanwhile started appearing when land prices fell after businesses moved out. Landowners turned vacant lots over to parking in order to at least stay afloat until something better came along. As a result, long before the advent of superhighways, the automobile began reducing available space downtown for businesses and for housing.

The second important characteristic of the automobile and the superhighway is that they were central to modernist plans. In 1916, Arthur Hale earned a patent for what has become known as the "cloverleaf" interchange, so named because its on-ramps and off-ramps resemble a lucky four-leaf clover. The first U.S. cloverleaf was built in 1928 at the intersection of Routes 1 and 35 in New Jersey and lasted until being replaced by a more modern example in 2001. World War I proved the need for better roads as rail lines clogged with matériel. A 1919 cross-country convoy intended to demonstrate motor transport's contribution to the war effort and support the good roads movement was hampered by inadequate roads and bridges, making a lasting impression on a young lieutenant colonel who participated, Dwight D. Eisenhower. (Later he would note how quickly cars and trucks moved along Hitler's autobahn.) The Pennsylvania Turnpike, generally considered the first American superhighway, was completed in 1940.

At the same time, metropolitan planners—especially in France, which had its own vibrant car culture in the early days, and the United States—began turning out visions of the automobile city. Typically, these had layers upon layers of traffic: rapid transit topped by automobile traffic, topped by pedestrian walkways. Airplanes would land atop roofs. (On my visit to the Shiodome area of Tokyo, I was struck by how much the area, built in this century, resembled these visions, absent the planes on the roof.) Le Corbusier's 1925 "Plan Voisin" envisioned a Paris in which slums had been cleared by wide roadways, pedestrians moved to elevated walkways, and housing and commerce were filed away in cruciform skyscrapers. He sought support from automakers to build and publish his plans, later recalling, "As it is the motor-car that has completely overturned all our old ideas of town planning, I thought of interesting the manufacturers of cars . . . I saw the heads of the Peugeot, Citroën, and Voisin companies and said to them: The motor has killed the great city. The motor must save the great city." (Only Gabriel Voisin, a maker of airplanes and truly breathtaking luxury cars, bit and got his name on the plan, if not much else.)

Frank Lloyd Wright took the problem of the automobile to its logical conclusion in Broadacre City, a 1930s concept he developed over many years at some length through books, articles, and models. To Wright, Le Corbusier had not gone far enough. High-density urban forms built at great expense with walkways above roadways above tunneling rail lines looked very modern, even futuristic. Yet he wondered, why preserve the skyscraper and the density of the nineteenth-century city when clearly the automobile rendered them obsolete? If the traditional city was measured in footsteps, Wright's modern city would be built on the scale of odometer clicks. It was, in a word, urban sprawl, though beautifully imagined.

Norman Bel Geddes popularized these prewar visions for the General Motors 1939 World's Fair exhibit, Futurama. In the city of 1960, according to the most popular exhibit at the fair, well-spaced skyscrapers and elevated walkways to carry pedestrian traffic over wide roads would provide plenty of open space. Staggeringly wide freeways would separate traffic by speed, with traffic being sent belowground once it reached downtown.

Bel Geddes too envisioned that his broad roads would cleanse the city: "Here is an American city replanned around a highly developed modern traffic system . . . Whenever possible the rights of way of these express city thoroughfares have been so routed as to displace outmoded business sections and undesirable slum areas."

In other words, in the United States and France, even in the 1930s, arguments for urban freeways emphasized the existing suburbanization and central-city "blight" that most people attribute to the postwar era. Thomas MacDonald, the longtime head of the U.S. Bureau of Public Roads, reported in 1939 that the motor vehicle had made it possible for the middle class to leave the city and commute to work by car. The streetcar suburbs had exploded into automobile suburbs, and it was hurting cities: "The former homes of the transferred population have descended by stages to lower and lower income groups, and some of them have now run the entire gamut. Almost untenable, occupied by the humblest citizens, they fringe the business district, and form the city's slums—a blight near its very core!" Farsighted highway builders tried to team up with urban planners and federal housing authorities to make highways part of comprehensive redevelopment plans. After all, slum clearance was also high on the federal affordable housing agenda.

In signing the 1949 Housing Act, President Truman declared, "This far-reaching measure . . . opens up the prospect of decent homes in wholesome surroundings for low-income families now living in the squalor of the slums." Cities would buy slum areas with federal funds and sell them on to private developers to build housing. The process became known as urban renewal and quickly drew critics. Most famously, Jane Jacobs criticized the program as just the latest example of modernist, rationalist planning, planning that ignored people and destroyed the vibrant, seemingly chaotic city. Her model was her own Greenwich Village, itself once a suburb. For Jacobs, the trouble really began when cities first passed zoning laws to separate industry, commerce, and housing. They thought they were imposing structure and safety (by moving toxic paint-producing factories outside residential areas, for example); in fact, according to Jacobs, they were destroying the natural fabric of city life.

Her critique of planning as a whole may overreach, yet looking back at the visionary plans of Le Corbusier and others reveals a striking lack of human beings amid all the cruciform skyscrapers and elevated streets. On the other hand, by the time the highway men came to town, the planners were all but a footnote. The lack of coordination between housing authorities and highway builders made the dislocation of poor communities especially dreadful as little assistance was offered for relocation. To make matters worse, public housing projects like Pruitt-Igoe in St. Louis, and Cabrini-Green in Chicago, looking for all the world as if they had been designed by Le Corbusier, quickly deteriorated into crime-filled, high-rise, concrete slums.

The plan to use broad streets to revamp the city has a long history. The first Neolithic protocity, Çatalhöyük, in what is now Turkey, had no streets at all. Houses shared walls and were entered through a door in the roof. Maybe they were onto something, because as cities grew, streets became dismal places. Only in the thirteenth century did the first Parisian street get a drain to carry raw sewage away, meaning that until then (and in most places for a long time to come) the street itself was the sewer. In overcrowded and unsanitary conditions, disease spread quickly. So too, according to the chroniclers of the age, did vice: prostitution, for one, was always associated with the street, as in "streetwalker," and "street urchin" refers to the especially grimy, indigent children who roamed the streets. Even in the era of sanitary sewers, streets in poorer districts remained crowded warrens. Planners offered radial boulevards to turn over these dismal streets every chance they got. Cleansing fires often gave them that chance. John Evelyn and Christopher Wren each offered a plan of radial avenues after the Great Fire of London in 1666. Pierre Charles L'Enfant's late-eighteenth-century plan for Washington, D.C., featured radial boulevards, and when Detroit burned in 1805, it was rebuilt to Augustus Woodward's imitation of L'Enfant.

When Haussmann renovated Paris beginning in the 1850s, he used wide boulevards to create air and light. We should not forget, however, that France had just gone through a revolution when Napoleon III hired Haussmann. Barricades are harder to build across wide boulevards than across narrow streets. Daniel Burnham's 1909 Plan of Chicago also featured radial boulevards. For him, traffic congestion, not revolutionaries, was the main problem. The comprehensive plan was first and foremost a program for better circulation. The same rationales—both transportation and land reform oriented—supported superhighway construction in the latter half of the twentieth century.

The high-minded goals of urban renewal, the desire of owners to boost property values, the need for deindustrializing cities to find a new source of revenue, the federal government's efforts to minimize right-of-way costs (the poorer the district you built the highway through, the less it would cost to buy the land via eminent domain), and the segregationist agendas of local elites combined powerfully. They ensured that the highways would be built right into the heart of the city to connect it to the national network on routes that divided, displaced, and destroyed poor, and mostly black, communities. If they'd been able to do it earlier, they'd have done it earlier, but it was only with postwar prosperity and a more powerful central government that the money finally came through.

During the Great Depression, the Works Progress Administration under Franklin Delano Roosevelt provided the unemployed work building roads and bridges. Even when the war put Americans back to work in the cause of freedom, Roosevelt continued to support planning for future highways as a form of countercyclical, or Keynesian, spending. The 1938 Federal-Aid Highway Act called for a report on creating a national network of toll roads. The resulting landmark report to Congress in 1939, "Toll Roads and Free Roads," concluded that many remote stretches of the planned national highway network would have too little traffic for tolls to cover costs. Some other funding mechanism would need to be in place. The Federal-Aid Highway Act of 1944 gave a congressional imprimatur to the report, though provided little funding for actual construction. The idea that states should bear a significant amount of the cost—an unfunded mandate—caused opposition, as did the proposal for a highway trust fund supported by a federal gas tax.

While various interest groups clashed at the federal level over how to pay for toll-free roads, states began building their own superhighways funded by tolls. Following the model of the Pennsylvania Turnpike, opened in 1940, Illinois created a tollway authority in 1941, New Jersey, a turnpike authority in 1949, and Massachusetts, in 1952. These authorities could issue bonds backed by future toll revenues to pay for road construction and maintenance. (A "turnpike" is a toll gate, so properly speaking a turnpike is a toll road, and a "freeway" is a toll-free superhighway, though the terms are often used interchangeably. The matter is further confused as many older turnpikes have since become toll-free. The terms "expressway" and "thruway" describe roads in terms of traffic, not funding.)

Finally, in 1956, a plan for a gas tax to support a highway trust fund along with a 90-10 federal-state split for costs won the day and gave rise to the Dwight D. Eisenhower National System of Interstate and Defense Highways.

Historians disagree about whether national defense was indeed a central role for the highways. "National Defense" appears in the 1944 legislation, the Pentagon reviewed state plans for routes, and inspiration came from Hitler's autobahn. But some argue that the military need was just a ruse to ensure support. In any case, defense was at most a secondary purpose and not one that significantly impacted the choice of routes or building of the interstates.

With the tidal wave of funding coming from the gas tax, highway engineers had relatively free rein. All the engineer had to do, in the words of one official, was to avoid "city halls, cemeteries, and governor's mansions." Routing decisions would necessarily affect property owners, those in the right-of-way and the immediate abutters, and even those farther afield. Middle-class families inside and outside cities suffered. No matter where you live, your property value will plummet when a highway moves in next door.

But without question African-Americans were hardest hit by the urban freeways. Interstate 95 cut through the mostly black city of Camden, New Jersey, displacing nearly thirteen hundred families. Farther south, state and local officials routed I-95 through the Overtown neighborhood of Miami, Florida. According to the historian Raymond Mohl, "One massive expressway interchange took up twenty square blocks of densely settled land and destroyed the housing of about 10,000 people. By the end of the 1960s, Overtown had become an urban wasteland dominated by the physical presence of the expressway. Little remained of the neighborhood . . . known as the Harlem of the South."

Richmond also claimed a "Harlem of the South," Jackson Ward, which was bisected and destroyed by I-95. What's left of the once thriving area is now on the National Historic Register and, according to *The New York Times*, is enjoying an influx of Brooklyn hipsters.

Highways cut through black communities in New Orleans, Birmingham and Montgomery, Alabama, and Columbia, South

Carolina. I-75 razed Cincinnati's mostly black West End. When planners routed Interstate 40 through a black community in Nashville, residents sued, claiming racial discrimination, and won a temporary restraining order. But they ultimately lost and the highway was built.

Detroit's Black Bottom district was destroyed to make way for I-75 and I-375 and the Lafayette Park housing project designed by the modernist architect Mies van der Rohe.

In Boston, it was the Italians and the Chinese who saw the elevated Central Artery, I-93, land atop their neighborhoods; in Providence, Rhode Island, Interstate 95 creates a wall between the Italian North End and the affluent East Side. After crossing the George Washington Bridge, I-95 becomes the Cross Bronx Expressway, perhaps the most notorious highway monster of them all.

The story of the story of the Cross Bronx shows how hard it is to arrive at a balanced view of our urban freeways.

The standard story of the Cross Bronx Expressway comes from Robert Caro's biography of Robert Moses, the chief urban planner of New York from the 1920s to the 1960s. Caro portrays Moses as a monomaniacal, unelected bureaucrat out to connect suburbanites with bridges and highways that run roughshod over New York City. Moses seems to have gone out of his way, in Caro's telling, to drive the Cross Bronx through a working-class Jewish neighborhood, East Tremont, when an alternative route existed farther south that would avoid displacing so many residents. This claim, if true, might tell us something about Moses. But it tells us little about the Cross Bronx, always part of a master plan for New York freeways. Moreover, shifting the highway a few blocks south would merely have shifted its destructive impact, not lessened it.

Moses would have continued his "sacking" of New York had not Jane Jacobs intervened. Expressways were only one of her targets; Lincoln Center was emblematic of the folly of planners. They had torn down a vibrant neighborhood—San Juan Hill—to build a sterile oasis for opera fans.

But Caro published his account of Moses in 1974, just a year before Gerald Ford told a bankrupt New York, according to the *Daily News*, "Drop dead." Today, with New York City having returned to prosperity, historians have rethought Robert Moses. Subsequent research has called into question many of Caro's claims, including the claim that racism was at the root of many of Moses's designs. Among the most intriguing stories Caro relates regards Jones Beach: Caro alleges that Moses built the parkways leading to the beach with overpasses too low for buses. He intended to reserve the new park for whites, excluding the poor and black. (Caro's story was given new life in 1980 when it was repeated in an influential essay by Langdon Winner.) But travelers could choose among several routes to Jones Beach, and in any case, the buses fit under the overpass just fine.

The Columbia professor Kenneth T. Jackson, no friend of sprawl, has suggested that Caro's view of Moses was shortsighted. Moses, the revisionists argue, should be praised, not denigrated, for helping to keep New York a modern city, connected to the rest of America through its bridges and, yes, its expressways. We cannot know how New York would be different today had the highways never been built or had the plans left on the drawing board been realized. Jane Jacobs and others stopped the Moses plan for a lower Manhattan expressway that would have obliterated SoHo. But would they be happy that the neighborhoods, including Jacobs's beloved Greenwich Village, have become enclaves for the ultrarich?

The highway builders always knew urban freeways would be difficult. "When you operate in an overbuilt metropolis," Moses famously said, "you have to hack your way with a meat ax." The highway builders moved quickly to get projects done to outrun the opponents. By the 1960s, however, the opponents caught up. The era of "highway revolts," as they have become known, began. Dozens of crosstown and linking highways were planned but never built. Civil rights activists stood with environmentalists to block them.

The modern city rests on a web of technologies, including sanitary sewers, distributed electricity, safe water supplies, steel-frame construction, and mechanized transport. Without these, cities would stretch no more than a few miles across—or about the distance a person can walk in an hour. They could be neither the teeming home to the diverse millions that are their purpose nor claim the prize as the most environmentally friendly living arrangement for those millions. Each of these technologies, all of this infrastructure, arose to solve urban problems. So it was too with the urban freeways, intended not to destroy the city but to save it.

It is easy to romanticize the city of your youth or the storied one of your grandparents' youth. I know New York always drew me in as a connection to my mother and uncle and grandparents, and hats and pipe cleaners and lace cookies in white boxes wrapped in candy-cane string pulled from a silver orb above the counter. But my Bronx-born mother always told us kids she was from Yonkers, though she only moved there at the age of sixteen. She never talked much about her time as a social worker in Harlem. She loves her house in the suburbs. In other words, if Robert Moses destroyed New York City to build the suburbs, Mom, and millions like her, were right behind him.

Today, the worst aspects of the highway in the city are being confronted. Boston buried its Central Artery (never a central vein) at a cost of over $1 billion per mile, and New Orleans seems set to tear down its elevated Claiborne Expressway. Tunneling has become so much less expensive and cumbersome that more urban freeways will be interred, and the public will celebrate, as it did when Seattle brought in "Bertha," the world's largest tunneling machine, to worm a new route under the viaduct. Could the Cross Bronx and the Bruckner be far behind? Technology is also making public transport more viable and less expensive, from Zipcars and ride-sharing apps to intelligent transportation infrastructure and driverless buses. The line between public and private transportation might one day be pretty blurry. We might trade owning cars to buying transportation services provided by individual autonomous vehicles.

The transportation problem, the problem of moving about, will remain. Dodge Street through Omaha may be riddled with strip malls and parking lots, a depressing realm. A few minutes west, however, it becomes Dodge Road, a grade-separated highway with city boulevards flying over it every mile as if it were part of Frank Lloyd Wright's Broadacre City. Dodge is also part of Route 6, dedicated to the Union army as the Grand Army of the Republic Highway. It's one of the longest roads in the country and the one on which Jack Kerouac first set out when he went "On the Road." For Kerouac, the road served as the antipode to consumerism and the American military might he saw on display in the nation's capital. Oddly, the interstates have destroyed Kerouac's road as surely as they have the city. The road trip, on the old two-lane highways a journey of serendipity, whimsy, and the chance to see something new, does not happen on the interstate, whose culture of hurtling speed punctuated by rest stops served by national chains provides a comforting conformity. The interstate highway is very much part and parcel of the military-industrial complex that Eisenhower himself warned of as he left office. The interstate is the ultimate closed road. But whereas the plan had always been for the superhighways to supplant the dangerous and unruly Route 6 and Route 66, they were supposed to have saved the city.

Interring the urban freeway may not reverse the urban agenda that created it in the first place. Some would call it a plan to revitalize the city; others, a plan to separate white from black, rich from poor. If the land freed by burying the road simply opens up more land for high-priced development or, as in Boston, for urban amenities to serve a high-value customer, it will only continue the process begun with the first horsecars. ("New York is a luxury product," as Michael Bloomberg, billionaire enemy of cars, put it.) Just as the highway could not save us from streetcar suburban development, nor resolve the socioeconomic conflicts of mid-century America, transportation policy alone cannot transform urban America into the city that we all seem to want.

The interstates are easy to hate. But at its best, the interstate is a new kind of creation. I challenge anyone to drive through Glenwood Canyon, Colorado, on Interstate 70 and not have a transcendent moment, or southbound I-295 as it rises over the Delaware Memorial Bridge and lifts you up out of the mire, on I-68 through the Sideling Hill cut in Maryland, or even heading north, on I-71, descending into the Ohio River valley in Cincinnati. These views, this feeling, is the height of the highway engineers' art. They are of their time, to be sure, so one can hope that the highways of our time will do better.

24

ATLANTA'S BELTLINE
MEETS THE VOTERS

ALEX SAYF CUMMINGS

Class has always been the shadow cast by New Urbanism. The idea of curbing sprawl and promoting greater urban density runs up against material realities time and time again. Consider Oregon's much-lauded urban growth boundary system, which set a limit for growth around the state's cities beginning in the 1970s. The policy was put in place by a liberal Republican governor, Tom McCall, who hoped to prevent "grasping wastrels" from gobbling up Oregon's farms and scenic countryside. It accomplished this while also promoting infill—intensive reuse of existing urban space, in lieu of expansion—contributing to the famously walkable and bike-friendly urban culture of cities such as Portland.

But setting a limit on growth necessarily restricts the amount of land available for development, making the remaining land both scarcer and dearer. Housing becomes smaller and more expensive. Working-class Oregonians have not been wrong to ask whether the New Urbanist ideal comes at too great a cost when they look in vain for homes they can afford to rent or buy. The walkable city, it turns out, might be a luxury of the upper-middle class.

If Atlanta is not America's least walkable city, it is close. Jacksonville, Florida, sprawls over 747 car-centric square miles, earning the dubious distinction of the "largest" city in the United States, while Phoenix, Dallas, and a few other Sunbelt metropolises are likely contenders. The curious truth is that Atlanta actually combines a core of semi-navigable urbanism with a broader metropolitan land-scape of sprawl that rivals any in the world. The city boasts three areas that look a lot like "downtowns," knotted along a north–south axis: at the bottom is Downtown, a dreary hodgepodge of conven-tion hotels, Hard Rock Cafes, government buildings, and 1970s modernism at its worst, where public housing and small businesses once stood before they were bulldozed to make way for the 1996 Olympics; above is Midtown, a sleek, shiny cluster of skyscrapers and high-rise apartments that is known as the region's gay mecca; and farther north is Buckhead, a tony area with jagged towers pointing to the skies, where the Swarovskis and the Escalades roam.

Around these three skylines is an archipelago of "in-town" neighborhoods—communities close to the city center and, cru-cially, not outside "the Perimeter" of I-285, a beltway that encir-cles the city and serves as the conventional border beyond which boundless suburbia unfurls. One can walk to bars and restaurants and even use public transit to get to work in neighborhoods such as the old mill village of Cabbagetown, which hipsters have renovated and repainted as a much-desired zip code, and Inman Park, where the earliest gentrifiers moved in in the 1970s and 1980s to fix up old Victorian homes that were abandoned in the haste of white flight.

But beyond this gentrifying inner Atlanta, there is the vast world of the suburbs: a ten-county area where the overwhelming majority of the metropolitan population lives. Only 440,000 or so souls live in the actual city limits of Atlanta, while another 5 million reside outside the Perimeter. The metro area is a jigsaw of municipalities—such as Lawrenceville, Marietta, McDonough, Peachtree City, and countless others—which, to the in-town urban-ite, resembles nothing so much as the blurry horizon of Kansas City, Los Angeles, and Japan in the famous *New Yorker* cover "View of the World from 9th Avenue." This is why Atlanta has been univer-sally recognized as a poster child for sprawl, traffic, and broken metropolitan governance at its finest.

For decades, Atlanta has grappled with how to deal with this gargantuan landscape. In the 1960s, there were battles over the founding of the city's mass transit system, MARTA—notoriously inadequate when compared with New York or Chicago but still the most extensive in the South, a region with a long-standing allergy to all things public. Today, the city continues to debate how to combat its unwieldy traffic and sprawl, which in early 2014 left thousands of motorists stranded on strangled interstates for as much as sixteen hours during an unexpected snowstorm.

The most recent transit melee involved the BeltLine, an ambitious plan to build a ring of parks, bike paths, and ultimately light-rail around the city's in-town neighborhoods. (The project mostly traces the path of old rail lines that have long been out of use.) The idea originated in a master's thesis by the Georgia Tech student Ryan Gravel, who sent his plan for a transit loop to a variety of influential Atlantans in 2000. A group called Friends of the BeltLine began to elicit community support in the early years of the twenty-first century; Mayor Shirley Franklin soon embraced the idea, and the city began to study options for funding a new transit corridor. The BeltLine has since won major support from banks, developers, and federal transit authorities, who have helped fund the construction of bike trails, parks, and playgrounds along the route where light-rail might someday be built. Meanwhile, planning enthusiasts have singled it out as one of "the country's most ambitious smart growth projects." "We can't think of a project more inspiring and forward-thinking," declared *Salon's* Will Doig in 2011.

In 2012, BeltLine supporters placed a referendum on the July ballot, asking if voters in the city of Atlanta and its surrounding counties would be willing to approve a ten-year, one-cent sales tax to raise $8 billion for the Transportation Investment Act (TIA), a grab bag of transit projects that included hundreds of millions of dollars to build light-rail along the BeltLine. And that is when a relatively uncontroversial, public-private partnership that was building parks and bike trails turned into an all-out political fight, with attacks on the BeltLine from both the Right and, more surprisingly, the Left.

The opposition of Tea Partyers in the suburbs is not hard to understand. They claim to hate all government spending, and none quite so passionately as liberal handouts to the people of color who are the biggest riders of public transit in the South. (MARTA is said to stand for "Moving Africans Rapidly Through Atlanta.") But opposition on the left was more interesting, as many progressives had previously been happy to see words like "light-rail" and "affordable housing" without subjecting the project to greater scrutiny. The Atlanta Public Sector Alliance, an activist group formerly associated with the Jobs with Justice movement, was particularly vocal during the run-up to the vote, claiming that the TIA was a Trojan horse for privatizing MARTA. Before people started saying the "devil is in the details," there was an earlier expression—"God is in the details"—and in the case of the BeltLine both may be true.

How I Learned to Start Worrying and Hate the BeltLine

Let's look at the specifics, as best we understand them. By its own definition, the BeltLine will create "a network of public parks, multi-use trails and transit along a historic 22-mile railroad corridor circling downtown and connecting 45 neighborhoods directly to each other." Like many public-private partnerships, the project is held together by a patchwork of federal funds, local government support, individual donations, volunteer work, and help from private entities like Bank of America. Understanding its myriad funding sources and the multiple arms of its projects is not easy to do.

The biggest critique centers on gentrification. According to Atlanta Indymedia, the BeltLine is a "gentrification project for white people," which involves the "forced displacement of Black families from the city." The argument here is twofold: the BeltLine runs through communities, such as the Old Fourth Ward and Reynoldstown, that have traditionally been working class and African-American but that have already begun to be transformed by largely white middle-class urban newcomers who fix up the housing stock and raise property values, eventually pricing out the older residents because of rising property taxes and rents.

In this sense, the BeltLine is a means to further a process already in motion. It is, as another Indymedia contributor puts it, "a line to serve not workers but, largely, a handful of tourists to view the newly gentrified (= de-blacked) areas along the loop to complete the process begun with the destruction of Atlanta's public housing that drove thousands out to South DeKalb and Clayton"— neighboring counties south and east of the city proper. (Atlanta, like many other American cities, began to dismantle traditional, large-scale public housing projects in the 1990s, giving former residents vouchers to seek private-market housing wherever they could find it.)

Concerns about gentrification are legitimate, albeit frustratingly complex, and we will return to them in a moment. Critics are upset not just that the BeltLine will foster rising property values along its path but that it will accelerate a process that has already transformed in-town neighborhoods like Candler Park into havens for the white middle class, who send their kids to "good" local schools, or Grant Park, where the new settlers are eager to get their children into the Neighborhood Charter School (that is, not mixed in with the poor and dysfunctional public schools in their district). But the gentrification issue is one that emerges pretty much anytime projects to improve quality of life in cities threaten to actually improve the quality of life—and thereby entice the home buyers who drive up property values.

The more worrisome critiques raised about the BeltLine involve funding and priorities. Critics allege that the project is pilfering funds that were diverted from property taxes meant for Atlanta Public Schools—in essence, making poor people of color pay for the amenities enjoyed by white home buyers who are pushing them out of their neighborhoods and putting their own children in charter schools, a choice that further saps city public schools of students and funds.

The core of the problem lies in a funding mechanism called a tax allocation district (TAD). Instead of just allocating public funds to pay for the project, the BeltLine depends on a scheme that essentially shaves off part of the anticipated increase of future property values to pay for transit and infrastructure. As the Georgia Tech planning professor Catherine Ross explained back in 2007,

> The TAD . . . uses the incremental increase in taxes due to increased property values in the district to repay TAD bonds used to fund capital improvements for the BeltLine. The TAD is expected to raise approximately $1.7 billion over a 25-year period; therefore, the publicly funded improvements, like park development, new infrastructure, brownfield cleanup, and workforce housing, will take place over time. Ultimately, the BeltLine is expected to result in an approximately $20 billion increase in the tax base over 25 years.

The trouble is that property taxes support Atlanta Public Schools, and critics are not wrong to suggest that the BeltLine is diverting funds earmarked for education to "build upscale yuppie residences and shopping, and pay corporate welfare to favored banksters and lawyers," as the Georgia Green Party activist Bruce Dixon put it. Proponents of the project argue that the TAD pays for itself through increases of property values that would not otherwise occur without the BeltLine, so it is not taking money from the schools that they would have if it didn't exist. Further, the Belt-Line claims that the development will ultimately help the Atlanta Public Schools by raising property values (and thus revenue) in general while rebuilding the city's tax base with "a stronger mix of households of varying incomes."

In any case, TAD-funded development remains risky, given that it mortgages current development on fantasies of future growth. It is like getting a home loan on the basis of a raise you think you might get a couple of years from now. Indeed, while property values have rebounded in many in-town neighborhoods, the collapse of the real estate market during the Great Recession hit Atlanta particularly hard, and prospects for future growth are nowhere near as rosy as they were in 2007, when many projections about BeltLine funding were being made. The TAD strategy also makes clear that the intent of the project is expressly to raise property values—the central driver of gentrification.

Moreover, critics argued that the majority of projects proposed in the sales tax referendum would actually have benefited the out-lying suburban areas much more than the urban core of Fulton and DeKalb Counties, which have African-American majorities and depend most heavily on MARTA's bus and train lines. Such projects included bike trails in Fayette County, bus rapid transit from the city limits to MARTA's in-town Lindbergh station, and a rail extension from there to the mostly white and affluent area around Emory University and the Centers for Disease Control. Critics on the left looked at such projects and saw something rather pernicious—a regressive sales tax that poor people of color would pay to support projects for affluent white people in the suburbs and an inner-city playground for gentrifying yuppies. Viewed from this perspective, the sales tax and the BeltLine looked pretty awful.

Ask the Local Gentry, and They Will Say It's Elementary

Is the BeltLine basically a redistribution of wealth from Atlanta's long-struggling communities of color to groups who are already privileged? Atlantans have already seen their schools and neighbor-hoods undermined from the age of urban renewal and white flight to the current epoch of gentrification. Atlanta is a textbook case of 1960s-era urban renewal at its most swaggering and destructive, sure to challenge New Haven or New York or any other American city where imperious white planners cut huge swaths through working-class communities in the name of fighting "blight." The building of Atlanta's interstate highways since the 1950s led to the demolition of homes occupied by both the white and the African-American working class in a large area near Downtown, where a huge and still barren gash remains, peopled only by the homeless who leave their bundles under overpasses. And while federal urban renewal laws required that the city provide new housing for those displaced by such projects, Atlanta's compliance was incomplete at best; a limited amount of public housing was built, some of which was subsequently torn down for the sake of another public-private boondoggle, the 1996 Olympics, which inaugurated much of the current push to prettify Downtown by cleansing it of its pesky black denizens (both housed and homeless).

Bitter memories remain, and they inevitably frame the issues for some critics. In the words of Robert Bullard, a leading environmental justice advocate and former professor at Clark Atlanta University: "To have people who promote the BeltLine say, 'Trust me, we're going to do it right this time'—I don't see anything in past experiences that would somehow allow African Americans and people who are transit-dependent to say that we trust you to do the right thing this time."

On the other hand, BeltLine supporters have tried to "do the right thing this time," hearing from local communities and outlining plans to ensure a degree of affordable housing exists around the loop. What exactly affordable housing means, though, is not entirely clear. Federal and corporate funds have made possible an extensive program of "down-payment support" to help low-to-middle-income home buyers purchase properties along the Belt-Line. The project helps teachers, firefighters, and the like gain access to homes that they may not otherwise have the savings or income to purchase, especially in areas where property values are expected to rise.

New housing projects built along the BeltLine, like the redevelopment of the old hulking structure of City Hall East along Ponce de Leon Avenue, promise to set aside a certain percentage of units at below-market rate, although it remains to be seen whether developers or the BeltLine will follow through on this. Such promises have disappointed elsewhere before, as Denver learned with its largely fruitless effort to mandate affordable housing as part of new development—a requirement that developers dodged, building as few as fifteen units between 2011 and 2013. Indeed, as many as three hundred communities across the United States have attempted either to require or to incentivize affordable housing in new developments, but if San Francisco or New York's experience with such policies is any indication, the results have been mixed to say the least.

The goal is to create a mixed-income corridor of housing on the BeltLine in order to offset the effects of gentrification, but such a project provides cold comfort for existing residents whose property taxes will rise along with increasing values or renters whose landlords pass on the costs to them. Here the essential conundrum of today's version of urban renewal comes into clearest resolution: we may not be wielding the wrecking ball like Robert Moses or Atlanta's past city fathers, but we are still aiming to create amenities—parks, light-rail, bike paths—that make the city more appealing to groups whose incomes and other resources will drive prices up and marginalize people who are already there. Call it the Quality of Life and Cost of Living Trap. If a place becomes "nicer," people with money will want to move there. The people who participate in the affordable housing initiatives may end up serving as a precious few fig leaves.

Does this mean that any efforts to beautify cities, enhance transit, and generally improve the experience of urban life are inevitably detrimental to the poor, working class, and people of color? Does this mean the better path is to do nothing that would make the city a more desirable place to live—in essence, to avoid raising property values anywhere, at all times, at any cost? This seems like a recipe for the same dystopian abandonment that wrecked cities such as New York and Atlanta during the age of white flight in the 1960s and 1970s, when middle-class families (largely, though not exclusively white) fled and took their tax base with them, leaving the cities to wither on less than a shoestring budget.

White flight, for better or worse, is over, and coffee shops and charter schools are in. They ease the way for middle-class white professionals to recolonize the urban space their parents and grand-parents once abandoned. What was once decried as a racist be-trayal of America's cities is slowly being reversed, but in ways that reproduce and perpetuate racist inequalities through a panoply of means: the educational system, tax incentives for development, the housing market, and so forth.

Where gentrification is concerned, the fundamental issue is housing—property taxes and rents—and here one finds that the BeltLine is ultimately not the true driver of change. Neighbor-hoods in Atlanta like Cabbagetown (which was once the home of white working-class families, before its tiny mill homes were reno-vated by bohemians) and Candler Park have already been almost totally gentrified, and areas such as Reynoldstown and East Atlanta are well on their way to being made over by a mostly college-educated, largely but not entirely white group of new residents. The property market follows the signals sent by people with the jobs and the family wealth necessary to purchase homes in the $150,000 to $300,000 range—a pittance in California, perhaps, but a pretty good chunk of change for working-class and middle-class families in Atlanta. This is where Reynoldstown and East Atlanta are at, regardless of the BeltLine. These are the areas where young people and families seeking a more diverse, urban experience and access to good food and music go when they don't want to move to the sub-urbs and prefer a home closer to Downtown and hip destinations like Little Five Points.

The truth is that market-rate housing will never provide ade-quate shelter for everyone. This is the unspoken fact that underlies all discussions of gentrification. Neighborhood change unfolds through many processes, such as the provision of public education, police protection, housing loans, and media depictions, but the ability of individuals to actually access decent housing will always be largely determined by market forces in a capitalist society. This is why the federal government stepped in to subsidize working-class and middle-class homeownership through Federal Housing Ad-ministration loans during the New Deal of the 1930s, and ever since—because a lot of people would not have the financial where-withal to borrow the kind of money necessary to pay for a home in a totally free market. And as the political scientist Ira Katznelson noted in his book *When Affirmative Action Was White*, for the first several decades of their existence these vital housing subsidies excluded people of color.

This is also the rationale behind public housing, because the market does not create houses or apartments priced at the level that people at the bottom of the wage scale can afford. It is simply not profitable to build and manage such properties for people at a cost that those of the most modest means can afford. The filmmaker Chad Freidrichs beautifully demonstrated this fact in *The Pruitt-Igoe Myth*, his 2011 documentary about the iconic failed housing project in St. Louis; the development was crippled by a lack of public financial support to supplement the meager amount tenants were able to pay in rent.

Until the problem of housing is solved, projects like the Belt-Line will inevitably disadvantage and exclude those who are less privileged than the newcomers who, presumably, will follow in the path of new developments. Government-subsidized public housing is the only way to remedy the inequities of a system that depends on property taxes to support public education and other services and makes ability to pay such levies a precondition to membership in a community.

True public housing does not appear to be on the BeltLine's menu of projects, but there is a promise—and right now it is only a promise, particularly for low-income renters—of new housing de-velopments expanding the number of housing options to Atlantans. The BeltLine says it will spend $240 million to create fifty-six hun-dred units of affordable owner-occupied and rental housing, which would be "the most significant investment in affordable workforce housing in Atlanta's history." Given Atlanta's past experience with urban renewal—and the poor record of affordable housing initiatives nationwide—this is a program that progressives ought to monitor as vigilantly as possible.

The other notable source of opposition to the referendum from the Left involved the lack of real funding in the proposed bill for the Atlanta public transit system, MARTA. Progressive activists argued that bolstering and enhancing MARTA should be our one and only focus in terms of transportation and that using a regressive sales tax to make the urban poor pay for bike paths in the suburbs is not just morally wrong but politically unwise for anyone who hopes to channel greater financial and political support into the city's basic public transit system in the future. With its $8 billion price tag, the sales tax might have sucked up all the oxygen available for transit funding for the foreseeable future, and MARTA advocates were understandably skeptical. They saw misaligned priorities and, indeed, a transfer of wealth from working people who depend on MARTA bus and rail service to suburban commuters and in-town gentrifiers who like the idea of catching a ride on the BeltLine from one yuppie colony to another. These strategic and ethical concerns merit consideration from progressives as we look at the future of the BeltLine, especially if we understand taxation and transit to be essentially a zero-sum game—that is, money for light-rail today means no money for MARTA tomorrow.

But Is It Bread?

In the end, the referendum went down by a crushing 63 percent to 37 percent vote, with only the city of Atlanta and its affluent suburb of Decatur registering support. The BeltLine will go forward, hobbled though it may be by the loss of potential funds and an aura of diminished political support. In December 2013, the BeltLine's board of directors laid out an ambitious plan to complete the entire project by 2030, but it will require billions of dollars—a sum that may be difficult to raise, given that a sales tax is now definitively off the table.

The debate about the referendum and the BeltLine comes back to one of the oldest political problems in the book: the choice between getting half a loaf or "no bread." Every law, every government program or policy decision, involves a maddeningly complex array of moving parts, as the 2009 debate over health-care reform revealed. We can argue over whether a project includes too many compromises or concedes too much to the opposition. Do we get enough of what we want in the deal? This discussion of the pros and cons of the BeltLine raises a deeper question, though: not whether we're getting enough bread ("half a loaf"), but whether what we're arguing over is bread at all. In other words, critics of the BeltLine force us to ask not whether the project does enough good but whether it does good at all.

The answer has to be yes. The BeltLine's aim is to create a denser, greener, more accessible Atlanta, and its work has already begun in new parks and greenways through pieces of its future corridor. In the African-American community of Peoplestown in South Atlanta, a new park has risen in an area where too many homes lie empty, with the windows boarded up. Neighborhood parents and children play around the colorful dinosaurs and art installations. A burned-out old barn sits in the background, next to a newish apartment building and high ridges of dangling kudzu. The BeltLine vision includes many such projects, including a *Parks and Recreation*–esque quarry that will be transformed into a space bigger than the epic Piedmont Park, Atlanta's premier public space.

The referendum was not a choice between a grab bag of projects and an ideal plan to improve and extend MARTA. It was an up-or-down vote on fixing these roads, building those bike paths, and— the biggest item of all—connecting in-town neighborhoods in north, south, east, and west Atlanta through light-rail.

Suburbanites were not having it, though, even with all the sweeteners. Anything that benefited mass transit, even peripherally, was beyond the pale—for the same evergreen reasons that suburbanites have always resented public transit. When MARTA was first proposed in the 1960s and 1970s, voters in Cobb and other suburban counties flatly rejected lines reaching into their communities—with the result being that workers who commute in and out of the city each day spend hours sitting in the sixteen-lane parking lot that is

I-75 each morning and night. As *The Atlanta Journal-Constitution* noted in the wake of the referendum's defeat, "A notable minority, 42 percent, believe that new mass transit would bring crime with it." Maybe it's reassuring that 58 percent of those polled apparently think otherwise.

Nearly six million people are spread over an incredible twenty-eight counties of the Atlanta metro area, and for most, cars are the only way to get to and from the necessities of life. The entire region desperately needs better transit, and anything that gets people out of their cars is a good thing: light-rail, streetcars, bike paths, and greenways. They may not directly or explicitly serve the cause of racial justice or economic equality, but in the absence of bigger solutions for such issues these projects remain valuable in their own right.

I find it hard to believe that building bike paths and light-rail to connect in-town neighborhoods that are otherwise ill-served by MARTA is a terrible thing. The BeltLine will ultimately link the arms of MARTA's limited, cross-shaped transit network with a loop, making it easier to get from the East Side to south Atlanta, the West Side to north. It will connect neighborhoods of widely divergent class and racial character, from upscale Midtown to gentrifying East Atlanta to working-class black neighborhoods like Pittsburgh and Mechanicsville in the west and the south. The very forces that might increase property values in less privileged neighborhoods are the ones that can help working people get to jobs in another part of the city without driving a car. In terms of access to transit, the BeltLine would hardly seem to be "no bread."

Moreover, the creation of new access to transit is not exactly a death ray of instant gentrification. If it were, then the poorer neighborhoods already served by MARTA would have been riddled with Citarellas and Whole Foods long ago. The introduction of rail transit in Atlanta since the 1970s has not turned everything it touches into white bourgeois enclaves. Anti-BeltLine activists have decried the project as "a tool of white supremacy" and "a massive and racist gentrification scheme." They argue that adding to the existing framework of MARTA would create far better access to transit and create more jobs than the BeltLine would. However, creating new parks, bike paths, and rail would not only put people to work but help get them to work. It seems beyond shortsighted to maintain that a plan to build parks and public transit is nothing but a class and race war against poor people of color.

We often lament that Americans don't do "big" projects anymore; a system as extensive as New York's magnificent subway would be nearly impossible to pull off today, if the seventy-five-year plan to build the Second Avenue subway line is any indication. The BeltLine is one such big project. The TIA proposal contained a vast number of programs, of which the BeltLine was only one part, and the BeltLine itself consists of numerous initiatives for housing, transit, and public amenities. Not just transit or housing or even gentrification, but also parks—those few democratic spots in the American landscape that remain open to all, charging no cost of admission. The TIA package might not have done everything we want, but it would have represented a drastic improvement over the status quo of Atlanta's notoriously impoverished public space.

BeltLining with Gulliver

I voted for the TIA referendum in 2012—a lonely vote, as even my progressive friends had their doubts and the local Sierra Club and NAACP joined with the Tea Party in urging a "no" vote. I want to see a denser, more navigable Atlanta. When I moved to the city, I was determined to live close to work and walking distance from bars and restaurants; I landed in East Atlanta Village (EAV), a gentrifying hipster enclave that might be described as the Bushwick of the South. While EAV and a handful of other in-town neighborhoods offer walkability and access to transit, getting around the city remains difficult without a car. To me, the TIA seemed like the only plausible way that better transit could be accomplished, especially when the metro area shows little political will to raise funds by any other means.

Consider my former home of Charlotte, North Carolina, Atlanta's small but plucky regional rival. Charlotte launched a plan for light-rail in 1998, when Mecklenburg County voters supported a referendum to fund transit with a half-cent sales tax. The resulting rail line, Lynx, is modest and primarily serves one north–south corridor, but the service is popular: ridership far surpassed expectations soon after the line opened in 2007. And despite a tenacious campaign to repeal the tax led by libertarians and antitax activists, Mecklenburg County voted to retain it by a lopsided 70 percent to 30 percent margin in a 2007 referendum—almost the mirror image of TIA's failure in Atlanta.

What made Charlotte different? The Queen City is hardly without its problems, but the city and suburbs have arguably had a less poisonous relationship than the city of Atlanta has had with its surrounding counties. Charlotteans in the 1970s and 1980s were significantly more proactive in working together to make school desegregation work—thanks in part to the consolidation of city and county schools under one system. No such identity of interest or unity of purpose has prevailed in Atlanta, where, for instance, the Atlanta Public Schools are separate and distinct from Decatur City Schools and DeKalb County Schools, among many others.

As is so often the case in the South—and America in general—much of this comes down to race. Charlotte has remained a predominantly white city and was able, thanks to North Carolina law, to annex outlying suburbs in a way that Atlanta never could. In contrast, Atlanta's regional politics have long been starkly divided between the liberal black city and the conservative white suburbs, meaning that the ugliest clichés about urban pathology and suburban virtue remain a familiar part of the debate here. And whatever the Queen City has been able to achieve was done on a much smaller scale; greater Atlanta is about the size of two or three Charlottes. Any attempt to deal with sprawl in Atlanta must contend with a dizzying array of competing authorities and interests over a vast metro area—or fail.

I hope the BeltLine will continue despite the electoral verdict. In all development, some will benefit more than others, and some may even be hurt. It is too cavalier to say "you have to break a few eggs to make an omelet"—the convenient refrain of the worst dictators as much as the garden-variety evildoer—but we also have to decide whether the prospect of gentrification means ruling out any kind of neighborhood improvement that might increase property values. The homeless people who have been living along the abandoned rail lines that the BeltLine plans to use will clearly not benefit; as *Creative Loafing*, a local alternative weekly, has reported, they are already being forced out of their hideaway in the liminal shadows of urban Atlanta.

But then again, the BeltLine is not the cause of homelessness, and it did not create the insane American system of property taxation that makes safe neighborhoods with access to grocery stores, decent schools, and other "amenities" inaccessible to many of the urban poor and working class. Renters are subject to rising rents, and even working-class homeowners find themselves shuffled around according to the whims of people with greater means—the middle class who fled the cities in the 1960s and 1970s and who have begun to migrate back since the 1990s, in one of American history's greatest and least understood ironies. This is a function of the way we support local government and schools through levies on property values, as well as the lack of any real effort to ensure good public housing in the United States, which could redress the economic dynamics that drive gentrification. To pin all these broader problems on the BeltLine seems wrongheaded if we really want to reduce traffic, increase density, and promote a future with fewer cars—for everyone.

The BeltLine story is about how one does politics in America's sprawling urban areas, where power and resources are broken up among a dizzying number of entities, from mayors to county commissioners to library boards—and in a country where assertive action by a strong, central authority has always been regarded with suspicion. The BeltLine bears the additional burden of evolving in a southern metropolitan context poisoned by race hatred and chronic, mutual suspicion between suburbs and cities.

It may be that the city of Atlanta itself cannot change deep, institutional injustices, even if it wanted to. And the lack of political will to do anything about traffic and sprawl bodes ill for the future of the metro area. It's no surprise that suburbanites in Cobb County—Newt Gingrich's old stomping ground—view public transit as a delivery service for black criminals; they opposed MARTA in the 1960s, and they oppose anything that smacks of a public service now. But the fact that environmentalists, civil rights activists, and advocates for the working poor can't agree on an agenda for remaking Atlanta's clogged, choked landscape is far more frustrating.

The city may carry on as a helpless giant, tied down by suburban lilliputians on all sides. Perhaps only a united and energetic Left could free it, but the outline of such a coalition is hard to discern in the fractured social landscape of metro Atlanta. If the BeltLine is to endure and change the city, it will need a bigger constituency than its current base of planners, hipsters, and other yuppies. I hope it gets one.

25

DIRE STRAITS

MICHELLE TEA

My mother calls me at home in San Francisco as I work on my computer in my kitchen. I live alone in a spacious one-bedroom. People visit and crane their heads, looking for my roommates. My monthly rent is more than I've ever paid, but only $300 more than I formerly paid to live with three twentysomethings—a bartender/ performance artist, a banker/drag queen, and a student. I decided to move out when I found our fridge filled with sickly, shriveled houseflies. They moved slowly in the cold, among the leftovers. I realized they must have been born there and that baby flies are maggots. I was thirty-nine years old and feared celebrating my fortieth birthday there. So I moved.

My mom calls from the lanai of her own home in Florida. She lives there with her husband. Because she is a graveyard-shift nurse and her husband suffers from a disease that interrupts his sleep with jolts of pain, their bedroom goes mostly unused. They take turns sleeping on the puffy, fake-leather couches in the living room. They sleep before the blaring television, always tuned to Fox News, though neither is a Republican. The television doesn't seem to bother them, nor do the cups of coffee they drink like water throughout the day.

My mother tells me that they've moved the futon from the spare room into the living room and are trying to sleep together again, there on the floor between the couches and the TV. Her husband's disease—his spinal cord is pocked with holes and stuffed with cysts—makes it hard for him to get out of a normal bed, but a futon on the floor is manageable. They haven't slept together in a very long time and seem to be excited, though he has already rolled off the futon once, bruising himself.

I leave my computer when my mother calls and lie down in bed to talk to her. My mother tells me her husband is probably experiencing the beginning stages of congestive heart failure. They're not sure. He doesn't have health care, and so attempts to understand what is making his feet swell up and his stomach bloat into a hard ball, what is making him short of breath, have not gone well.

"It's just an awful situation with the health care," my mother says. Her voice betrays forty or so years on the North Shore of Boston, where the accents run thick. No r's to speak of, and certain words—say, "half"—have a refined pronunciation that reveals the dialect's English roots. My mother is from *New* England, specifically the city of Chelsea, a place that made national news when it went into state receivership in the early 1990s. The proportion of people living below the poverty line is more than double the state average.

My mother has health insurance, and her husband doesn't. The cost of putting him on her plan is too much, but he was turned away from their local free clinic because my mother's income is too high. I don't ask my mother how much money she makes; it seems rude. On occasion, my sister and I send her checks, most recently when she broke her knee at work and needed groceries. Through a series of bureaucratic bamboozlements, my mother was not given any paid leave for her accident. Her time away uncompensated, she returned to work too soon, on painkillers and in a wheelchair, to care for a ward full of seniors, some younger than she. She'd hurt herself slipping in a puddle of urine.

My mother's friends tell her to lie and say that she and her husband are separated. He can get a post office box and redirect his mail there. My mother can say that she allows him to stay in the house at night while she is at work but kicks him out in the daytime. This could help him get better health care.

"I can't do all that lying," my mother says. "You shouldn't have to go there."

In San Francisco, where I have lived for almost twenty years, I have had health insurance three times: for one year while working at a housing clinic, facilitating lead removal from low-income apartments in the Tenderloin; for one year while working at Mills College, teaching fiction; and for the past five months, since my partner put me on the insurance she gets through her employer. The majority of my care has been through the city's free clinic system. I could walk into any clinic, wait all day, and eventually be seen; with a little paper card, my medicine was $5. The staff worked to find ways to cover patient costs. Though I am a lesbian, for years my annual gynecological checkups were covered through a federal family-planning fund. The free clinic closest to my mother and her husband is open just one day a week, on a first-come, first-served basis.

My mother's husband was just rejected for Social Security benefits for the third time. She says that having more than a high school education worked against him, as well as how much money he'd made the year before he got sick.

Both my mother and her husband attended the School of Practical Nursing offered by the Soldiers' Home in Chelsea, a vets' hospital. The program is free, and you work at the home after graduation. My mother graduated when I was nine years old, then promptly divorced my father; I often think of the program as a way of giving the city's many uneducated women in bad marriages the tools and the income to get out.

It was while working at the home that my mother met her husband. He was an orderly with homemade tattoos on his fingers and an earring. She was scared of him. They married a year after her divorce, and within another year he too attended the Soldiers' Home and got his LPN.

My mother has continued to work in geriatric nursing, even though she dreamed of being a pediatric nurse. The extra year or two of schooling needed to get her RN, with its attendant pay scale and increased opportunities, has been decided against; my mother has said she doesn't want to be like "those people."

"What people?" I cried. "People who make more money? People who live more comfortably?"

"They think they're better than everyone," my mother said. "Plus, I'm too old to go back to school."

Recently, my mother tried and failed to get a part-time job at the BigLots! near her home. The management feared she would be bored. She dreams of working at a bookshop or as a Walmart greeter. Something that seems light and easy after decades of caring for the dying.

Before he became sick, my mother's husband was promoted to manager at the assisted-living facility where he worked. He had to wear a tie, which disturbed him. He was asked to overcharge patients from wealthier families to make up for the drag of the poorer residents. He also was expected to discipline his fellow nurses and aides. He quit. My family is not cut out for positions of authority; because we have spent too much of our lives resenting those in charge, the transition into such a role is psychologically impossible. For years, I thought that my own raging against the upper classes, my resistance to bettering my standing, was a punk-Marxist stance born of my own moral spirit. It wasn't until my thirties that I realized I was parroting everything I'd heard at home.

After leaving the management position, my mother's husband found work as a home-care nurse. He would drive to different housebound patients, administering medicines and routine care. Apparently, he was a favorite. Both he and my mother are proud of what good nurses they are. My mother has told me the very first thing she does when she gets to work is wash her patients' eyeglasses with warm water and soap, an image I can't dwell on too heavily. The tenderness and the duty of it strike my heart.

Both my mother and her husband talk to their charges like

equals. They treat them with compassion and respect. They possess a certain snobbery about having received their training in New England—in "Boston," my mother will stress. Not in Florida or any of the other Podunk regions where her co-workers were certified. My mother did internships at Brigham and Women's Hospital, at Beth Israel. A New England health-care education is world-class.

When he was still working as a home-care nurse, my mother's husband began to chafe at his job. He did love the freedom, alone in his truck listening to Aerosmith on his way to his next patient, goofing and palling around while administering care. But management wasn't reimbursing his mileage, and gas is expensive. Plus the wear and tear on his truck. Although the agency he worked for sometimes wouldn't have work for him, it forbade him to sign up with other agencies. Then he became sick, and a job was no longer an option.

A combination of shames keeps my mother from sharing her and her husband's problems. She doesn't want to be a burden on her children. Parents are supposed to give their children money, support, help, not the reverse. She doesn't want me to worry. I've had a strained relationship with her husband, and perhaps she doesn't want to give me more reasons to wish they weren't together. Her husband, too, can be secretive. Sometimes I think they're both shady. It can seem as if they're hiding things, not telling the full story. Maybe they're not.

The last time my mother's husband left Florida was Christmas 2007, when they came to San Francisco. My sister came as well, with her husband and his family. My sister and I put my mother and stepfather up at a hotel in Union Square, in the middle of the hustle-bustle, where the cable cars clang all day. We hadn't expected him to be so sickly. The three blocks down Powell to grab a hamburger in the mall food court almost killed him. He seemed to be in tremendous pain as he walked, the kind of pain that evicts you from your body. He seemed both intensely focused on moving forward and totally checked out, ignoring his body's command to *stop*.

"What's wrong with him?" my sister asked in the hotel lobby. "He's going to need a wheelchair."

"Oh, he'll shoot himself before he ends up in a wheelchair," my mother said, fearful and defensive. "Or winds up in a home, God forbid. He'll kill himself."

Suicide as a sane response to a more draggy ending is something my family has always championed. "A bottle of Seconal and a six-pack," my grandmother would say about her time, should her time come preceded by cancer or dementia. And it did, by lung cancer at the age of fifty-four, and there were no barbiturates or alcohol, just a painful, drawn-out death at Massachusetts General, where she lay in bed convulsing, bald from chemotherapy, her body shrunk and whittled into something resembling a Chinatown chicken.

My mother shared her depressive death wishes with me until I ordered her to stop, and still she lives.

In San Francisco, my mother took her husband to a traveler's doctor downtown. He saw a doctor after hours, late in the night, and was given a prescription for painkillers that could only be filled at the twenty-four-hour pharmacy in the Castro. She took a cab there and back to fill it. I learned this the next morning, when it was all done and her husband was floating on a cloud of pills. Actually, he wasn't floating, not in the way narcotics lift you when you don't actually need them. He was just normal. The medicine had absorbed his body's struggle, and he could be among us on Christmas Day, smiling, excited to see San Francisco, hanging off the side of the cable car that took us into Nob Hill, to the French bistro where we ate our holiday dinner. He had beef Wellington for the first time and found it pleasing, as did I. We both enjoyed the lobster risotto. We'd agreed on a "Secret Santa" plan to stop everyone from spending money on everyone, but my mother cheated and gave me a light blue sweater from Old Navy. My sister's mother-in-law picked up the bill; on the cable car back downtown, she shoved a pocketful of bills into the operator's gloved fist and expressed sympathy for his having to work on Christmas. He dinged the bell at her.

In the hotel lobby, I said, "Ma, you should have called me, I could have gone to the Castro for you, I could have come to the doctor's." But my mother didn't want to worry me; she was too busy worrying *about* me: my recent breakup, my new AA sponsee. My mother was happy I wasn't drinking anymore, but she didn't like me hanging out with so many alcoholics.

All we want to do is feed our mother when she visits and buy her things, as if we could save her with tuna sandwiches and hamburgers and tchotchkes from the Disney Store. But she is our mother, and all she wants to do is take care of us, pay for lunches and dinners, and buy me cast-iron pans and glittering silicone spatulas from the fancy kitchen shop by the water. It is hard to accept things from my mother, but to refuse them robs her of her dignity, her desire to be a mom taking care of her kids. It would take from her the feeling that all is right with us, that our family demonstrates the natural order of things. Kids don't take care of parents, not until they're very old, anyway, and even then you inherit something, don't you?

My mother and her husband make ridiculous decisions with money. The way that she came into any at all was by throwing out her back at work in the 1990s. Her settlement was enough to buy a house in Massachusetts. Soon after, my sister and I confronted her husband about his creepy behavior when we were younger, drilling holes in walls around the house in order to spy on us. The family fell apart for a while, which my mother dealt with by maxing out her credit cards on trips to Disney World. Her husband became a certified diver and took trips off the Keys, swimming with whale sharks. Eventually, they decided to live inside their vacation and moved to Florida. She sold her home to her husband's brother at a deep discount, not even bothering to get what they paid for it. Her brother-in-law had been struggling, with a lazy wife who wouldn't work and two teenage boys, plus houses in Florida were cheaper.

About a year after they moved, the brother-in-law sold the house at a profit and joined them in Florida. The next house he bought was bigger and had a cage pool.

When a hurricane ripped apart their town, my mother's house was spared, but she was traumatized by the experience. The windows on her floor of the managed-care facility imploded, spraying glass on her patients. The tornado in the parking lot created an otherworldly atmosphere that popped her ears and sucked the elderly toward the hole in the wall. She found her staff, a group of certified nursing assistants from Trinidad, holed up in a nurses' lounge holding hands and crying out to Jesus and ordered them back into the ward. When she returned home, her house was so obscured by fallen trees she thought it was gone. She cried with relief to see it wasn't, and she cried for the next month, erratically bursting into tears while buying a flat of water at Home Depot and while talking to me on the phone from her house, a dark and oily place powered by generators, the windows boarded, fans replacing air-conditioning, weakly trying to push out the Florida swamp. When a man came around offering to haul downed trees out of their yard, she paid him up front for three days' work. He was a stranger, but he had a little girl with him and seemed like he needed money, and she felt bad. She gave the little girl lemonade. The man worked for half a day and never returned.

When my sister got married, my mother's anxiety about the cost of the wedding consumed her. She decided to sell the lot that came with her house. It didn't matter that the wedding was paid for or that her plane tickets and housing would be taken care of. She wanted to help. She wanted to buy a dress and pay for a lunch the day after the wedding. The possibility of a sale rose and fell, rose and fell.

"Do you know about Joseph-in-the-Ground?" my mother asked me. European Catholic nuns once buried statues of Saint Joseph outside property they wanted for their convents. Now people buried the statues on their own property when they hoped to sell their homes. She'd purchased a Saint Joseph home-selling kit from a

Catholic supply center and dug him into the lot. She signed off on a fast sale, less money than she could have gotten had she waited, but the wedding was coming.

My sister tried to block my mother from spending any of the lot money on the wedding. She wanted her to put it in the bank. I told my sister that she needed to let our mother pay for the lunch. "It's important to her," I said. "She needs the dignity to make her own decisions with her money." My sister's therapist said this was true, and so my mother paid for the lunch.

My mother's husband's medicine runs her $400 a month. It is harder and harder for him to get his prescriptions filled, as their region of Florida is plagued by "pill mills," illegitimate pain clinics staffed by doctors who will prescribe morphine and OxyContin to addicts. Morphine and OxyContin are his medications. The pain clinics have become tiny police states, with all patients presumed to be guilty addicts by the cops who patrol and raid the places. Squad cars idle in the parking lot.

Because he is not insured, her husband can get his prescription at the pain clinic, but he can't get it filled there, as they don't take cash. He goes to the pharmacy at Walmart, but they are clean out of narcotics. He finds a private pharmacist who is scared to take on a pain-pill client. My mother's husband talks him into it.

Why do some people have really, really hard lives while other people's lives are easy? Why don't I have a degenerative spine disease? My mother learned from another friend from Chelsea that three other men of her husband's generation have strange spinal disorders. They all grew up in the same neighborhood, a series of streets that dead-end into a large waste dump.

"What are you gonna do," my mother says, and it's not a question. "It's just what's going on." She's talking about her husband's body. "It is what it is."

My mother and her husband are the least healthy health-care professionals on earth. They have done nothing to supplement the education they received in the 1980s. They chain-smoke and have resigned themselves to the deaths they'll be rewarded with. My mother reacts with fury against the antismoking legislation popping up around the country. When she arrives in California, she's not allowed to smoke outside the airport. In San Francisco, she cannot smoke in parks. "Before you know it, they won't let you smoke in your own house," she rails.

"Mom, you're paranoid," I say. "People just don't want to breathe in cigarettes, it's gross."

"I know," she says, slightly ashamed. "It's terrible." Her addiction butts up against her desire to make everyone happy or not make anyone mad.

Her husband has a high white blood cell count. "What does that mean?" I ask. "How did you find that out?"

"When we went to the free clinic and they told me I made too much money," she says, scoffing. "They handed him an inhaler and sent him home."

"How is he doing today?"

"He's down in the dumps." Her husband has been depressed about his condition, about his inability to contribute to their life. To compensate, he'll mow the lawn or take on a chore beyond his ability, which results in falls and increased pain. He has burst into tears, afraid that she will leave him. For years, my sister and I have wanted her to leave him. Now if she leaves, he'll die.

"If his feet swell up bad again, we'll go to the emergency room," she tells me. "He's not in dire straits, like I need to call 911 or anything." "Dire straits" is something my mother will say a lot. They're waiting for him to reach this level to bring him in. But I wonder if they are able to accurately recognize what "dire straits" look like. To me, they have been in dire straits for quite some time.

"His feet came down some once he put them up on pillows," she explains. "They were so red and shiny."

It is hard for my mother to explain a situation in a straightforward manner. I think she is in a state of perpetual overwhelm. "Why are there fluids in his feet?" I ask her. "It's a congestive heart failure thing," she says. "The heart's not pumping, and the fluids pool in the feet. I noticed Thursday or Friday, he took a shower and came to sit down. I said, 'You don't look good.' He was huffing and puffing." My mother got one of her nurse tools, an oximeter. "It's a little gizmo you put on your finger and it tells you how much oxygen is in your blood. I said, 'Put it on and go walk into the kitchen.'"

He shuffled into the kitchen, where their untrained Maltese, Kira, pees on newspapers on the floor. He shuffled back.

"Ninety-one," she said. "Not good. We put people on oxygen at ninety-two. But then it went back up again. He's not in dire straits."

Who says "dire straits"? They're a band. There are all sorts of old, regional phrases that my mother carries on. "Not for nothing." As in, "Not for nothing, but I should have looked into the situation for nurses before I moved to Florida. There's no union. It's a right-to-work state, meaning you have the 'right' to work, and they have the 'right' to fire you." Or, "Light dawns on Marblehead." Marblehead is a fancy town by the sea in Massachusetts, but it is also your own thickheaded noggin, slow to understand.

"He's going to talk to his doctor," my mother continues. "He wants to get off some of his medication."

"Wait, I thought he doesn't have a doctor," I said.

"His pain-management doctor, at the pain clinic. She does labs, but she's not his primary care. He doesn't have that. I could have him go to Mapatan"—that's her doctor—"but he won't do shit. He'll say, 'Put your feet up and watch your salt.'"

"You don't know that," I said. Is it because my life is so comparatively easy that I'm quick to access hope? Because my life has turned out well, do I presume everyone else's will, too? "Why don't you just try Mapatan?"

"Because he doesn't have insurance. They don't take uninsured patients."

I begin a rant about the Hippocratic oath. Don't all doctors take a pledge not to let people die? I am ruined from a life in San Francisco, where people like to do good things.

"We'll see," my mother says. "Like I said, he's okay right now. I'm a realist, Michelle. He's got a disease process in his back. He's a heavy smoker, though he's cut his smoking way down, and people get sick."

I am relieved that my mother is so detached, because I fear her being in emotional pain over her husband's dying before her eyes. And I am chilled by her detachment. When they found a cancer in my grandfather's nose, my mother was also a realist. "He's an old man," she repeated. She didn't think surgery was a good idea. But they fixed the cancer, and he lived another decade.

"I don't think I'm exaggerating," she says. "I just know what I see. And his belly's gotten huge."

I would never think that my mother was exaggerating. My mother, and our whole family, downplay everything; they do not exaggerate. For years, my mother would play the lottery, elaborating humbly on how she would spend the money. "I'd keep some," she'd say, "but I'd give it to you kids, I'd give it to Papa and Willie"—Papa's girlfriend—"I'd give it to Darlene and the kids, I'd give some to Carlie." It was a prayer of sorts. My mother is truly Catholic and believes that selfless altruism is rewarded with the granting of more selfish desires. The pagan roots of her Irish Catholicism exist within her without her knowledge, her prayers often resembling spells. In her cold acceptance of death, she is a Scorpio; in her work, she is Hecate, ushering the dying out of life.

My mother is explaining her husband's body to me. "It's just that your heart doesn't pump right, so the fluid in your body, instead of it moving, it stagnates. You got valves in your legs that pump the blood back into your heart."

"What is the fluid?"

"Blood, plasma, lymph fluid. Your blood isn't just blood."

"What does he want to do about his meds?"

"I think he wants to get off all of them and start all over again and see how he does without them. They don't know enough about syringomyelia." That is her husband's disease. When he was diagnosed, my mother called and asked me to look it up on the Internet, something she didn't have. I printed out pages of information and sent them off to Florida in an envelope. "Duke, UCLA, and

Mass General are just starting to do tests." There is a new medicine available, called Neurontin. "It's for neuropathy pain, from nerves. It's not a narcotic."

"The whole thing is no health insurance," my mother says. "You can't even go in and get it straightened out. We'll see what we can do. It seems to be a chronic thing; it's not like, 'Oh my God, I've got to call 911, he can't breathe.' But the shortness of breath is new." When Obamacare was rolled out, my sister and I had a flare of hope that this could be what they needed, a way to save my mother's money and get her husband actual care. But their state, Florida, has one of the more complicated systems. Their aversion to the Internet, to paperwork and authority, to the government, doesn't help.

Her husband doesn't want to go to the hospital anyway. "'Oh yeah, and there's another bill for you,'" she mimics him. "'And I can't contribute.' But I don't care about that. You think I care if I get a $2,000 bill from the ER? Seriously, I'm sixty-two, what are you gonna do about it? I'll give you $10 a month, as long as you give them something, what are they gonna do?"

"There's no debtors' prison," my mother is fond of saying, and good thing. She went bankrupt traveling to Disney, moving to Florida, installing a hot tub inside the house they eventually lost.

"I'm reading a lot about that generation," she says, referring to her husband, a decade or so younger than she. "The '60s and '70s. People did a lot of shit, and it took a toll on them, their livers and hearts, and it's showing up now."

I wonder if he could have hepatitis C, like a lot of people who once shot drugs.

"They were wild childs," my mother says, and shifts from vaguely cavalier yet agitated to somber and guilty. "Part of me feels bad for talking to you about it. I haven't even talked to you in a week, and now I just dump all this on you."

The doorbell rings, and Kira the Maltese begins to bark wildly. "Hold on, it's my pizza," my mother says. I wait on the phone while she pays the delivery guy. My mother doesn't have many people to talk with. Maybe some casual friends at work. A couple old flames from childhood she's reconnected with on the Internet, which she now has, both with sickly wives. They commiserate. Her parents are dead, and her only brother is a mentally ill drug addict so far gone that it's impossible to tell when he is high and when he is having an episode. She comes back on the line.

"I think you need to talk about it," I say to her, and she says, "I guess I do."

We have confusing boundaries, my mother and I. I have forbidden her to share so much of her pain with me, because I didn't want to hear how she wanted to die. When I wouldn't speak to her husband, I didn't want to hear about how hard it was for her.

My mother's pizza is getting cold; she has to go and eat it.

"I love you," I tell her, and she counters with "I love you more." It's what she always says. "Kisses and hugs," she singsongs, and makes a bunch of squishy kissing noises into the phone, and hangs up.

26

FEAR AND AGGRESSION IN PALM COAST

ELIAS RODRIQUES

Most of the unsubstantiated stories I heard in high school focused on violence. The time someone pulled a knife on BD at the eighth-grade dance and how his boys jumped the guy afterward. The time someone pulled a knife on Jackson in the hallway and how, grabbing the knife-holding hand in one fist, Jackson punched with the other until blood splattered the ceiling. The time some kids jumped some other kid with a spiked bat outside the library. Were these stories true? I don't know. But the possibility that they were lurked beneath every argument, encouraging us to consider hurting one another in advance.

Few of us were native to Palm Coast, Florida. Most of the seventy-five thousand people suspended in that suburban stretch alongside the Atlantic between Jacksonville and Orlando came from elsewhere. When I arrived from New York, the ambient climate of violence surprised me. The local teenage boys, ever the putative aggressors, seemed normal: we played sports, worked restaurants part-time, shamed any outbreak of feminine behavior, and chased girls. When it was warm, we surfed. Still, the town had a fierce atmosphere.

In 2005, the year I started high school there, Florida passed a law repealing a defender's "duty to retreat." Stand Your Ground sanctified deadly force in any situation where a person felt threatened, even beyond the boundaries of his or her home or property.

My mother worried about this law as she had about its predecessor, the Castle Doctrine. Many people feel threatened by black males, she warned me, even skinny, studious ones like me; I could lose my life for stepping on the wrong lawn.

My response was a fear that has never left. I remember the first time I wore my extra (extra) large black hoodie in fall of freshman year. Walking to the bus, I imagined my white neighbors peering through their blinds into the early morning dark. What would they see when they saw me? If they saw a thief, then they would call the cops. Bad as that might be, it would be worse if they decided to handle things themselves. I took my sweatshirt off and braved the cold. Later, a white friend confessed that my hoodie scared him and that was why we hadn't spoken on the bus. I must have looked ridiculous, a boy swimming in cotton, but fear has a way of making dark skin appear older than it is.

I hated that walk to the bus. For a while, I tried carpooling with a friend, but he dropped out of school. My mom bought a used Dodge and drove me until gas prices spiked and I went back to my morning walk. Unable to afford a jacket, I wore my hoodie again when frost settled on my neighbors' lawns.

As we got older, the paranoia sown by Stand Your Ground became a permanent fantasy of provocation. People often said, "I wish so-and-so would show up to my house." If so-and-so had done so, people would have a reason to deploy the weapon of their choice. Some days, when the brawny white guy in the back of our bus spouted slurs, I thought, "I wish you would." Then I pictured him at my house and me unloading a pistol on him. My Florida daydreams typically featured a house filled with an endless supply of pistols.

Stand Your Ground, like its predecessor the Castle Doctrine, made it rational to err on the side of aggression. For my black friends, hostility was ever present, and so we endlessly prepared for battle. As teenagers, we bragged about our strength, about how nobody could hurt us, how we would win any fight. Even when we didn't believe ourselves, we sometimes fooled each other.

On the track team, I became friends with Justin, a self-identified redneck, who helped me to the school bus when my leg cramped at our first practice. He explained the difference between niggers and black people. "See, there's white trash and regular white folks," said Justin, "and there are niggers and black folks. Niggers are just the white trash of black folks."

A few weeks later, a friend wore a Confederate flag T-shirt to practice. When someone confronted him, he said it had nothing to do with slavery; the shirt just represented southern pride. He couldn't see why it bothered anyone. The ensuing discussion went nowhere. In Flagler Beach and others nearby, you see the Stars and Bars on bikinis. Occasionally, my mother and I would drive through a neighborhood filled with trailers and farmhouses proudly flying the flag itself. I always glanced around to see if any cars were tailing us. After all, we were in their neighborhood. Could they claim self-defense because they didn't recognize us? And even if they couldn't, even if they weren't acquitted, would that matter if we were dead?

The fear was worst at night, and especially when I walked the half mile home from my friend Jerome's. Not wanting to arouse suspicion, I stared straight ahead while the world throbbed in the periphery. Everything looked as if it could kill you. Countless specters smoked cigarettes in their yards, watching me. Every barking dog became a Doberman about to be unleashed. Eyes straight, pace steady, my calves awaited their teeth.

I plotted escape routes and assured myself that I could outrun anything; I could dash into the nature preserve with the alligators and the snakes. If I needed to hide, I would jump into the gully and lie flat in the sickly yellow-brown gutter water. Worried about leading someone to my house and endangering my mother, I planned my routes in order to lose my pursuer. Unlike my other black friends, who always planned on hopping fences if things went down, I vowed never to step on someone else's property.

Sometimes, when I ran the half mile home, my mom would ask why I was out of breath. I told her I was trying to stay in shape.

Once, two white policemen stopped me. After they stepped out of the car—I don't know if I imagined it, I refused to look—one of them had his hand poised by the gun on his waist.

"What're you doing around here?" he asked.

"Going home."

"This late at night?"

It was 10:00 p.m. on a Saturday.

"Yes, sir."

"Do you live around here?"

I remembered the time some cops stopped a black friend on his way home, shoved his face to the ground, and handcuffed him. Maybe tonight was my night. I had been handcuffed without reason before. In Los Angeles in the 1980s, the police beat a cousin of mine who was running to catch his school bus.

"Around the block," I said.

"I've never seen you around here," said the hand by the holster, "and I live just down that street. How long have you lived here?"

It didn't seem as if they were going to let me off without a few bruises. I considered running, but didn't want to be shot in the back.

"About three years, but I don't get outside much," I said.

"Where are you coming from?"

"A friend's house."

The holster stepped forward and said, "Are you lying to us?"

"No, sir."

This went on for twenty minutes, as they waited for me to contradict myself. It never occurred to me that this law enforcement was my law enforcement, paid for by my taxes, charged with protecting me from criminals. These were not my police. Eventually, they let me go. As they stepped into the car, the one with his hand by his holster said, "You shouldn't be out this late at night anymore."

That night, I listened to 2Pac's "Thugz Mansion" in my bedroom. I recalled that scene from *Boyz n the Hood* where the crooked cops stop Tre, the protagonist, and one puts a gun to his neck for no reason. When Tre arrives at his girlfriend's house, he says, "I'm tired of this shit. I'll kill all these motherfuckers." Then he sobs and swings at nothing, repeating, "I'm sick and fucking tired of this shit. I'm sick of this shit." After wearing himself out, he sits down, holding his girlfriend and crying.

I hadn't cried in years, I never felt comfortable punching at people or shadows, and I had nobody to sob with. Callous and cold, I lay in bed, contemplating what would happen if I stayed in the South.

Junior year I fell hard for a thin white girl named Kelly who smoked cigarettes and skipped every third day of school. She had never dated a black boy, but I thought she might make an exception for me. After she broke up with her boyfriend, I visited her house to work on a school project, sure that a hookup was imminent. As we sat on her bed, I recalled Kelly's temper: she often screamed on the phone with her ex and would call you a nigger if you upset her. Did her parents own a gun? I imagined her standing in the drive-way and shooting as I zigzagged down the street, searching for cover. I won't lie: I found the danger erotic, even thrilling. I'd like to say that fear for my life or revulsion at her racism kept us from kissing, but the truth is I was nervous and wasn't sure she had feelings for me.

Senior year, Marco showed me the Magnum under his seat.

"Just in case anyone fucks with me." He paused. "Check under your seat."

I found a pipe.

"That's for you, or whoever's in the seat, in case we get into some shit."

We were driving to his house to play video games.

In contrast to Marco's aggression, which felt rational, I was baf-fled by the way my white friends moved around, untouched by fear. One night, a friend suggested ringing the large bell on an unsus-pecting neighbor who would emerge to find a flaming bag of dog shit. As usual, the plan unnerved me more than it did them. As-suming the cops would pursue the only black kid first, I tried to dissuade them; I did not want to get arrested.

"Have you been listening to the I Love Penis soundtrack?" someone asked.

When we arrived at the house, I was nauseated and short of breath. Because I was the fastest runner and because I never stood up for myself, they made me shake the large bell until the ringing hurt my ears. As lights turned on in adjacent houses, we ran away. One friend hopped a fence into a neighbor's yard while most of us sprinted down the street. If anyone came outside, I was going straight into the woods.

Running, I was both vulnerable and invincible. At first, the rush of the wind as I outpaced everyone; then the image of the police shooting. I would be hit in the back and crawl on hands and knees toward the woods. When we made it back to the car, my friends boasted, laughing as if after a heist. I demanded to be taken home.

Years later, when George Zimmerman killed Trayvon Martin an hour from Palm Coast, I was not surprised. My white friends asked what I would have done. I've thought about it. If I was walking alone at night, being trailed by a white man would terrify me. Not wanting to be another victim of self-defense, I would run. Maybe I'm faster than Trayvon.

But I'm not faster than bullets; better to wait and let him interrogate me. Who cares if I'm humiliated for a few minutes or even a few hours? And if he beats me, clench my teeth and know that it can't last forever.

That would be my response, but it isn't the only one. Marco would have killed Zimmerman immediately and taken his chances in court. I, on the other hand, would wait passively for the violence to end. During the trial of Trayvon's killer, the prosecution attempted to cast Trayvon as a black kid like the one that I was, a studious teen, destined for a good school, just trying to make his way home. Nobody bothered to point out that if Trayvon had had a gun and shot Zimmerman, he would have had the law on his side, that he would have been doing exactly what the Florida legislature told him to, that he would have been standing his ground. How many other times had he been stopped for nothing? How long be-fore fear ferments into aggression and violence starts to promise relief? Sometimes I envy those whose first instinct is to attack. By hitting back, they take an active role in shaping their lives. I have chosen fear—or rather, fear chose me—and it has kept me breath-ing. But every time a cop car comes slowly to a stop, I wonder if today is my day.

27

MIAMI PARTY BOOM

EMILY WITT

Villa Vizcaya

DATE: July 2005
VENUE: Villa Vizcaya
LIQUOR SPONSOR: Flor de Caña rum

The Villa Vizcaya is one of those Gatsbyesque single-family mansions that have been converted to event spaces. The new owners installed an industrial kitchen to accommodate catering companies and an HVAC system to dissipate the warmth generated by large groups of people. They removed the permanent furniture so gilt chairs could be trucked in for weddings. Guests still had the run of the extensive gardens, but there was no longer anything particularly Gatsbyesque about the place, just a rental tab of $10,000 for a weekend evening.

The Vizcaya was still a very nice event space. From the parking lot, a jungle of banyans and broad-leafed foliage obscured the house. At night, when picking one's way down a path lit with honeycomb floodlights around the ground, there was a feeling of tropical intrigue, followed by awe when the coral mansion finally emerged from the fronds and the vines, a floodlit beacon in the night. This used to be a Xanadu, a neo-Italianate castle built before Miami was even a city, before Miami Beach was even solid land. Where one person saw a mangrove swamp, the mind behind the Vizcaya saw greatness. Thus the first real estate boom began.

Now another real estate boom was happening, here in Miami, where I had just settled (in the gravitational rather than pioneering sense of the word: for several years I had been sinking in a southerly direction, like the pulp in a glass of orange juice). This was my first party. I don't remember much—not even what the party was intended to celebrate—and I took bad notes. The mosquitoes were formidable. I was plastered in sweat. The night was thick and hot, and the concrete steps in back descended into still, inky water. The moon hung over all of it: the bay, the stone barge, the topiaries. Corporations were the sponsors. They hung banner ads promoting Clamato; girls in miniskirt uniforms served free mojitos with Flor de Caña rum. I picked up a free copy of a magazine called *Yachts International*. A real-life yacht was moored to the dock out back, and its passengers were drunk and tan.

I stood with my friend Krishna, watching fireworks explode over Biscayne Bay, over the girls serving rum, over the maze hedge and the moss-covered cherubs and the coral gazebos. We sipped our drinks and scratched our mosquito bites. He gazed at the explosions and said, "The fireworks were so much better at the condo opening I went to last weekend."

Spa Opening

DATE: July 2005
VENUE: Hotel Victor
GIFT BAG: Ylang-ylang-scented bath cube, thong underwear

I moved to Miami from Arkansas to work at an alt-weekly newspaper. My first order of business, after finding an apartment, was to make friends. I appealed to a girl from work to rescue me from loneliness, and she sent me an e-mail about a spa opening at a new boutique hotel on Ocean Drive, steps away from the mansion where Gianni Versace had met his violent end.

I walked up from my new apartment past the Deco and neon, past Lummus Park and the homeless people and mounds of malt liquor bottles beneath the stands of palm trees. It wasn't yet dark; this was an early weeknight party. My co-worker checked us in with the tan girl at the door with the clipboard. From then on, there would always be tan girls with clipboards. We were led to an elevator past tanks filled with pulsing jellyfish lit a glowing indigo. The elevator went down to the basement area where the spa was, and when the door slid open, an impossibly tall drag queen greeted us, dressed only in white towels except for the diamonds that twinkled from her earlobes.

Petrova, a woman with a thick Russian accent, stepped in front of the towel-bedecked drag queen and handed us champagne glasses. She said they contained cucumber martinis, but I think it might have been cucumber and 7UP. "Welcome," murmured Petrova. She took us on a tour that was like a ride at Disney World. Curtains were pulled aside: Behind one was a naked man on a slab of heated marble. Behind the next was a woman having her breasts gently massaged. "Ew," said my co-worker. We stayed twenty minutes, then collected our gift bags, which contained thong underwear and an effervescent bath cube. I didn't have a bathtub.

Hurricane Katrina

DATE: August 2005
VENUE: My apartment building, South Beach
LIQUOR SPONSOR: My next-door neighbor Brett
PHARMACEUTICAL SPONSOR: Idem
FOOD: Frozen pizza
ATTIRE: Sweatpants

Maybe nobody remembers now that Hurricane Katrina hit Miami before New Orleans, but it did, as a baby hurricane. Then it crawled over to the Gulf of Mexico and turned into a monster.

On the afternoon of Katrina, I waited too long to wrap my computer in a trash bag and leave work, and the outer bands of the storm were laying into the city by the time I drove across the causeway from downtown to Miami Beach, my car shuddering in the wind. I understood I was to buy nonperishable food items.

The grocery store was chaos, and I was completely soaked from the trip across the parking lot. While I considered the selection of almonds, the power went out. A dramatic hush fell upon us. One minute the store was all beeping scanners and fluorescent lights, the next darkness and total silence but for the wind and rain. I ate some almonds. In the darkness, someone broke a wine bottle.

We were told to move to the front of the store. Minutes passed. Rain pounded, wind howled. Suddenly a generator turned on, creating just enough electricity to bathe the store in low-key mood lighting, enough for us to grab bottled water and get out but not enough to forget that the hurricane was something to be taken seriously.

Outside, Biscayne Bay, normally tranquil, was a mountainous expanse of gray and white in extreme motion. Plastic bags flew through the air. The high-rises looked exposed and frail, the dozens of cranes in Miami's skyline like toothpick structures that would come crashing down with the first gust of storm. Once safely home, I put on my pajamas and uncorked a bottle of wine. I opened my door to a blast of wind, rain, and sand that filled my apartment with leaves. I ran across to my neighbor Brett's place, on the other side of the stoop. He opened his door, and his apartment filled with leaves.

A friend in Miami once referred to Florida as "America's funnel," and that's what I'd thought of when I met Brett. He was in his mid-thirties and had dyed-black hair, stained teeth, and a permanent sunburn and was almost always smoking on our building's stoop and drinking from a bottle of Sauza Tequila. His apartment was draped in fabric of different psychedelic patterns. He had been looking forward to Burning Man. He had played in an early-1990s grunge rock band of some repute—they had toured with the Smashing Pumpkins—but things hadn't worked out very well. In a moment of idle gossip one afternoon, my landlord Dave told me that Brett had woken up one morning after a night of substance

abuse in New York and found his girlfriend dead next to him.
So he took their cat and moved to Miami, and now the cat was
in its waning days, and Brett was selling boats on the Internet,
supposedly.

Once I left him my rent check to give to Dave, because I was at
the office most days. The next morning Dave, a tan surfer type from
Boca Raton who never seemed upset about anything, knocked on
my door. "Um," he said, embarrassed. "Don't give your rent check
to Brett."

But Brett was the social nexus of our building, which was a low-
rent holdout in a neighborhood at the bottom tip of South Beach
that had gotten much, much fancier since Brett moved in. Our
building was funny; the walls of most of the apartments had vari-
ously themed murals: underwater scenes, jungle scenes, and, my
favorite, in the studio behind mine, hot-air balloons and clouds.
My guess is that the landlords originally painted the murals as a
sort of spell against the crack-addicted undead that were said to
have ruled the neighborhood in the early 1990s. The building even
used to have some kind of tiki setup on the roof, but the door to the
roof was padlocked when the rule of law finally arrived, sometime
around the turn of the century. My apartment was painted the colors of a beach ball and included sloping wood floors, bamboo
shades, and a mosaic-tile counter. It was a one-room studio and a
total dump, but it had beach style.

Our two-story baby-blue building was surrounded by towering
new condominiums of gleaming white stucco, one of which had a
helicopter landing pad. I saw a helicopter land exactly once in the
two years I lived there. Rent was month to month, which meant
I was the only person in the building with a salary.

Upstairs lived a call girl with whom Brett was good friends. She
would come down sometimes in her evening finery and ask Brett if
he would "do her," meaning would he please fasten her black-lace
bustier to maximize the lift of her fake breasts. Brett would flash
his tobacco-stained teeth, hook her into her corset, pat her bum,

and reassure her that he would do her anytime. They were fond of each other.

She didn't like me, with good reason. She lived above me, in a jungle-themed studio. Once, when I was sitting on my couch on a Saturday morning, a thin stream of amber-colored liquid began to patter steadily on my windowsill from somewhere upstairs. Fuck this, I thought. I went upstairs and banged on her door, asking why somebody was peeing out the window. It was that kind of building. She said that she had spilled a cup of tea. "Peeing out the window!" she yelled. "What kind of trash do you think I am?" I apologized, but the damage was done. Later she moved back home to Michigan, leaving in a sweatshirt, with no makeup on. But that was much later, when everyone was leaving.

Brett's friends were always hanging around, none of them model citizens, but I would regularly cross our foyer to chat with them, because being alone at the end of the day sometimes felt unbearable. Two months in, my friend-making campaign was going only so-so.

The night Hurricane Katrina hit Miami, Brett had a pizza defrosting in the oven—the power wasn't yet knocked out—and he dispensed Tombstone, Percocet, and beer. This combo hit me quickly, and I soon staggered home. It was raining so hard that a puddle had seeped under my door. As the streetlights flickered and the eye of the storm passed over the city, I slept.

I woke up the next morning and drove to work. I assumed that the rest of the city still had electricity, but it turned out that almost nobody did; some wouldn't get it back for two weeks. Downtown Miami was deserted. The stoplights were out. The only movement was that of a tribe of vagrants deeply concerned with the transportation of fallen palm fronds scattered across sidewalks and intersections. I arrived at the *New Times* building. Its parking lot was empty except for palm fronds. I sat there for a full minute, engine idling, before turning around and driving back down the Biscayne Corridor. Even the windows of the Latin American Café were darkened, the spy shop shuttered, the sidewalks damp and empty but for the Sisyphean struggle of man versus palm frond. You wouldn't think electricity makes that much of a difference during the day, but it makes a world of difference.

The MTV Video Music Awards

DATE: August 2005

VENUES: Pawnshop lounge, the Redroom at Shore Club, backseat of a police car, La Carreta twenty-four-hour take-out window, Hibiscus Island, someone's yacht

LIQUOR SPONSORS: Various

FOOD: Empanadas, roast suckling pig, cigarettes

ATTIRE: Cowboy boots

CELEBRITIES: Kanye West, Carmen Electra, Jessica Simpson, Black Eyed Peas

GIFT BAG: One Slim Jim, one Slim Jim T-shirt

Brett was closing on a big Internet boat deal "with some Mexicans" the weekend of the MTV Video Music Awards, and the one party I'd been invited to was canceled because of storm damage. The publicity buildup for the awards had been extensive. I kept seeing press releases on the fax machine at work that said things like, "HOTEL VICTOR LANDS A SPACE IN THIS YEAR'S MOST COVETED GIFT BAG." P. Diddy had flown in to a local marina wearing a rocket pack and a white linen suit to announce the nominees. I couldn't go outside without returning with souvenirs like a free Trick Daddy Frisbee handed to me from the trunk of a Louis Vuitton–upholstered muscle car. But my lack of party invitations made me feel sorry for myself. When an event happens in Miami and you have no parties to attend, you start to doubt your own self-worth, even if you're a pale myopic person with the salary of a rookie civil servant who has no business at any Miami party, let alone the fancy ones.

Then a friend called from Los Angeles to see if I would go out with his friend, who was in town for the awards. This friend was a Jewish rapper in a hip-hop group called Blood of Abraham who also co-owned something called a "lifestyle store" in Miami's Design District. The Design District, much like the Wynwood Arts District, was more of a semiotic hypothesis than a reality. Most people still knew it as Little Haiti, and in spite of skyrocketing housing prices it was one of the poorest urban zip codes in America. Average T-shirt price at the store, which closed down within the year: $70.

This friend of a friend, whose emcee name was Mazik, picked me up with a cousin or two in a shiny white Land Rover. He was wearing a pink polka-dotted shirt and a green sweater vest. He announced that Kanye West was performing downtown and that we were going to see him. I was wearing cowboy boots and a dress I'd bought at a Savers in Little Rock, but somehow Mazik and the cousins and I managed to talk our way into a pawnshop-cum-nightclub through leggy models in stilettos. Kanye West showed up for five minutes, and then Carmen Electra performed a choreographed dance with four anemic-looking girls in spangled costumes. The free drinks tasted like lemon drops, and when we left, we were presented with a gift bag containing a Slim Jim and a Slim Jim T-shirt.

We continued on to the beach, to a hotel called Shore Club. Mazik again was on the list. Outside, under a cluster of Moroccan lanterns, I saw Jessica Simpson sitting on a bench looking lonely. She was very small—midget-size, almost, tan and tiny. In the VIP room, I saw a member of the Black Eyed Peas get into a fight. My new friends got peripherally involved, in a drunken inept way, but at least they didn't take off their shirts. Somebody else did, at which point Jessica Simpson was whisked away by what looked like a bodyguard detail dressed up as county sheriffs. We left. The following night, Suge Knight would be shot in the kneecap in that very spot.

Miami is connected to the island of Miami Beach by a series of causeways. The MacArthur Causeway, I-395, is the main artery into South Beach, the palm-tree-lined promenade that Crockett and Tubbs were always driving down on *Miami Vice*. I drove back and forth across the causeway almost every day of my time in Miami, and it never lost its air of serenity. Because of Florida's flatness, the sky is bigger there; the clouds pile into endless stacks of white Persian cats and mohair bunnies. The MacArthur is bordered on one side by the port of Miami, where massive cruise ships and freighters come and go. When I was heading toward the beach, the view was of glittering white condominiums and yachts. When I was heading toward the city, it was of downtown: luminous skyscrapers growing up from a rickety forest of cranes, half-finished high-rises, and canvas-draped rebar skeletons.

At night, sometimes the moon would rise large and yellow over the water, and packs of scarab-like motorcyclists on Yamahas would whir around my car, occasionally doing wheelies. Even when traffic was bad, the environment was glossy: the shiny surfaces of moonlight on the water, of streetlights on freshly waxed cars; the palm fronds rustling and the revving of German motors and the glow of LCD screens showing pornography through tinted windows.

At the end of the night, inside the marshmallow-white Land Rover, I clutched my Slim Jim gift bag. A row of blue lights flashed behind us. We pulled over, and a group of police cars somehow screeched into formation around us, cutting us off in front, reducing traffic on the causeway to a single lane, and leaving our car with two-thirds of the highway and a very wide berth on all sides. I'd lost count of how many lemon-drop cocktails I'd had, but I was drunk. We were all drunk. I can say fairly confidently that the driver was drunk and that all the other drivers on the causeway were drunk too. It was 4:30 on a Saturday morning, and now we were going to be arrested.

The police had their weapons drawn and emerged from their cars shielded by bulletproof car doors. They yelled into a loudspeaker, and we followed their instructions. I stepped out of the car and held my hands in the air. I walked backward, a breeze rippling the palm fronds and my dress, my eyes on the asphalt where normally cars sped and now all was quiet. I knelt, gazing up at the soft purple sky. Then I was cuffed and put into the back of a police car next to an empty pizza box, where a lady cop began demanding information about our firearms.

I was suddenly a lot more impressed with the people I'd been hanging out with. They had weapons? I quickly confessed that there had, in fact, been a fistfight. But then it emerged that, no, the police had simply confused our car with another white Land Rover. Someone in *that* Land Rover had fired shots at a police officer. We were sheepishly released, our drunkenness apparently not enough to merit attention from the law. We drove to Little Havana and ate empanadas.

There was one more party that weekend, on Hibiscus Island. We were transported by boat, and the theme was sort of luau meets Vegas: tiki torches, roasted suckling pig, and girls in uniform carrying around piles of loose cigarettes on silver platters. I think American Spirit sponsored the party, but maybe it was Lucky Strike. We removed our shoes and climbed onto a yacht moored against the mansion's back dock. Out in the gulf, Katrina was growing and New Orleanians were preparing to flee, but the Atlantic was quiet now. It was pretty, with the lights and the palm trees and the views of South Beach, and a little rain that would fall for a minute and stop.

Driving Brett and Andy to the Airport

DATE: September 2005
VENUE: Toyota Corolla
PHARMACEUTICAL SPONSOR: Brett
GIFT BAG: A very small Ziploc

Brett and a friend of his, an Australian male model named Andy, were going to Burning Man. I agreed to drive them to the airport. Their flight left early, and when I knocked on his door, Brett emerged baggy-eyed and smelling like a mildewed sponge soaked in tequila. We picked up Andy at his girlfriend's. She was also a model, tawny with dark brown eyes and a minimalist figure. As they said goodbye, they were orbited by what seemed like a dozen tea-cup Chihuahuas but might only have been two very light-footed teacup Chihuahuas.

We merged onto the highway. Brett, in the backseat, began emptying his pockets, pulling out bags of pills and empty mini-Ziplocs coated in a residue of white dust.

"Should I put those pills in a container?" asked Andy.

"I guess. I don't know. You think?"

"I guess."

Brett passed a baggie of prescription pills to the front seat, and Andy put it into an orange case with a prescription on it.

"But what about the cocaine?"

"The cocaine?"

"The *cocaine*?" I shouted.

"Somebody gave me all this coke last night. I can't bring it?"

"Don't bring it on the airplane."

"*Really?*"

They decided there was only one thing to do with the cocaine. As I nervously pulled up to the airport, Brett put what remained in the well next to the gearshift. He looked at his nostrils in the rear-view mirror and took a Percocet. I quickly put the baggie in the glove compartment. Off to Burning Man! We waved to each other. I drove to work feeling lonely.

Hurricane Wilma

DATE: October 2005
VENUE: Ted's Hideaway, South Beach

Wilma hit Miami in the middle of the night, and by the time I woke in the morning, the city was silent, void of electricity. The air felt a way that it would never feel again in Miami: crisp, dry, and cool like a New England fall day. I walked to the beach. Men with surfboards ran past me to catch the only surfable waves there would ever be on South Beach. The wind was still blowing and pelicans loitered miserably, too worn out to flap their wings even when the surfers barreled toward them. Somebody spoke up for the pelicans and ordered everyone to leave them alone while they were tame like this, docile with exhaustion.

People wandered the streets with cameras, taking photographs of smashed cars under fallen trees. One parking lot between two buildings had formed a wind tunnel. The cars had piled up like leaves. This was a popular spot with the photographers. My trunk, which had been stuck shut since a British woman in a gleaming chrome SUV rear-ended me, was suddenly open and filled with the branches of a nearby ginkgo tree.

A curfew was called for nightfall, and the city forbade driving after dark. My neighborhood bar was crowded and candlelit, but outside the strange autumnal chill remained. My neighbors picked their way through the darkness, stepping over fallen trees. They held flashlights and lanterns, and the landscape seemed odd, as if they were going to a Halloween party in Sleepy Hollow. The stars were bright over the darkened city.

Some parts of the city were without electricity for weeks, but my place regained power after three days. Miami Beach with its tourists is always a priority. For the remainder of the time I lived in Florida, skyscrapers had plywood over the places where windows had broken. In poorer neighborhoods, blue tarps covered damaged roofs for years. But the significance of Wilma didn't register at the time. Now people say that was the moment when the manna curdled in Miami, when the fragility of its physical location started to affect property values, when the logic of building taller and taller high-rises in a natural-disaster-prone peninsula started to seem suspect. Wilma wasn't even a real storm, it wasn't an Andrew or a Katrina in New Orleans, but it was enough.

Art Basel Miami Beach

DATE: December 2005
VENUE: Miami Beach Convention Center, my apartment
CELEBRITIES: Jeffrey Deitch, David LaChapelle (rumored), Madonna (rumored), Sofia Coppola (rumored)

Art Basel Miami Beach is perhaps the only time each year when New York aesthetes bother with Miami. The art fair is an offshoot of Art Basel in Switzerland, and it attracts a lot of very wealthy people. These were a different sort of wealthy people from the banana-yellow-Hummer-driving, highly leveraged "rich people" who were always cutting each other off on I-95. Suddenly my neighborhood hamlet of fake tans, silicone breasts, and hair gel was invaded by pale androgynous people with Italian glasses. The first rule of fashion in Miami was that you wear nothing that might make you look androgynous or poor. These people all looked like shit, but wonderfully so, expensively so.

I spoke with my friends on staff at various hotels, who told me that Sofia Coppola had been spotted at the Delano and that Madonna was at the *Visionaire* party last night and that David LaChapelle's poolside installation at the Setai had a drag queen lounging naked in a glass house in the middle of a swimming pool.

New Year's Eve

DATE: January 2006
VENUE: Delano hotel
FOOD: Surf and turf
LIQUOR SPONSOR: Dom Pérignon
CELEBRITIES: Billy Joel, Snoop Dogg, Jamie Foxx, Ludacris

I ended up at Jamie Foxx's album-release party on New Year's Eve because I accepted an invitation from a man twenty years older than I who was the local correspondent for a prominent celebrity tabloid. "You're the only person I know who is superficial enough to actually enjoy this," he said kindly.

I decided I would enjoy myself. The problem was that as soon as I stepped into the lobby of the Delano, with its gossamer curtains and high ceilings, and as soon as I was served champagne by models dressed in silver angel outfits, and primal hunter-gatherer food (fire-blackened meat, stone crab claws, oysters, caviar, lobster tails) by a waiter dressed in tennis whites, I was overwhelmed by a profound sadness.

But 2006 was going to be a good year, or so promised Jamie Foxx when his press handler escorted him over to us. He was covered in distracting surfaces—mirrored sunglasses, diamond earrings, polka-dotted shirt—and graciously shook our hands.

"An excellent year," he promised, and I believed him.

Then he performed the song "Gold Digger" against a backdrop of more gossamer curtains and dancing angels and pewter candelabras, while we watched from the lawn around the pool, where the grass was cut short like a tennis lawn and tiny white edelweiss-like flowers sprouted. I held my glass of Dom, and my high heels sank into the soil. Snoop performed, looking shy and grinning goofily, then Ludacris, and then fireworks exploded over the Atlantic Ocean and a new year began.

I ended the night without my escort at a bar called Club Deuce. In Florida, unlike in Brooklyn, the dives are really dives: neon lights shaped like naked ladies, wrinkly alcoholics, obese bartenders, all in New Year's crowns, blowing horns and throwing confetti. I was in a cab heading home alone by 4:00 a.m., my gold shoes somehow full of sand.

My Twenty-Fifth Birthday

DATE: April 2006
VENUE: Stand of palm trees, Key Biscayne Beach
LIQUOR SPONSOR: BYOB

I celebrated this birthday with my friend Krishna, who made close to six figures a year as a waiter at the most expensive hotel in South Beach. Krishna had grown up in a yoga ashram in central Florida and then gone to Brown. The son of his ashram's guru was now a big-time real estate broker in Miami Beach with a boat and a BMW and an apartment in the Mondrian. Krishna was gay and surrounded himself with down-to-earth, interesting people. He was a real friend, not a fake friend. Things were changing for me. For example, I started taking tennis lessons. I started hanging out with people I actually liked. I stopped shooting the shit with Brett. I would nod on my way out the door, when he was sitting there having a cigarette, but I didn't go swimming with all his friends in the evenings, and their parties got so depressing. One night, I agreed to drive one of them to "pick something up." I was just trying to be neighborly. On the way, the guy failed to warn me about a helpless animal crossing the road. I know that as the driver it was technically my fault, but he saw this animal, this doomed raccoon, and he just let out a slow "Whoa." Then I ran over the raccoon. In the rearview mirror, I watched the raccoon drag itself toward the curb. I hadn't even properly killed it. I was furious. I was furious at this poor creature for trying to live on Miami Beach, at myself for having maimed it, and especially at this guy for being too much of a stoner to stop me. It wasn't quite fair, but that's how I felt. From then on, when Brett's drug-dealer friends offered cocaine when I stepped out of my apartment in the morning, I would be outright rude. At some point, Brett had lost his job selling boats.

My relationship with Miami changed. I went to fewer parties at hotels. The gift bag influx slowed. I stopped being around so many people who sold real estate, who picked me up in luxury vehicles, who drank lychee martinis and said things like, "Well, I was talking about this with John Stamos at Mansion the other night." I still pursued unlikely friendships out of curiosity: I went on a date with a paparazzo who had netted his fortune from a single portrait of Paris Hilton with her tiny dog. The funny thing was that this paparazzo had a tiny dog of his own that would nuzzle and burrow under your arm when you held it, like a little cat.

I stopped writing e-mails to my friends in New York about my mirth at outrageous Floridian real estate nonsense. The billboard advertising a condominium project on I-95 that was simply a photograph of a man's hands unhooking a woman's bra was no longer delightfully symbolic of everything that was wrong with the real estate boom, just depressingly so.

To live in a place like Florida is to destroy the earth. I watched snowy egrets and great blue herons picking their way through drainage ditches outside Costco. I covered county commission meetings where the merits of building suburbs in the Everglades were proclaimed and posters of digitally rendered high-rises were offered in exchange for slackening of the zoning laws. I went to the Everglades and saw anhingas flitting under the boardwalk, their tails expanding like fans in water stained brown like tea. I thought about how in Florida, a bird like the anhinga was only useful insofar as it provided local color in the names of housing developments. The names of new housing developments grew more and more offensive. I started keeping a list. The idea was to make some sort of game out of it, like that Internet game that generated Wu-Tang names. I thought I could make a Florida subdivision name generator.

Here is an excerpt of my list: Villa Encantada. Gables Estates. Old Cutler Bay. Journey's End. Hammock Oaks. Cutler Oaks. Pine Bay. Deering Bay Estates. Old Cutler Glen. Cocoplum. Saga Bay. Serena Lakes. Lakes by the Bay. Three Lakes. Cutler Estates. Swan Lake. Arabesque. Arboretum Estates. The Sanctuary at Pinecrest. Gables by the Sea. Tahiti Beach Island. Snapper Creek Lakes. Banyans by the Gables. Coco Ibiza Villas. Kumquat Village. The Imperial. The Moorings. Trocadero in the Grove. Gladewinds Heights. Killian Oaks Estates. The Palms at Kendall. Poinciana at Sunset Lake. Villas of Briar Bay. Las Brisas at Doral. The Courts at Doral Isles. Porto Vita. The Terraces at Turnberry. Lychee Nut Grove. Flamingo Gardens Estates. L'Hermitage. The Palace.

Nightly Barbecue, Guantánamo Bay

DATE: May 2006
VENUE: Leeward dormitories, Guantánamo Bay Naval Base
LIQUOR SPONSOR: Navy PX

A senior reporter at the paper quit, and they sent me in her stead to report on the detention facilities at Guantánamo Bay. Cuba fell under our purview as a Miami newspaper, even if Gitmo was four hundred miles away. Before I left, I watched *A Few Good Men*, the basic-cable mainstay about a military cover-up at Guantánamo. When Demi Moore and Tom Cruise visit the island to look for evidence, Demi, in curve-hugging navy whites, accuses a flippant Tom of goofing around. "Are you going to do any investigating," she demands, "or did you just come here for the tour?" I came for the tour.

I flew Air Sunshine. A lawyer, a frequent flier on Air Sunshine propeller planes, had told me that taking the airline's shuttles from Fort Lauderdale to Guantánamo Bay was like traveling in a "minivan with wings." The nine-seater's decor was peeling blue pleather accentuated with protruding bits of orange foam. A front-row seat afforded a detailed view of the cockpit, because one sat practically inside it. The windows were pockmarked and scratched. The engine thrummed a steady bass vibrato. The air smelled acrid with fumes. As the plane tilted to land, a container of shoe polish rolled across the floor.

I spent ten days at Guantánamo, most of it by myself on the deserted leeward side, where I rented a bicycle from a Jamaican contract worker and went swimming on a rocky beach overseen by marine guard towers. The detention facilities were on the windward side, where we could go only with military escorts. I toured the camps twice, going through the motions of journalism. The tour was a farce. We saw the prisoners only from a distance. The cells they showed us were stocked with "comfort items" like soap, the "interrogation room" furnished with a plush armchair and an espresso machine. The troops we spoke with told us about their scuba-diving lessons. They lived in a suburb devoid of a city, like an amputated limb with a life of its own, with Pizza Hut and Ben & Jerry's and outdoor screenings of *The Hills Have Eyes*. When inside the camp, the military personnel removed the Velcro name tags attached to their uniforms and emphasized that detainees have been known to make threats. On one of the tours, our guide was the naval commander Catie Hanft, deputy commander of the Joint Detention Group. Commander Hanft's previous job was commanding the naval brig in Charleston, South Carolina, where José Padilla was jailed in an environment of almost-total sensory deprivation, never allowed to see the faces of his captors, until his transfer to a federal prison in Miami. Hanft had short hair and a tan. When one of our escorts accidentally called her by name, she smiled and interrupted: "Colonel, don't say my name in the camp, please." The mood curdled slightly.

Most nights we would pick up some meat and alcohol at the navy PX before they escorted us back to the deserted side of the bay. Then we would drink alcohol and grill meat, "we" being an assortment of human rights lawyers, Pashto translators, and journalists. Joshua Colangelo-Bryan, one of the lawyers, told of walking in on his Bahraini client, Juma Al Dosari, as he attempted suicide during a bathroom break the previous year. Al Dosari, who had made twelve serious attempts, had cut one wrist and tried to hang himself. On this visit, although Colangelo-Bryan noted a couple of new scars, Dosari seemed in better spirits.

On the night before I left, there was a bigger group than usual at the barbecue. Around midnight, when everyone was slightly drunk, a plane came in to land on the base's runway, which was also on the deserted side of the bay. Sleek and floodlit against the night sky, the plane gleamed white and bore the green insignia of the Saudi royal family on its tail. The Saudis had come for some of the prisoners. In the morning, the plane was gone.

NBA Finals

DATE: June 2006
VENUE: Street in Coconut Grove

The Miami Heat had had a good season, and as the team advanced to the play-offs, people actually started going to Miami Heat games. Everybody in the stands wore white to these games. Later I was informed that the entire sports blogosphere made fun of Miami for doing that. The Heat beat the Mavericks in the finals. I went to an outdoor screening of the last game and watched Dirk Nowitzki run backward chewing his mouth guard with an increasingly frantic air of frustration. Lots of Miami players seemed to be wearing special injury-preventing compression kneesocks and sleeves. After the team won, a friend who was visiting observed the cheering hordes in white on the street. "The most hard-core Miami Heat fan is like one of those girls who wears a pink Red Sox shirt," he said.

Fidel Puts Raúl in Charge

DATE: July 2006
VENUE: Calle Ocho

Everybody wanted to be in Miami when Castro fell. *The Miami Herald* supposedly had a plan, or rather *the* plan, for the moment of Castro's death. Then nothing turned out as planned. Castro showed up on television in an Adidas tracksuit, looking ill. Then he made his brother acting president. The streets outside Café Versailles were full of people honking horns and waving flags, but Fidel wasn't really dead. *Fidel Castro was no longer running Cuba*, he was attached to a colostomy bag and being fed through a tube, but the Berlin Wall moment everyone in Miami expected didn't happen. For the first time, it seemed possible that it might not ever happen. Then again, he's not dead yet.

Dinner with a Psychic

DATE: September 2006
VENUE: The home of Univision's morning show's visiting psychic

I was writing about the first homosexual love triangle in an American-made Spanish-language telenovela. One of the actors, who was straight (it was unclear whether the show's tolerance extended into telenovela casting practices), invited me to dinner at the house of a Spanish-language television psychic named Frances. I had a friend of a friend in town so I invited him, too, thinking he would enjoy the cultural experience. He did not enjoy it. The evening ended with Frances's waving a wand around a warbling vibratory instrument called a meditation bowl and ordering the friend of a friend to hug a palm tree. "I'm an atheist," he kept repeating, his face pressed against the palm tree. The next week I got an e-mail inviting me to a gathering at Frances's with some Tibetan monks. I have many regrets, but few loom so large as my decision not to attend.

Weeknight Shindig at Brett's

DATE: September 2006
VENUE: Our apartment building

This year Brett came back from Burning Man with an announcement: he had fallen in love. Kellie, an eighteen-year-old from Truckee, California, arrived shortly thereafter. She immediately found work as a cocktail waitress and started supporting him. I gave her my old driver's license so she could get into bars. We had other news as well: our building was going condo.

Art Basel Miami Beach

DATE: December 2006
VENUE: Shore Club

This year I went out a little more at Art Basel. I went to a *Vanity Fair* party. We got rubber bracelets, like Lance Armstrong testicular cancer bracelets, but hot pink and stamped VANITY FAIR. My aunt, who lives in southwest Florida and paints pictures of children flying kites on beaches, came to see the art, but what excited her most was watching someone write a $400,000 check in a particleboard boothlet.

A Celebration of the Jade Collection of Thi-Nga, Vietnamese Princess in Exile

DATE: February 2007
VENUE: The Setai, Collins Avenue

The paper assigned me an investigative piece: discover the true identity of Princess Thi-Nga, a Miami Beach philanthropist and supposed member of the exiled imperial family of Vietnam. She was on the board of the Bass Museum of Art, where the parties were always sponsored by Absolut Vodka. Her collection of ancient jade sculpture was on display at the Bass at the time, which some people saw as a conflict of interest. My editor thought she might be a fraud. I failed to uncover much evidence of this. I failed to uncover much evidence at all, actually. It appeared nobody was paying close attention to the lineage of the former royal family of Vietnam. I too didn't really care.

I met Thi-Nga at the Setai, the hotel where my friend Krishna worked. A room at the Setai cost upwards of $1,000 a night. Its bar was inlaid with mother-of-pearl and its couches upholstered with manta ray skins, or something like that. According to Krishna, when a guest of the Setai arrived at Miami International Airport, he or she had the choice of being chauffeured in a Bentley or a Hummer (a question of personal style). In the car was a wide selection of bottled-water brands and an iPod.

Thi-Nga was launching her jade sculpture exhibition with an

elaborate party at the hotel. I met her there for breakfast the day before the party. I ate a $12 bowl of muesli. It was the most delicious bowl of muesli I have ever eaten.

For her party, Thi-Nga had rented an elephant named Judy. Adorned with gemstones, Judy led a parade down Collins Avenue on Miami Beach that also included dancers: Thai ones with pointy golden hats and splayed fingers and a Chinese lion that batted its paper eyelashes to the rhythm of cymbals. The princess rode in a silver Jaguar convertible behind them, seated next to the mayor of Miami Beach, waving to confused pedestrians who tentatively waved back. Then all her guests went to the Setai and ate salmon.

Brett Moves Out

DATE: April 2007

This party is in fact only theoretical. My neighborly relationship with Brett had deteriorated to the point of mere formality, so I'm not sure if he had a goodbye party or not. I hope he had a big party, where the lava lamps oozed and the cigarette butts accumulated and the dollar bills were dusted in cocaine. Our building was de-populated now. The call girl was gone; the dumb stoner who had been my accomplice in the murder of the raccoon was gone. The apartments upstairs had sold for phenomenal amounts of money. My apartment had been purchased by a tennis pro, who informed me that I could consider him a landlord upgrade. I took him at his word and purchased the air-conditioning unit with the highest *Consumer Reports* rating, paid the alcoholic handyman who hung around the neighborhood to install it, and deducted the whole pro-duction from my rent check. Going condo was amazing.

Unless you were Brett. Things weren't going well for Brett, who was still unemployed and being supported by his teenage girlfriend. He and Kellie had recently been arrested for driving someone else's car that happened to have a felony-size quantity of crystal meth in the glove compartment. I encountered them on our stoop after they had been released on bail. Apparently, everything would be all right; they had agreed to rat on some drug dealer. But still, this on top of moving. They were heading up to Eighth Street, a part of South Beach that remarkably had retained its seedy character and whose apartments, though as expensive as everything else in Miami, were terrible to live in. I'd had a friend who lived on Brett's new block; her floor was often inexplicably littered with millipede exoskeletons. She would gamely sweep up the hard brown shells and claim that they were harmless, but I vowed that I would draw the line of shitty apartment living at mysterious worm infestations.

Then one day Brett was gone, and the landlords were happily ripping out the interior of his apartment. One of them, Dave, told me it had been a relief.

"You should have seen the bathroom. Drug addicts. It's disgusting."

Very stupidly, I had never thought of Brett as an *addict*, just as a guy who did drugs. A certain kind of Miami guy who liked to party. But now Brett was gone. All traces of him were replaced, in a matter of weeks, with granite countertops and track lighting.

I saw him one more time that summer, on Fifth Street, when I knew I would be leaving Miami. I was walking home from the gym when I was waylaid by a torrential downpour, the kind where I could see the violent wall of water approaching from across the street. I waited under an overhang, staring at nothing, until it retreated. In the dripping aftermath, the sidewalks gray and clean, the palm trees still quivering, I encountered Brett on a street corner. Brett wasn't a pessimist. Everything was going great, he said, the new apartment was fantastic. Later, when the recession came, I took comfort in knowing that, like me, Brett was probably all right, because Brett owned nothing.

That was the thing about boom times that later became clear: We now know that boom times don't feel like boom times. They feel like normal times, and then they end. Particularly if one is not a direct beneficiary of the excess wealth and one's salary is measly to nonexistent, boom times are just the spectacle of other people's reckless spending. Their gluttony was my gluttony of course—only a bore would have abstained from the festivities—but their downfall was little more than an abstraction from the vantage point of one with no assets.

Our downfalls would not involve grand narratives of repossession or foreclosure, just a steadily diminishing ability to keep some fundamental part of the city at bay. In heady days, we conquered Miami, carving out the mangroves, digging up the ocean bottom and slathering it on a sandbar, molding concrete into skyscrapers, pumping refrigerated air through miles of metal windpipes and over glass coffee tables and white couches. But here, now, as those with no assets fled to low-rent holdouts, inland from the beach to paved-over swamps, recession only meant a slow infiltration: worms burrowing through the floor and dying, spores drifting through vents, and terra-cotta roof tiles uplifted by the autumn winds.

My Last Day

DATE: August 2007

The Corolla was packed up, and as I was about to leave, one of those terrific summer rainstorms hit. I lay next to my boyfriend on his bed (for by then I had a boyfriend), watching the rain pound against the windows, the palms lean into the wind, and the cat purr between us. Of the whole tableau, the only thing I anticipated missing was the cat. The relationship was ending, my job was ending, and the real estate boom had already ended. I had gotten ornery in the last months in Miami. If another interviewee told me, as we drove in his golf cart through a maze of pink stucco on top of a leveled mangrove grotto, that he "lived in paradise," I thought I might wrestle the wheel from him and plunge us both into the algae blooms of a fertilizer-polluted drainage canal. So I left the place where baby sea turtles mistake the floodlights of condos for the rising sun, where the dogs are small, the breasts are big, and the parties are ornamented with drag queens in bubble baths.

When the rain stopped, I drove past suburbs until I hit the Everglades, then emerged into suburbs again on the other side.

28

LEHIGH ACRES, DESIGNATED PLACE

SPENCER FLEURY

I think when the end finally comes to America, it will look like Lehigh Acres. It never suffered a cataclysmic implosion, like the one that broke Detroit. It has no grand urban ruins to serve as reminders of a great city that was. There is instead virgin space and frustration, weeds and snakes and slowly crumbling tract homes. At ninety-five square miles, Lehigh Acres, Florida, is a vast and largely empty preserve for the roughly eighty-six thousand souls believed by the Census Bureau to live there. This is more space than is contained within the city limits of San Francisco or Boston or Miami. It is slightly smaller than Orlando or Tampa, two nearby cities with three and four times the population, respectively.

Then again, Lehigh Acres may well be even bigger. Or maybe smaller. We don't know for sure, because there are no actual city limits for Lehigh Acres. It is categorized as a "census-designated place," which seems to mean only that people agree it has a name.

But *is* Lehigh Acres a place? I'm not entirely sure. It is freestanding sprawl. It cannot be a suburb in the literal sense of the word, because it doesn't have an *urb* to be subordinate to. Nevertheless, even if it is not one, Lehigh Acres has the physical form of a standard-issue Florida suburb: meandering streets converge at a single entry point to avoid giving access to those who don't belong; there are no sidewalks, because there is nothing to walk to. Few if any old-growth trees, because trees slow down the process of grafting row after row of identical stuccoed boxes onto the landscape. Deep front yards and generous setbacks keep company with expensive fences amid a lonely, indifferent quiet, broken only by a passing car or a far-off lawn mower, never by a human voice.

In Lehigh Acres, the effect is amplified by the unintended empty spaces between homes. Unused lots have long since reverted back to nature, and much of the built environment is uninhabited. It is the only ghost town of eighty-six thousand I've ever seen.

To a geographer, "place" is something distinct from "location." Events and processes define a place. Place *includes* location but is not limited to it. It also signifies human influence and interaction. A single location can also be two different places on two different days or even simultaneously. But location itself is immutable, and it seems that location is all there is in Lehigh Acres.

With its enormous sky and broad stretches of wire grass and scrub palmetto, southwest Florida has the look of a frontier. When the sun is high and the cicadas are whirring, it is a bright and lonely landscape. In the 1950s, ads for Lehigh Acres ran in northern newspapers promising a brand-new home for "only $10 down and $10 a month." The developers took the typical approach to infrastructure in Florida—grow fast and let the rest take care of itself—but applied it on an impossible scale. As a result, it is easy to drive through Lehigh Acres and not realize it. The emptiness sneaks up on you, uncoiling behind the generic trappings of Florida exurbia: scattered fast-food outlets, a handful of newish shopping plazas with plastic banners rippling from the rooftops in place of permanent signs, the commercial plumage of transition or decline.

Take a random right turn off Lee Boulevard, the main drag, and pull in to almost any driveway. You will find an abandoned house surrounded by a chain-link fence and wheeled gate, which itself is padlocked shut and secured by a thick, rusty chain. Weeds and wild grasses infest the yard and wedge the driveway apart, reclaiming everything for the snakes. Some houses have plywood nailed over the windows, as if the owners were hunkered down inside, waiting to ride out the next storm with their plastic jugs of water and pyramids of canned beans and peaches. Often they are separated from each other by a stretch of empty lots, parcels that were plotted but never developed. These lots are now just over-growth, wide fields of knee-high grasses tended by no one, dry and brown from the lack of rain, gratefully bending to even the gentlest breeze. Sometimes houses interrupt the spread of the weeds; in other spots, these subtropical meadows spill across entire blocks.

If you drive around long enough, you may also stumble across one of the handful of gated communities—lonely outposts in an encroaching wilderness, their gates often mere yards away from blighted starter homes and lakes of wild grass. But those gates are porous; beyond the guard shack, you might spot a patchy lawn or two, or faded green streaks of pollen caked onto someone's pastel-yellow stucco, or a garage door that doesn't close properly.

Lehigh Acres is not a place like Paris or Portland or Las Vegas or even Royal Oak, Michigan. It is not a neighborhood, because this would require neighbors. There are no public spaces to speak of. "Place" implies the existence of something unique, something that a visitor can latch onto and say, "Aha, yes, you see? This is unmistakably Lehigh Acres." Yet nobody could ever, will ever, say this.

29

DISAPPEARING IN DULUTH

SHAWN WEN

We all wanted to leave. Eventually, most of us did. But she left first.

She left home without her cell phone or her engagement ring. She was wearing a gray sweatshirt and blue sweatpants. She ran in New Balance sneakers.

Two hours later, her fiancé started to retrace her route. West Lawrenceville is a winding road. In April, the crape myrtles were in bloom. He drove as far as the Town Green and then back toward Joan Glancy Memorial Hospital, before heading home and calling the police.

Officer in Training Rodney Harris arrived at the Mason residence at half past midnight. He found that Mr. Mason was "confused" and "upset, very cooperative." The house appeared "organized, well maintained." Harris wrote that he found no evidence relating to suspicious activity. He called his superiors. Soon several units of the Duluth police were searching the surrounding area.

I first saw her when I was driving home from school. A woman in the search party waved me down. She held up a photograph of a slender white woman who was smiling and wide-eyed. Jennifer disappeared three nights before her wedding, on her regular evening jog. She lived here. Right in this neighborhood. Had I seen her?

It wasn't a small town anymore. And though we rarely talked about race, we openly discussed the constant threat of "gang violence." At school, we couldn't wear bandannas or scarves in our hair. We weren't allowed to roll up our pant legs. These were gang symbols. In driver's ed, we were instructed to never flash our headlights at other cars, even as a courtesy. Mr. Mays said that gang members cruise around with their headlights off, waiting for you to flash yours at them. Once you do, they'll jump you.

Gang members throw eggs at your car window. When you turn on your windshield wipers, the egg smears. You can't see anything, and that's when they attack. If you spot a baby carriage or a box of puppies on the side of the road, never try to save it, Mrs. Vaughn told me. It's a gang initiation ritual. Once you step out of your car, they'll beat you up. Maybe worse if you're a woman.

Though we all felt that Duluth was changing rapidly, the census data bore it out. In 1970, fewer than 2,000 people lived in the Duluth city limits. The county was 95 percent white.

In 2005, the year that Jennifer disappeared, we wondered when white people would be outnumbered in Duluth. My high school history teacher had warned us that it was coming. Five years later, in the 2010 census, 26,600 residents lived in Duluth, and 41.5 percent of them were white.

On April 29, the night before Jennifer Wilbanks and John Mason were supposed to get married, five of her fourteen bridesmaids appeared on Greta Van Susteren's show on Fox.

"This is not how you're supposed to be spending tonight, is it?"

"No."

"Lindsey, what do you think happened?"

"I wish we knew. I mean, we've—we don't know, and we're not giving up hope. And we're just—we're still searching."

At this point, 250 people had joined the search party for Jennifer Wilbanks. Neighbors, wedding guests, and police officers scoured neighborhoods and riverbanks. They passed out flyers. Her family was busy planning a candlelight vigil. They announced a $100,000 reward.

Van Susteren leaned forward, her face puckered with concern. "Jamie, anything going on in her life, any ex-boyfriends, anything like that?"

"No."

"Nothing at all?"

"Not at all."

The first search for her covered five square miles. The search party expanded its search when her family told Chief Randy Belcher that Jennifer Wilbanks liked to run in marathons.

"Marlene, tomorrow is the wedding. Postponed, not canceled."

"Yes."

"The cake is all ordered; everything's ready to go. What can you tell me about the wedding plans? Because obviously, they have to be put on hold."

"She planned this for a long time. She was happy, excited. And we were going to get together and celebrate her joy and her love with John."

"You got the dresses?" asked Van Susteren.

"Yes. They're all at the house waiting."

Major Donald L. Woodruff of the City of Duluth Police Department said in a press conference that the police had no explanations. They had brought in the Georgia Bureau of Investigation, the FBI, bloodhounds, and German shepherds. They took the dogs out to Gainesville, Jennifer's hometown, to pick up the scent of the wedding dress. Jennifer Wilbanks's disappearance was being handled as a criminal investigation.

Van Susteren said, "Marlene, anytime anyone disappears, the last person to see the person who's vanished is going to be put under the microscope. Jennifer's father, totally behind John. Are you behind John?"

"He's part of our family."

"All of you behind John? A hundred percent, no doubt?"

"No doubt."

"No doubt."

"She was so in love with him."

•

A handsome neighbor once told me over a bottle of gin that the great thing about New York is that people know how to live with one another. That you have all these disparate groups who are capable of sharing space. He insisted that you don't get hate crimes in New York the way you do in the South and the Midwest, just crime. Although he and I aren't in touch anymore, I often think about what he said. Every time I see a homeless man on the subway muttering to himself, I think about how great we are at sharing space on this train car.

It's easy to tell a friend over a drink in New York that the North is more racist than the South. When I say it, what I lack in conviction, I make up for with force. And a part of me believes it. I did have more black friends when I lived in Georgia. There's a larger middle-class black population.

But then I recall the smaller things we did and said, heard, and saw. An elbow glides over the inside door panel to lock the car as a Latino man walks down the center lane of traffic. A classmate says, "If they move here, they need to try to fit in. They should at least learn English."

In 1821, while the rest of the country looked west, Evan Howell of North Carolina talked some friends into venturing south with him. He found an area empty of white settlers. Some of our oldest families were these first, brave pioneers: the Knoxes, the Summerours, the Lawrences. Imagine their dismay—these farmers who were used to the rich brown Carolinian soil—when they dipped their shovels into the ground and pulled out red clay.

The Cherokee and the Creek were here first. And though the Trail of Tears wiped them out of the region so thoroughly, children I grew up with still dug for arrowheads in their backyards. At the Duluth Historical Society, I looked at photographs of beech trees marked by the Cherokee on their way out. A volunteer at the museum told me they had chosen beech because the bark never peels. And they intended to find their way back and retrieve the buried treasure. Of course, the Cherokee still haven't made it back, and the volunteer didn't mention what happened to the buried treasure.

The red clay proved fertile for cotton. And the railroads moved in. At its peak, Duluth had three cotton gins, three mule-trading barns, and three blacksmiths. The warehouses so overflowed with bales of cotton that the streets were nearly impassable.

The Atlanta Daily Sun printed on its front page on February 28, 1871, "The geografical condition of her peple, and the fiscal location of the immediate place in question, and the surrounding cuntry generly, will all culminate to cap this the Climax City of the up cuntry. 'Tis true, sur, that Ganesville and Norcross have extended parts, but Duluth will ride over them as the tornado rideth the over cuntry. To this, let us all open out, amen."

John Mason never really looks camera ready. Chief Belcher, Major Woodruff, and his dad were all better in interviews and press conferences. But the producers wanted John, so he tucked in his shirt and gave a statement: "She left out of here with just a radio and her clothes that she had on. Her cell phone's in there, her credit cards, her pocketbook, her money, her keys, her car, her diamond, and everything that she owns is in the home. If it's cold feet, it's the weirdest case of cold feet I've ever seen."

I remember watching TV with my parents when we saw Duluth on national news for the first time. The camera panned across the faces of elderly white people swaying on rocking chairs.

A reporter stood at the Town Green, the city's most photogenic site. She used words like "small town" and "Mayberry." In days, this was the top story on the major networks and cable stations, tag teaming the twenty-four-hour news cycle along with Michael Jackson's child molestation case.

The stories detailed Jennifer's wedding registry: pure white china with a band of platinum by Lenox, Waterford crystal, Grande

Baroque sterling from Wallace. Her wedding planner appeared on CNN to say that, no, six hundred people is not a particularly large wedding. Yes, fourteen bridesmaids does seem a bit much. Her height and weight came up over and over. On flyers, in articles, in the mouths of TV reporters: five feet eight, 120 pounds. Strikingly tall, admirably light. As if the numbers themselves bore power. As if the numbers could bring her home.

The police found a clump of brown hair. The CNN correspondent Jonathan Freed went on *Nancy Grace* to say, "It was not a clump of hair that you would expect to find if somebody was in a fight, for example, looking like it was ripped out of somebody's scalp with follicles at the end of it. It looked like somebody simply cut their hair, you know, held two fingers together, snipped a lock of hair off."

A pair of dark blue sweatpants turned up in Duluth. Two gray sweatshirts were found, one in the Suwannee and the other twenty miles away in Cumming, Georgia.

Jennifer's fiancé, John, underwent a polygraph test. Police called this "standard procedure." And he passed.

The saying goes something like, "You never know what comes up the Buford." Buford Highway is the main thruway of Duluth, connecting the town to Atlanta proper. It's a seven-lane road with no median, few sidewalks. Two hundred and fifty people were injured crossing Buford between 2000 and 2010. Another thirty died. Still, there are no plans to change it.

Tim from the planning department told me that Buford Highway was probably older than Duluth. That it used to be an old Indian road. Then we came in, spilled concrete over dirt, and gave it a name. But he couldn't verify this.

If you go south on Buford, the street signs turn to first Korean, then Spanish, then Chinese. There are sprinkles of Vietnamese, Indian, and Ethiopian. Closer to Atlanta, there's a stretch of strip clubs and sex video stores. When I was in high school, I dated a guy who lived in a nice neighborhood across the street from the biggest strip club nearby. The building was lined with blinking purple lights. Though I had never seen it, my then boyfriend claimed a helicopter sometimes parked on the roof and strippers dangled from its blades. He said, "I like to drive by and yell out the window, 'Hey, get those girls off them copters.'" He raised his voice as he explained this last part.

But the part of Buford Highway near the house that Jennifer Wilbanks and John Mason shared was different. The original Rexall diner and the old Parsons general store were still there. From your car window, you could look out at the Town Green and its terraces. There's a Victorian pavilion. A fountain shoots water seventy feet up in the air. The park was just three years old in 2005, the year Jennifer Wilbanks disappeared.

The Town Green was where Jennifer ran on her nightly jog. It was where John first searched for her and where TV crews aimed their cameras.

He told the press, "I went out looking for her and never found her anywhere."

John Mason's stepfather picked up the ringing phone. Jennifer was on the other line. She was calling from a 7-Eleven in Albuquerque. She wore the clothes she was last seen in: a gray sweatshirt, blue sweatpants, and New Balance sneakers.

The man on the phone was elated. He told her that she was all over the news. TVs across the country were tuned in to her story. People were praying for her. He told her to hold on, he's handing the phone to John.

John was crying and laughing. What happened? he asked her. Call the police, he told her.

A 911 operator picked up.

"What's your emergency?"

"I'm at the—um, I don't know where I am. I'm right here at Solano Street [sic] at the 7-Eleven."

"Okay, what's going on?"

"I was kidnapped earlier this week."

"What is your name, ma'am?"

"Jennifer."

"Okay, and who did this to you?"

"I don't know."

"Okay. And the person who did this to you. Was it a he or she?"

"It was a Hispanic man and a Caucasian woman. It happened in Duluth."

"About how old?"

"I would say in their forties, maybe."

"Okay, how tall was he?"

"Oh, God, I don't know, probably my height, about five nine."

"What color shirt did he have when you last saw him?"

"He had on a maroon jacket, and I don't know what color shirt under it."

"What kind of vehicle was he driving?"

"It was a blue van, like a dark van."

"Was it a conversion van or a small minivan?"

"It wasn't a minivan. It was like a painter work van."

The police picked Jennifer up. In custody, she told them that the Hispanic man and the white woman were a couple. He didn't speak any English, so the woman translated.

The couple bound her hands with rope and placed her on the floor of the van. Where in the van? On the right side, facing backward. The man drove as the woman stayed beside her.

"Who took your clothes off?" the policeman asked Jennifer.

"She did."

"Did you resist at that point when they were trying to take your clothes off?"

"I just, you know, I said, please don't, I said, please don't do this, but I didn't put up a fight."

And then she told police that the interracial couple raped her. She described the sexual assault in details that NBC called "too graphic to repeat" and "all of them untrue."

Everything Jennifer told the police was untrue: the kidnapping, the physical restraints, the rape. She made it up. She had run away.

Jennifer and John were devout Christians. Though they were living together while they planned the wedding, they promised to be chaste. Chaste until they made their vows in front of God and six hundred wedding guests. Her father, Harris Wilbanks, said, "He did it the old-fashioned way. I couldn't ask for a finer Christian son-in-law."

Hours into questioning, the FBI agent said, "Jen, I've been doing this job for a long time. Jennifer, I think something happened, and you said, 'I just can't do this on Saturday.'"

"I just cracked under all this pressure, and I—I just—I mean, I couldn't do it all, I just couldn't, and have the perfect wedding that everybody thought that I was supposed to have."

"Mm-hmm. Yes."

"Oh my gosh—oh my gosh. You know, and then I was like, 'I only have Friday off. I've got to get my pedicure and manicure done. I've got to pack for this honeymoon that I don't even know where I'm going.'"

She bought a Greyhound ticket a week earlier. And before the run, she withdrew $40 from an ATM and packed a few snacks. She changed into her jogging clothes and called a taxi and met the driver at the Duluth Public Library. The first bus took her from Atlanta to Austin. She chatted with a Hispanic man and a white woman who befriended her on the ride. The second bus went to Las Vegas. And then, on the last leg of her trip, she stepped off at the bus station in New Mexico. She was out of money. She called home.

"Based on Jennifer's own statement of the entire incident being false, this case will be considered closed, unfounded," Officer Michael Medrano wrote in the police report.

There was only one question: Why?

And she couldn't give a satisfying answer.

•

Construction was the only constant in Duluth's landscape. More than any one building or road, I remember bulldozers, upturned dirt, and cracked concrete. In the South, there isn't the same sense of finitude as I've seen up north. No preservationist bent, no urge to build upward, but rather a tireless renegotiation with the land. Every time I come home, more woods have been cleared away; another building has been torn down and rebuilt bigger.

When I lived there, Pleasant Hill Road and Buford Highway intersected near the railroad tracks. Traffic was painful in the late afternoon. Worse after they closed down two regular Walmarts across town from each other and built one Walmart Supercenter on Pleasant Hill.

I remember watching freight trains pass at dusk. The cars moved so slowly. Sometimes they would stop and go backward, then forward again, shifting onto different tracks. It could take twenty minutes. I used to turn off my car engine and prop my feet up on the dashboard. As I fixed my lipstick in the rearview mirror, I could see the river of cars behind me.

Then one day when I came home for winter break in college, the intersection at the railroad tracks was gone. Pleasant Hill and Buford were now two separate roads, one running over the other. A system of four on-ramps and off-ramps channeled cars between them. The first time I drove on the ramp, it was morning and happened to be overcast. Cars kicked up gravel that was still loose from recent construction.

And, of course, who built these new roads? Who came in and crowded our streets? Who drove up the gas prices and the crime rates? Who migrated up the Buford Highway? Who is that man, splattered by paint and dirt, walking along the shoulder of the road?

Traffic moves faster now, and Duluth is just one place on the way to another place.

It wasn't enough for Jennifer to say "I'm truly sorry" or "I was scared to death. I didn't know what was going on."

Everyone was still mad at her. She secluded herself in her child-hood home. She refused media interviews, and for a time she only saw her family, her minister, and John.

John said to Katie Couric that he was "angry for about five minutes."

And he went on, "She just was scared. She had a lot of confu-sion and a lot of hurt for herself, I think. And she'll uncover a lot more of that as we get through the next phases of our life. But she is very loving, very caring, never met a stranger, just loves people, and little kids in particular. Her mom always said she was put on this earth to be a mother, so we're looking forward to that one day."

The community was less forgiving.

Meg Marston of Snellville wrote a letter to *The Atlanta Journal-Constitution*: "She's a selfish, self-centered brat who thinks of no-body but herself. What a shame character is no longer rewarded in our society. But bad behavior? It reaps bountiful rewards."

The media was more vicious. Multiple outlets reported that she had been caught shoplifting three times. Was she in the habit of running away? The *New York Post* suggested she was trying to see an ex-boyfriend. The ex denied it. But he added that if he had the chance, he would have turned her in. "And then I'd have asked for the $100,000 reward," he said.

People magazine printed that she ran away because she was sexually frustrated. John Mason was, after all, a born-again virgin. They circled a photograph of her chest and suggested she had breast implants. Sanjay Gupta stood in front of a giant projection of her face on *Anderson Cooper 360°*. He pointed to the whites of her eyes. He saw signs of Graves' disease, an overactive thyroid. Is that why she's so thin? Is that why she ran away?

In the end, she received two years of probation, a $2,250 fine, and 120 hours of community service. A stranger approached her as she cut grass.

"Are you feeling okay about life?"

"I'm getting there."

"Yeah. Is the public—how are the public treating you?"

"I need to get back to work, please. I don't want to get in trouble."

"Are you used to mowing the lawn?" the woman asked her.

Until recently, race in the South has been a black-and-white story. Which is to say, until recently, race in the South has been a white story. So many southern cities like Duluth look longingly to the past. But when Duluth looks back on the small town that it used to be, the white town that it used to be, it is looking at a town that existed ever so briefly. Just over a hundred years. Native Americans border the time line on one end, Latinos and Asians on the other.

When Jennifer Wilbanks disappeared, when we all thought she had been kidnapped, when we sat in front of our TV sets waiting for news, when she lied and said she'd been abducted and raped by an interracial couple—these were the manifestations of our anxiety. This is how we regarded white women. This is how we felt about whites becoming the minority.

This is a land that is accustomed to rebuilding, albeit begrudgingly. General Sherman burned most of Georgia in his march from Atlanta to the sea. He spared Savannah because, as my high school history teacher told us, his girlfriends lived there. Two of them.

Aside from Atlanta, I honestly can't imagine there was very much for Sherman to destroy. I remember the scene of Scarlett O'Hara clinging to Rhett Butler's lapel as they drive a horse-drawn wagon out of the burning city. And then when I pop in the second VHS tape, Scarlett is meaner and more savvy. Her hands are coarse. She is a businesswoman. And Georgia is beginning Reconstruction.

Before there could be Reconstruction, there had to be destruction. Before the New South could rise, the antebellum South had to burn.

Just over a year after her disappearance, Jennifer Wilbanks and John Mason broke off their engagement. They filed lawsuits against each other. She sued for money. He sued for emotional distress. They have since dropped the lawsuits and moved on with other people. And they've also left Duluth.

When I researched this story, visiting city hall, the planning department, the police station, I was told again and again, "You can ask about Jennifer Wilbanks, but nobody likes to talk about it." I think that's a sign of rebuilding. There's no memory here. Does fire breed amnesia? All of our buildings are new.

30

WHITE OAK DENIM, GREENSBORO

AARON LAKE SMITH

The Cone Mills White Oak denim factory sits out past the college football stadium and baseball diamonds on the nether edge of downtown Greensboro, North Carolina. Named for a large tree on the property, it is bordered by narrow, numbered streets cluttered with eyeless and empty ranch-style houses that seem to clamber up to the factory gates, dusty FOR RENT signs swaying in their freshly seeded front yards. An asphalt bridge on a hill bordering the plant crosses over a single lonely railroad track, and from there you can see the factory's berth; it goes back for miles, buffeted on its southern edge by farmland, creeks, and historically black North Carolina A&T State University. Rusted water towers and three grimy smokestacks loom overhead; just across a small drainage creek sits Cone Mills' twin facility, all boarded up and abandoned, windows slowly shattering themselves out of boredom while crumbling ledges collect dust and crows. At White Oak's main administrative office, 1970s-style white block letters slowly rot off the ruined facade. On my first visit to the plant, I pulled my car up beside a little guardhouse, dust billowing around my tires. I rolled down my window and reached for the big yellow telephone, seeking permission to pass through the barbed-wire gate. It seemed as if a disembodied voice on the other end of the line had always been there waiting for my call.

"HE-LLO?" a voice warbled on the other end. "Can I help you?"

"It's Aaron?" I responded. "I'm the new security guard?"

A hundred years ago, the White Oak plant employed upwards of twenty-five hundred people; late in the first decade of the twenty-first century, that number dwindled to four hundred, and as of 2014, to two hundred. Strange circumstances had landed me the job. After an initial, virile thrust of résumé mailing followed by several weeks of unemployed despondency, I received an unexpected call from a man with a syrupy North Carolina drawl named Sam Whitey. Whitey asked if I was still interested in the position as a security guard. I didn't remember applying for the job, and the name of Whitey's contracting company didn't sound familiar, but I said yes. Whitey explained that he had a contract to secure White Oak and that he needed to hire a stable of warm bodies to watch the barely operational factory, freelance, for minimum wage and no benefits. An hour later, I was driving down four-lane Benjamin Parkway, which cinches around Greensboro like an oversize belt, to endure the ritualized humiliations of tax paperwork and drug testing at a nondescript strip mall office. Sam Whitey turned out to be as ruddy-faced and polo-shirted as he had sounded over the phone. (Smiling, ruddy, polo-shirted middle-aged men with white baseball caps asking everyone "Howya doing?" are as North Carolinian as vinegar-based BBQ.) We shook hands, and he shuffled me into a small room where I was administered a state security guard licensing exam. The computer flashed questions: "Is it OK to do a full-body search on someone because they're wearing a turban?" and "Is telling someone they are 'looking good' sexual harassment?" I was to rate these on a scale from 1 ("don't agree at all") to 5 ("completely and totally agree"). My answers (1 and 5 to the questions above, respectively) must have been satisfactory, because Whitey led me to a wardrobe, said, "Welcome to my team," and left me alone to get suited up. The rows of starched shirts and crisp, pleated slacks swished around as I put on a pair of slacks, a white shirt, and a glistening black bomber jacket, large American flag embroidered on the sleeve. As a finishing touch, I pinned the heavy copper security badge onto my lapel. Looking in the mirror, I could hardly recognize the clean-cut stranger staring back. The North Carolina state motto, "Esse quam videri" (To be rather than to seem), seemed applicable. I liked the stark anonymity that the uniform achieved.

Throughout the nineteenth century, American textile production was centered in New England, but after the Civil War mill owners began to reconsider their strategy in the South. To the Alamance County textile manufacturer E. M. Holt, "it seemed a geographical and economical inconsistence and perversity" that cotton "should be carried thousands of miles away from the place of its growth to be made into cloth . . . to clothe the very people who had produced it," wrote one biographer. In the opening years of the twentieth century, two brothers, Moses and Ceasar Cone, built the White Oak mill and another flannel-production factory called Revolution Cotton Mills in Greensboro. By 1908, White Oak was the largest denim factory in the world. In 1915, the brothers partnered with Levi Strauss and became the jean company's primary supplier. At the time, bringing a factory to the South was considered a form of philanthropy, a Gilded Age gift to yeomen farmers still reeling from Reconstruction. The turn-of-the-century South possessed an irresistible draw for the hungry magnate: it was then, as now, anti-union, business-friendly, with an eager, exploitable workforce, and dotted with towns competing fervidly to offer the largest land grants and biggest tax breaks to window-shopping corporations. A prominent Baltimore textile investor wrote, priggishly, "Every little town wanted a mill. If it couldn't get a big one, it would take a small one; if not a sheeting, then a spinning mill," a statement that remains true of the South today, if you replace the word "mill" with "server farm."

In the red clay of the Piedmont, the Cone brothers built five paternalistic mill villages around their Greensboro factories. Each of these settlements had its own churches, medical facilities, pool halls, and company stores. White Oak had its own hotel. By the early 1940s, the Cone brothers had built at least eleven plants and subsidiaries across the Carolinas. Cone was the world's leading supplier of denim, Greensboro's largest employer, and its most lavish patron. Even now, a decade after Cone Mills went bankrupt and was absorbed into an international textile conglomerate, the Cone family has remained the city's second-largest employer through Cone Health, a network of hospitals and outpatient health-care providers. Most of its former plants are rusting, hulking monuments to a former grandeur. But people still whisper when Cone heirs arrive at parties, and their name is synonymous with the city their great-grandfathers bottom-lined, from the wide, empty Cone Boulevard to the Moses H. Cone Memorial Hospital.

My first week at the White Oak plant was spent training with an upbeat middle-aged woman named Judy, who explained that she worked at the factory "not because I have to. My husband's old and rich. I just need something to do to pass the time while he's out on the boat." Judy took me on my first security round through the factory. I was surprised to find that cinema had not deceived me. An old factory really is a fun house of red exit signs and retractable doors that yank open with the pull of a cord. *Terminator 2* really nailed the vats and chains, the smoke, chemicals, and decay. It got the catwalks and metal grates and most of all the lengthening shadows. Judy and I wandered past vats spewing steam linked up to mysterious-looking monitors. We heard our footsteps echoing on the hardwood floors of stadium-size rooms storing massive carpet rolls of denim. These were cataloged on distorted shelves that crawled up thirty feet to the corroded scrap metal ceiling. Large rooms were named for the processes required to transform raw cotton into denim—weaving, slashing, beaming, warping, link spinning, and the ominous-sounding dye house. Big, worn doors opened onto smokestacks and huge pill-shaped tanks of chemicals emblazoned with rust and bright EPA hazard diamonds. The darkened recesses of the factory were a mechanized tangle of pipes blowing steam and incomprehensible machines pumping away like some living, anodized Cthulhu. This was the two-mile round I was to make six times a day, Judy and I taking turns on the hour to fill the twelve-hour shift.

"I'm so glad you're with me now, Aaron!" Judy shrieked in exaggerated fear, dotting her flashlight around empty cavernous chambers. "It gets lonely in here!" I jumped when loud machinery hissed unexpectedly, and we passed huge, bowl-like plastic containers filled with velvety spools of cotton. "This is the part of the round where I have to walk with Jesus," Judy began to shout as we ran through a decrepit expanse of wires and exhaust in the pitch. "Say it with me! Walk with Jesus! Walk with Jesus!" We emerged in a polyurethane-floored room filled with glowing, oven-like glass furnaces that looked like alien pods, their chutes blinking red in the darkness, and made our way up a short set of grated stairs out to the safety of the pipe-lined breezeway.

In the following weeks, I memorized the lonely, serpentine walk through the living factory. Down inside the darkened departments with my flashlight, surrounded by whirring machinery, I shuffled from one security checkpoint to the next, following the bar codes that were the trail of bread crumbs leading me, eventually, to the safety of an exit. When I got lost, I would start running, eager to finish the round as quickly as I could. I occasionally imagined giant inflatable demons floating through the wide-open doorways or specter-like goat-men hoofing around in the dark just beyond my flashlight. I shouted down long, dark corridors where no one could hear me. I jumped and danced and screamed and like an undertaker became reconciled to the grim solitude of the job. The factory maze began to infiltrate my dreams. I had visions of shuffling hands and bodies. On the even hours of my shift, while Judy made her rounds, I sat in the guard shack, passing time with crossword puzzles and endless pots of coffee, watching the gurgling Technicolor sunsets on the worn-out surveillance monitors

the way one stares at a lava lamp, lost in the incandescent mono-
chrome. I looked out at the empty parking lot or at filed time cards,
collating them into a neat stack beside the antiquated punching
machine. I drifted in and out of thousand-page books whose plots I
no longer remember. I would get knots in my stomach from worrying, prickles of fear rising in preparation for the next tour through
the building's innards, the satanic subbasement. Occasionally, I
would collect passes and clock out the exhausted workers who filed
out of the barbed-wire gates when the horn, blaring, announced a
shift change.

When I called my mother and told her I was working at the factory, she was initially disappointed that I was squandering my college education at the kind of place she had worked so her children
wouldn't have to. But after a while, she grew sentimental. "I just
love the smell of an old cotton mill," she said. "It reminds me of
being a girl back in Mississippi." I tried to appreciate her nostalgia
but kept thinking of a W. H. Auden quotation I had read somewhere: "One cannot walk through a mass-production factory and
not feel that one is in Hell." Completing factory rounds, I could
feel a long sweaty chapter of industrial history coming to a close. I
began to prefer the company of books to people. Phone calls and
e-mails became unbearable. There didn't seem to be much left
once you stripped the anecdotal varnish off everyday life. It was all
just long walks past smoking vats and dyeing machines. When I
came home after a twelve-hour shift and my considerate housemates
would ask, "How was work?" a mumbled "Fine" was all I could
muster before shuffling to my bedroom and shutting the door.

"The dream of organizing the South," Si Kahn, folksinger and labor activist, once wrote, "has always been that drain in the bathtub
through which progressive movements just kind of drain away."
The South remains the least unionized region of the country, with
North Carolina clocking in dead last, with less than 3 percent of its
workforce paying union dues. In the 1920s, as cotton prices tanked

and profits began to shrink, mill owners began what was to be a long clampdown on textile workers. Random firings and layoffs increased, and employees were made to operate many more looms without an increase in wages. In response, wildcat textile strikes spread rapidly through the Piedmont South in the late 1920s. In 1929, there were eighty-one textile strikes in South Carolina alone. The most bitter conflict was the five-and-a-half-month-long standoff at the Loray Mill, in tiny Gastonia, North Carolina, just outside Charlotte. A young Massachusetts Communist named Fred E. Beal, sent down to the mill by the National Textile Workers Union, called a strike after several union men at Loray were arbitrarily fired. Two days later, the governor of North Carolina, a mill owner himself, called in the National Guard, who combined with local anti-Communist vigilantes to turn Gastonia into a war zone. When strikers were evicted from company housing, the Workers International Relief set up a tent colony for the newly homeless. On June 7, a small army of police officers invaded the makeshift city and engaged the union's armed guards in a firefight that left the Gastonia chief of police mortally wounded. Sixteen strikers were indicted for the murder. They were defended by the International Labor Defense and the ACLU, until the apparent insanity of the juror Joseph C. Campbell forced the judge to declare a mistrial.

Soon after, vigilantes murdered the beloved organizer and single mother of five Ella Mae Wiggins in broad daylight, effectively bringing an end to the long strike. Despite numerous witnesses, no one was ever convicted in Wiggins's death, which nonetheless prompted enough of an outcry to get the number of defendants charged with Chief Orville F. Aderholt's murder reduced to seven, Fred Beal among them. All seven defendants were convicted, and all seven jumped bail and followed Beal to the nascent Soviet Union. Beal gave lectures, wrote articles, and got a job picking cotton in Uzbekistan, until famine, bureaucracy, and the liquidation of the kulaks soured him on Communism. He returned to the United States, where he went into hiding. After spending four years running from the police and his former comrades (and writing his autobiography, *Proletarian Journey*), Beal was caught and sent to prison in Raleigh. Paroled after a year, he recanted his Communism before the Dies Committee in exchange for the reinstatement of his U.S. citizenship.

Throughout the 1930s, mills closed, wages plummeted, and organized labor suffered a number of bitter defeats, even as FDR moved to reform labor laws. In 1933, FDR's National Industrial Recovery Act established the Cotton Textile Code, which set up a baseline of regulation to protect textile workers: a minimum weekly wage, a maximum number of hours per week the mill could run, and a ban on child labor. Mill owners quickly found ways to skirt the regulations. In an early precedent to "permalancing," tens of thousands of workers were "stretched out" and reclassified to assistant and apprentice positions, which allowed mill owners to get away with giving them substandard wages.

Strife between owners and workers continued throughout the Depression and flared up again after World War II. In 1947, after five million American workers went out on strike and stayed out longer than ever before, Congress passed the Taft-Hartley Act, a deathblow to organized labor: it let states pass "right-to-work" laws that allowed individual employees to decide whether or not to join a union. In right-to-work states, employees who don't join the union still receive the contract benefits of collective bargaining, even as they undermine the solidarity of their co-workers. Many right-to-work states also make it illegal for public employees to strike. Today, twenty-four states have right-to-work laws on the books, including every state in the South.

The primary duties of a security guard are antagonizing people and trying to look busy. We stopped workers at the gates, demanded hall passes, ticketed their cars, asked for multiple forms of identification. Our presence at the factory was less a matter of security than of shrewd corporate accounting: the cost of maintaining a stable of warm patrolling bodies is simply less than the cost of damages or lost production if a fire or theft in progress is not discovered. One evening, Judy and I were staring out at a pink sunset when we heard the sound of glass breaking. I jumped up and pressed my face to the window, squinting out over the parking lot just in time to see a pack of dot-size teenagers running away from the old church across the road. As I got up to go out after them, Judy jumped from her swivel chair. "Don't you even think about going out there, Aaron! We're staying right here. We don't get paid enough to go mess with that shit!" Judy carried a golf club with her on her security rounds, saying she had seen wild dogs prowling around the outdoor sections of the plant. Down by the railroad tracks, where trains brought in baled cotton, I chased stray cats around creaky wooden barns. Once, in the machine shop, Judy's flashlight landed on a possum standing upright and hissing on a golf cart, and she screamed over the walkie-talkie for me to come save her. One Sunday, while making my way through the hissing sub-basement for the thousandth time, I found myself stooping down beside a noisy boiler unit to cry, blinking red lights and grays swirling in my tears.

One afternoon, I came in to find my co-workers Stacy and Jamie hollow-eyed and exhausted. Overnight they had had to drag an employee out of the plant after a vat of chemicals boiled over on top of him. Stacy recounted the accident clinically, her eyes glazed over: "He was going into shock, covered from head to toe in blisters, and the heel of his foot? It was like, hanging off, liquefied, not even attached anymore." When I asked Stacy what to do if I was faced with a similar situation, she shrugged. "Open the gates. Fill out an incident report. Help carry them out on a stretcher if necessary. The company lawyers will be hovering around trying to get the employee's family to sign the waiver so they can't sue. And if they're bleeding, for God's sake, don't forget to put on gloves."

Earlier, while rooting around the guard shack for something to read, I had stumbled upon a large yellowing binder labeled

"Incident Reports," a kind of greatest-hits collection of factory trauma: all the fights, animal attacks, trespasses, assaults, fires, vandalism, and falls on staircases elaborately recounted in a security officer's tight, neutral prose. Throughout the factory, there were dusty light-up LED boards that said, "This Department has been accident-free for ___ days!" They attempted to make not getting injured into a team-building exercise. Walking through the factory after the incident, I found it depressing to see one of the injury LED tickers set back to zero. About a week later, I noticed a memorial set off in the grass near the factory entrance. Etched into stone were the names of four Cone Mills executives. It read: IN MEMORIAM. PERISHED IN A PLANE WHILE ON BUSINESS TRIP TO SWITZERLAND.

I shook my head. Where was the stone monument to the third-shift mill worker who had never left Guilford County? Perhaps the company felt it had already done enough. After all, on the walls of every department were grimy mirrors with a line of faded text running across the top, reminding employees who would be paying the bills if they got hurt. The mirrors all read: MEET THE PERSON RESPONSIBLE FOR YOUR SAFETY.

One can't speak of Greensboro without noting the periodic gusts of radicalism that blow through the town. Throughout the 1970s, young people from the North on track for promising careers took blue-collar jobs in the North Carolina mills in an attempt to awaken the southern working class. They formed a subgroup of the Communist Workers Party, dubbed the Workers Viewpoint Organization, and distributed thousands of copies of their newspaper, *Workers Viewpoint*. During one particularly long shift in the guard shack, I read a memoir about the southern Marxist movement in the 1970s that told the story of Bill Sampson, a young man with a master of divinity from Harvard who got a job at my factory. He started the White Oak Organizing Committee while working in the dye house—the most toxic department, where spools of cotton are dipped into noxious vats of indigo. Sampson produced a short pamphlet to hand out to White Oak employees that described a typical accident at the plant:

> Chemical fire in the dye house. Dangerous chemical fumes started to spread . . . Meanwhile several workers in the finishing room started throwing up from breathing in the fumes. Naturally, many workers wanted to go home . . . But the supervisor told them, "If you value your job you better get back to work."

Sampson and his comrades were successful enough in establishing a union at the factory that Cone management sent out a letter to White Oak's workers warning, "A small group of radical employees is threatening your job security."

By 1979, the Workers Viewpoint had organized six strikes across North Carolina and established a substantial presence in the local mills. Along the way, it engaged in an escalating struggle against the resurgent Ku Klux Klan. The Workers Viewpoint led a Death to the Klan march in China Grove, North Carolina, and disrupted a Klan viewing of *The Birth of a Nation* sixty miles to the south of Greensboro, burning a Confederate flag and chanting, "Kill the Klan!" On November 3, 1979, it organized another Death to the Klan rally. This one was held in a predominantly African-American housing project in Greensboro called Morningside Homes. This time, the Klan and the American Nazi Party showed up ready to meet the protesters: a small caravan of good ol' boys stood behind their cars and placidly unloaded their rifles and shotguns into the crowd. Five organizers were killed: Cesar Cauce, an immigrant from Cuba and recent Duke graduate; Dr. Michael Nathan, chief of pediatrics at Lincoln Community Health Center in Durham; Sandi Smith; Jim Waller; and Bill Sampson. The massacre was captured on film; it later emerged that an undercover police agent had accompanied the neo-Nazis and the Klan and knew what they were going to do but did nothing to stop them. A police detective and police photographer were also present at the shoot-out but made no attempt to intervene. Of the approximately forty Klansmen involved, only twelve were arrested. Of those twelve, only six were brought to trial. All six were acquitted by an all-white jury.

Dams have to be built, and coal has to be burned. Sewage systems have to be kept running. Water and electricity have to be pumped in to power machinery. Chemicals have to be manufactured to be put in food and products and then be delivered in trucks that use gasoline, and grease has to coat the cogs of conveyor belts. Cotton has to be packed onto freight trains and cross dewy fields at night. Factory employees run hazardous machines to dye and process cotton into denim, while others roll it up and put it on planes. Once it arrives at its destination, other workers unload it and drive it to factories where it is sewn into blue jeans. The product is then loaded back up onto planes and shipped to the United States and driven by truckers to stores. Jeans are bought by people who work hard and deserve to have nice things. They are sold by people who have pretty smiles but no health insurance. Department by department, the lights were shut off throughout White Oak, and the outsize machinery was quietly bubble-wrapped, put on planes, and shipped to Nicaragua, to a doppelgänger factory that would be manned by a more pliant workforce. Huge boxes addressed in Chinese lettering sat in gymnasium-like rooms. In the 1970s, when Bill Sampson was fighting the capitalists and the Klan, North Carolina had been a contender, a textile leader. But as the market became glutted with foreign products, Cone Mills couldn't compete. The company sold, converted, or liquidated ten of its mills between 1977 and 1990. The textile industry made one last-ditch effort with an optimistic "Buy American!" campaign, but it was too little, too late.

After about seven months at the factory, I realized my life had degenerated into a kind of early retirement, full of remembering and repetition. It was time to go. I put in my two weeks and drove away from my final shift at dusk, past the construction and tiny strip malls, toward the unusually bright glow of downtown Greensboro. The roads were cordoned off: a local booster organization had organized a "Get downtown, Greensboro!" day, but attendance was sparse. A few dozen corporate sponsors and volunteers shifted around and chatted anxiously, trying to determine the fate of dozens of boxes of promotional T-shirts. Middle-aged gallery owners stood outside their empty opening nights with folded arms and pensive smiles on their faces. Sunny 93.9 blasted tepid radio rock from a hastily thrown-up tent. These people too were like undertakers, administering last rites to the dream of a new city—one fed by fiber-optic cables and servers, stored on key-chain zip drives; allergen-free, air-conditioned, lit up twenty-four hours a day by cheerless fluorescence. Meanwhile, warehouses and old mills rotted on the edge of town.

But I was no Fred Beal or Bill Sampson. A few weeks after quitting, I moved back to New York to join the pale, information-age multitudes huddled in front of computers, breathing the menthol-cold air pumped into offices by great, rumbling HVAC units. But in the early mornings before heading to work, I made coffee and took long aimless walks, as if my feet had come to expect a certain number of miles be covered per day. I would leave my apartment and head east to where the squatty vinyl-sided apartments of "East Williamsburg" abruptly give way to the brick factories and cobble-stoned streets of Bushwick. Walking past those quiet warehouses, in the perfectly contrasting geometries of morning light and receding shadow, I stared up at the sooty chimneys and centuries-old smokestacks, looking for smoke.

31

WASHINGTON, D.C., BROTHEL

MICHAEL MERRIAM

This floor was entirely asleep; others were roaming, and the last of us wouldn't be back from work until nearly dawn; the Pimp (hereinafter referred to as [Name Withheld]) was snoring to the south, and the dear three-hundred-pound, peach-complected Commander (navy, retired), who owned the whorehouse, was snuggled with his boyfriend to the north. To be fair, we did not call it a whorehouse, even though escorts lived and worked here. It was simply the House. It was like Disney's Haunted Mansion: thick drapes, creaking halls, many, many stairs, plus "discretion," exaggerated in a Dickensian way to mean something more like "occult secrecy."

I had been there a week. Apparently, [Name Withheld] wished to retire and the House needed a madam. I dubbed myself Madam Mike, but the name didn't stick. All the escorts had fake names. Escort Rich would not call me Madam Mike. He would not go on the museum outing I'd arranged, either. "It's bad for the business," he said. "One of them will be the queen; the others will wanna be princesses." I lived on the third floor. It was implied that I'd get a salary as well as a small commission on every completed call; that is, if I could get the client to agree on the price and the escort, facilitate the meet up (either at the House or at the client's hotel), and collect the House's share (generally 50 percent) from the client, then I'd have succeeded. I found the salary part hard to believe, especially because the number was either $1,000 or $1,500 a month, but I wasn't in it for the money.

The details of my job ranged from the eye-rollingly menial (changing sheets in the downstairs rooms between calls) to the much more interesting (answering the phone and matching the client with the escort). Most clients were direct and boring. Maybe a little shy, seldom rich, they were sometimes middle class, sometimes below. One client wanted a rebate—complained that the escort just wasn't very good at it and said that he'd had to make a choice that month between making a car payment and using our service. (He didn't get the rebate, but afterward [Name Withheld] yelled at the escort for not being dominant enough in the bedroom and letting the client down.) If the client was shy, it was usually because his fetish involved either feet or water sports.

I wasn't particularly good at working the phones. I sent an African-American transsexual, Regina, over to see an African-American client. Bad move. Regina called me in a huff. "I'm sure [Name Withheld] told you that I prefer not to see African-American men."

"I understand, and will respect that, of course. Would you mind telling me why?"

"That is my *pref*erence, and that is how I *choose* to *work*." Her tone was insistent. I'd encountered this kind of attitude before, when I was the personal assistant to an actress in New York. Reality isn't good enough. Why didn't I fix it before she stepped on it? I get it. And I agree.

In-calls were less frequent; that was more for the regulars, the old guard, or people referred by the old guard. People who were likely to sit on the porch for an hour or so afterward and chat with everyone. But the real money came in changing a one-hour visit to an overnight visit. Some boys were better at this than others. One, named Jeremy, was pure magic: He would always try to meet the client at a restaurant first and memorize the locations of ATMs on the way. Over dinner, he'd find a way to express to the client how much he would rather stay all night than just an hour. Because the connection was strong, unusually strong. He would love to stay overnight . . . but [Name Withheld] had firm rules about that. If the client could give him $1,500 instead of just $250 . . . then [Name Withheld] would let him stay. While the client hemmed and hawed, Jeremy would tell him where all the nearby ATMs were. A few years after the time I am describing, during Passover, Jeremy would lose his shit and draw a big X on all the doors in the House and have to be hospitalized.

Fifteen hundred dollars was a baseline for us, for overnights. Some people went higher. Janet charged $3,500 for an overnight.

It was my first time in our nation's capital.

I asked the Commander, "Could I do it? You know, it?" He sighed. He asked me to stand up, take my shirt off, turn around a couple times. "To be honest, I wouldn't wanna send you out there before you spent a couple weeks in the gym. Now, that's not to offend you or to say that on the civilian level you're unattractive. But this business is all about repeat clients."

"Got it."

As I put my shirt back on, it was explained to me that there used to be more women, "born women," in this escort service. A lot of clients will want one, I was told, and we'll run out early. Try to "up-sell" them. I assumed this meant to a transsexual, but the Commander said you can send a boy to a client who wants a girl.

"You can?"

He shrugged. "Once in a while. I usually just tell 'em, 'Hey, a blow job's a blow job.'"

"Does that work?"

"It has worked."

It was not a well-run business. In fact, only seven women remained on the books—five of whom were trans—and sixty-eight men, though it used to be almost even. How I got the job is complicated and not interesting. A creepy guy asked me whether I'd like to make $250 an hour. I said, "Wha . . . ?" Then he asked me what percent of the male population my age could do that, make that kind of money, did I think. Two percent, he said. Shouldn't I take advantage of that? When I heard this escort service worked out of an actual house, I was intrigued, and like many things that begin with intrigue, it ended in an administrative job. I stayed because I was incredibly curious and thought at least I could work on my novel, a Western set in "the American subconscious," a Jungian wonderland of heterodoxies. Mary Todd Lincoln was the villain; she was an evil sorceress. I don't know how long I was there, but it's safe to say a month. Probably longer. I usually remember it as "a summer," but that doesn't seem right.

In the evening of the first day, an escort named Jeffrey was fired. "You ripped out my soul," he'd screamed before leaving. Then I went to the roof with the Commander and his boyfriend. We drank champagne and looked out over the neighborhood of —— and could clearly see the Capitol dome. It remains the only moment in my life of perfect, transcendent happiness. They asked me about my novel, but I was already very drunk and had taken some of my pills. I babbled a bit about cowboys, time travel, wizards, magic realism, who knows what else.

The next morning, a new escort arrived from New York. He wore Gucci sunglasses and was all attitude. From Venezuela. "Now," said [Name Withheld], "in a minute, Michael will show you around and give you the rundown of how this works. Your first call is one of our easiest clients, Dan. He'll probably just want you to strip down to your underwear and do jumping jacks."

Leon nodded and kept nodding, a figure of attentive competence, as if he were starting a high-level position at a fashion magazine.

"We're putting you on the roster as 'European' instead of 'Hispanic.'"

At this, Leon stopped nodding, not because he was offended, but because he was confused. "Am I from Spain?"

"We just say European."

Leon resumed nodding, with marginally less confidence.

I showed him to his room. We fell immediately into gossip. He asked me if I was going to do some escorting myself, and I said no.

He became shy, withdrawn, and asked me if it was because I didn't want to get involved in that kind of thing. I laughed and said I'd do it if I thought I'd be good at it. He warmed to me again, said we should go grocery shopping; he'd show me how to be confident, if I decided to hook.

In the store, he turned to me. "Enemas," he said. "You have to use enemas. So many escorts, they don't do nothing. It's disgusting! However they are, however they look, they just go to work. Nothing." He shook his head. "Also," he said, "you must not brush your teeth before a call. You must use peroxide." He held up the bottle to show me. "Because if you brush your teeth, you possibly will bleed, in your gums. And you could get sick if you kiss the clients. You cannot have blood in your mouth."

Leon's disdain for the other escorts softened over the two non-consecutive weeks he worked at the House. One evening, an escort named Ahmed and I were talking while Leon prepared for an out-call at a hotel. He invited us to continue our conversation while he took a shower. Ahmed, who was nineteen, asked Leon, "Do you wax your ass?" Leon nodded and got into the shower, closing the curtain. Ahmed asked further, "Is that not incredibly painful?"

Leon opened the shower curtain again. "It is painful. But I have to have clients call me again and again."

Ahmed, with no prompting, removed his shirt. "I occasionally use Nair on my back," he said.

"Your chest?" I asked.

"I trim," he says.

"Is Janet coming back?" (Janet was the House's most successful escort, a male-to-female postoperative transsexual.)

I laughed. "She did four calls today. I think she's done." (This was almost unheard of. Most escorts were exhausted after two.)

Leon rolled his eyes. "Janet is whore," he said, and closed the shower curtain again.

We went to a museum. Maxx met us there. Typically, escorts don't like to hang around each other, but it was good to see Maxx and Leon talking shop. Maxx's motto is "Say it, they'll pay it." He told us how to fake an orgasm: pearl-colored shampoo slipped into the tip of your condom. You can take more calls per day that way.

There was one weeknight, I think it was about midway through my tenure there, when we were drinking on the porch. Well, I drank. It was me, a few boys, and the Commander's eighty-year-old aunt, Opal. Janet was inside watching TV with a textbook open, studying. It was just like a big friendly house where a lot of friends lived and had guests over. On the porch, Leon was still trying to use oblique language in front of Aunt Opal, to speak in code. He gave it up. "This is surreal," he said. "Everyone knows this is whorehouse. The workmen know. She know," he nodded toward Opal, who was pretending to be deaf and rocking in her rocker. "She know everything."

Yet no one seemed to want to shut us down. The closest we ever came to getting busted was when a dominatrix named Erin sat smoking on the porch, in full regalia, and ashed onto the neighbor's lawn. He saw her do it and asked her not to. "Fuck you," she said (she's a dominatrix), and the authorities became involved. But they didn't have much interest in getting too involved. The cops don't want to bust prostitution, really. A vice cop once gave me a seminar, of sorts, on how not to get arrested for vice. If, say, your client is giving you some kind of problem, and you fear for your safety, and you really need the police, this is what you say: you met this guy, you liked him, you went home with him, he started the problem. The cop will know you're lying, but he has more interest in arresting your assailant than in arresting you. Thus the vice squad is refigured as a sort of immune system, as the very force of differentiation between actual vice and, you know, the gold-hearted hooker and the charming scamp.

We had rules about what not to do:

1. Refer to the escorts as hookers, hustlers, or prostitutes.
2. Refer to transsexuals as "he."
3. Drink to excess.
4. Encourage (or even allow, I guess) intimacy between resident escorts.

As I worked in the office, I would often hear odd, upsetting noises. "Must be Janet's two o'clock," I'd think. Then a deep-throated "I'm sorry, sir—auuughh!" and I would remind myself not to judge the whack jobs Janet had as clients. Ah, but does she not usually work downstairs? Perhaps that noise . . . wasn't she . . .

And where did Rich go? Wasn't he in the living room? Was I hearing [Name Withheld] claiming some kind of employee discount? How does one establish consent in this arena? I went to the living room and turned the pages of a magazine. I heard a thud. A series of slaps and no response.

Later, I made an oblique reference to the noises to [Name Withheld], and it was explained to me that Rich borrowed money and hadn't paid it back yet. That's where the S-M came in, said [Name Withheld].

"Is that—his thing, is he into that?" I asked, sipping coffee and staring at the floor and knowing that had Rich been into S-M, it would have been in his file.

[Name Withheld] shrugged. "It's always more fun if they're not into it."

One day the phone rang; it was one of our most popular escorts, the street-looking, straight-acting Chris, calling to renegotiate his rate to $450 an hour, which is ridiculous.

"And you still don't take it, you only give it?" I asked.

"This is my asshole: you can put your tongue in there, or your fingers in there, if you want to. That's it."

"And you still won't kiss the client?"

"Naw."

"If you're getting 450 an hour for freelancing, I encourage you to keep charging that while you're still young enough, but what you're asking [Name Withheld] to do is—"

"Mike—you haven't had my mouth on you. I'm sayin'—"

"Chris, listen—"

"Naw, Mike, you listen. I have guys tellin' me all the time they can't even believe how good they just got their dick sucked. Now, if you want me to get with a girl? Okay, 250 an hour, fine by me, but for guys? No offense."

"How about this—we put you at 350 an hour, take our cut down to 100, no kissing, but—"

"But you gotta tell these people, prices may vary. Like, if you're fat and you stink."

"What if it's just one or the other?" I asked, hoping to resolve this.

"What?"

"What if they're fat but they don't stink, or they kinda stink, but, you know, they're not fat?"

A long, exasperated pause. "If I'm tryin' to suck dick and there's a fat man's stomach bouncin' on my fuckin' head, that fat guy better have some fuckin' money on 'im is what I'm sayin'."

"We'll pay for the chiropractor, if that happens."

Pause. Then, wearily, "Okay, buddy, bye."

We hung up. (Well, "we" might be stretching it.)

I do honor what these boys are doing; I wish there were some way to protect them better. On a good night, they get taken to the theater and to dinner, and they're well treated. It's not always a good night.

We had a client who had once forced a kid to strip naked and threw him out into the snow. In another incident, he beat a hand-cuffed escort black and blue, and I don't remember what his third strike was, but it was loathsome. That client was dangerous; we usually sent him R., our twenty-seven-year-old S-M top. R. wore military clothes and was very combative. Nobody gave R. any shit.

I dated a hooker once. He was a nice guy, had been in a porno. (Actually, he was an asshole.) I've known people who've done it; it's not very demanding. And people who say it sucks your soul are as wrong as those who claim, on the other end of the spectrum, that doing, say, retail is basically prostituting yourself. Oh, but it's not—not basically, not even in any way—metaphors just don't stretch that far.

One night, at 2:00 a.m., I woke up to the sound of the Commander, banging on the door. He held out a cordless phone. "Deal with this," he said, and practically dropped it into my hand.

He glared at me while I talked. The guy on the other end was almost as drunk as I was and more incoherent. He wanted someone who looked like Beyoncé. I tried to help him out, but he wasn't interested in a transsexual. I knew there was nothing I could do for him. The Commander watched me attempt to negotiate this situation. But it didn't take long before I just hung up.

I got some kind of a mini-lecture. I don't remember the words. I wasn't supposed to be asleep. People were still out and about. The Commander's hands were in the air as he turned his back on me, indicating that my conduct was so ludicrously inappropriate that he couldn't even address it, that indeed no normal person would. He made surprisingly little noise descending the stairs, I noted, watching his vast body ferry his swollen soul.

I discovered the next day that I was fired. For alcoholism.

I was fired from a brothel for alcoholism.

It wasn't just that I'd gone to bed too early. Apparently, I dialed people at 2:00 in the afternoon to tell them how miserable I was, but I don't remember this. I ranted about something, offended some people, and the next day [Name Withheld] called me into his office and asked me about it. "What got into you last night?"

I had no idea what he was talking about. I told him so, nodding patiently and professionally as he described the events of the evening. I'd said some things about how whatever had befallen Jeffrey, who had been missing ever since he'd been kicked out that first night, was the Commander's fault. How Jeffrey had been right about all of them. How, given that they knew so many restaurateurs (who, like pimps, demand long hours for very low pay), it seemed Jeffrey would have been better off as a waiter or something. I'd made remarks, too, about the decor. Apparently, the Commander and Jeffrey had been close; the Commander had been hurt that I thought they were bad people.

They were right to kick me out of there: they knew something about me I didn't know myself. Whatever they said about me, to me, they were right. I don't remember a word of it. The Commander offered me a ride to the train station, which I didn't take. "We are good people," he insisted, as I shook his hand for the last time.

I always hesitate and breathe deeply before I tell any of these stories. I don't really know what they mean. Looking back, despite all my understandable enthusiasm, I never really made it deep enough in. I thought for some reason that I grasped what was happening and what it meant, but now I see I failed to penetrate the place. I was like every journalist in Washington that way.

32

CHRISTMAS IN BALTIMORE

LAWRENCE JACKSON

The funeral came off without a hitch, in spite of the snow. It was as dignified as we could have hoped for, and no one at the altar mentioned what had happened.

I had parked my rental car on Argyle Avenue, a bit more alert than usual. In Atlanta, just after Thanksgiving, two men had robbed me of my station wagon and wallet at gunpoint; now, two days before Christmas, I didn't want to invite fate's wrath a second time. I was back home in Baltimore.

In 1975, civic boosters had tried to improve the city's image by giving it the name Charm City. Teenagers, the real victims of a forty-year cycle of surreal open-air shootings, stabbings, beatings, and narcotics use and sale, renamed the place Harm City. I footed through the slush toward the church, marveling at the irony. My generation had considered Atlanta a great promised land, the Zion of prosperity, the chance for a life nestled in the grassy suburbs away from the crumbling brick and mortar of our youth. Being robbed at gunpoint there made me want to go home to Baltimore for Christmas, not only to see my mother and reconnect with the familiarity of home, but also for the greater security of Harm City.

When my two little sons settled down to play by themselves during my visit, I passed a few hours reading one of my college books, *A Hazard of New Fortunes*, a William Dean Howells novel about the seductive powers of Gilded Age society. When he was finishing the book, Howells wrote a letter to his friend Henry James in which he worried that American society was "coming out all wrong in the end, unless it bases itself anew on a real equality." Despite the impressive rise of President Obama and the "real equality" he registers, I fear an American society coming out all wrong too. And I feel compromised, just like Howells, whose next sentence in his letter to James is "Meantime, I wear a fur-lined overcoat, and live in all the luxury money can buy." Americans in general and black Americans specifically live in an era of unparalleled access to power and bling, but, like Howells, some of us "tingle with shame and horror for what we are doing."

The homegoing took place at a historic African Methodist Episcopal Zion church on Pennsylvania Avenue. In the 1920s, when my grandmother sparked her family's exodus to Baltimore from a little tobacco town in southern Virginia, "the Avenue," as it was then known, was home to scenes of great African-American optimism and Jazz Age prosperity. It was the legendary destination for most of our ancestors who migrated from the rural South during the World War I era, a migration that sputtered to an end for that part of the city shortly after World War II. Concerned about its appeal to the younger crowd, the AME Zion in the 1970s rebuilt the church in an Art Deco style of sharp angles and finished the exterior in rough-edged cement grooves. The optimism of the durable modernist structure remains, but the neighborhood surrounding it has washed away. The most obvious culprit is heroin. There is also residential segregation, the collapse of the market for skilled labor, and the destruction of the public schools, but these are not as visible as what bubbles on the street corner.

Years of architectural revision and neighborhood decay aside, the minister of the church produced a soloist who sang a manly, conservatory-trained tenor that crescendoed in "All is well!" and brought the crowd to its feet. The minister, a tall, powerful-looking man, then topped this performance in elegance and carriage with a sermon that quoted Frederick Douglass and parsed the distinctions among ethics, passion, and duty. He did all this in immaculate English; he'd completed his training at Yale.

Heroin, and the police's response to it, have claimed several generations, and our task at the church was to try to get home to God one of our lost brethren. A bright childhood friend, a boy with a mocking adolescent wit, a student at one of the venerable Catholic high schools for boys, had lost his life. Our families live next door to each other on the same block. We had the same childhood and high school friends. We suffered many of the same enemies. A week before, Chris had battled police officers and been slain. Because of my own relationship with the local police dating back twenty-five years, I believed immediately that he was the victim of trigger-happy whites with badges.

I wasn't shocked by Chris's fate, as I hadn't been shocked when a small young man produced a pistol and started shouting, "Give up the check!" at me in November. But both times I was deeply saddened.

My homeboy is buried at a cemetery with a swan lake where we used to take our girls at night because it was a park with a lake and it was just over the line in Baltimore County. "The County" meant safety and comfort to us. Two days after the funeral, my closest friend, David, and his older brother—first cousins to the deceased— and I take our children sledding at the bucolic swan lake, in the park facing the cemetery. I had attended the funeral above all to support David, who is like a brother, and his uncle and aunt, Chris's father and stepmother, who still live next door to my mother. David and I ran after girls together, faced terrifying bullies and more terrifying gunmen, and waded through the rivers of alcohol and drugs. We have been shot at together. We arrived at plateaus of stability in our own lives for reasons we can't be completely certain about. It had something to do, though, we are both sure, with the murder of our comrade Donald Bentley in 1989. My own pursuit of moderation, or balance perhaps, also had something to do with the loss of my father six months later.

The children enjoy themselves with abandon, and my four-year-old son fits in easily and accepts avuncular guidance from two men I have known my entire life. My boy even surprises me by thoroughly embracing a plastic box top as a makeshift sled. It's curious, because although we certainly had carts of plastic store-bought toys in the 1970s, it was still an era when boys coveted makeshift toys, especially go-karts and stickball bats. I have been worried about Nathaniel fitting in with other black children, because so much of the environment I provide for him in Atlanta is lily-white, even though he lives in a city with a large and flamboyant black middle class.

My old homeboys from the neighborhood honored our man down, the source of a week's worth of news coverage praising the use of lethal police force. Chris was armed when he died, and the police claimed he shot at them. There were, it seemed to me, different tiers of men at the homegoing. About a dozen of his mates from Hagerstown made their way to the left side of the church, away from his parents. The majority of the crowd were relatives and friends from the neighborhood. There were about eight or nine of us born in 1968, one or two from 1969, and then eight or nine from 1970, his year. Chris's brother's group from the mid-1960s was there too. The 1970 guys who had been in his class were the most deeply emotional. A couple of them had been running the streets together when he died. Despite some solid elements in his upbringing, Chris had spent virtually all his adult life behind bars and had said he was not going back to prison.

In the church, after I took a last glance at Chris, I passed CB, an impressively sized man with a lion's mane of hair. I asked about his older brother Sean, my classmate, who'd had a child with a girl I knew from church. Surprised to see me, CB smiled through his tears and shook my hand. "Sean locked up, but he be home soon," he said. David used to give me the same update about Chris; Jason, farther down our block, would say that his uncle, who had murdered his girlfriend, was due home any day. CB's brother, Sean, is, just like Chris, an intelligent, winning, sensitive, and slender young man. I loved visiting with the group of outgoing, clever, oddly amusing guys and redbone-fine sisters along their street, sheltered by a canopy of marvelous oak and maple trees. Like me, they all grew up firmly middle class.

Harriet Jacobs once wrote that beauty was a slave girl's curse, and to paraphrase a famous Louis Farrakhan speech from 1990, intelligence for a black boy is its own kind of curse. My favorite running buddy, Courtney, from P.S. 66, my old elementary school, where I was the pet, who wouldn't always let me run with him, apparently was unable to do much with his great gift. I heard once that he was in Sing Sing, in New York, which maybe for a Baltimore guy is a certain kind of achievement.

When I'd walked into the church, I'd greeted Rock, another classmate of mine from 66 who had lived on my block and who had conquered his checkered past. Rock gave me intimate details about what led to Chris's shooting, the kinds of things people who serve prison terms know. I've never told Rock that shortly before he lost ten years of his life, he shamed me away from drugs.

During the funeral, I sat next to another old friend from my block. In high school, we had an exclusive club that used to throw parties at nightclubs downtown. Now an Iraq veteran with a bad back—he slipped a disk lifting corpses—he works as a correctional officer at a state facility in Anne Arundel County. I asked him if he selected a prison in the southern part of the state to avoid having to deal with an inmate population from our old neighborhood, which is typically housed in Jessup, in Hagerstown, or at the Eastern Shore. He said no, but I had my own thoughts. Throughout the viewing of the body, he bantered and giggled and talked about people from where we grew up. His mood was light, but he saw it as a duty to be there, as did a few of Chris's other friends who had become police officers. He checked his watch, because he was on his way to a food shelter to prepare Christmas meals for the needy. Chris was a loose affiliate of our group, which later lent itself, after college didn't work out for much of our crew, to a kind of loose-knit brotherhood in nod. My buddy, the officer, moved away from partying after a car accident nearly took his life and left him in an intensive care ward. I got away to college.

The twenty-five-car funeral procession to the cemetery was joined along McCulloh Street and Liberty Heights Avenue by gutsy African-American drivers gaining advantage in the rough jousting of cars through the city streets. It struck me as willful heedlessness, as if the land held nothing sacred. The cortege led us inadvertently through the old neighborhood. We drove down Liberty Heights, and I recognized the old Our Lady of Lourdes yard where we played football and the barbershop at Edgewood where Mr. Barnes and Mr. Ratliff expertly tapered our fades; the "bars"— cut-rate carryouts—where we first copped malt liquor and fortified wine and the stoops and alleyways and corners where we tried ourselves. Farther down Liberty Heights, we passed more of the churches. The last time I stood in All Saints it was for Donald's nighttime funeral. He was born the same year as Chris. I noticed the fast-food restaurant that people said Chris robbed back in the day, which became a Johns Hopkins health-care community outlet, which has now been bought by Leroy Dyett, the neighborhood undertaker.

Once I was home, I didn't look at the police reports or the newspaper stories of what happened. I was unable to spend much time with Chris's family; it seemed as if words were a tepid remedy for sorrow. I remembered the moments when our innocence began to fade. I was again walking from the No. 28 bus stop on Liberty Heights, past Chris's mother's house on a summer day in my young manhood. Chris, his brother, their cousin, and some of the fellas from their block were around a picnic bench passing a quart of beer and a joint. This is the common man's Arcadia, commemorated in lyric after lyric since before Geoffrey Chaucer's time. The evening of drinking ended with our running a G on an older woman, a quintet that she initiated. Chris was only sixteen, and he accepted the boon with a savoir faire that I could not muster. I don't think I saw her face among the crowd at the funeral.

I was once briefly jailed for a motor vehicle offense. If you are black and locked behind bars in America, you rapidly lose the distance between what you have done to land in the cell and what is happening to you and the way it is being done to you on account of your race, on account especially of who you have been, where you have lived, who your relatives and friends are, right down to exactly how common your name is. No one wants to accept this in a country based on upward mobility and the hope of individual distinction, but it is a fact: blackness still causes the distance to evaporate between who you are and what you have done and what the society has made you.

There was a funny twist when I gassed up at a filling station down the street from my mother's house on the way out of town. Since the proprietors seemed new to me, I asked where they were from. For a time, I'd thought they were Korean, but now I noticed that the man looked Indian. I asked if he was Hindu, since it was the eve of the great Christian holy day. The cashier said no, he was a Buddhist, but since he looked like whatever I had in my mind for an Indian from southern Asia, and since he was working at a gas station in what had been redefined as the inner city, I was filled with a bit of insolence and continued my queries. Are you from Nepal? Tibet, he said, on the mountains near China.

I wanted the Tibetan Buddhist to know that our natural curiosity and our observation of the immigration patterns to these places we are locked into were not dead. The last time I got gas and returned to the Plexiglas window to purchase Utz and Tastykake snacks, I let the Tibetan Buddhist know that I had had the opportunity to have contact with the Dalai Lama; in fact, I had helped him cross a street with several other monks. I wanted to see, I guess, if I could arouse his engagement with the complex humanity that emerged from the subway stop at Cold Spring Lane and Wabash

Avenue, an intersection of laboring black American life where families' dreams go up and come down. He opened his mouth to register something between surprise and amusement and said there had been problems with the Dalai Lama. A man beside me was asking for Kool cigarettes, and because I didn't want the customer to become impatient on account of what was really only an indulgent whim, I left the young Buddhist without learning more. Outside, a white teenager driving a luxury car was serially asking the African-American patrons of the gas station for a dollar. In a gray hoodie and jeans, not weighing 120 pounds, the gaunt white boy looked ever so much like a heroin addict from a good family, not in the worst possible circumstance yet but approaching it quickly. I told the boy that I couldn't help him.

On my way back to Atlanta, I stopped at Colonial Williamsburg with my children and my mother and sister. The preserved Virginia town bustling with the living story of our national origins is the kind of experience that I want my children to have chiseled into their earliest memories, right at the joint of their sense of what it means to be Americans. Of course, the going-back-in-time-at-Colonial-Williamsburg experience is highly bizarre for us because we descend from the enslaved, and though you do see an occasional black historical interpreter, slavery and Africans are definitely erased from Colonial Williamsburg. Fifty-two percent of the people in the town during the colonial era were enslaved Africans and first- and second-generation Creoles. By my count, about nine of ten tourists here are white, and the Colonial Williamsburg trustees seem to have decided that whites aren't interested in visiting a place that doesn't mainly represent them.

We paid an extra $10 apiece to visit the restored colonial governor's mansion. My sister, a colonel in the U.S. Army, was disappointed when I asked the historical interpreter about Lord Dunmore's relationship to his slaves. It occurred to me that he might have had some ties to them that shaped his famous proclamation of freedom that caused five thousand blacks to flee the patriots for the British. She thought it was a kind of impolite game that I was playing with white people and the situation; calling attention to slavery in an audience of whites made her uncomfortable. The interpreter responded a bit defensively, and correctively too, as if it were impossible for the owner of the forty-seven human beings who worked in the colonial Virginia governor's mansion to have been influenced by them. But she did later, in a kind of pre-emptive strike, insert the enslaved in her narrative on bric-a-brac and chamber pots. In a way, my sister is further along than I am in her Americanness.

The last time I saw Chris alive I was walking into my mother's house with my sons. It was May, and we had just come from the airport for my mother's retirement party. She had worked twenty-five years for the Baltimore County Department of Social Services, her last five years as an employment and training counselor, helping social assistance recipients prepare résumés. I thought then that Chris would put the touch on me; I wanted to give him something because I knew he was having a hard time finding work, but I could smell wine on his breath, and I thought fresh dollars might have burned a hole in his pocket. I just dapped him and grinned and went into my mother's house with the kids.

A year before, when I had seen Chris's older brother Jimmy, I had given him something. I'd run into him around the way, on a bus stop at Reisterstown and Belvedere, a kind of crossroads of the northwest Baltimore ghetto. Since the time I was in high school, Jimmy has always called me "the Genius," and in that same manner he greeted me from his pew during the funeral. When I talked to him at the bus stop in 2008, I was making the rounds of the neighborhood in the car of a man I had known growing up, a convicted felon, who I knew had just picked up a package, from another black man in an alley, that he kept in the waistband of his shorts under his white T-shirt. It is easy to fall into old patterns, and all it takes is an afternoon.

At the grave site, the old crew walked the casket from the hearse to the bier under the direction of the ditcher, who was roughly the same age, complexion, and slender build as the man who lay inside the casket. He gave us sincere directions to load and unload the dolly and to get the weight of our burden into the ground. I was standing at the front, closest to this man in a hooded sweatshirt, and he seemed intoxicated to me; the word I would actually use is "nice." It was a cold day, bitterly cold, and the man was insulated against this lonely world, digging into the snowy hillside. It was obvious that the ditcher was only recently home from prison. I could hear it in his speech, his practiced country manner intended to mimic sobriety. I could see it in the sparkling quicksilver behind his muddy eyes that yearned for the numbing rest from all known pain in a bag of dope.

On the snowy hill, we learned that the funeral sermon of the profoundly dignified AME Zion minister was impromptu. He had substituted for Chris's real minister, who'd been stuck in traffic. His extemporaneous talent astounded me. At the grave site, Chris's preacher, a man who knew him well, arrived to offer a benediction. But the graveside prayer was not short; naturally, it was the sermon he'd been unable to give. He warmed a Bible under his arm, and his full-length camel hair coat swung open while he paced back and forth along a piece of pine board covered by a runner of green all-weather carpet. Turned backward on his head was a baseball cap with the logo "Jesus saves," and as he opened his mouth to address us, I got the impression that, like Chris, he had been institutionalized at a time when he needed better dental care. He was not a Yale man. These two facts alone would have disturbed many of Chris's family, elegantly dressed and shod, driving exclusive automobiles. But the trouble was more explicit. The earthy minister moved immediately to the heart of the matter, which had been avoided: Was our beloved burning in hellfire for having lived the life of an outlaw, a highwayman? Who was responsible for having made him into this man, or, rather, precisely how responsible was the assembly—his parents, his comrades, some of them felons, some still frosting with numbness?

There was a dynamic between the two ministers: one expertly shielded us from the evil, and the other called it forth in order to defeat it. The Ivy League man knew that the congregation preferred not to have its wickedness exposed; the uneducated prophet insisted that we touch the flaws of our beloved, assured us that salvation was still reserved for him, and demanded that our own transgressions be addressed.

I found that I was seared emotionally by this rough-and-tumble, spittle-spewing man, who swung about most unsteadily on the scaffolding between the earth and the suspended coffin. At the peak of his ministerial fury, he shouted that God told him in the early morning that Chris had made it to paradise. He looked skyward and cried that Chris's mother "raised him right!" and never condoned his wrongdoing, that she put him out when she thought he was not looking hard enough for work or that he held weapons or kept up his ties to the hard lost men.

When it was over, my peers kissed the casket and laid flowers and lingered in silence.

There is something larger here, I know. There is something larger about the presidency of a black American man who admitted that he had sniffed illegal street drugs and who demoted the "drug czar" from a cabinet-level position to signal an end to the Twenty Years' War. There is something more profound about a year in which I found myself on the ground in Virginia where my last ancestor walked in chains; on the wrong side of the barrel of a .25 automatic held by a black hand in Atlanta, not so far from where a Spelman coed and an Olympic gold medalist had been felled by gunmen; and at the funeral in Baltimore of an old friend shot four times while exiting an appointment with his probation officer in the city of our birth. But I am not sure what it is, or that it has not come out all wrong in the end.

33

PHILLY SCHOOL REFORM

JESSE MONTGOMERY

On a spring afternoon in 2013, hundreds of parents, students, teachers, and activists stood at the headquarters of the Philadelphia School District to protest the worst school budget in Philadelphia history. The press had already taken to calling it a "doomsday budget," a seriocomic term that obscured as much as it expressed. The proposed budget would leave schools with only the barest signs of education: a principal and a core group of teachers. Counselors, sports, secretaries, librarians, and music and art teachers, as well as all support safety staff, would be eliminated. Dressed in red (the color of the teachers' union, but also, of course, of a deficit budget), waving signs, and holding banners, the protesters massed on the stairs of the squat concrete building. They spilled out into Broad Street, in clear view of city hall, chanting, "Save our schools!" Near the front of the rush, a student pep band performed under the direction of its teacher, who faced layoff.

Inside the building, in the auditorium of the School District Education Center, the public school district's state-imposed governing body, Philadelphia's School Reform Commission, was preparing to vote on the controversial budget. The auditorium, too, overflowed with protesters, many of them prepared to deliver comment on the proposal before the vote. Four of the five members of the commission were joined by Superintendent William Hite behind a long row of tables topped by microphones, name placards, and bottled water. The fifth commissioner, Joseph Dworetzky, participated via teleconference. As the doors were closed and the last people jostled for room, the district leaders talked quietly among themselves and even smiled.

But as the meeting came to order, they took on the grave, nervous expressions they would wear for the duration of the evening. The bulk of time had been set aside for public testimony on the proposed budget, during which the commission could field questions and respond to concerns. One by one, parents, teachers, and students delivered indignant, anguished, oftentimes tearful speeches. Many spoke about crucial programs that would be cut from the schools, the importance of counselors and cafeteria workers, and the already vulnerable populations that would be hit hardest by the cuts. Others attacked the commission directly, calling the budget, and the process of its creation, hurried, callous, and racist.

The commissioners listened to all of this quietly, their faces drawn. It seemed clear that the issue had been resolved in their minds and that the public comment period could do little to change the hard decisions they felt had to be made. Pedro Ramos, the chair of the commission, was a lawyer who had served as president of the Philadelphia School Board and as city solicitor and had been chief of staff to the president of UPenn. He had grown up in one of the poorest neighborhoods in Philadelphia. But he had been appointed by the Republican governor, Tom Corbett, to be his man on the commission and was now dutifully executing orders from Harrisburg.

After two hours of comment from the public, Ramos proposed a vote. The budget passed, 4–1. The immediate question was whether what remained after the thousands of cuts could really be considered "schools." Before casting the sole dissenting vote, Dworetzky stated that "wherever the line falls between a school and not a school, what's being proposed here is very close to the line." But the question was treated as academic. His four fellow commissioners cited their legal obligation to approve a budget and voted yes. One week later, it was announced that layoff notices were being sent to 3,783 district employees.

Public schools in Pennsylvania have been a site of conflict for decades. Until the 1970s, teachers in the commonwealth held no collective bargaining rights. Once teachers acquired them, after many years of intense organizing around issues of low pay and poor working conditions, teachers' strikes proliferated. Between 1970 and 1988, one of every five public school strikes in the country took place in Pennsylvania. Their frequency helped make them unpopular; a sense that teachers were protecting their own rights against the needs of students took hold among parents and the broader community. In the early 1990s, the state stepped in and managed to roll back many of the rights previously achieved by the unions. These struggles were especially pitched in Philadelphia, a city whose public school system suffered exceptional levels of poverty and economic stratification resulting from white flight. Years of conflict had created a racially charged antagonism between Harrisburg and the city, and the remote state government took the first opportunity to turn the city into a kind of laboratory for school "reform."

The current struggles faced by the city's schools began in the late 1990s, when a state senate overseen by the Republican governor, Tom Ridge, changed the state school-funding formula, untethering it from poverty levels and choking off much-needed funds for Philadelphia schools. In 1998, the district superintendent, David Hornbeck, in a fit of indignant activism, threatened to shut down Philadelphia's public schools unless the district received the additional funding from the state he deemed necessary for operations. Hornbeck's move was audacious, and the members of the Republican-led Pennsylvania General Assembly did not like it. They responded by passing Act 46, which gave the secretary of education power to declare any school district in the state "under distress" should it sink to below specified standards of conduct. Once a district was named distressed, an administrative machine would take over. The local (usually elected) board of education would be dissolved and placed under the control of a five-person school reform commission, staffed with members appointed by the governor and unaccountable to the public. In a preview of future attacks on public-sector unions, Act 46 would also limit collective bargaining between teachers and the commission, strip teachers of their right to strike, and allow the state to impose a contract if they did (all of this despite the fact that Hornbeck, not the teachers' union, had threatened the shutdown).

In the fall of 2001, citing abysmal test scores, staffing shortages, and a multimillion-dollar budget deficit, Governor Mark Schweiker (a Republican who had taken over after his predecessor, Tom Ridge, was appointed to the newly created Department of Homeland Security) revived Act 46 and initiated the state takeover of what was at that point the fifth-largest school district in America. Schweiker initially sought to turn control of all district schools over to Edison Inc., a for-profit school management group, effectively privatizing the entire school district. After months of student protests, negotiations with the city, and lawsuits filed by a host of organizations, including the Philadelphia Student Union and the NAACP, a compromise was reached. In the end, Edison Inc. was awarded only twenty schools (a failure that sent its Wall Street stock plummeting), and Mayor John Street managed to wrest two appointees to the reform commission from the state. What began with Hornbeck's attempt to demand equitable funding three years prior had led to the largest state takeover of public education this country has ever seen.

In the years since—which coincided with another systematic intrusion into the lives of schoolchildren, the passage of the No Child Left Behind Act—the performance of the school district has been discouraging. While test scores saw small gains each year, they remained far below the state average; high school graduation rates hovered around 60 percent. In keeping with national trends, the school district also encouraged systematic deprofessionalization and championed "choice" in its public schools. Charter school growth exploded, skilled teachers were replaced with temporary workers from Teach for America, scripted curricula were made mandatory in many schools, and the number of precarious workers in the district more generally seemed to grow.

I wound up working in the school district almost by accident during the fall of 2010. I had graduated from college in the Midwest and spent the summer reading on a bench in front of the student union while my bank account dwindled and everyone I'd known for the last four years trickled out of town and toward the coasts. When this arrangement became untenable, I made an arbitrary move to Philadelphia with a few friends. With the Great Recession proceeding unabated and no connections in the city, I answered an ad on Craigslist for an AmeriCorps position tutoring English in the public schools. I was hired within days.

EducationWorks, the nonprofit that was my direct employer and the largest AmeriCorps program in Pennsylvania, assigned me to work at Frankford, a public high school located in the Northeast Philadelphia neighborhood of the same name. My job was to act as a classroom tutor for ninth-grade English classes serving high-risk students (those testing two to four years behind in reading). The pay was bad—we were given a stipend of $1,150 a month, which worked out to about $7.20 an hour before taxes—but I was excited to work with kids and motivated by the opportunity to do meaningful work.

When I arrived in October 2010, Frankford had been classified by the terms of No Child Left Behind as a "persistently dangerous school" every year since 2006—a designation based on a sustained ratio of more than five "dangerous incidents" per 250 students. There are currently six such schools in the state, all of them in the city of Philadelphia. Frankford enrolled close to 2,000 students—nearly 90 percent of them black and Latino—but on a given day only 75 percent attended school, and an even smaller number actually made it to class, electing instead to wander the halls or disappear after signing in. Standardized test scores fell well below the district's already low average. Over 85 percent of the student body was considered economically disadvantaged. One hundred percent were eligible for free lunch.

Issues of "school climate," as the euphemism has it, tended to dominate the attention of the administration. This was made apparent to me on the first day, when my already short orientation ended abruptly after my new supervisor, an assistant principal, bolted from her office mid-sentence in order to chase down a truant student. From the beginning, I maintained a low profile, because of the flexible nature of my position and the general hum of chaos that permeated the building. I retained this weird, liminal status throughout my tenure at Frankford. I wasn't a teacher; I wasn't even an employee of the school district. As an AmeriCorps member, I was on the books but somewhere in the margins: academic support staff without much accountability or real supervision (let alone real pay) best used to plug holes left by budget cuts and understaffing. My job was at once highly ambiguous and paradigmatic: flexible, unprofessional, supported by an unpredictable source of funding, its existence was a testament to what the system needed and what it could afford. The district employed thousands of us.

I was ostensibly a tutor, and in a few of the classes I was attached to—typically better-run classes with more engaged students—I did a lot of tutoring: one-on-one work with kids who were struggling, small group homework help, essay workshops, and the like. But in other classes (or in the halls), I played different roles, mostly out of necessity. I would sit and attend to a particularly distractible student, for example, or play backup disciplinarian if a teacher needed support. Once or twice I broke up a fight; often I was a chaperone or a shrink. Some of this work seemed tangential to what I was supposed to be doing. As the months passed, I came to realize that the extra tasks were my job, that I was there simply to be a body, to sustain a vague sense of order or calm, and that this was, to varying degrees, the job of every single adult employed in one of these schools. From veteran teachers to school safety officers, everyone's first priority was to create an environment where one could teach.

At this small task we often failed. The school was dysfunctional. There was a lot of bullying, and fights happened frequently. Many students I knew felt unsafe; several transferred after getting jumped or robbed. Still more had grown inured to it all. For them, things popping off were a respite from the intense boredom that constituted the school day. Part of this was the result of poor leadership: I remember the principal, bemoaning the disorder in his halls, comparing students who roamed between classrooms to cockroaches. "Turn on the lights, catch them in the act," he told us, "and BOOM! they're gone." But it was hard not to suspect that the problem was systematic, district-wide. Still, it was good work. I learned a lot about working with students, thanks chiefly to mentoring by excellent, experienced teachers who were very good at a very difficult job, and I felt like an important, positive part of some of the classes I worked with. But the overall lack of support was exhausting, and many days I left Frankford dispirited and at a loss.

By the end of the 2010–11 school year, rumors began to circulate that the district would lay off 16 percent of its workforce, including 12 percent of its teachers, as a result of the governor's budget. Few of the teachers I worked with were sure that they would have a job in the fall, let alone jobs at Frankford, and the students all knew it, too. There were walkouts at Audenried, a district school slated to be turned into a charter as part of a turnaround initiative. Two of the three students I had worked with every day, sweet, thoughtful guys who never missed our after-school program, had been jumped on or near school grounds by their classmates. One of them wouldn't return in the fall, and the other simply disappeared—transferred, probably, but I'll never know for sure. The kids who beat and robbed him kept attending school, despite being suspended; evidently, there was something about school they liked.

I was saved the trouble of quitting when the federal stimulus money funding our program ran out. Were the program to continue in the fall, already strapped schools would have to pay my wage, and there was talk that I might be put to work in the cafeterias when

I wasn't tutoring. I bowed out, somewhat deflated and not a little relieved. It was strange to leave an environment where you felt, all at the same time, terribly needed but entirely powerless.

There are three fundamental tenets of the modern school reform movement: some schools are beyond saving; the teachers are largely to blame; and children can essentially be saved from the very communities they come out of through the intervention of various highly motivated wealthy individuals and their surrogates in the multiarmed school bureaucracy.

The American public school system as a whole is, even on the terms of the school reformers, a decently performing system, if nowhere near the levels of northern European countries such as Finland, with their highly paid, deeply professionalized—and densely unionized—teaching staff. In fact, when you adjust for child poverty, American public schools perform about on par with any other system. But at least since the late 1970s, when Americans began to feel their competitive advantage in all things, including smarts, slipping in the face of rising East Asian nations, the idea of the American school system as "broken" has taken hold—thanks to the ideological campaign of school "reform."

Beginning in the early 1980s, when Ronald Reagan's National Commission on Excellence in Education published its famous report *A Nation at Risk*, conservative voices became increasingly dominant in discussions of school reform. The report was intended to be a clarion call to American politicians, enjoining them to save a public school system that was supposedly adrift, unable to produce students equipped to compete in the global economy. Many of the report's recommendations are familiar to us today: that the schools focus on standardized testing; that the school day be made longer and that more homework be given; that schoolchildren be held to higher standards of academic performance; and that teacher salaries be made "professionally competitive, market-sensitive, and performance-based."

The report was intended to ensure the federal government remained deeply involved in setting goals for schools as well as dealing out sanctions and demerits. But the punitive thrust of the rules helped open new and lucrative inroads for the private sector, as districts across the country failed to meet benchmarks and sought fixes and scapegoats. The school reform movement is an alliance of business-savvy technocrats and self-styled education crusaders intent on disrupting what they see as an ossified system. It paints itself as nimble and entrepreneurial: committed to testing and meritocracy, with teaching staff flitting in and out, and governance of the school given over to a charter board, often composed of the well-heeled—not unlike the board of directors for a publicly traded company.

By most measures, charter schools perform, as a whole, on par with or even worse than traditional public schools. Yet they exert a tremendous attraction for many parents in urban districts, who have seen the costs borne by underfunded schools. So, too, do the believers who staff the movement—with its many para-organizations, such as Michelle Rhee's StudentsFirst and Wendy Kopp's Teach for America—see the wide-ranging program of school reform as ultimately progressive. Their world is one in which continual innovation in pedagogical methods anticipates disruption in the global economy. It is a world in which progress, assured by constant assessment and adherence to metrics (the ideals of the most admired quarters of American capitalism, such as Silicon Valley), will eventually triumph over a decadent, outdated, bureaucratic structure that tenures weak teachers at the expense of the students, who will soon be competing for jobs with each other and, what's more, competing in a flat world with the Chinese, Indians, and South Koreans. This message doesn't only resonate with the power elite; refined over generations, it has come to carry real weight with many city dwellers, whose consent or vocal approval the movement, and its allies among elected officials, at least partly depend on.

The routes to the actual "reforms" are sometimes circuitous and dependent on local circumstances and personalities, but in the end they tend to look pretty much alike; in other words, they look like business strategies. The latest round of cuts in Philadelphia came after the commission ordered a report on the schools under its charge from the infamous Boston Consulting Group (BCG), a firm publicly famous for its studies of consumer shopping habits, *Trading Up and Down Around the World*. The BCG promised to "right-size" the district and "return [it] to structural balance." Hired for a five-week engagement for a presumably enormous sum— partly bankrolled by the charter-school-friendly William Penn Foundation—BCG developed a blueprint for the future of public education in Philadelphia that would dismantle and reconstruct the entire system in the name of efficiency. Asked to focus on developing a "portfolio model" for managing the schools and identifying areas where costs could be cut, BCG came up with a plan that called for the closure of forty schools by 2013 and sixty-four by 2017. It also recommended "modernizing" operations by replacing transportation, cafeteria, maintenance, and custodial workers with subcontracted, nonunionized labor; significantly reducing the district's central office staff (also unionized); and splitting the centralized school district into a series of de facto mini-districts so that they could be awarded competitively to charter management organizations, nonprofits, and groups of educators. According to BCG, the district should focus "on expanding high performing schools," excising those that lagged, "and attracting high-quality leadership and operators, rather than directly managing schools."

A year after the BCG report, the commission announced its plan to destroy the beleaguered district in order to save it. Around the same time, the district opened contract negotiations with the Philadelphia Federation of Teachers with what Diane Ravitch called "the most insulting, most demeaning contract ever offered in any school district to my knowledge." It called for pay cuts of 13 percent for those who earn more than $55,000 and 5 percent cuts for those making $25,000 or less. The contract would eliminate stepped raises and freeze salaries until 2017, extend the school day by an hour, eliminate seniority, require that teachers be available for conferences with parents and students outside the normal workday (unpaid), allow for unlimited evening meetings (also unpaid), and eliminate the district's responsibility to provide librarians (for schools with a thousand students or more), counselors for each school, employee lounges, water fountains, parking facilities, desks for teachers, and "a sufficient number of instructional materials and textbooks." Superintendent Hite said that such protections do not belong in a professional contract.

You would be hard-pressed to find a set of terms more representative of the strategy and aims of school reformers today. The cuts in wages, the end of seniority, and the thoroughgoing elimination of services deemed "inessential" by wealthy non-educators are the hallmarks of today's reform agenda. Their aim is to further distress the system, which in turn pushes out teachers who won't stand for the conditions and makes alternatives like charter schools increasingly attractive in comparison. Similar agendas are being pushed through in districts across the country as politicians call for merit-based pay and data-centric evaluation in all things. But even in an environment where these types of reforms are the status quo, school closures on the scale seen in Philadelphia are alarming.

Ultimately, the commission voted to close twenty-four of the city's schools and merge or relocate five others. The argument behind the closings was that the schools were underutilized, expensive to maintain, and academically underperforming. Their closure was framed as a sacrifice for the sake of the district. But it is overwhelmingly young people of color, and those who work in their schools, who bear the brunt of these closings and witness the worst effects of the budget cuts: of the fourteen thousand students affected by the decision, 81 percent of students in now-closed schools were black, and 93 percent came from low-income households. For decades now, the district and the state of Pennsylvania have decided, again and again, that austerity measures that disproportionally affect poor students of color are the only means for balancing budgets.

The rationale cited by the commission when it voted to accept the unacceptable budget was that the school system had run out of money—the suggestion being that it had been profligate with the money that it had. But a poor school district will *always* run out of money; that is what happens when schools are paid for by local property taxes. In every state in the Union, therefore, the state government subsidizes the school districts with greater need. But these systems are highly variable from state to state, running the gamut from progressive to regressive, and Pennsylvania's over the last two decades has gone from bad to one of the worst. Poor areas here get significantly less overall funding per student than do richer ones, and the percentage of aid provided by the state is estimated to be the second lowest in the country. This is a problem for districts across the state, but Philadelphia has one of the worst poverty rates of any large American city. Its tax base is weak, and its school system heavily dependent on state and federal aid. As a result, big cuts to state education spending have devastating effects.

I started writing about school reform in the district during the spring of 2012 after the district announced its insolvency and initial plans to follow the BCG's recommendation and dismantle the district, but after a few months of following the increasingly grim and convoluted story, I felt exhausted and put it down. When I returned to it almost a year later, as the school closures were being finalized and contract negotiations began, I was struck by what little progress had been made. Again, hundreds of district employees were being threatened with layoffs. Again, the schools might not open at all.

In the three years I have been following the apparently perpetual collapse of the Philadelphia School District, the cyclical nature of the crisis has become undeniable. At the time of this writing [2014], the city is attempting to pass a tax on cigarettes in order to fill most—but not all—of its budget gap. Superintendent Hite has indicated his intention to open the schools fully staffed and run them as such until the money runs out. And in Harrisburg, Governor Corbett is attempting to use the crisis to extract concessions from Philadelphia in order to improve his abysmal approval ratings ahead of November elections.

Most of the problems the district faces today are the same problems it has faced since the state takeover, and the annual nature of the funding fights and mass layoffs makes it difficult to tell if progress is being made. Resistance to the closures and outside control has been growing. Since spring 2011, when the governor proposed massive cuts to basic education spending, a coalition of parents, teachers, and students fighting the closings and the defunding has had some effect. Various high-profile actions—such as a two-week hunger strike in May 2013—drew national attention to the Philadelphia school crisis and forced a recalcitrant governor and a chastened legislature to scare up money for the city, while the School Reform Commission retracted some of its layoffs. But Governor Corbett and the senate have time and again found ways to maintain control of the district.

As in many cities, the weak link in Philadelphia is the teachers' union—the one force that could lend clarity and power to a struggling coalition. Teachers' unions, the chief target of school reform movements, are also in the best position to make the strong case against school reform and for full funding. But for decades, teachers' unions in cities everywhere have settled into defensive postures, occasionally going on major strikes to preserve wages and benefits— tactics that the school reformers have, time and again, succeeded in painting as selfish and harmful. The reformers are wrong, but the goal for teachers must be to neutralize the reformers' message, not simply to feel they are in the right. Teachers' unions have every right to fight for first-rate working conditions and to negotiate fair contracts, but politically they have often failed to make these fights seem like struggles on behalf of an entire community or a public. The salient exception has been the strike of the Chicago Teachers Union in the summer of 2012, a direct result of a reform movement *within* the union. Its strike, over issues strictly confined to the classroom and to the environment that students faced, not only galvanized a public to take its side but also made a sizable dent in the political power and influence of the city's mayor, Rahm Emanuel. Chicago has inspired union movements everywhere, including Philadelphia, where the union's Caucus of

Working Educators could very well become the leading voice for responsible reform. As of this writing, a reform slate has taken over the union in Los Angeles, while contract fights in Portland, Oregon, and St. Paul, Minnesota, have successfully brought community leaders and rank-and-file union members together. These movements are the most promising counter to school reform yet.

In Philadelphia, *real* school reform—one that provides fair and reliable funding, restores local control of the district, and reaffirms the state's responsibility to provide for the health and safety of all its children—cannot come quickly enough. The district now averages one nurse per thousand students and places no counselors at schools with fewer than six hundred students. During the 2013–14 school year, two young students died in schools without nurses on duty. Counselors who remained in the schools report declines in the number of their students attending college. There is still no money for books, supplies, or librarians.

Without more money from the state that is regular, reliable, and born of a commitment to the equitable funding of poor districts, the public schools in Philadelphia are going to get much worse; if school funding isn't restored soon, stripped of safety officers and counselors and support staff, they will get exponentially worse and quickly. And what then? Perhaps the further degradation of public schools feeds a panicked enthusiasm for even more charters or voucher programs. Perhaps total deprofessionalization. Certainly more of it. Perhaps these reformers get so good at starving these public schools that your own city decides to hire them. Perhaps they are already there.

34

BED-STUY

BRANDON HARRIS

Early on the morning of July 4, 2006, was the only time anyone ever tried to mug me on the streets of my adopted home, Brooklyn, New York. I was walking south on Taaffe Place in camp counselor clothes—a blue polo, cheap white sneakers, and tight green shorts—on a nearly deserted block leading to my building's front door. It was just after midnight. I was having a phone conversation with a friend in California. Half a block from home, a man in a white T-shirt offered me a cigarette, his voice escaping his mouth in a low, dreadful mumble. I didn't notice it at first, but as I passed him, shaking off the invitation to smoke, I glimpsed what appeared to be a sawed-off bike handle in his right hand. As I continued walking up the block, I gleaned that he was following me from the play of his shadow on a brick wall to my right.

I'm a light-skinned Negro who weighs over two hundred pounds. I used to play offensive guard on a half-decent high school football team. But I was dressed like a buffoon, almost never get in fights, and had a man-purse with a brand-new black MacBook in it. Mark. When I realized the man was following me, I was saddened by the prospect of having to smack a motherfucker in the face with my new laptop, the one I'm currently writing this essay on seven years later. So I ran.

Across the street, up the block. He pursued me to my building's front door, but I was able to open the door and pivot into the building before the man could strike me with his peculiar improvised weapon. He lashed the sawed-off end of the bike handle at me, but I got out of the way and proceeded to smash his arm, several times, as hard as I humanly could, with the very heavy glass and metal door that led to 227-241 Taaffe Place.

A tall, thirtysomething white man looked on in horror as my attacker removed his now surely injured limb from the door. I slammed it shut, my assailant cursing loudly from the other side of the glass, his slender body shuddering. He was in great pain. I never hung up the phone, so my friend in California, hearing the commotion, was loudly asking me if I was all right as I held the phone near my chest, breathing hard, staring at this man who had meant me harm.

He was clearly much worse off than I was, for reasons no doubt of his (and our) own making, long before the possibility of stealing from me was something he tried to act on. Now, from the other side of the glass door, he said, tears in his eyes, "Fuck you, fuck you, yella ass nigga, I gonna get y'all mothafuckin' shit, this is Bed-Stuy, bitch." Then he sauntered off. I went upstairs, to the seventh-story loft I lived in, smoked a spliff, and got ready to face the phony celebration of national independence that the day promised to offer.

"This is Bed-Stuy, bitch." That's not what everyone else was saying.

It's difficult to say exactly how long I've lived in Bedford-Stuyvesant. It's not for lack of trying. For some time, I believed I first moved to the neighborhood in the summer of 2008, but by any honest accounting of the neighborhood's actual geography I first moved there in the summer of 2004, into a stuffy two-bedroom apartment on Throop Avenue, just south of the Flushing Avenue border with "East Williamsburg," across the street from the notoriously shoddy Woodhull Medical Center. I only lived there for four months before a year-and-a-half-long tour of quasi-illegal Manhattan dwellings (Battery Park City! Inwood!), but then I came back. I now believe I have resided in what is geographically Bedford-

Stuyvesant, the most historically African-American of all Brooklyn neighborhoods and now the fastest gentrifying, for fifty-seven months over the past nine years.

When I moved into the apartment on Taaffe in the summer of 2006, I thought, and my roommate thought, that we were moving to Clinton Hill. This had been one of my roommate's stipulations when we started our search. My wealthy childhood friend, the type who was awkward, bookish, and intense in middle school, the type who somewhat iconoclastically befriended the *Star Trek*–obsessed, nerdy, overweight child of black middle-class Cincinnati strivers, simply rebuffed the idea of living in Bed-Stuy. He didn't want to do it. I blinked twice as he said this, unsure how to respond as he spun out his logic. He preferred somewhere already gentrified, and if not the ragingly hip precincts to our north (Williamsburg!) or the increasingly refined enclave to our west (Fort Greene!), then at least somewhere that wasn't Bedford-Stuyvesant.

He grimaced and shook his head when I mentioned it again, a bit further into our apartment search. This is a rich midwestern white man who would go on to vote for Obama and has seen *Belly* and *Don't Be a Menace to South Central While Drinking Your Juice in the Hood* at least three times, who beneath his cool patrician vibe is a genuinely searching and tortured and open person, a lover of jazz and boxing and 1960s soul—who could still passively assume in conversation over dinner with a mutual friend that of course black celebrity X or Y "would squander all his money, they always do." No one seems to call this double consciousness, but someone should.

I'm an agreeable person, perhaps to a fault, so after some time, as it began to look as if we might end up staying at our parents' if we didn't say yes to an apartment, I relented and agreed to live above my means on Taaffe Place. When walking into the office to sign the lease agreement, I remember saying to my old friend, "I'm going to really have to hustle to make this rent." He nodded past me, as if a passerby had said something vaguely interesting that he hadn't quite heard.

I had a bachelor's degree in film and film history, and I wanted to make movies, but in the meantime I could teach. That summer I taught film history at an arts summer camp in Long Island. This involved driving an ailing mid-1990s Ford sedan from my "Clinton Hill" loft seventy-two miles round trip in rush hour traffic on the Long Island Expressway to teach spoiled kids about movies they had no business watching. Still, we watched *The Passenger* and *Pierrot le fou* and *Clerks II*. In a way, it was worth it.

And I liked Taaffe Place, whether it was in Clinton Hill or Bed-Stuy. Anyway the idea that an amorphous, systematic conspiracy concerning the geography of central Brooklyn was afoot seemed implausible. I wasn't deluded enough to think that lofts inhabited by kids with mysteriously inexhaustible checking accounts and spliff-smoking wannabe filmmakers had always existed on Taaffe Place, across the street from the Lafayette Gardens and kitty-corner to the police station where Spike Lee shot the exteriors for that underrated Brooklyn hood/cop/drug/redemption Harvey Keitel drama *Clockers* (that cop station rests on the Clinton Hill side of Classon Avenue, BTW). But one could step into Sputnik, the Leninist-themed hip-hop bar across the street from my building, which occasionally hosted some of the late greats from a previous era of central Brooklyn rap culture (DJ Premier, M-1, et cetera), and think that some multiracial, class-diverse utopia had found its way to this tucked-away part of the borough.

Those were months, which soon turned into years, of magical thinking. "You were middle class in college," my godmother had said to me after I graduated, "but now you enter the world a poor Negro for the first time in your life." Maybe so. But in the Brooklyn night, I smelled opportunities to make lasting things, and I chose to believe that they would open themselves effortlessly, that I wouldn't have to struggle, that grinding class and status anxieties would not have to define my way of encountering the world.

•

As 2006 became 2007, my roommate spent increasingly more time inside our home with his bass, trying to attain perfect pitch by playing incredibly slow chord progressions over and over and over, to the great, unending annoyance of his roommate, who was trying to think. At first, it really didn't seem possible that he would never get a job in the two years I lived there, or even so much as appear to be looking for one, eventually allowing the sheer fact of his effortless affluence to overwhelm our shared space and, in the end, our friendship. For one thing, I didn't think his parents would allow it.

I saw the same looks of exasperation on their faces every holiday when they asked me about his job prospects. Really? I thought. Where was the good ol' boys' club when you needed it? Surely this intelligent young man, who read real literature and thought about things with seriousness, would find his way in the world. Surely.

After my summer teaching at the arts camp, I took a job managing the office of a well-respected if not well-financed independent film production company for $800 a month—which meant I needed one other job, or several, to make the rent. Although I wasn't a technician, I took jobs on sets in my spare time, driving trucks for $100 a day on bad indie movies that would sell at Sundance for millions. I edited Web videos about dirt biking in Mexico, produced short films about lovelorn redheaded bike messengers, made documentaries about bookstores for travel websites, and ghostwrote a lot: papers on Ermanno Olmi for college students, artificially humane director's statements for debutant filmmakers, and a comedic screenplay about the conquest of Colombia for John Leguizamo. I drove people I found on Craigslist to odd corners of New York to shoot documentary footage of old trains. But it was never enough to lift me out of poverty; my rent was just too damn high.

Many days, especially after I moved on from the production company job in mid-2007 at the behest of my employers (I would make a "better employer than employee," they said with odd affection, allowing me to keep the keys and use their office for casting or taking a meeting or even, a few times, a late-night joint), I wished

I simply had the time to attempt to make meaningful art of my own. I rarely found it anymore. Most of the free time I did have I passed smoking weed in my stairwell or Fort Greene Park, all in order to avoid my melancholy home. It was not the life that had been sold to me in the film school brochures.

We never once admitted to each other that we lived in an over-priced *Bedford-Stuyvesant* loft, one that was slowly choking away my desires and our friendship. And I never once admitted that despite all this I loved my roommate, so much. I'd never had a brother, and he had become one to me. I didn't want to move out. So I kept borrowing money on credit cards and deferring my student loans.

Would it have mattered if we'd known we were in Bed-Stuy? I don't know. It might not have meant much to me then. But maybe it would have helped. "Clinton Hill" was bullshit, but Bed-Stuy was a place of black history; the site of one of the first communities of black freedmen in the nineteenth century, it later became the "Harlem of Brooklyn" and then, more recently, Spike Lee's Bed-Stuy and Biggie Smalls's Bed-Stuy. The Marcy Houses, where Jay-Z grew up, were just a fifteen-minute walk north of where we lived. "Cough up a lung / where I'm from / Marcy son / ain't nothing nice." I don't know that any of this would have mattered. But it might have given me the gumption to say to my friend, "Look, I'm drowning. Either we find a cheaper place to live, or help me with my rent." Of course I never said that, and eventually we moved out, separately.

What was Bed-Stuy? When I brought it up with my family in Ohio, they always mentioned Spike Lee. He was synonymous with Bed-Stuy, even if he'd never actually lived there. And I'm sure the worlds of *Crooklyn* and *Joe's Bed-Stuy Barbershop: We Cut Heads*, forty and thirty years gone, respectively, have some bearing on the Bed-Stuy I've lived in, but I haven't found it. The black barbers and jazz musicians I know don't live in such elegance; nor do they have such striver-centric social anxiety. Why would they? The brownstone on Arlington Place that Spike and company shot *Crooklyn* in recently sold for $1.7 million. In these days of the form's increasing cultural irrelevance, there isn't a hit jazz record on earth that would sustain for its creator that kind of mortgage. Or a haircut.

After I left Taaffe Place and moved deeper into Bed-Stuy, I frequently walked down the Bed-Stuy block, Stuyvesant between Lexington and Quincy, where *Do the Right Thing*, Lee's sole narrative masterpiece, was shot. Whenever I'd ask a young man who was more or less the age Martin Lawrence was in that film if he'd ever seen it, he'd shake his head no or pass me by without a word. It's almost always empty in the middle of the summer, that block. The busy and bustling community depicted in that film was a fantasy. Which is not to say those early Lee films don't represent a certain reality of the place. But it was a vision of Bed-Stuy as much less poor and desperate and sad than it actually must have been in those years, a Bed-Stuy that was more like the liberal, middle-class neighborhood where Lee himself grew up: Fort Greene.

When *Do the Right Thing* came out in the summer of 1989, the media worried that it would cause race riots. They shouldn't have. In Lee's films—like in the blaxploitation films he generally found wanting despite his affection for some of the performers—the nationalists, the Muslim rabble-rousers, the dudes who "want some brothers on the wall," always get short shrift at the end: they are embarrassed or jailed or, in the case of Radio Raheem in *Do the Right Thing*, die a violent death. In his more nuanced films (including *Malcolm X*), they transform into more complicated individuals, people willing to grasp the ambivalence of Negro existence and understand that the white man is only part of the problem and naturally an even bigger part of any lasting solution. Watch the films. That's actually what's in them, from *Joe's Bed-Stuy Barbershop* (Mr. Lovejoy, the sharply dressed, black nationalist gangster antagonist, is seen as a shark and charlatan) through *Bamboozled* (where Mos Def's nationalist meets a violent, undignified end). The revolution never comes, only imperfect compromise with the nefarious forces of racial animus or institutional corruption. Those forces are rendered benign not through greater understanding but through mutual resignation to the status quo. Neither Lee nor his cinema has ever been revolutionary. The resilient but embattled Negro middle class consumed Lee's images for years, letting him give the nationalists just enough rope to hang themselves with. Lee was the middle class's champion no less than Bill Cosby, the scion of their aspirations and the troubadour of their anxieties. But they didn't show up for his more difficult Brooklyn tales, like *He Got Game* and *Clockers*. And eventually he was begging all of us for money on Kickstarter.

The rapper Lil' Kim's younger brother Bo was my third Bed-Stuy landlord. He grew up in the neighborhood, knew Biggie Smalls personally, and, like many a young man I got to know in my time there, was from a broken home. Along with his more famous sister, as an adolescent he cared for himself on those unforgiving corners. He had long since decamped for Queens, although early each month he'd sail by in his Lexus SUV, one with rims that spin on their own, to collect our rent. It was kind of a shock when I first met him; he's diminutive, like his sister, but with a warm manner, speaking New Yorkese with a velocity that rivals Korean. He counts cash, which is how we paid for the place, faster than any human being I'd ever seen. Never once did he replace or fix anything in our crumbling Brooklyn digs; we'd simply do it ourselves and take money out of the rent for it. Still, I thought it was neat having a black landlord in our mostly black neighborhood. I was beginning to think by law you had to be a Hasidic Jew to own a piece of property in this part of town.

This was at 551 Kosciuszko Street, between Malcolm X and Stuyvesant, just a block and a half south of the Bushwick border. It's one of the poorest zip codes in the borough; much of the neighborhood is dominated by a series of decaying row houses and brick walk-ups filled with immigrants from the Western Hemisphere's most impoverished countries. I lived in a four-bedroom town house with a hard-drinking white lighting technician friend from film school, who'd given up on making art of his own, and an assortment of other clowns from various stages of our lives. The place cost half what I'd paid in "Clinton Hill," and the constant, unspoken class antagonism that had taken hold of me and my well-heeled friend no longer existed. I bought nickels from young Haitian or Dominican kids on our block or from a skinny, gold-grilled thirtyish black dealer named G., who lived around the corner, on Pulaski, with his two kids and Spanish wife. I had been introduced to him by JP, a charismatic Haitian teenager, already the father of a young child himself, who lived with his mother and younger brothers in a squalid apartment across the street. Crackheads lived in the basement apartment beneath them. I'd spy them from my window sweeping the sidewalk or taking out the trash gingerly each dawn before their morning beer, leering at one another and the new day outside in that serene, docile way they seem to have when they aren't screaming their heads off. From my window, I once watched JP, who couldn't have been much older than eighteen when I met him, drop-kick one of them as I entertained a friend from college.

JP was a good man to know in the neighborhood. When he went to jail for a couple years after assaulting a drunk white kid with a Taser and trying to coerce him into going to an ATM and giving him and his friend some cash, my home became a de facto day-care center for JP's little brothers, Roland and Mordecai.

I didn't really put down roots, though, because as the housing crisis reached a fever pitch, my landlord, Bo, found himself significantly underwater. We were served with eviction papers pretty routinely, always accompanied by Bo's easygoing assurances that his lawyers were "handling it." I noticed the mid-six-figure number the bank claimed he owed it and thought there was no surer sign the country had lost its collective mind than the idea that this crumbling home was worth that much to anyone. Especially, I'd think (in bad faith, I know), in this neighborhood.

I wanted, very badly, to ask Bo about Biggie Smalls, a.k.a. the Notorious B.I.G., a.k.a. Christopher Wallace, but I couldn't figure out how. In general, he was a very open guy, but I knew he was guarded about (a) the status of our ever-impending eviction and (b) his family. His sister Lil' Kim had a rocky relationship with Wallace and had been involved in a well-publicized love triangle involving Wallace and the singer Faith Evans, whom he'd married in 1994. All this was dramatized in *Notorious*, a 2009 biopic about Biggie, and I had to content myself with watching that, several times, while living under Bo's roof.

It's not a great movie, or even a good one. Keeping a biopic of a tragic public figure hopeful and reverent, especially one about a hip-hop musician who met with such a swift rise and violent end, is a troubling proposition; in the case of the largely compromised but never less than fascinating *Notorious*, it's one that pretty much sinks the entire enterprise. Still, before the phony redemption tale, there are some good scenes of life in Bed-Stuy circa 1990. We see a young Biggie rocking headphones as he sits listlessly on his building's stairwell, consuming the jams of DJ Marley Marl and Slick Rick. As he gets older, as with so many youths in my zip code, the lure of easy money proves too much, too quickly; Chris begins dealing crack (in front of the Fat Albert on Broadway, under the JMZ track, no less!), but after a brief stint in jail and the birth of his first child he tries his hand at rapping. Pretty soon his demo draws the attention of an ambitious young producer and promoter (Derek Luke gets the dubious honor of portraying Puffy Combs, the film's executive producer and the picture's voice of personal growth/ moral reasoning, in a truly astounding, sickening performance— "We can't change the world unless we change ourselves"), and the rest is history.

As the film draws to a close, Biggie, in "Generating Cinematic Tragedy 101" fashion, proves what a stand-up guy he is, realizing the faults of his ways and making amends to everyone he's fucked over. This includes his first girlfriend: overweight and dark brown with nappy hair, she's the jilted mother of his largely ignored child. That he left her for a thinner, lighter-skinned woman (my landlord's sister!), whom he then left for a prettier, even lighter-skinned woman, whom he then cheated on with a blond-haired white woman (who, in the film's only legitimately gruesome scene of violence, is beaten up by Faith Evans after she catches Biggie in the act), is never explored as a symptom of the sexual neurosis the darker-than-midnight Wallace probably suffered from. Then, on a March night in Los Angeles, Biggie is shot. Suge Knight, as in Nick Broomfield's documentary *Biggie and Tupac* (2002), makes an easy fall guy, while Puffy gets to be a mentor and executive producer of this film. The winners do get to write history.

But does *Notorious* do an injustice to Biggie's memory? Yes— and no. Because it was, unfortunately, exactly how Biggie would have wanted it. Have a look online, if you can, at some old rap videos from the 1990s. It was the golden age of the genre, with real auteurs emerging in the format and lavish production values, totally unimaginable in our era of austerity, being put to use in their making. When you watch them again, it's clear how governed by a type of repression, a persistent need to deny social reality, Wallace and his handlers were—much more so than their counterparts on the West Coast in the early 1990s, who were much more interested in displaying that social reality in their own three-minute MTV fever dreams. The music videos for Wallace's tracks from that era, the ones that also introduced young teenagers like me to more enduring, unmartyred, now remarkably wealthy rap icons like Shawn Carter and Sean Combs, never dwell on the realities of the streets from which these men came; they're always too busy depicting themselves throwing money around some impossibly well-lit island nightclub stuffed with beautiful, barely dressed women or lip-synching on a yacht while some well-dressed but clearly overmatched goons on Kawasaki Jet Skis chase Mariah Carey to no avail.

It was Biggie's great achievement in his remarkably dexterous lyrics to express this other kind of double consciousness. The songs are rife with tales of Bed-Stuy violence and social decay, even as Biggie clearly yearns for a different kind of world—one that he claims to have already reached by robbing and drug dealing but actually hopes to reach through his art. It wasn't just the Craigslist hustlers and neighborhood-inventing realtors who had an agenda of obfuscation. Come to think of it, Biggie was from Clinton Hill.

In 2008, when Obama was elected, I was still at 551 Kosciuszko, working as a critic and festival correspondent for *Filmmaker* magazine and a few other dying film publications, and I still didn't have any money. After the election, I finally signed up for food stamps, now known as the Supplemental Nutrition Assistance Program, at 500 DeKalb Avenue, a mordant-looking, mostly windowless five-story brick structure that would have been at home in 1970s Minsk. It was a stone's throw from our old loft on Taaffe Place.

I waited among the multiple strollers, pushed by either Hasidic women or blacks from various Caribbean nations, a few slumming hipsters in beat-up New Balances, a few tatted-up Crips in throwback Brooklyn Dodgers hats, and then the polo-wearing men with unshakably weary faces, faces that had seen two- and three-hour waits at 500 DeKalb many times. This collection of diverse human misery and mundane suffering was mostly muted by the white cinder-block walls and the seemingly sterile, almost clinical quality of the building, but occasionally an eruption of emotion, usually over denied benefits because of a lost wages report or a botched falsification of income, jolted us all back into consciousness, away from our private tales of trying and failing to make it in a new, winner-take-all America. I had found Bed-Stuy at last.

35

PROVIDENCE, YOU'RE LOOKING GOOD

IAN MacDOUGALL

At first glance, Luigi Manocchio looks like any retiree. Louie to family, the eighty-seven-year-old wears his gray hair slicked back from his balding pate and favors understated herringbone sport coats. As a younger man, after World War II, he did a brief stint in the army. For vacations, he tends toward places like Italy and Florida. Until recently, he lived in an apartment, described by some as "small," on the upper floor of a house swathed in seafoam vinyl siding—an exterior design style ubiquitous in Providence—on the edge of Federal Hill, the city's Little Italy. On its ground level is a Laundromat called Addie's. He's known to be a regular next door, at Euro Bistro, the kind of small Italian restaurant one finds all over Federal Hill.

Look a little closer, and he starts to stand out from the blue-plate-special crowd. Before his retirement, Manocchio claimed a variety of disparate professions on passport applications—real estate agent, restaurant manager, jewelry worker—but there's not much evidence he ever actually had a job to retire from. His brother Anthony, with whom he is close, has said he "was a salesman at one point," adding, for good measure, "but I don't really know." A federal investigation into his finances turned up only one asset in his name: a prepaid funeral plan. And then there's his criminal record. In 1969, Manocchio was indicted on charges that he masterminded a brazen daytime hit that left two men dead. He fled the charges and spent the next decade on the lam. By some accounts—though evidence is thin—he dressed as a woman at one point to elude law enforcement. Manocchio returned to Providence only after Alzheimer's had so ravaged the memory of a key witness against him that after a protracted court battle, he wound up serving only two and a half years in prison. As for Euro Bistro, its appeal may not be its early-bird buffet. Manocchio's niece owns the place, and according to court filings it's a place of business for the octogenarian, who until 2009 was, federal prosecutors say, the head of the leading family in the New England mob, the Patriarca clan.

Manocchio was arrested in early 2011, shortly before I moved to Providence to cover cops and courts for a news agency. He was eventually charged with extortion and racketeering. Here, in Providence, he's known as Baby Shacks—one of several underworld aliases prosecutors and mob investigators tack onto his name atop indictments. Conventional wisdom has it that the alias refers to his baby-faced good looks and his propensity for "shacking up" with women. That reputation isn't entirely surprising. In photographs from his younger days, Baby Shacks's dark eyes radiate a movie-star brightness, his coy smile conveying charm across the years. His unflappable style—call it mob-boss cool—can't have hurt his popularity with the fairer sex. But figuring out mob nicknames is an imprecise science, and some people think that actually his nickname is the more sinister Baby Shanks, as in someone who shanks people. In 1996, a state police detective named Brendan Doherty, who had just arrested Manocchio, asked him to clarify the confusion. In handcuffs, Manocchio looked at the detective matter-of-factly and said, "Brendan, what does it really matter?"

As I watched Manocchio's case start to work its way through federal court in Providence, his prosecution seemed to me representative of the city's recent transformation. For more than a decade now, Providence has made regular appearances on a smattering of "best city" lists. In its November 2010 issue, GQ called it one of "the coolest small cities in America." That same year, Providence was ranked the second-best American city for theater and performance art, after New York, and third best for "neighborhood joints and cafes" in a *Travel + Leisure* survey. In 2010, the magazine named it the tenth-best city in America for singles, making particular mention of Federal Hill. (Baby Shacks might have agreed.) In order to transform itself into an up-and-coming arts mecca and a good place to meet singles, Providence first had to shed its old reputation—of being a corrupt and dying city and a good place to meet mobsters. Small cities, which tend to dress up political and social insularity as local solidarity, are slow to change. That makes the extent of change in Providence all the more remarkable.

In 1524, the Italian explorer Giovanni da Verrazano met a tribe of coastal Algonquin Indians—the Narragansett—near the hilly shoreline on which Providence would be built. "These people are the most beautiful and have the most civil customs that we have found on this voyage," he wrote of the encounter. "Their manner is sweet and gentle, very like the manner of the ancients." By the time of Providence's founding, in 1636, European disease had decimated the Narragansett, and the East Coast was increasingly populated by refugees not from declining Italy but from ascendant Great Britain. The city's founder was Roger Williams, whose religious beliefs had gotten him kicked out of Puritan Massachusetts. This early emphasis on religious freedom attracted all manner of individualists—including, in time, sea pirates, who found the long, narrow Narragansett Bay an ideal place to hide from the law. Privateers and smugglers came to call the city home. Industrialization replaced them with a different kind of crook: robber barons, who tended to be blue-blooded Protestants, made millions running textile mills and factories on the backs of underpaid Catholic immigrants, mostly from Italy and Ireland. In 1905, the muckraker Lincoln Steffens visited Rhode Island for *McClure's Magazine* and found it "a state for sale." Steffens conceded that a state run by a corrupt "oligarchy" was hardly unusual. But Rhode Island was unique for the poll taxes that remained in place long after most northeastern states had lifted them. "There is one peculiarity about the Rhode Island oligarchy," Steffens wrote. "It is constitutional." Eventually, those kept off the voting rolls—chiefly Italian Catholic immigrants—began to find other ways to improve their lives.

The Mafia in the United States grew out of a confluence of four strands that came together in the early twentieth century: first, mass immigration from Italy to large and midsize American cities; second, discrimination against immigrants by the native Anglo-Saxons; third, the prohibition against alcohol passed by Congress in 1919, which put an enormous industry into the realm of illegitimacy. The fourth, more controversial strand, historically speaking, was the tradition of the Sicilian Mafia, which had first formed—as Eric Hobsbawm writes in his book on the subject, *Primitive Rebels*—in the anarchic cauldron of Italian unification, when local networks of authority began to fail but federal power had not yet reached the island. (A process, some would say, that is still ongoing.) As per Hobsbawm, too, the early American Mafia saw itself at least partly as a form of social rebellion. Especially in a place like Providence, where Italian-Americans had long been kept from power by the Yankee plutocracy, this description of the mob has particular validity.

Of course, none of this predestined the increasingly powerful Italian street gangs of the 1920s to become a giant nationwide organization, with a strict set of rules and procedures. That achievement was largely the work of one man, New York's Charles "Lucky" Luciano (who is, incidentally, a character on *Boardwalk Empire*, portrayed as a younger man by Vincent Piazza). In 1931, Al Capone, then among the nation's richest and most powerful gangsters, hosted a nationwide mob meeting in Chicago, a lavish affair that by some accounts included a closing dinner of Roman proportions, orgy and all. There, Luciano proposed what he called the Commission. The Commission was, as Selwyn Raab puts it in his seminal mob history, *Five Families*, at once analogous to a Mafia "national board of directors" and "an underworld Supreme Court." The Commission consisted of representatives from New York's

Five Families, as well as the families in Chicago and Buffalo and, later, New England. They laid out general policies for mob families across the country. They decided, for instance, whether families could be involved in selling drugs and who could be involved in which drugs where. They also adjudicated disputes between families, both territorial and personal. Luciano was a true Mafia innovator. At the same time as he set up the Commission, he also introduced the code of silence, the *omertà*, a concept borrowed from the nineteenth-century Sicilian Mafia, and the hierarchy that persists today—a boss, an underboss, and a consigliere to serve as an internal counselor and a diplomat in dealings with other families. One of the key aspects of the *omertà* was that the very existence of the Commission had to be denied. From a law enforcement perspective, it was one thing if some Italian-Americans stole a truckful of goods or illegally imported liquor, in which case you locked those guys up for a while, and quite another thing if those guys were part of a national criminal syndicate, in which case you needed to look further up. It was therefore vital for the Mafia to continue to insist that the Mafia did not, in fact, exist.

In the beginning, the Mafia was mostly involved in illegal businesses: bookmaking, numbers games, fencing stolen goods, protection rackets, loan-sharking. Later, as the labor unions that were formed in some of the same historical currents as the Mafia—immigration, urbanization, and industrialization—became bigger and more powerful, the mob infiltrated those as well. It also moved into truck hijackings, liquor during Prohibition, and then the drug trade. It operated in businesses that were explicitly illegal and on the edges of businesses that were legitimate. Of course, even the apparently legitimate tended toward the illegitimate. In Providence over the years, Mafia-run businesses bribed city property tax assessors to bump them down a few brackets. Contractors bribed city inspectors to overlook the fact that they smashed up the sidewalks the city would then pay them to fix. The mob boss Raymond

L. S. Patriarca's legitimate vending machine company—Coin-O-Matic—laundered dirty cash on the side. The mob's goal was to get its hands into as many revenue streams as possible, then divert a small part of those streams for itself. It functioned through violence, coercion, and guilt-tripping. Patriarca's son, also Raymond, summed up the method in a Mafia induction ceremony he presided over in 1989, which was caught on a federal wiretap: "If I'm in the garbage business and you own a dump, before you go to ah, BFI, and go do business with them, if you know anybody at this table can aid you in a business, legitimate or illegitimate, your obligation is to come to us first." If you knew the Patriarca family and certainly if you were an associate of the Patriarca family, it was incumbent upon you to see if maybe the Patriarca family couldn't "aid" you in the business—by negotiating a better deal with your customers, for example, or by helping you cut some corners, or you name it. They were there to help.

Providence was fertile ground for the Mafia because of its large Italian-American population, its thriving port, and its location. It was close enough to Boston and the rest of New England without being Boston, where the sizable Irish community produced a powerful Irish gang presence. An underboss—a Mafia family's second-in-command—was retained in Boston to preserve that faction's loyalty.

This hierarchical principle emerged under the elder Patriarca, the first truly powerful boss of the New England Mafia and whose name it now bears. Patriarca grew up on Federal Hill and rose quickly through the ranks of an ill-defined New England mob, which he took over in 1954. As cover for his criminal enterprise, Patriarca bought the Coin-O-Matic vending machine company on Federal Hill. (The family got its alias, "the Office," because Patriarca ran his rackets out of the back office.) Patriarca had a reputation for being a fair but ruthless leader. He was politically savvy, forging close ties with New York's Five Families, whose disputes he was known to arbitrate, and buying Rhode Island and Massachusetts officials of all kinds.

Although Patriarca's reach grew long, he never took his eye off Providence. As retail stores and theaters followed the demographic shift to the suburbs in the 1950s and 1960s, Patriarca sought to expand Mafia entertainment operations, horse racing, and gambling. Exercising his local influence, he got the governor to approve nighttime horse racing, over widespread public opposition. When the head of the state police cracked down on illegal gambling, Patriarca had the governor replace him. At the same time, Providence's industrial base—its textile mills and machine tool factories—also fled to the suburbs, where land was cheap and newly accessible by the interstate highway system. Patriarca sought a piece of what commerce remained, seeking control, for example, of a car rental company and a fish delivery firm. As the city responded with redevelopment efforts, Patriarca mobilized government and union connections to keep business swift among Mafia associates in the construction industry. Mob manipulation surely did little to get Providence back on its feet.

Still, Patriarca and his heirs are remembered fondly by some citizens, who view him as a patron of the Italian-American community. One afternoon, as I was standing outside the courthouse after a bail hearing for Manocchio, an older man in a Borsalino hat approached me, having wandered over from a park across the street. He asked who was in court. I told him.

"It wasn't so bad when they were in charge. Things got done," he told me. Meaning what? "Ah," he muttered, "the economy's gone to shit." True enough, but what did that have to do with the mob? "Where are you from?" he asked me. I told him Virginia. He waved a hand in the air, dismissively, and headed back toward the park.

Interstate 95—I-95—blasted an elevated concrete path through Providence in the late 1950s, dividing the city's wealthy East Side and its struggling West Side. College Hill, home of Brown University, clapboard New England houses, and narrow, leafy streets, was on the East Side. Federal Hill, the Italian neighborhood, with its one- and two-story houses and storefronts filled, at the time, with pool halls and liquor stores, was on the West Side.

"The Mayor of Providence," as Patriarca was sometimes called, ruled from the West. An FBI wiretap of his office in the 1960s revealed that he had politicians, judges, police, and union officials in his pocket. In 1985, the chief justice of the Rhode Island Supreme Court, who had officiated at the wedding of Patriarca's chauffeur, would resign over allegations of deep mob ties. Patriarca's reach was remarkable. He owned a horse track in which Frank Sinatra had an ownership stake and was a silent partner in the Dunes hotel in Las Vegas. The Mafia was a legitimate national force. One allegation, never corroborated, held that the CIA had approached Patriarca and other dons in 1960, offering them several million dollars to arrange the assassination of Fidel Castro.

By the 1960s, though, there was trouble on the horizon. In 1957, state police raided a meeting of high-level mafiosi, including Patriarca family members, in the upstate New York hamlet of Apalachin, sending dapper criminal masterminds skittering across soggy meadows like high schoolers from a busted keg party. The raid forced national law enforcement skeptics—the longtime FBI director J. Edgar Hoover foremost among them—to acknowledge the Mafia's existence. A series of congressional hearings, some nationally televised, and further investigation left little doubt that the Mafia existed as a nationwide crime syndicate. The trouble was that the structure Luciano set up insulated the upper tiers of mob families from prosecutable wrongdoing. The money might ultimately flow to them, but by the time it wended its way there, often through serpentine laundering operations, it was hard to prove that it was money stemming from criminal activity. The orders went out from lower-level capos. They left no paper trail to follow. Famously, the feds could only get Al Capone on tax evasion. His successors proved just as difficult to indict.

In the wake of these revelations, Senator John L. McClellan, a Democrat from Arkansas, began drafting legislation to fill the legal lacunae that allowed mob bosses to operate with de facto immunity. McClellan had spent the 1950s on subcommittees investigating what at the time was called subversive political activity—though objecting mightily to McCarthyism—and illegal activity within labor unions. He had found that the labor unions—not to mention other business enterprises—were shot through with Mafia influence. With the Soviets sharpening their tractors across the ocean, the integrity and superiority of the American workforce became a matter of domestic and international political legitimacy.

Although the legislative process took time, McClellan was successful in two ways. First, in 1968, Congress passed legislation he drafted that created a process for obtaining legally admissible wiretaps, letting the FBI dig beneath the stone wall of *omertà*. Hoover's FBI had been using wiretaps for years, but despite the mob-boss wrongdoing they revealed—including that of Patriarca—a patchwork of federal laws and U.S. Supreme Court decisions left the evidence derived from wiretaps largely inadmissible in court. Then, in 1970, Congress passed McClellan's Racketeer Influenced and Corrupt Organizations Act, or RICO. RICO effectively made mere association with a criminal enterprise, like the Mafia, a federal crime, with each member potentially liable for the crimes of every other member. The mob hierarchy had insulated itself from criminal liability by delegating oversight of its dirty work to capos. Dubbed the "godfather law," RICO exposed that hierarchy to a range of criminal charges—and lengthy sentences—unimaginable before the passage of RICO. Prosecutors would take time to grasp the profundity of the complex RICO statutes, but the message of their passage was clear: dismantle the mob from the top.

Patriarca faced RICO only in the last years of his life—he was charged with labor racketeering—but he died of a heart attack, in 1984, without standing trial. Still, he was no stranger to courtrooms. Many of the early mob prosecutions occurred in state court, and that's where Patriarca found himself in the early 1970s, facing an accessory-to-murder charge. The Rhode Island assistant attorney general running the case was a young lawyer named Vincent Cianci Jr., who preferred to go by Buddy. An ebullient man with a round face and a receding hairline, Cianci failed to secure a conviction, but his work, which included discrediting Patriarca's alibi—courtesy of a friendly Catholic priest—won him esteem all the same. It wasn't every day a prosecutor went after "the Mayor of Providence."

Less than two years later, that prosecutor would be elected the actual mayor of Providence. Running on an anti-mob, anticorruption platform—and capitalizing on a rusting, mob-friendly Democratic machine stalled by infighting—Cianci entered city hall in 1975 as the first Republican elected to the office since 1938, and the city's first-ever Italian-American mayor. He inherited a postindustrial city in deep decline. Railway lines ran like a fracture through downtown; mills and factories stood empty, cracked monuments to the pre–World War II boom years, when Providence churned out everything from cotton textiles and costume jewelry to steam engines and rubber catheters. The city was hemorrhaging people. Even God was deserting Providence. "The American Bible Society, one of the last successful businesses we had, had packed its Bibles and moved out of town," Cianci writes in his 2011 memoir. During his roughly two decades in power, Cianci would oversee what came to be called the Providence renaissance. He moved the railroad tracks and set up a commission to help private developers put the newly liberated heart of Providence to use. Like a municipal god, he relocated the rivers that run through Providence, removed the cement that had covered them for decades, and laid down idyllic promenades along their banks. He shepherded the construction of a convention center and a shopping mall, refurbished the city zoo—from which animals were literally escaping the night of his election—and put in place tax policies and subsidies that encouraged Rhode Island School of Design graduates, and artists generally, to create arts spaces out of the city's many unoccupied lofts. Cianci became expert at getting the city's hands on federal funding, which he deployed to convert old industrial zones into commercial districts replete with fancy restaurants and boutiques. He launched initiatives to fix sidewalks and roads.

Cianci took a break from office after he pleaded no contest in 1984 to torturing a man he believed was sleeping with his ex-wife, burning the man with a lit cigarette, hurling an ashtray at him, and threatening to murder him. He didn't have to go to jail, though, and his popularity was undiminished, so Cianci regained office in 1990, keeping the renaissance humming along. Still, allegations of corruption plagued his administration—some of his associates were convicted of selling no-show city jobs—and although he escaped direct scrutiny the first time around, he wouldn't the second. In 2001, federal prosecutors indicted Cianci on RICO charges. The indictment laid out more than two dozen counts, alleging the mayor took kickbacks for awarding city contracts, sought to sell city jobs, and extorted bribes from tow-truck operators. A media circus surrounded his trial, at the end of which he was acquitted of all but one RICO charge—conspiring, in the words of federal prosecutors, to run city hall like an organized crime enterprise. (And the mob wasn't too far off. One of Cianci's codefendants was a reputed associate of the Patriarca family.) Released in 2007, after serving a five-year prison term in Fort Dix, which Cianci called "a federally funded gated community," the fallen mayor's former constituency has reinstalled him, crowning him a different kind of urban prince—one of the city's top-rated talk radio hosts.

Nobody has ever proved that Cianci had direct ties to the Mafia, and given the record, I think it's unlikely that he reached out to them directly, unlike some of his predecessors. But there were several incidents of mob involvement in the activities of city officials and Cianci associates during his time in office. One alleged mobster, William "Billy Black" DelSanto, was a city sidewalk inspector. Another, Frank "Bobo" Marrapese, was awarded city snowplowing and paving contracts, despite Cianci's prosecution of him in the 1970s. (The trial included colorful testimony from Marrapese's girlfriend: after she fed him Italian wedding soup infused with her own urine in retaliation for his hitting her, Bobo broke her arm.)

Such contracts apparently stemmed from the appointment, in 1980 (five years after Cianci became mayor), of DelSanto's brother and Edward "Buckles" Melise—both known to law enforcement as mob associates—to top positions at the city Department of Public Works. All those beautiful projects—the Waterplace Park lagoon and WaterFire, where dozens of large cressets set in the river are lit on Saturday evenings throughout the summer and fall—got their start with the help, or the hindrance, of the old Providence mob.

Cianci calls the Mafia links to his administration the product of the "inbred corruption that went on in every major city in America, and there was very little the mayor could do to stop it." That may be true. And Cianci's antipathy toward the mob seems genuine. When asked as mayor to help promote *The Sopranos* in Providence, Cianci declined. "When I was a kid, I always felt that [the Mafia] was a stain on Italian Americans," he writes. "I got sick and tired of seeing the Italian stereotypes."

And yet it's hard to believe that a former mob prosecutor was unaware of the mob ties of his top public works officials. It's particularly hard to believe given the importance of public works to his administration. The first step in cleaning up Providence was fixing its sidewalks and roads, which Cianci did in 1982 through a campaign that cost the city well over $1 million and bore the tagline "Providence, you're looking good." Again, Melise and Marrapese were involved. Did they inspect the sidewalks and pave and plow the streets better than anyone else could have? Maybe; maybe not. Probably not. But their participation might have been the price extracted for another kind of help. A large public works project like this required the cooperation of the labor unions, and it was an open secret that some of them had deep mob connections, including the Laborers' International Union, widely believed to have been overseen by a shadow leader, Raymond Patriarca.

On its face, then, Cianci's appears to be a municipal Jekyll-and-Hyde story. With one self—plump, smiling, hairpiece set just so— Cianci pumped hands and secured funding for many of the initiatives that remade Providence during his reign, converting a depressed postindustrial dump into an arts and culture hub. Meanwhile, his other self—corpulent, snarling, face bathed in the sinister red glow of some neon sign downtown—spent evenings rubbing his hands together, plotting to turn city hall into the nexus of a citywide network of rackets. But the truth seems to be that Buddy did what he had to do. By the time Cianci was elected, the way prosecutors would later accuse him of getting things done was, simply, how things got done. The only way to change that was to clean up the city, and to clean up the city, one had to play the game. Cianci turned the game into a double game, reforming with one hand while racketeering with the other. But as a city grows nicer, it also grows less tolerant of its old corrupt ways, and Cianci had to go.

While Cianci was cleaning up Providence—or sullying it, or both—gradually, patiently, Luigi "Baby Shacks" Manocchio was working his way through the ranks of the Patriarca family, rising to the top in the middle of the 1990s. It was a long, slow climb from relative obscurity, and just as he reached the top, the bottom fell out. The FBI and federal prosecutors had, in the mid-1980s, figured out how to use RICO, with its lengthy sentences and broad reach, to bring down Mafia families, and they were going about it with aplomb. By the 1990s, *omertà* had collapsed. In New York, underbosses had become cooperating witnesses. The bosses of the Five Families were in prison or on their way there. But Manocchio was undeterred. In 1992, he set about shaking down the Cadillac Lounge, a strip club in Providence. Under threat of retaliation, Manocchio had the owner of the club hire a mob associate, Thomas Iafrate, as bookkeeper. His real job was to set aside $125 per day. The money came from what the girls brought in, girls with stage names like Austyn and Haze and Gemini, who, when not slipping out of bikinis onstage, sometimes pose for the club's wall of fame, draped topless over vintage Packards and Merkel motorcycles. The racket, according to court filings, came to include an adult bookstore and another strip club, the Satin Doll, owned by the same proprietor.

Manocchio was arrested while on vacation in Florida. I first saw him in a federal courthouse in Providence, awaiting the first of several days of bail hearings. Just before the hearing, a prosecutor had filed a seventeen-page memorandum in an effort to show why Baby Shacks, given his fugitive past, should be denied bail. To illustrate Manocchio's deceptive style, the memorandum noted that his cell phone number is registered to a forty-three-year-old Warwick, Rhode Island, resident named William Smith, incidentally the name of the federal judge assigned to Manocchio's trial. As she looked over the filing for the first time, Manocchio's attorney swept her bangs off her forehead compulsively.

Manocchio "enjoys remarkably good health and is well known for his dedication to remaining physically fit," the prosecutor had written in his memorandum. It showed. In a green prison jumpsuit, his corona of gray hair fastidiously slicked back, Manocchio moved with the ease of a man half his age. He didn't look much different than he did in decade-old photographs. His eyes retained their screen-star brightness, and I could still make out Baby Shacks's baby face, which betrayed no emotion as he took his seat.

His lawyer, still fussing with her bangs, whispered something to her client and passed him the prosecution memorandum. Manocchio shrugged and started reading. Page after page, he remained impassive. The biography contained in the document—granular details of his travels, his habits, his relationships—evidently did not surprise him. Then Manocchio hit something that gave him pause. His eyebrows arched in surprise, and he let his mouth fall open slightly. Turning to his lawyer, he pointed at the paper in front of him. "That's my number!" he exclaimed. His lawyer said something to him quietly. Manocchio leaned back in his chair, the brightness drained from his still-wide eyes. He stayed this way for a while, staring into the middle distance or, maybe, into a future less certain than he had thought.

•

The detection of his phone number wasn't the only thing that caught Manocchio by surprise. The FBI, it emerged, had planted a bug in the back office of the Cadillac Lounge. One day in court, prosecutors played some of what the bug had picked up. In it, a bouncer at the lounge who was charged with being Manocchio's enforcer screamed expletive-laced threats over the phone at an unknown interlocutor. A nervous-looking man in his fifties with a thinning ponytail, the bouncer, who was in court for a bail hearing, winced as the tape played. It's a sad state of affairs when even the muscle is over the hill. Sadder still was having to watch a young girl in the gallery, his daughter, cry quietly as she listened to tapes of her father's threatening to slit another man's throat. Whether she cried because she had never heard her father this way before or she cried precisely because she had heard her father this way before, I don't know.

Manocchio, meanwhile, was denied bail.

"What we have here is a defendant who has in the past fled," a federal judge said before ordering him held pending trial. "Don't forget Bulger. Whitey Bulger. How long has he been gone?"

"Long time," Manocchio's lawyer said.

Then, in February, after two codefendants pleaded out, Manocchio admitted not only to racketeering but to his role as a former Patriarca family boss. In exchange, prosecutors dropped the extortion charges. His admission—a major betrayal—surprised me. Maybe Manocchio came to realize that Providence's future isn't Providence's past. Betrayal is of no great consequence if there's nobody around to avenge it. Indeed, after Manocchio's arrest, several other Patriarca family members were indicted in the strip club protection racket. Hardly any remain free. Manocchio, serving his time in a low-security prison in North Carolina, is scheduled for release on November 4, 2015, at the age of eighty-eight.

Hobsbawm writes of movements like the Sicilian Mafia that they are "exceedingly primitive . . . in so much as they tend to disappear as soon as more highly developed movements arise." In America, the more highly developed movement was not, as in Italy, new forms of social and political protest as embodied by the huge political movements of the twentieth century, Communism and Fascism. Here, it was capitalism. As a former NYPD mob detective says in Raab's *Five Families*, "At one time, not so long ago, there was a supply of young Italian-Americans who wanted to be in the families. Now, they want to be CEOs of legitimate corporations." Michael Corleone would have known what to make of the word "legitimate." It's a good racket if you can get into it, the legitimacy racket. Just ask the big banks.

Still, the change in Providence has had an effect. A cleaned-up Providence, whose small size leaves organized crime with fewer options than its larger counterparts, like New York and Chicago, is today inhospitable to mobsters. Without a culture of corruption and graft to inspire them, the politicians, the union leaders—those left anyway—the judges, and the cops aren't so easy to buy off. And if you can't buy them off, how's a crime family to pay the bills?

The answer was to shake down two sad, bunker-like strip clubs for a few thousand dollars a month. The desperation may run deeper still. Even after Manocchio's indictment, other Patriarca family members, now in prison or awaiting trial, tried to continue shaking down the strip clubs. Idiocy might be to blame, but a more likely explanation is that, as one FBI agent put it, these are "people with no money, living scam to scam, and just trying to get by."

With the citywide ambit of mob enterprise contracted to the dingy confines of a couple of strip clubs, even the old mob stronghold, Federal Hill, is cleaning up its act. Young mothers park baby strollers outside cute bakeries where men in dark suits once parked black Coupe de Villes. Bookish Brown students sip iced lattes where wiseguys in undershirts once played sidewalk pinochle in collapsible lawn chairs. Arts spaces have replaced safe houses. It's pretty sad—if also pretty nice.

36

BOSTON BUYS RESISTANCE

INTERVIEW WITH STEVE MEACHAM

Between September 2008 and July 2014, there were more than five million completed foreclosures in the United States, displacing more than ten million people. Many were initiated by institutions—either Fannie Mae, Freddie Mac, or various banks—that had received large government bailouts at the height of the crisis. As evidence of fraud and criminal behavior on the part of lenders piled up, resisting foreclosure became a centerpiece of community organizing. City Life / Vida Urbana (CL/VU) is an affordable housing and tenants' rights organization located in Jamaica Plain, Boston, whose methods have influenced similar groups nationwide. Steve Meacham has been working for CL/VU for fourteen years. He spoke with us at CL/VU's office in a converted brewery in the fall of 2013.

n+1: Let's just start with when were you born and where are you from?

SM: I was born in Baltimore in 1948, and I grew up in New Jersey. I went to Lehigh, came to Boston to go to graduate school in city planning, and then dropped out. I was having trouble wrapping my head around myself as a city planner, and I took a course in community organizing in the local neighborhood. And then I kind of felt, "Well, this is what I want to do." So I dropped out of school and just did it. I got a job as a school bus driver to support myself and, you know, never looked back.

n+1: Is there a version of city planning that is good?

SM: Well, it's not so much that there's something bad called "city planning"; it's that pursuing it professionally precluded my politics. I had thought that a professional course would follow up on my involvement in the antiwar movement and my interest in cities and social justice. And that turned out not to be the case.

n+1: Talk about the antiwar movement.

SM: When I went to college in 1966, I was pro-war, and I was one of millions of people who changed in the subsequent years. A year and a half after I got to school, I was going to rallies everywhere. And that became a part of a more general movement involvement: supporting the black liberation movement after I left college; reading about and supporting the feminist movement; a beginning involvement in economic and social justice activities when I was still in school. So, becoming an organizer at that point in a neighborhood was part of a general shift that was happening.

City Life was founded in 1973 as a community-based, socialist organization, and the people who founded City Life were members of all those radical movements I just mentioned. And they decided that they wanted to implement those broad politics in a specific, urban setting and take up class. A lot of groups were similarly founded in that period and were doing that, and almost all of them, almost with the sole exception of City Life, broke apart due to Left sectarianism.

n+1: Why was that? Was there an official party affiliation?

SM: No, it was more like City Life was really committed—and this is probably something I disagreed with at the time, and they turned out to be right—but they were really against "vanguardism."

n+1: What's that?

SM: Vanguardism is the idea that there is one organization that is the leader of the working class—but there were many organizations competing for the title. City Life opposed the whole idea, so they weren't destroyed by infighting. That's one reason they survived.

n+1: Was there a moment when you got to school that you remember as being key to the shift from being pro-war to antiwar?

SM: Well, I would visit the SDS table and argue with them. And then, of course, other people were there arguing with them, people who I thought were complete jerks. And then I would argue with those people. Until I said, "Wait a minute, I should just be on the other side of the table."

n+1: So then you graduated, went into urban planning, had this feeling that that wasn't it, and then took this class on community organizing? Or was it at the school?

SM: It was at the school, but it was a practical thing. I mean, you were out in the field, doing either community organizing or what they were calling advocate planning at the time.

We were assembling a group of neighborhood residents that we were lending our planning skills to to help them formulate a vision for the neighborhood. But the process of doing that, of getting to know the people involved, you know, quickly went way beyond lending planning skills. It became much more of "Well, here's a nice vision, but how do we fight for this?" Yeah, we want neighborhood health clinics, but it's not enough just to have a colorfully done planning vision; you've got to get out on the street and fight for it. And at some point in there, I said, "You know, I could do this the rest of my life." And nobody could ever take it away from me: I don't have to get hired to do it; I can't be laid off. It could be something that is my life's commitment. I don't know where, at quite what point that happened, but by the end of the course I was saying, "This, yes, and the school, no."

So I left school to become an organizer. I was doing a neighborhood-based community group called the Cambridgeport Homeowners and Tenants Association. And they were focused on displacement and housing and evictions and stuff like that, but they also were multi-issue. They would take up workers' struggles and support city workers and take up issues of desegregation. And one of those things that became a pivotal moment for a lot of those groups was the 1975 busing crisis. All the groups, wherever they were, were deciding how to relate to that struggle for desegregation.

n+1: Can you talk about the busing crisis?

SM: Well, despite what I just said, it wasn't really a busing crisis; it was a desegregation movement. The school desegregation was part of it but not the whole thing, not by any means. For example, we participated in a march designed to desegregate Carson Beach, which was halfway between white South Boston and black Columbia Point but was controlled by South Boston. And any attempt by people of color to swim there would be met with violence. So there was a big march on parts of the beach. And the fight for school desegregation, protecting buses against stonings were part of it.

But the groups that were doing community-based work had to decide how to relate to that. And one of the things they had to decide was whether issues of racial oppression were subsumed under class issues, or whether they were independent and existed in their own right. And our group in Cambridge and City Life and a bunch of other groups went the second way and said, "Look, we have to be involved in this desegregation fight." Trying to protect working-class unity by not dealing with racial injustice is wrong and doesn't work anyway.

n+1: How does City Life address these things?

SM: City Life's mission statement clearly articulates our understanding that there are multiple oppressions. But there's a million ways to interpret what to do with that. I tend to be somebody who says, well, all these multiple oppressions exist and each oppression generates its own movement of resistance in response. All these oppressions flow through the dominant system of the moment, which is capitalism. That doesn't mean they don't predate capitalism or that they won't exist after capitalism, but we have to do something about all of them.

City Life is not a Left group in that it doesn't have a really coherent analysis that we all share. We do have a clear view linking race, class, and gender oppression and the responses to them. A lot of our organizing is based on that understanding. The bank tenant movement and tenant asssociations we organize are almost by definition class formations because they say "Look, any of you who want to fight the banks come into our ranks." On the other hand, most of the people who come in the room are people of color, and the articulation of that class demand against the banks takes the specific form of defending communities of color and articulating the ways in which the banks' foreclosure prices will specifically affect communities of color.

n+1: You said City Life opposed vanguardism. Where did you stand on that in the 1970s?

SM: I haven't always seen the wisdom of City Life's position. So after the busing crisis, I went to the shipyard to be a welder. I worked in the shipyard for nine years. There were many workplaces in the Boston area and around the country where leftists were doing that. It was typical that the shipyard, this workplace of six thousand workers, had eight or nine different Left groups and formations in there.

n+1: Which one were you in?

SM: October League. We were less than the sum of our parts. Or something like that. I can give you a list of criticisms of my own sectarianism that would be as long as my arm. On the other hand, we didn't know what we were doing. The previous Left had been vanquished from the working-class movement. We were going in there, trying to figure it out, and made a shitload of mistakes. And did some amazing things too.

What I learned is that you needed to have a broad radical criticism of how the system operates. A lot of people actually wanted to talk about that in the shipyard. Even if they didn't, that broad understanding would form around everyday things in profound ways. An example: the shipyard was dependent on navy work. We were building ships for the Rapid Deployment Force. And I'm an antiwar activist. So do I say, as some religious activist in the antiwar movement would have said, it's immoral for me to be here, I have to leave? Or do I say, this is a very important place to be as a leftist? Do I just make a moral argument against our huge defense budget, or do I somehow try to integrate myself into the demand for jobs and interpret it in a new way? We wanted to take the jobs argument out of the defense budget debate.

So we came to this idea of economic conversion. We launched a movement in the shipyard that became a national movement for economic conversion. The idea was to create nonmilitary products that could keep military facilities going. And more than that, that could create products that weren't apparently the normal product for that facility. So the non-ship products, in the case of the shipyard, could keep the facility going, someday, without making weapons.

That had a lot to do with industrial policy, planning for the future, having to build labor solidarity among different shipyards rather than compete with them for work. I, as an antiwar activist, would mute my moral criticism of navy work in order to build a movement that really had a chance of organizing an alternative. The goal was for the union to say, "Look, we don't care which one of our locals gets the navy work. We want to make sure the local that doesn't get it still has a future." So we pursued that and spoke about it all over. And we ran for a union election based partly on that premise of using conversion as a way to fight the shipyard closing. We lost the election either narrowly or perhaps by fraud. As a result, the closing of the shipyard didn't have nearly the struggle associated with it that it should have.

n+1: How is a shipyard different from a city?

SM: There's something special about urban environments, especially now that our economy has moved from being centered on production—where cities were warehouses for industrial workers—to one where one of the key resources to capitalist profit is real estate investment.

Therefore we have to pay enormous attention to real estate value. It's a very conscious process. There are various formations in the real estate industry that are constantly trying to create real estate value. The large banks very deliberately created the real estate bubble. That fits in with the idea of a modern, mature capitalist economy that's focused more on speculation than production. Land value speculation is a key part of that.

This is why a lot of what we've done at City Life uses a collective bargaining model for tenant organizing. City Life has popularized that in the last ten years. We're doing it now in some buildings. People will get a big rent increase, and we'll organize them not to pay the rent increase. Then we'll seek a collective bargaining contract.

n+1: I didn't know that.

SM: Such a contract will establish rent for, say, three to four to five years in the same way that labor contracts establish wages. It makes a similar critique of the market: a fair rent is not market rent, in the same way that the implied critique of any union bargaining effort is that a fair wage is not a market wage, and so any collective bargaining by unions is a radical anticapitalist thing.

But unions became pretty good at de-emphasizing or ignoring the radical implications of what they do. So along comes tenant organizing in the housing justice movement, where the idea of collective bargaining is very radical. There's a story that illustrates this.

We had done a lot of collective bargaining. We had a thousand units under contract. We were fighting building by building. So we said, we need some legislation to codify this right of tenants to collective bargaining. We had failed to pass any rent regulation. The Boston City Council would consistently vote against it, mostly on racial lines, actually. The class demand of the tenants was being rejected by the white councilors, so we decided we had to go the route of an ordinance that was not rent regulation.

We chose collective bargaining. The ordinance simply said that any landlord who owned more than twenty units—no small landlords—had to sit down and talk to the tenant association, if one existed, twice a year. The landlords didn't have to do anything. No good faith bargaining or anything like that, they just had to talk to us. Councilor Charles Yancey said, "This is the mildest piece of housing legislation I've ever seen." There were no teeth in it.

But then billion-dollar real estate firms like Avalon came out and said, "We will stop investing in your city if you pass this." Why would they prioritize defeating a bill with no teeth? The answer is that any policy that even mentioned an alternative to maximum profit as a guiding principle, anything that recognized that there's another side with a legitimate stake to negotiate, would have been a huge ideological defeat for large real estate interests. Because what they really want is a real estate system where omnipresent all around you, in the air, is the idea that fair rent is the market rent so nobody has to defend it. As soon as they have to defend it, they can't defend it.

n+1: Talk about the threat of de-investment.

SM: Yes, the capitalist version of a general strike.

n+1: That's exactly what it is. So why rely on capital at all? Why not build our own buildings or our own institutions that are from the beginning organized around these alternative principles?

SM: This is a historic debate. And I think that we should do that. And City Life and our tenant organizing is always raising the demand to the effect that "we'd like to see this building purchased by a nonprofit," to get it out of the market. Either you're gonna regulate the market, or you're going to get stuff out of the market. De-commodification. And de-commodification is an important principle of City Life.

On the other hand, getting a building de-commodified, or for that matter setting up a workers' cooperative, can be a labor of such intensity, so many person-hours, and those hours are probably taking away from prosecuting the struggle in other ways.

So ironically, what's happened a lot is that the demand—not for de-commodification, but for limits on profit, for regulation, like the demand that a specific landlord give a five-year deal—is a more radical demand in the movement-building sense—in terms of the movement it creates—even though it's a much less radical demand in terms of its ultimate outcome.

Whereas for the demand for de-commodification to actually work in practice, you have to get involved with some community development corporations, somebody who's actually going to buy the thing for us (the tenants, the movement). And they are of necessity not a radical entity because they're dealing all the time with banks and investors. They see this as a completely technical thing. Their people are good people; they want to get it out of the market, but they're not seeing it as a movement-building exercise.

So it becomes a sinkhole of time. Even though it's a radical thing to de-commodify, it doesn't build a movement. So we see de-commodification as something that we're fighting for at a successful rate, but we're not going to put huge energy into making sure that it happens. Every time we get such a place, we'll take it. I mean, I live in a cooperative myself in Cambridge. I pay $725 for a two-bedroom.

n+1: Do you?

SM: Central Square.

n+1: We should talk.

SM: So I can testify to what happens when you take profit out of real estate. There's hundreds of units in Jamaica Plain that City Life organized, and those buildings were purchased by a nonprofit. But those buildings are not the basis of the resistance. Those facing displacement are the base of the resistance. So what do you do with that? This creative tension is one of those organizing conundrums that you're constantly trying to solve.

n+1: Antagonism is useful in that respect; to successfully de-commodify, in some sense, would destroy the conflict pushing people to organize in the first place.

SM: Well, if you could de-commodify on a large scale . . . If you win, you win.

There's an old dilemma: You imagine a society where we're in organized cooperatives and we're not trying to outdo one another. We're in cooperation, not competition. But our critics will say, "People aren't like that. We don't have the people that would inhabit such a society. We aren't ready to inhabit such a society." Where do such people come from?

The people who inhabit the new society come from the struggle to change the old. This is revolutionary praxis, as I understand it. And that transforms not only society but transforms the people who fight for it. We become the people that we need in order to inhabit that society. And that's kind of how it is in housing. People come into our tenant association meetings to fight rent increases, and, man, they're just all over the place. They're like, "I know I can't fight the rent increase. Just give me a little time to move." Or,

"Just fix up the building a little bit before you raise the rent," or, "If it wasn't for those bad Section 8 tenants bringing down the building, everything would be okay." A million things. So the process of the struggle is not just to fight the enemy but to work out all the stuff inside.

n+1: When do you go to the law? What is the relationship of the kind of struggle on the ground and the struggle in the courts?

SM: Well, we use the imagery of the sword and shield to symbolize that; the legal defense is the shield, and the public protest is the sword. But it's also meant to remind you that you're in a fight with an enemy that's trying to destroy you. Let's shed all illusions: you need your weapons. If you just have the sword, you better win with your first blow, otherwise they're gonna kill you. And if you just have a shield, then they're going to wear you down and kill you. So you need both.

n+1: I see.

SM: I'll give you an example: When a foreclosed home is auctioned off, the auction happens at the house, often with the family still inside. Investors show up and bid, and the bank sometimes has a representative there too. And so we often protest these auctions, to make it clear to investors that they will be buying resistance in addition to an asset. That's actually our chant: "If you buy here, you buy resistance." So we had an auction protest in the city of Brockton recently, and it was kind of new for some people. We didn't have any veterans there; ten people came who were part of our Brockton formation, the Brockton Bank Tenant Association. I could tell, you know: They get in front of the house, and the homeowner is really nervous. I knock on the homeowner's door—who's invited us to come—and I have my signs that say WE SHALL NOT BE MOVED, and I say, "Put these up all over the house." She says, "Really?" and I say, "Yeah, six to a window."

So pretty soon the signs are going up, and other people are arriving, and they're kind of nervously laughing. And we get a chant going, and people are kind of warming to the chant. And then the auctioneer comes over and starts reading his thing, this official document, and the rest of us are hovering around. And we're starting to breathe fire now, we're chanting loud, we're singing, we're drowning out the auctioneer. There's anger there, and yet it's an act of love and empowerment. The bank had the auction and seized the property, but we won because the investors all left; they didn't want to have any part of this. We'll have a much better chance to get the house back and . . . And, you know, the woman invited us all in, and people are *thrilled*. There's been this moral space that's created that didn't exist. People felt they challenged this giant power structure and eked out a small victory.

n+1: Can you tell me about the process a little bit? You have meetings; people come when they're in trouble with the landlord or facing eviction. How does the outreach process start?

SM: Well, we have this process called the five masses, and on our website there's this long, gigantic manual that describes it. But the five masses are mass outreach, mass meetings, mass casework, mass action, mass political education.

For mass outreach, we visit every house that goes into foreclosure. Through this kind of canvassing, through word of mouth, through social media and many other ways, we find the people in trouble and get them into the meeting. The mass meetings provide information about legal rights, but they are designed to have a lot of functions that aren't normal to community meetings by organizers. They have a revival aspect to them; there are many rituals that overcome isolation and alienation and shame, which are really nice. Then the mass casework is creating space for people to understand how their case is linked to everyone else's, but also to get the immediate help they need as individuals. After all, I might have a lot of solidarity with my neighbors, but it's still my house—I don't want to lose it!

n+1: Yeah, of course!

SM: But we try to do that casework in a way that links all these cases together. So, you know, you have a protest against somebody being evicted by Freddie Mac. [Freddie Mac and Fannie Mae own over 50 percent of all mortgages in the United States, so their behavior affects millions of people. They continued evicting thousands of people, even though they were 79 percent publicly owned after being bailed out in 2008.] So you assemble other Freddie Mac or Fannie Mae cases there to say, "And I'm gonna fight mine too!" And you try to link them all together. We had a long-running battle to defend a longtime friend who I worked with in the shipyard—Olivé Hendricks. He's a Fannie Mae borrower and evictee. In Roslindale, we had a standoff with the bank after the judge issued the eviction order. They knew we were ready to do mass demonstrations and civil disobedience to stop the truck, and they didn't want the publicity associated with that. After twenty-two days, Fannie Mae insisted that the police evict, and nine of us got arrested. The arresting officer held us in the police wagon for an hour while the furniture was moved out, then drove us around the corner and released us. He declared it a case of "savage capitalism."

But we took all the energy from that blockade and had a series of protests in front of the housing court, and thirteen more people were arrested there. And then, as a result of all that, we went to city council and got an emergency resolution passed, calling on Fannie and Freddie to stop all no-fault evictions. And then we went to Senator Warren and Markey's aides, and they promised to do a press conference. So all this is kind of building, and that's probably why we were finally able to get rid of Ed DeMarco, the Bush-appointed head of FHFA [the Federal Housing Finance Agency], overseeing Fannie and Freddie, who was standing in the way of any policy change. This was a major achievement.

So in that sense, we're trying to use all these cases, but we're going to do it in a way that builds the movement and *you're* going to benefit. And, ironically, what's happened is that people who fight with us to the end and lose are more likely to stay involved than people who fight with us and win quickly. 'Cause they're thinking, "I won my house back; now I can kind of be normal." But the people who fought and lost, all they've got is their history of fight. And they keep coming.

37

DestiNY, SYRACUSE, USA

STEVE FEATHERSTONE

One frigid winter afternoon, at the height of the Great Recession, I went to the Carousel Center mall to look for the future of Syracuse. The last time I'd checked, it was on the sixth-floor Skydeck, sitting on a large pedestal bearing the label "DestiNY USA." The mall was in a postholiday slump. At the top of the escalator, an old man wearing a burgundy blazer stood gripping a velvet rope as the riderless horses of the eponymous carousel spun slowly behind him. Organ music echoed in the empty food court. I got on an elevator in the glittering chrome and glass atrium and pushed the Skydeck button. It'd been deactivated. I tried the stairwell on the fourth floor instead. But the door to it was locked. A security guard peered at me from behind a slot cut in a heavy steel door next to the stairwell.

"Can I help you?" he said.

"Can I get to the Skydeck from here?"

"Skydeck's closed," he said. He eyeballed the bag hanging on my shoulder.

"Camera," I said, patting the bag. "Who do I need to talk to for permission to go up there?" The guard tilted his chin toward a set of double glass doors leading to offices of the mall's management. I pushed open the doors with purpose, as if I were late for an appointment, and asked the receptionist if I could please speak to somebody about visiting the Skydeck.

"Ohh-kaay," she said. "And who are you with?"

I told her that I was a freelance photographer. Freelance writer was closer to the truth, but in my experience people are much more accommodating to photographers than they are to writers. The last "writer" to visit the Skydeck was a troubled twenty-one-year-old poet and cough syrup addict who jumped a hundred feet to his death. I told the receptionist that I wanted to take a few photographs of Onondaga Lake while the light was still good. The view of the lake from the Skydeck was the best in the city. What I really wanted to do was photograph the scale model of DestiNY USA. The receptionist circled her desk and disappeared into a glassed-in office suite. Moments later she came out and shook her head.

"I'm sorry," she said, "the Skydeck is closed."

I gave up and went outside. All along the length of Hiawatha Boulevard, the southern boundary of the mall, snowcapped mounds of excavated dirt stood over DestiNY USA's aborted foundation.

Any story about Syracuse begins and ends with Onondaga Lake. The city would not exist without it. Both sit in a wide bowl on the northern end of Onondaga Valley, which extends south from the city limits for about fifteen miles. If you rolled a giant marble down one side of the valley, it would roll up the other side, and back again, until it came to rest in Onondaga Lake.

The lake, the valley, and much of the surrounding territory were once the ancestral homeland of the Onondaga tribe. What's left of the Onondaga, about five hundred tribe members, still live in Onondaga Valley on a swampy parcel of bottomland known as the Onondaga Nation. (I grew up a block away from the Onondaga Nation, although we always called it the rez.) The Onondaga are founding members of the powerful Haudenosaunee, or Iroquois Confederacy, a political entity consisting of six tribes whose territory encompassed what is now upstate New York and parts of Pennsylvania and Ohio. Onondaga Lake is sacred to the Iroquois. It's said that the Haudenosaunee was founded on its shores under the visionary leadership of an Onondaga chief named Hiawatha. The Haudenosaunee was the first form of representative government on the continent, and many historians cite its influence on the democratic principles enshrined in the U.S. Constitution.

Over the past few years, I've spent a lot of time in the Onondaga County Courthouse, attending custody hearings between my sister and her ex-boyfriend. Most of the time, nothing happens at these hearings. But I've learned a few things from staring at the walls in the courthouse's vaulted second-floor vestibule, which has been restored to its full Beaux Arts glory with lots of polished marble and gilded plaster. Large oil paintings hang high on the walls, depicting early episodes in Syracuse's history. One of them shows the Hiawatha of legend standing upright in a white birch-bark canoe, his arms outstretched and his face turned to the sky like Christ on the cross.

I've often sat at one of the heavy wooden tables in the vestibule while my sister's ex-boyfriend, a member of the Onondaga tribe, sat at an adjacent table, both of us staring at the murals as a way of avoiding eye contact. I couldn't help but wonder what he saw when he looked at the portrait of Hiawatha. An idealized version of himself? Sentimental white man bullshit? The painting reminded me of my days as a Boy Scout, paddling an overloaded canoe on Saranac Lake in the Adirondack Mountains. Why the hell was Hiawatha standing up in a canoe? The greenest of greenhorns, to say nothing about Native American demigods, knows better than to stand up in a canoe.

A mural on the wall opposite Hiawatha's portrait depicts the 1654 discovery of Onondaga Lake's salt springs by the French. A black-robed Jesuit priest and an explorer wearing a feathered cap stand over a kneeling, bare-chested Onondaga brave who offers them springwater in his cupped hands. Aside from the genteel racism on display in the foreground, the background of the painting contains a sublime feat of historical revisionism. Sheer white cliffs rise from the shores of Onondaga Lake, towering high above the shoulders of the priest and the explorer. But there were no white cliffs anywhere near Onondaga Lake in 1654. So how'd they get in the painting?

I have a theory. The muralist William de Leftwich Dodge completed the courthouse paintings in 1904. At that time, the biggest business in Syracuse was the Solvay Process Company, a chemical manufacturer of soda ash, which had been dumping industrial waste into Onondaga Lake for decades. Mountains of a chalky-white compound from the company's chemical factory could be found all along the southwest shore of the lake. But maybe Dodge, who wasn't a Syracuse native, actually believed the white mounds were natural features. His decision to include them was prophetic, for in a single frame he managed to memorialize the founding moment in Syracuse's history—the discovery of salt—while retroactively fouling the pristine landscape with the very industrial waste that the discovery would lead to.

In 1656, the Jesuits built a mission on a knoll overlooking Onondaga Lake. They came to collect souls, not salt, declaring the wild country outside their palisades the "heart of a land destined to become holy." Two years later, they fled the holy land under the cover of night when Onondagas threatened to massacre them. The mission fell into ruin. White settlers didn't return to the region until after the Revolutionary War. This time they came for salt, building a few ramshackle dwellings on fetid swamplands near the salt springs (the Onondaga had always sited their longhouses on higher ground south of the lake). They named the settlement Salina, after the commodity that created it. By the nineteenth century, most of the salt consumed in the United States would come from Onondaga Lake's springs. But it didn't happen overnight. The historian and newspaper editor William L. Stone ventured to Salina in 1820, before Syracuse was a name on a map. He spoke to Joshua Forman, one of Syracuse's founding fathers, and made these observations:

I lodged for the night at a miserable tavern, thronged by a company of salt boilers from Salina, forming a group of about as rough-looking specimens of humanity as I had ever seen. Their wild visages, beards thick and long, and matted hair even now rise up in dark, distant, and picturesque effect before me. I passed a restless night, disturbed by strange fancies, as I yet well remember. It was in October, and a flurry of snow during the night had rendered the morning aspect of the country more dreary than the evening before. The few houses . . . standing upon low and almost marshy ground, and surrounded by trees and entangled thickets, presented a very uninviting scene. "Mr. Forman," said I, "do you call this a village? It would make an owl weep to fly over it." "Never mind," said he, in reply, "you will live to see it a city yet."

I first became aware of Onondaga Lake as a physical presence when I was about six years old. I knew it was *there*, of course. I could see it from the distant hills south of the city. Depending on the season, the lake appeared blue in color, or pewter, or white, or as a band of gold glinting behind the city's modest silhouette of office buildings and churches. On hot summer days, my three siblings and I would pile into the backseat of the family car to go swimming at Oneida Lake or fishing on the St. Lawrence River. It never occurred to me that Onondaga Lake, much closer to home, might also be a good place to swim and fish. In the geographic index of my mind, Onondaga Lake shared a slot alongside the junkyard on the rez that I often explored, a forbidden land that existed somewhere between the natural and the man-made worlds.

Those summer fishing trips took us north through the heart of Syracuse on an elevated highway that soared over the black tar rooftops of old factories made of crumbling red brick. As the lake grew near, we could see Oil City's white storage tanks, sprouting like a colony of giant toadstools along the overgrown banks of the torpid barge canal. Here, the highway descends to ground level and rounds the southwest corner of Onondaga Lake. It was on this short stretch of road, with only a narrow corridor of shrub willow separating our car from the cloudy green water, that Onondaga Lake asserted itself. At that moment, my father cranked his window closed. In the back, we followed suit. But the vaporous miasma drifting off the lake had already infiltrated the car.

The smell of Onondaga Lake hits your sinuses like cheap cologne, a nauseating one-two punch of flaming mothballs and something stronger . . . more organic. I have tried many times to pinpoint exactly what it is, but I think it smells like armpit. The vile stench emanates from twenty-two acres of tar beds adjacent to the lake's western shoreline, across the highway. According to the Environmental Protection Agency's Superfund report on Onondaga Lake, the tar beds, which the report refers to as "Semet residue ponds," are filled with waste products of benzol manufacturing, a sticky black stew similar in consistency to driveway sealant. It consists of benzene, toluene, xylene, diphenyl ethanes, and the stuff mothballs are made of—naphthalene. These chemicals have leached into the lake for nearly a century. But the tar beds are hardly the only, or worst, source of toxins in the lake. Onondaga Lake's sediments are a carcinogenic brew of heavy metals (mercury, cadmium, chromium, antimony, manganese, copper, lead, nickel, cobalt, vanadium, thallium, selenium, and zinc), polychlorinated biphenyls, polyaromatic hydrocarbons, chlorinated and non-chlorinated benzenes, dioxins, furans, and shit—regular ol' human shit, which flows into the lake from the Metro wastewater treatment plant.

Sewage levels in Onondaga Lake led to a ban on swimming in 1940 that's still in effect today. By 1972, mercury levels were so high that the state banned fishing as well. A "health advisory" replaced the fishing ban in 1986, allowing people to catch fish but not eat them. It had no practical impact. Nobody fished in Onondaga Lake anyway.

•

During the dot-com boom of the late 1990s, I worked in New York City as a public relations flack for various technology companies. I got laid off after the tech bubble burst in the spring of 2001 and returned to Syracuse one month after the 9/11 attacks. My girlfriend—and future wife—had just moved back to Syracuse to take a job as an emergency physician at the main hospital in town. We got an apartment in the city together, and I started looking for a job. I thought my big-city experience would vault me to the top of Syracuse's white-collar labor pool, but it turned out to be a stigma that required explanation. Potential employers couldn't understand why I'd come back. Syracuse is the lover you leave for more attractive prospects. If you can't leave, you dream about leaving. If you leave and come back, there's something wrong with you. No offers came my way, so I gave up the job search and began freelance writing.

For one magazine assignment, I spent two weeks in the Gulf of Alaska aboard a National Oceanic and Atmospheric Administration research vessel. One day, I accompanied crew members to an uninhabited island. While they unpacked their GPS equipment, I wandered the rocky shoreline, mindful of bears. A bright fleck of white among the gray stones caught my eye. It was a thick fragment of ceramic. Rinsing it off in the cold surf, I turned it over to reveal a green stamp that read, "Syracuse China." How strange, fated almost, that I should travel over three thousand miles to this remote island, only to find a broken bit of Syracuse's history. But it's not so strange when you consider that a hundred years ago Syracuse China supplied most of the tableware for the hotel and restaurant industries. The island, I later learned, once had a hotel on it.

At the turn of the twentieth century, Syracuse was what business analysts today would call an industrial "incubator." People came here to make stuff and to invent new ways to make it. It was the center of manufacturing for candles, typewriters, ball bearings, and so on. Sports fans will recognize Syracuse University's iconic Carrier Dome, even if they don't know that Carrier Corporation, the inventor of air-conditioning, was one of the largest employers in Onondaga County for half a century. Then, in the postwar era, Syracuse shed residents and factory jobs faster than it could replace them. By the time I was growing up in the 1970s, the city was long past its prime. Our glam, globe-trotting, four-term mayor milked the state to pay for parking garages and other public works boondoggles, for which he received bags of cash, gold coins, and six years in federal prison.

At the turn of the twenty-first century, the dinosaurs of Syracuse's industrial age had all but gone extinct. Carrier shuttered its manufacturing operations in 2003. That same year, the Marsellus Casket Company, unofficial coffin maker for U.S. presidents—Truman, JFK, Nixon—gave up the ghost. In 2009, Syracuse China's kilns in Salina went cold. (You can still buy dinner plates with "Syracuse China" stamped on the back, but now they're actually made in China.) Assembly lines at the massive New Process Gear plant, which made transfer cases for Detroit's auto industry, fell silent in 2012. Those four companies alone provided good jobs to tens of thousands of Syracusans for nearly *five hundred years* combined.

Today, Syracuse staggers toward a dim future, feeding off its sick and dying in order to sustain itself. Marsellus Casket Company's historic west-side factory, torched and partially gutted by vandals, is being turned into the regional headquarters of an ambulance service. Three of the top six employers in the city are hospitals, and another is an old folks' home. One of the largest for-profit companies in the top ten that pays its full tax burden is the defense contractor Lockheed Martin, and it's dependent on a dwindling military budget. To many, it would appear that Syracuse is, in fact, already dead. When bricks from an old tin factory fell onto the northbound lanes of Interstate 81 in 2010, a highway so integral to Syracuse's identity as the crossroads of New York State that it's featured on the official city seal, the state transportation department shut down the highway for three whole weeks while it rifled through the city's pockets for cleanup money.

So it was with morbid fascination that I watched the saga of DestiNY USA unfold against this backdrop of dilapidation and despair. It all began with the announcement of DestiNY USA's name, a product of committee thinking if there ever was one. Saying it aloud conjures up the image of executives awkwardly high-fiving each other around a dry-erase board. DestiNY USA. As a PR professional, I would've cringed every time I had to utter that ridiculous name to a journalist—*yes, it's two words, and "NY" and "USA" are all caps*—but it was a perfect distillation of its time, a pompous cheer for the home team that crystallized the sloganeering of the post-9/11 era, when shopping was elevated to a solemn patriotic duty.

DestiNY USA was the brainchild of Bob Congel, a native son of Syracuse who amassed a fortune building malls across upstate New York and western Massachusetts, before plunking one down along the shores of Onondaga Lake in 1990. Carousel Center, as it was called, was a win-win for everyone. The city rid itself of an industrial waste dump and received a cut of the mall's sales tax revenue. In return, Congel didn't have to pay property taxes on the mall for fifteen years. But there were unfortunate side effects. Carousel Center killed off retail in downtown Syracuse, which had struggled for years as suburban malls siphoned off shoppers. Eventually, Carousel strangled the life out of the suburban malls, too.

In 2000, with his original tax deal coming to a close, Congel announced plans to expand Carousel Center into what would eventually be known as DestiNY USA, a massive tax loophole disguised as Disney World. It would be a "destination product," not a mall, complete with hotels, amusement park attractions, a hi-tech research park, and upscale shopping. Economic impact studies declared that DestiNY USA would create tens of thousands of new jobs, attract millions of visitors to the region, and rescue Syracuse from the postindustrial malaise it had been wallowing in for decades. The price for this civic resurrection was a new thirty-year tax deal. Some city officials were hesitant to give up tax revenue on a mall that was already a city unto itself, with no connection to the crumbling neighborhoods surrounding it. But Syracuse is a one-mogul town. No one else was proposing to build a billion-dollar retail utopia on a brownfield site overlooking Onondaga Lake. Congel got his tax deal, but that was only his opening gambit. Soon he would demand much more, threatening to build DestiNY USA elsewhere if he didn't get it.

In the fall of 2002, Congel held a groundbreaking ceremony for the Grand Destiny Hotel at a Carousel Center parking lot. Surrounded by his seventeen grandchildren, he doled out gold-colored shovels. In the background, an enormous pile driver pounded a steel support beam into the ground with a monotonous clang. The beam, like the ceremonial shovels, had no real purpose. Blueprints for a hotel, much less a new parking garage, did not exist. But that didn't matter. The DestiNY USA promotional blitz had entered a new realm of pure abstraction where anything was possible with enough tax credits, and all the politicians who could make that happen for Congel were on hand that day to congratulate each other for saving Syracuse.

What began as a relatively modest 800,000-square-foot expansion of Carousel Center quickly mutated into a hundred-million-square-foot Frankenmall that would cost $20 billion to build, making it one of the the the largest building projects in U.S. history, according to *Architectural Record*. And it was going to save not just Syracuse but the entire world. In the pages of *The New York Times Magazine*, Congel crowed that DestiNY USA would "produce more benefit for humanity than any one thing that private enterprise has ever done."

Below is a partial list of DestiNY USA's humanitarian benefits:

- Five-star restaurants, including Jimmy Buffett's Margaritaville
- Twenty-five-thousand-square-foot off-Broadway theater designed to host premier acts such as David Blaine Magic and Blue Man Group

- Onondaga Dunes, an eighteen-hole golf course to be built over the Solvay waste beds
- Swim-with-the-Fish Experience, with dolphins, tropical fish, and stingrays
- Torch-lined historical re-creation of the Erie Canal
- Four miles of jogging and biking trails
- Butterfly sanctuary
- Rain-forest habitat, with real tropical plants and animatronics
- Five-acre extreme-sports complex

The local newspaper published a series of conceptual renderings of the project that might as well have been printed with disappearing ink. Any firm notion of what it was supposed to be evaporated with each new illustration. These weren't functional architectural drawings but broadsides designed to showcase Congel's bold vision. Albert Speer's sketches showed less ambition. The Grand Destiny Hotel started out as two identical towers reminiscent of the World Trade Center (this was in 2002). Congel dumped the design in favor of one featuring emerald-green spires last seen on matte paintings for *The Wizard of Oz*. In its final iteration, the thirteen-hundred-room Grand Destiny Hotel disappeared altogether, replaced by six or more—the renderings aren't clear—tube-shaped glass towers accounting for eighty thousand hotel rooms, equal to the hotel capacity of New York City at the time.

As Congel's marketing team tinkered with DestiNY USA's features, one element remained constant: the big glass dome. *Architectural Record* described it as "the world's largest glass canopy roof." The dome changed from one rendering to the next. Sometimes it was wavy, other times curved. The illustrators sketched the dome's structural lattice as lightly as possible, but it could not be ignored, and that was the whole point. The sunny, swanky shopping paradise depicted in the renderings was the anti-Syracuse, sealed off from the stinky lake and grimy city surrounding it by a glittering glass bubble.

•

The rusty support beams erected during DestiNY USA's ground-breaking ceremony cast long shadows over Carousel Center's parking lot for five years while Congel lobbied for additional government subsidies. His best hustle was persuading officials to rezone DestiNY USA so that he could reap $10 million a year from the state on property taxes that he never had to pay in the first place. Not a penny went to pay for the police or fire department or any other essential city service. Public opinion about DestiNY USA began to sour. Where were all the jobs Congel promised in exchange for the mountains of public money he was raking in? Sensitive to growing outrage over the tax deal, Syracuse's new mayor refused to implement it and put the mall back on the tax rolls. But instead of pouring concrete, Congel sued the city and poured millions of dollars into a massive public relations campaign to renew enthusiasm in the project and to smear officials who opposed him as enemies of progress.

Congel launched his attack from Carousel Center. Displays on every level of the mall enumerated the multitude of economic benefits and luxury attractions that he promised to lavish upon his beloved hometown. In 2003, before DestiNY USA entered its chimerical phase, Congel's marketing team sponsored a bass-fishing tournament on Onondaga Lake to get people excited about the project. Top prize was $1 million for whoever caught the fish with the magic tag.

I decided this was as good a time as any to learn a bit more about Onondaga Lake, so I went for a boat ride with an aquatic biologist named Bruce Wagner. Bruce works for Upstate Freshwater Institute, a nonprofit scientific organization dedicated to studying the lake. Steering the aluminum skiff with one hand on the throttle, he pointed out landmarks, his pinched, nasally voice marking him as a native central New Yorker. Four and a half miles long, one mile wide, with an average depth of thirty-five feet, Onondaga

Lake is relatively small. As we skimmed across its placid surface, I made adjustments to my mental map of Syracuse. I grew up south of the city. I was accustomed to seeing it from an elevated vantage point, looking northward on winter nights so cold and clear that it seemed as if the air might crack. The city's streets glowed like strings of pearls laid out on a rumpled swatch of black velvet. Or racing up Interstate 81 from New York City on a Friday night, half-asleep at the wheel, I'd hit a bend in the road right before Exit 16 and rouse at the sight of Syracuse's skyline materializing in the gap of Onondaga Valley.

Looking at the city from the low angle of a boat floating in the middle of Onondaga Lake was a minor revelation. It was like seeing the back of my head in a barber's mirror. Just by turning my chin a few degrees, I could take in the entire east–west axis of the city stretched across the middle horizon. Church steeples and reservoir standpipes I'd never noticed before poked above the tree-tops. A white slice of the Carrier Dome's pillow-topped roof lay half hidden behind the pale flanks of parking garages. It took me a moment to locate the MONY towers (formerly owned by the MONY Life Insurance Company, now owned by AXA Equitable, although Syracusans still call them the money towers). Resembling two up-ended shoe boxes clad in smoked glass, the towers are the most visible buildings in the city. But viewed from Onondaga Lake, they appear flattened against the hills rising above them to the south, like carvings in an old woodcut of a cityscape.

"You can see the whole city from out here," I shouted to Bruce over the drone of the outboard motor. "Beautiful!"

"It's really a shame," Bruce replied. "I just can't understand what the politicians, the people that controlled the community, were thinking back then." He seemed to want to say more.

"They were probably saying the same stuff that they're saying about Destiny now," I said, goading him a little. "Future of the city!" Bruce didn't bite. His job was to give decision makers facts about the condition of the lake, not opinions about the biggest and most controversial lakefront development project in the city's history. That was a sure way to lose funding. He just smiled ruefully and steered the skiff into a shallow little bay.

"Weirdest thing I ever saw on the lake was an inflatable woman," Bruce said. "It came down Onondaga Creek and ended up in the harbor and was circulating around. We just watched it."

There was nothing on the lake that day. No boats, no geese, no inflatable sex dolls. It was possible to picture the scene as the Jesuits did 350 years ago, gliding through the water in their birch-bark canoes. Onondaga Lake has been so thoroughly despoiled for so long that much of the waterfront is undeveloped and now exists in a post-natural state of sylvan tranquillity. The salt industry's vast infrastructure of pump houses, solar sheds, and boiling blocks was razed long ago. Oil City's ugly tank farm replaced the salt mills, but it, too, was bulldozed in 2000 to make room for DestiNY USA. The factories that once treated the lake as their private sump are either gone or far enough removed that all you can see of them is a distant smokestack. A sure sign that something might be terribly wrong with the lake is the conspicuous absence of pricey condos, or any private dwelling, crowding the shoreline, 90 percent of which is owned by the county.

Bruce throttled back on the outboard, and we coasted toward a row of rotten wood pilings—remnants of an old pier—that peeked above the surface of the bay. They were all that was left of Onondaga Lake's heyday, a period around the turn of the twentieth century when elegant resorts with names like White City and Iron Pier and Rockaway Beach drew tens of thousands of people to these shores. The lake was already in decline by then. Salmon, lake trout, and whitefish had been wiped out. Lake water was so dirty that the city banned ice harvesting. But it was still a great place to hear marching bands perform, play a game of tenpins, or ride the water flume. Bruce maneuvered us closer to shore. Bank swallows darted in and out of holes in a white bluff that rose thirty feet out of the water—the same white bluffs that William de Leftwich Dodge repurposed as dramatic backdrops in his courthouse murals.

"We call this the White Cliffs of Dover," Bruce said.

"It's actually kind of pretty," I said.

"Yeah, it's a waste bed." Bruce swept his arm the length of the shoreline. "All this—waste beds." The white stuff, he explained, was calcium carbonate, the same material that clamshells and Rolaids are made of. The Solvay Process Company obliterated the natural shoreline on this stretch of the lake long ago, burying it beneath eight square kilometers of calcium carbonate mountains that range up to seventy feet in height. Carousel Center was built on top of them. But for the most part, the waste beds remain undeveloped, a curious ecosystem of scrubland sandwiched between the highway and the lake. The waste beds are the only place east of the Mississippi River where tumbleweeds occur naturally, Bruce said. But their chalky substructure makes them unstable. On Thanksgiving Day in 1943, some waste beds liquefied and broke through containment dikes. Industrial waste flowed knee-deep into the streets of the Lakeland neighborhood, carrying away vehicles. The waste beds also contribute directly to the lake's salinity and pH levels. Calcium carbonate is a strong alkali. During the 1950s and 1960s, researchers tried to neutralize it by tilling treated sewage into the waste beds. The experiment produced a bumper crop of tomatoes and squash that sprouted from undigested seeds in the sewage. History doesn't record whether anybody harvested this cornucopia.

"But the woodchucks sure liked it," Bruce said. Eager to show me what calcium carbonate sediment looked like, he reached into the water. "The consistency varies from, like, Jell-O to concrete in this stuff," he said, "and it's very slippery." His hand emerged from the lake gripping a large black chunk of the lake bottom encrusted with razor-sharp zebra mussels, an invasive species from Eurasia. Zebra mussels have been wreaking havoc on marine ecosystems and infrastructure all throughout the Great Lakes for the past thirty years. When the zebra mussel scourge arrived in Onondaga Lake in 1992, it got more than it bargained for. The virulent little bivalves couldn't gain a foothold in the lake's poisonous waters.

Since then, improvements to the Metro sewage treatment plant have reduced the amount of ammonia and phosphorous discharged into the lake, and as a result zebra mussel colonies have sprouted up everywhere. Here, it's a sign of progress.

Bruce heaved the zebra-encrusted chunk of waste bed overboard, then steered us to another little cove. I asked him if the cove had a name. He shrugged. "We just call it the blue ooze area."

"Blue ooze?"

"Where you break through the crust"—Bruce jabbed an oar into the lake bottom—"the blue ooze comes up. Ah, there we go. There's some nice blue."

Plumes of sediment cleared to reveal an electric-blue substance seeping from the gash he'd made with his oar. It had the consistency of toothpaste, and the rotten egg smell of it made me recoil.

"What the hell is that stuff?"

Bruce didn't know. Nobody did, not even the Department of Environmental Conservation. Whatever it was, the blue ooze is unique to Onondaga Lake. Judging from the stench of hydrogen sulfide, Bruce speculated that it consisted of partially decayed sewage, rotting plant material, and finely ground limestone from soda ash. One time, he said, he was sloshing around the cove, collecting zooplankton, when he broke through the crust on the lake bottom and sank up to his waist in the muck. A colleague had to pull him out, leaving a bubbling hole of hydrogen sulfide and blue ooze.

We drifted toward a weedy stub of land poking into the lake that Bruce called White Trash Point. It was a popular spot for teens to hang out, drink beer, and toss their empties into the lake. A pair of white panties hung on a willow branch. I could hear the rush of traffic on the highway over the embankment behind the point, where the Semet residue ponds were located. "This will be really nasty," Bruce said, plunging his hand into the lake again. He dislodged an oncolite stone made of calcium carbonate, causing the soft sediment trapped beneath it to swirl to the surface. "See the oil slick? And the bubbles? Oh, that's pretty bad!"

"Jesus!" I gagged. The overwhelming stench of mothballs and sweaty armpits evoked childhood memories of trips around the lake. Bruce fired up the outboard and peeled away. He skirted the southern shore, taking us past a shallow reef made from thousands of old tires, "a haven for carp and catfish," he said, past the Metro effluent pipe, wide enough to drive a car through, and up the east side of the lake to the outlet of Bloody Brook, the smallest of Onondaga Lake's seven tributaries. Bloody Brook runs through the city's northeastern suburbs, where General Electric's old Electronics Park factory was once located, now the home of the defense contractor Lockheed Martin. In the late 1990s, high levels of cadmium, a toxic heavy metal used to coat television picture tubes at GE's plant, were discovered in Bloody Brook's sediments and cleaned up at great expense. Samples taken years afterward showed that cadmium levels in the sediment hadn't declined.

Bruce cut the motor, and we bobbed for a while near the marina, waves lapping gently against the side of the boat. We exchanged local lore about the lake as people walked dogs and rode bikes on the parkway that follows the eastern shoreline. Bruce was from the city's west side, near the village of Solvay and the chemical factory that the village was named after.

"When I was a kid, my elementary school teachers threatened a punishment of throwing you in Onondaga Lake if you didn't behave in class," he said. "That was their way of intimidating us."

Like most Syracusans, Bruce and I grew up believing that Onondaga Lake was the most polluted body of water in the country, if not the world. It's part of our civic identity, like our interminable winters. Dr. Steven Effler, Upstate Freshwater Institute's chief scientist and Bruce's boss, told me that there was no objective yardstick to measure such a claim. Besides, he said, there were much dirtier lakes in some former Eastern bloc countries. The news was disappointing, but I took some pride in knowing that it took Soviet levels of apathy and incompetence to top us.

•

The day of the bass tournament was hot and muggy and blessedly odor-free because of the lack of wind. I walked around the lake, talking to contestants. Most were residents of Syracuse's blue-collar neighborhoods, hoping to catch the magic smallmouth bass with the $1 million tag clipped to its fin. Ida Mae Evans, an elderly black woman with a southern accent, sat in the shade beneath the state thruway overpass.

"Call me the Fish Lady," she said, cackling gleefully. "Here come the Fish Lady!" I asked her what she would do with the prize money. "I wanna go to Vegas. Honest to God," she said, placing her hand over her heart. "I really wanna go to Vegas. I wanna go to Vegas and catch that handle on that machine and pull it down. And when I pull it down, I hope all the change start a-falling."

"Then they can call you the Slot Lady," I said.

"No," she said, "they gonna call me the Mississippi Chicken Scratch Lady!"

Zoran Nukic and Goldic Nermin, two shirtless immigrants from Bosnia, occupied a rocky point on the north end of the lake. They'd caught a few bass, but none was tagged.

"For us, only luck is when you go work and make a good paycheck," said Zoran. "This is best lucky." By which he meant impossible luck. Lottery luck. Still, I said, what would you do with the prize money? "Oh!" Zoran exclaimed and laughed. When he saw that I was serious, he gave it some thought. "I go visit to Germany my family," he said. He liked Germany. He liked Syracuse, too. Both places had a lot in common with Bosnia. "Because have good people, friendly. Have same winter, you know? It's almost everything same, like us country. Lot of people come here from Bosnia. About three thousand people is come, is now living in Syracuse." I asked him if they liked to fish in Onondaga Lake. Zoran turned to Goldic and said something in Bosnian that made both men snort with laughter. I didn't need a translator. Onondaga Lake is an eternal spring of black humor from which all Syracusans drink.

Max Rhodes didn't get the joke. Maybe because his sense of humor had been bought by the sponsors who'd hired him to organize the tournament, or perhaps because he was from Texas. I met Rhodes near the check-in station, where I was attempting to bribe a group of skeptical onlookers to eat one of the tagged fish splashing around in a big orange bucket. My offer had peaked at $500 with no takers when he sidled up next to me. "Show me your money, big boy!" he bellowed into my ear. "This ain't my first rodeo!" For $500, he'd sushi one of those fish right here, right now, with his own knife. Onondaga Lake was dirty? What did we know from dirty? "I spent ten years in the Marine Corps dragging a canteen through rice paddies—I'll show you dirty," he growled. "This is a great lake!"

I knew when I was beaten. I slinked away to my car and drove out to White Trash Point to see if anybody was fishing near the tar beds. It was empty. A stagnant marine funk hung in the air, wafting off the scummy effluvium of dead fish and rotting algae that floated around the boat launch. I wasn't far from the spot where Bruce Wagner had broken off a chunk of calcified sediment. Using a piece of steel rebar that I found lying on the ground, I began poking the lake bottom. Just then, two young men on dirt bikes careened out of the willow and skidded to a stop. They stared at me, revving their bikes. Once they determined that I wasn't a narc, they took their helmets off. One of them popped the tab on a forty-ounce can of beer. They introduced themselves as Dave Williams and T-Bone the Corrupter.

"Lose something?" T-Bone said. I shook my head and jammed the piece of rebar into the lake a few more times.

"What's that smell like to you?" I said, gesturing toward the cloudy hole I'd made in the crust. Dave and T-Bone bent over the side of the boat launch and sniffed.

"Ass," said T-Bone, wrinkling his nose.

"Armpit," Dave said.

"Armpit!" I shouted, perhaps too enthusiastically. T-Bone cocked his eyebrow at his friend and took a swig of beer. "That's what I always thought it smelled like," I said. "It's actually chemicals, from the tar beds across the road." Dave and T-Bone weren't impressed by the distinction.

"Smells worse up by Bristol-Myers," said T-Bone, referring to the pharmaceutical plant in East Syracuse. "Cooking them monkeys up there."

"You can get a monkey to eat dirt, but they don't like it," Dave added.

"They cook monkeys at Bristol-Myers?"

"Sure," T-Bone said, as if this were common knowledge. "In the incinerator there, after they're done testing them."

"Just their bones," Dave said. "It's like a big Crock-Pot." He tossed the empty beer can in the weeds, kick-started his bike, and tore off into the thicket. I stood on White Trash Point as the high-pitched whine of Dave and T-Bone's dirt bikes faded into the steady whoosh of traffic on the bypass. Fishing boats crisscrossed the lake. The concrete and glass ramparts of Carousel Center shone in the dull, hazy light. I wondered how different the scene would look after DestiNY USA had been built. Would the prosperity that the developers promised save Syracuse? Ten years later, the answer to that question is obvious, but before we get to it, it's worth mentioning that nobody caught the million-dollar fish.

In 2007, I caught a glimpse of a scale model of DestiNY USA in Carousel Center's Skydeck, which had been converted into a multimedia showcase for the project. It was sitting on a platform, surrounded by bright watercolor renderings. I recognized the tube-shaped hotels right away. Each hotel anchored a section of DestiNY USA characterized by a theme. The mansard-style buildings of the Marquis District, for instance, evoked a fashionable Paris neighborhood stocked with "the latest season's hot trends and personal shopping assistants" to help guide well-heeled "visitors desiring a more enhanced level of service." If concierge retail wasn't your thing, you could get your culture on in the Tuscan Hill Town, a twenty-five-acre enclave of rustic villas situated on a terraced hillside above a man-made river where you could stroll among the shops and museums "while sipping espresso" in a "cozy village atmosphere."

To those concerned about the carbon footprint created by this kingdom of conspicuous consumption, to those skeptical of the giant green DestiNY USA banners flapping in the wind outside Carousel Center or the new coat of green paint on the railings inside the mall or the funky green wind turbines displayed prominently on the mall's roof, Congel vowed that DestiNY USA would run on 100 percent renewable energy. To demonstrate the depth of his commitment, he commissioned a new round of conceptual renderings, including a 3-D fly-through of a futuristic research and development complex adjacent to DestiNY USA called the Petroleum Addiction Rehabilitation Park, or PARP. Green technologies developed at PARP would be tested at DestiNY USA, and DestiNY USA would in turn attract top tech talent from around the world. Onondaga Valley would become the Silicon Valley of the twenty-first century. We might not have a Mediterranean climate, but we would soon have a Tuscan Hill Town with monorail service.

The city settled its legal battle with Congel over construction delays by taking $60 million in exchange for leaving the thirty-year tax deal intact. In the summer of 2007, workers finally began digging the foundation for DestiNY USA's first phase. But in less than a year, the bottom fell out of the U.S. economy. Credit markets dried up. Citigroup froze Congel's construction loan, silencing the pile drivers and bulldozers. As the Great Recession deepened, Congel fought Citigroup in court. Something happened to DestiNY USA during this period. Hotel construction was pushed off to phase two; phase one would be limited to an expansion of Carousel Center. The gallery of DestiNY USA ephemera in Carousel Center's Skydeck closed, and the conceptual renderings disappeared from the mall's concourses. Any mention or depiction of what the project used to be was scrubbed from DestiNY USA's website. While the $228 million in tax-exempt "green" bonds that the federal government awarded the project still required Congel to wave his eco flag, he stopped hyping PARP and renewable energy. Instead of helping wean the world off fossil fuels, DestiNY USA's newest tech initiative would help retailers glean customer data from shoppers carrying wireless data transmitters around the mall. Even DestiNY USA's name shrank to match its narrowing scope, as "NY" quietly reverted to lowercase letters in all company communications.

Congel won his lawsuit against Citigroup and resumed construction in 2011. That summer, a decade after it first announced plans for Destiny USA, Congel's marketing team invited people to tour the unfinished project on an appointment-only basis. I booked one of the first slots. Marc Strang, Destiny USA's director of marketing, escorted our small group of mostly middle-aged suburbanites up to the Skydeck. The reporter's notebook protruding from my shirt pocket seemed to make Strang apprehensive. He asked what newspaper I was from. The notes were just for me, I assured him. I had a hard time keeping all the different versions of Destiny USA straight. Strang gave me a puzzled smile and went into the conference room to set up a projector. We milled around the Skydeck for a few minutes. I'd half hoped to find a stack of conceptual renderings leaning against a wall or, better yet, the scale model of the old DestiNY USA project hidden beneath a tarp in the corner. But it was all gone.

We sat around a conference table as Strang narrated a Power-Point presentation that began with the history of Carousel Center, a tale so familiar that it had achieved the status of an origin myth. Everybody in Syracuse knew it by heart. It goes like this: One day, Bob Congel decided to do something special for his hometown. He'd done so much already, turning empty factories into offices and apartments, renovating an abandoned downtown landmark for the headquarters of his mall empire. He owned malls in every corner of the state, except Syracuse. So that would be his gift to the city, a brand-new mall. But where would he build this mall? On a suburban greenfield site with good highway access? That's what an ordinary developer would do. But Bob Congel is no ordinary developer. He's a man of vision, the Hiawatha of developers. He would erect a superregional mall that would unite shoppers from Canada to Pennsylvania, from Buffalo to Albany, and he would put it in the heart of the city, on a scarred brownfield site occupied by a run-down scrap yard next to the dirtiest lake in the country.

"He grew up near this neighborhood and actually saw the opportunity to create something really transformational in the community," Strang said, clicking through slides of the old Marley Scrap Yard and Oil City. Strang reminded us that Congel now had nineteen grandchildren. What inspired Congel to build Destiny USA was his desire to make Syracuse a place where future generations of Congels would want to raise their own grandchildren. If Carousel Center was his gift to Syracuse, Destiny USA was his legacy. Strang ticked off a list of all the different stores and restaurants Destiny USA had signed on as tenants. At the end of the presentation, he handed out "real pretend gold" coins commemorating the twentieth anniversary of Carousel Center. Then he opened the floor to questions. A woman wearing a pink knit top and white shorts looked around the table.

"I have a *comment*," she said nervously. Strang smiled.

"Please, go ahead."

"The Melting Pot is going to do really good," the woman blurted out.

"Oh yeah?" Strang said. "Have you been to the Melting Pot?"

"My daughter lives in Wisconsin, and that place is just— *every*body raves about that place," the woman said. Other members of the tour started whispering to each other and shrugging. Melting Pot? What's a Melting Pot?

"It's a fondue restaurant," said a man in a suit who'd been sitting quietly in the corner. Strang introduced him as the mall's manager. "See, it's set up with these individual kind of cubbies,

·and they do seatings of seven and nine," the manager said, then realized that this level of detail probably wasn't necessary. He crossed his arms, raised his eyebrows, and said, "It's an *experience.*"

"We have them in a number of our properties," Strang said. "If anybody's driven by Buffalo in the last few years, we just did a renovation there. And they have a Melting Pot, a P. F. Chang's, a Cheesecake Factory—" The woman in pink clapped her hands.

"Oh, see, that too, a Cheesecake Factory!" I stared at the notebook on the table in front of me. In it, I'd written a list of Destiny USA amenities that had gone by the wayside over the years. My plan was to ask questions as if I'd just stepped out of a time machine from 2002. How much did it cost to play the back nine on Onondaga Dunes? Stuff like that. But I didn't have the courage to do it. For some reason, I figured that a mall tour scheduled for the middle of a weekday would coax other unemployed cranks like me from their caves for the rare opportunity to harangue Destiny USA executives in person. But my compatriots were nice people, the kind who came to the mall on a summer afternoon to buy presents for their grandchildren. My bitterness dissolved inside a steaming pot of gooey cheese.

A woman with a smoker's raspy voice asked about the number of jobs Destiny USA would add to the local economy. Strang fumbled the question and passed it off to the mall manager. The manager estimated that Destiny USA, when completed and flush with tenants, would bring 2,000 retail jobs to the city. I flipped through the pages of my notebook, looking for the jobs figure that Congel had boasted about in the past. The number ranged anywhere from 100,000 to 200,000, including a fair percentage of high-paying white-collar jobs. As I formulated a follow-up question, the raspy-voiced woman said, apropos of nothing, "I know I always sound like a cheerleader for Congel and company. I just happen to like these guys." Everyone around the table chuckled, which encouraged her to continue. "My family is from the Hudson Valley. When they get a chance to come up here, they always want to come to Carousel. *I* don't make them do that. They just say, 'Great, we'll come up to you because we want to come to Carousel.' I don't know why. It's the light in here, it's the . . . something, you know?" Strang and the mall manager nodded as if they, too, appreciated the magical quality of the light in Carousel Center.

"Wait until you see the Canyon," Strang said.

The walking tour of Destiny USA was all drywall dust, deafening power tools, and deathly stares from construction workers unhappy with dorky tourists in green Destiny USA hard hats and fluorescent green vests tramping through their work site. The high point occurred when we passed two old men wearing identical hard hats and vests. Surprised, Marc and the mall manager stopped the tour and introduced one of the men to the group as Bruce Kenan, Congel's right-hand man and part owner of Destiny USA.

"Hi, everybody," Kenan said, grinning. "Next time you come, spend some money here!"

The tour concluded with a viewing of the Canyon, a three-level concourse wrapped around a courtyard covered in glass. The summer light pouring through the ceiling got swallowed up by all the empty storefronts and gray, unfinished concrete. We stood at a railing and gazed at a branched metal sculpture rising up from the floor of the Canyon's courtyard. It looked like a lightning-struck tree. Strang pointed out where the Melting Pot restaurant was going to be located, in case we didn't notice the enormous banner draped above the restaurant's cavernous entrance. When it came time to leave, he encouraged us to hang on to the commemorative coins. "They're very valuable," he said, "at least they will be in, like, fifty years." I couldn't tell if he was joking. Halfway to the parking lot, I discovered that I was still wearing my hard hat. I thought about returning it but then decided that it needed to be preserved. The logo on the hard hat was an artifact from the "DestiNY" era of imprudent capitalization. It even had a little shooting star arcing over the top of "NY" and, underneath, a catchphrase that Congel's marketeers had dropped early on: "Nothing like it in the world."

•

One morning in June 2012, a courier walked up the limestone steps of city hall in downtown Syracuse and handed a letter to a security guard. The letter was from Bruce Kenan. The first phase of the "Expansion Project" was finished, Kenan declared. It was also the last phase. The announcement triggered a clause in the fine print of the city's agreement with Destiny USA that allowed Congel to begin reaping the tax windfall that the city, county, state, and federal governments had promised him in exchange for saving Syracuse. In other words, the Destiny USA saga was over. There would be no hotel, no golf course, no Tuscan Hill Town. From the outside, the textured concrete facade of the mall expansion resembled one of the many maximum-security prisons that dot the north country, except this one had a Toby Keith's I Love This Bar and Grill franchise. And for that the city had to give up only $600 million in tax revenue on the single most valuable property in Syracuse. In its final act of expectations management, Congel's marketing team revised the company logo yet again. New signs over the mall's entrances welcomed shoppers to a diminished "destiny usa."

The following August, Congel spoke at Carousel Center's brief rebranding ceremony. He stood beside Bruce Kenan, his grandchildren having better things to do that day. "I'm a proud man," Congel said, his voice echoing in the hollow chamber of the Canyon. "I'm not sure I'm awed about any of our malls. I'm awed by this mall." The Onondaga County executive, Joanie Mahoney, took the podium after Congel. "We owe a real debt of gratitude to . . . the Congel family in particular," she said. "This could have happened anywhere."

Many Syracusans share Mahoney's feckless sentiment. It's an integral part of the Congel mythos. Okay, so Destiny USA is a mere shadow of the grand vision Congel sold us. Sure, he got a lot of public money to build it. So what? Isn't that what developers do? Overpromise, under-deliver, and build things with other people's money? In the end, Congel broke no laws, and he created something where there was nothing in a town that has been edging closer to nothing for a long time. I could not agree more, and Mahoney could not be more wrong.

Destiny USA, and Carousel Center before it, could not have "happened" anywhere else *but* here. And not just here, in Syracuse, but on the frothy, stinking shores of Onondaga Lake. If it wasn't the most polluted lake in the country, if it didn't sit smack in the middle of a Rust Belt city verging on bankruptcy, Congel would have no abandoned land to grab nor the political leverage to exploit it. Had he hawked his megamall to any community located on any of the other Finger Lakes—the affluent resort town of Skaneateles, say, where the Congel clan owns multimillion-dollar mansions—it would've told him to take a hike.

Every awful thing you've ever heard about central New York winters is true. They're snowy, dark, and unspeakably long. You don't hear as much about central New York's glorious summers, though. They're short and bright, like a sharp blow to the head that makes you forget all about winter. I don't think I spent a single summer weekend in New York City when I lived there. On Fridays, I left work early and drove straight to Syracuse.

We spend as much time as we can outside during the summer, usually near water. Within a ten-minute drive of our house, there are three public beaches, four waterfalls, and too many creeks to count, including one in our backyard where our kids hunt for salamanders and crayfish. Sometimes we go north to Lake Ontario or the St. Lawrence River, on the same route that my father used to take up the western shore of Onondaga Lake, and sometimes we go to Onondaga Lake itself, which my father never would've done, and with good reason.

"When we used to go out there in the early '70s on a hot summer day, the lake sort of had the appearance of a green champagne cocktail," Dr. Steven Effler recalled. "A lot of bubbles rising to the surface all the time." Onondaga Lake today is not the fizzy cauldron of poisons that it was when I was a kid. It's not the lake of

Hayden Carruth's ode "The Oldest Killed Lake in North America," which the poet describes as "a great fallen sickly and silent harp" reflecting the "gleaming wires" of lights shining atop smokestacks. It's not even the same Onondaga Lake that it was a few years ago. The health of the lake has improved in inverse proportion to the city's health. But to understand how much it's changed, you have to go below the surface.

In the summer of 2011, Effler and a team of scientists from Upstate Freshwater Institute injected agricultural fertilizer into the bottom of the lake. They had a hunch that bacteria in the fertilizer would displace other bacteria that feed on the lake's enormous reservoir of toxic mercury. The experiment worked. Without host bacteria to disperse it throughout the water column, mercury levels in the lake dropped by 95 percent. The mercury didn't magically disappear. It's still there, immobilized in the muck, where it can't so easily get into the food chain. Mercury levels in fish have also dropped. That's great news for the bald eagles that have been coming here in recent winters. You can see them from the parking deck at Carousel (nobody calls it Destiny USA), swooping over the Metro plant's steaming sewer outflow, which doesn't ice up like the rest of the lake.

Effler's experiment is a small but important part of Onondaga Lake's court-ordered billion-dollar cleanup. Honeywell International, the company that inherited legal responsibility for polluting the lake, is doing the heavy lifting. The company's "dredging and capping" operations will cost half a billion dollars. When the winter ice melts, Honeywell's barges ply the west side of the lake, sucking up contaminated muck from the bottom. A big black pipe snakes aboveground for miles along the shore, past the state fairgrounds, carrying the slurry to a disposal site. There, it's pumped into long fabric tubes and left to dry like cured sausages.

T-Bone the Corrupter wouldn't recognize Onondaga Lake's western shoreline today. Construction equipment rumbles over waste beds once crisscrossed with dirt bike trails. Honeywell is restoring the lake's natural tributaries and wetlands there. The company is also installing a barrier wall to prevent tar bed residues from seeping into the lake. It even cleared the shrub willow from White Trash Point and built a visitors' center. If you're discreet, you can pop a tab on a forty-ounce and watch the barges gulping up the muck.

Honeywell is doing the bare minimum required by law, which amounts to sweeping the worst of the contamination under a very small rug. The company will dredge only 6 percent of the lake nearest the waste beds, including the blue ooze area and the White Cliffs of Dover. Then it'll cap the most contaminated portions of the bottom, about 14 percent of the lake's total area, in a three-foot layer of sand and dirt. Whether or not the cleanup goes far enough, it's undeniably a watershed event for Onondaga Lake, reversing two hundred years of nonstop spoliation and neglect. But progress abhors a vacuum. Already there's talk in the corridors of city hall about what to do with the west side of the lake. The latest idea, backed by a $30 million contribution from the state, is a waterfront amphitheater that will be carved out of the waste beds. I suppose it's an attempt to rebrand Syracuse as a vanguard of culture in upstate New York, an idea with special appeal among those who believe the city of Syracuse stops at the foot of University Hill. I'm not so sure that Zoran Nukic or T-Bone the Corrupter or the waitress at the Melting Pot will be lining up behind English professors to buy tickets for a Shakespeare festival, though. Syracuse isn't Saratoga. We've never gotten by on our charm. I think we should leave the lake alone for the next two hundred years and allow it to recover. Then we can decide what to do with it, if that decision will even be ours to make. Who knows, if current trends hold, in two hundred years Syracuse could be a pile of bricks and rust.

Our kids like to ride their scooters on the wide pedestrian parkway that runs along the eastern shoreline of Onondaga Lake. We often stop to sit on a bench in the shade or to throw stones in the lake. Last summer, my son pried a fragment of pottery from the dirt at the base of a large maple tree near the shore. Using sticks, we dug for more fragments. The root-heaved earth around the tree was full of them. Many bore Syracuse China stamps. We collected about a dozen ear-shaped finger rings from old teacups and one whole piece of white, unglazed earthenware that might have been a creamer. My son asked me where it all came from. I told him that restaurant dishes and cups used to be made right here in Syracuse and that we'd probably found a spot where factory remnants were dumped as fill. I tried to make the connection between the pottery fragments, Syracuse's industrial history, and the dredging barges on the far side of the lake. My son humored me with a thoughtful nod and resumed excavating.

The creamer sits on a shelf in his bedroom now, next to a fraying bird's nest. Does he remember what I told him about it? Will he remember years from now, after he's left Syracuse, and he finds it at the bottom of a box? Probably not. That's why he and I both collect junk, as a substitute for memory. If the creamer reminds him of anything at all, it'll be the weird habit his dad had of flipping over the plates every time we went out to eat. But I've got a plan. This summer I'm going to teach him how to ride a bike. I'm going to tighten the chin strap on his helmet and give him a shove down the bike path at Onondaga Lake. He'll fall and cry; I'll help him up and utter a few words of encouragement. And we'll repeat the cycle, over and over again, up the lakeshore, from the marina to the lunch truck at the north end of the lake. Afterward, we'll get soft ice cream and eat it under the tree where we found all the pottery fragments last year. And later, much later, when he's unpacking boxes in some distant city, and he comes across that creamer, he'll hold it in his hand and remember the day his dad taught him how to ride a bike on the shore of Onondaga Lake, in the city of Syracuse, his home.

CONTRIBUTORS

Greg Afinogenov is a Ph.D. candidate in Russian history at Harvard.

Dan Albert holds a Ph.D. in history and is a longtime contributor to *n+1*. He lives in Marblehead, Massachusetts.

Gar Alperovitz is the Lionel R. Bauman Professor of Political Economy at the University of Maryland and co-founder of the Democracy Collaborative. He is the author, most recently, of *What Then Must We Do?*

Chanelle Benz's fiction has appeared in *Granta, The O. Henry Prize Stories 2014, The American Reader, Fence,* and other publications. She lives in Houston.

Sam Biederman is a publicist and writer. He lives in Brooklyn.

Alex Sayf Cummings is a historian at Georgia State University and author of the book *Democracy of Sound.*

Moira Donegan is an associate editor of *n+1*.

Steve Featherstone is a writer and photographer from Syracuse, New York.

Spencer Fleury is a writer and geographer living in Florida.

Keith Gessen is a journalist, novelist, and translator living in New York. He is a founding editor of *n+1*.

Emily Gogolak is a journalist living in New York. She is on the editorial staff of *The New Yorker*.

Brandon Harris is a visiting assistant professor of film at SUNY Purchase and a contributing editor of *Filmmaker* magazine.

Jenny Hendrix is a Brooklyn-based writer and critic. Her work has appeared in *Slate*, *The Believer*, *The New York Times Book Review*, and *The Paris Review Daily*, among other places.

Lawrence Jackson is a biographer and historian teaching at Emory University. He lives in Atlanta.

Jordan Kisner is a writer living in New York, where she teaches in the Undergraduate Writing Program at Columbia University.

Simone Landon was born and raised in Detroit.

Katy Lederer is a poet and memoirist currently living in Brooklyn. Previously, she has lived in Concord, New Hampshire; Berkeley, California; Iowa City, Iowa; and Las Vegas, Nevada.

Ryann Liebenthal is an editor at *Harper's Magazine*.

Ian MacDougall has written about crime and legal affairs for *Slate*, *The Guardian*, *Newsweek*, and *n+1*. He formerly worked as a reporter in the Providence, Rhode Island, bureau of the Associated Press.

Steve Meacham is an organizing coordinator at City Life / Viola Urbana, a community organization that works with distressed homeowners.

Michael Merriam is an archaeologist living in New York City.

Ben Merriman, a native Kansan, is a doctoral candidate in sociology at the University of Chicago.

Jesse Montgomery is a Ph.D. student in English at Vanderbilt University and a founding editor of *Full Stop*. He was born and raised in Kentucky.

Debbie Nathan is a journalist and author living in Texas and New York City.

Gary Percesepe is a writer, minister, activist, and associate editor of *New World Writing*. He lives in White Plains, New York.

James Pogue has written for *The New Yorker* and the *London Review of Books*, among other publications.

Chris Reitz is a curator, critic, and historian of modern and contemporary art.

Elias Rodriques is a writer and high school English teacher living in Philadelphia.

Nikil Saval is an editor of *n+1* and the author of *Cubed: A Secret History of the Workplace*. He lives in Philadelphia.

Erin Sheehy is a writer living in New York.

Aaron Lake Smith is a writer and editor from North Carolina.

Stephen Squibb is a Ph.D. candidate in English at Harvard and a writer living in New York.

Michelle Tea is a writer living in San Francisco.

Michael Thomsen is a writer in New York. He has written for *The New Yorker*, *The Atlantic*, *Forbes*, *Slate*, and *The Paris Review* and is the author of *Levitate the Primate: Handjobs, Internet Dating, and Other Issues for Men*.

Nicky Tiso is an M.F.A. poetry candidate and English TA at the University of Minnesota.

Dayna Tortorici is an editor of *n+1*.

Shawn Wen is a writer, radio producer, and multimedia artist. She lives in San Francisco.

Emily Witt's book *Future Sex* is forthcoming from Farrar, Straus and Giroux.

Annie Julia Wyman is a writer living on both coasts and a Ph.D. candidate at Harvard.

ACKNOWLEDGMENTS

n+1 would like to thank Aaron Braun, Laura Cremer, Nora DeLigter, Moira Donegan, Max Donnewald, Jeffrey Feldman, Joseph Frischmuth, Rebecca Jacobs, Jo Livingstone, Yen Pham, Samantha Schuyler, Doreen St. Felix, and Katia Zorich for their scrupulous attention in fact-checking this book.

Permissions Acknowledgments

Many of the essays in this collection were previously published, in different forms, in the following periodicals:

Michael Thomsen's "Modern Fresno" was first published on www.nplusonemag .com on May 18, 2012, as "Fresno," © 2012 by Michael Thomsen. Reprinted by permission of the author and *n+1*.

Jenny Hendrix's "Bankrupt in Seattle" was first published on www.nplus onemag.com on August 17, 2011, © 2011 by Jenny Hendrix. Reprinted by permission of the author and *n+1*.

Erin Sheehy's "Gold Rush Whittier" was first published on www.nplusonemag .com on March 25, 2013, as "Gold Rush Alaska," © 2013 by Erin Sheehy. Reprinted by permission of the author and *n+1*.

Ryann Liebenthal's "The Making of Local Boise" was first published on www .nplusonemag.com on March 19, 2014, as "Boise, Idaho," © 2014 by Ryann Liebenthal. Reprinted by permission of the author and *n+1*.

Debbie Nathan's "Crossing El Paso" was first published on www.nplusonemag .com on May 15, 2013, as "El Paso," © 2013 by Debbie Nathan. Reprinted by permission of the author and *n+1*.

Moira Donegan's "The Kindness of Strangers in New Orleans" was first published on www.nplusonemag.com on March 12, 2014, as "New Orleans," © 2014 by Moira Donegan. Reprinted by permission of the author and *n+1*.

Gary Percesepe's "M., Northern Kentucky" was first published on www.nplus onemag.com on May 26, 2011, © 2011 by Gary Percesepe. Reprinted by permission of the author and *n+1*.

Sam Biederman's "Six Houses in Hyde Park" was first published on www.nplus onemag.com on August 19, 2011, as "Six Houses in Chicago," © 2011 by Sam Biederman. Reprinted by permission of the author and *n+1*.

Greg Afinogenov's "Milwaukee's Gilded Age and Aftermath" was first published on www.nplusonemag.com on May 24, 2011, © 2011 by Greg Afinogenov. Reprinted by permission of the author and *n+1*.

James Pogue's "Neighborhoods of Cincinnati" was first published on www.nplus onemag.com on August 8, 2011, as "Cincinnati," © 2011 by James Pogue. Reprinted by permission of the author and *n+1*.

Chris Reitz's "Five Jobs in Reading" was first published on www.nplusonemag .com on December 10, 2012, © 2012 by Chris Reitz. Reprinted by permission of the author and *n+1*.

Alex Sayf Cummings's "Atlanta's BeltLine Meets the Voters" was first published on *Tropics of Meta* (http://tropicsofmeta.wordpress.com/) as "Is the Beltline Bad for Atlanta?" on April 9, 2012, © 2012 by Alex Sayf Cummings. Reprinted by permission of the author and *Tropics of Meta*.

Michelle Tea's "Dire Straits" was first published in *n+1*, issue 20 (Fall 2014), © 2014 by Michelle Tea. Reprinted by permission of the author and *n+1*.

Elias Rodriques's "Fear and Aggression in Palm Coast" was first published on www.nplusonemag.com on March 19, 2014, as "Fear and Aggression in Florida," © 2014 by Elias Rodriques. Reprinted by permission of the author and *n+1*.

Emily Witt's "Miami Party Boom" was first published in *n+1*, issue 9 (Spring 2010), © 2010 by Emily Witt. Reprinted by permission of the author and *n+1*.

Aaron Lake Smith's "White Oak Denim, Greensboro" was first published on www.nplusonemag.com on May 27, 2011, © 2011 by Aaron Lake Smith. Reprinted by permission of the author and *n+1*.

Michael Merriam's "Washington, D.C., Brothel" was first published on www.nplusonemag.com on May 17, 2012, as "Brothel, Washington DC," © 2012 by Michael Merriam. Reprinted by permission of the author and *n+1*.

Lawrence Jackson's "Christmas in Baltimore" was first published in *n+1*, issue 12 (Fall 2011), as "Christmas in Baltimore 2009," © 2011 by Lawrence Jackson. Reprinted by permission of the author and *n+1*.

Jesse Montgomery's "Philly School Reform" was first published on www.nplus onemag.com on September 11, 2013, as "On Philly Schools," © 2013 by Jesse Montgomery. Reprinted by permission of the author and *n+1*.

Brandon Harris's "Bed-Stuy" was first published in *n+1*, issue 18 (Winter 2013), © 2013 by Brandon Harris. Reprinted by permission of the author and *n+1*.

Ian MacDougall's "Providence, You're Looking Good" was first published on www.nplusonemag.com on November 16, 2012, © 2012 by Ian MacDougall. Reprinted by permission of the author and *n+1*.

Steve Featherstone's "DestiNY Syracuse, USA" was first published in *n+1*, issue 21 (Winter 2014), © 2014 by Steve Featherstone. Reprinted by permission of the author and *n+1*.

Grateful acknowledgment is made for permission to reprint an excerpt from the poem "On Thinking About Hell" from *Poems, 1913–1956* by Bertolt Brecht. Copyright © by Bertolt Brecht. Reproduced with permission of Theatre Arts Books via Copyright Clearance Center. English translation as "Contemplating Hell" by Henry Erik Butler. Printed with permission of the translator.